HISTORY AFTER HOBSBAWM

History after Hobsbawm

Writing the Past for the Twenty-First Century

Edited by
JOHN H. ARNOLD
MATTHEW HILTON
and
JAN RÜGER

OXFORD
UNIVERSITY PRESS

OXFORD
UNIVERSITY PRESS

Great Clarendon Street, Oxford, OX2 6DP,
United Kingdom

Oxford University Press is a department of the University of Oxford.
It furthers the University's objective of excellence in research, scholarship,
and education by publishing worldwide. Oxford is a registered trade mark of
Oxford University Press in the UK and in certain other countries

First Edition published in 2018

Impression: 1

Published in the United States of America by Oxford University Press
198 Madison Avenue, New York, NY 10016, United States of America

British Library Cataloguing in Publication Data
Data available

Library of Congress Control Number: 2017936760

ISBN 978–0–19–876878–4

Printed and bound by
CPI Group (UK) Ltd, Croydon, CR0 4YY

Acknowledgements

The majority of the chapters in this collection were originally presented at the conference 'History after Hobsbawm' held at Senate House, University of London, 29 April–1 May 2014. The editors would like to express their thanks for the contribution made by the many other speakers at this event, as well as the extensive comments from the audience. They acknowledge too the generous support provided by Birkbeck College, the Institute for Historical Research, and the Past and Present Society.

Contents

III. PEOPLE AND POLITICS

CONCLUSION

List of Plates

List of Maps and Table

INTRODUCTION

1

The Challenges of History

John H. Arnold, Matthew Hilton, and Jan Rüger

What does it mean to write history in the twenty-first century? The past has seemingly never mattered more—it is everywhere, in the media, in public debate, in popular entertainment. Given this interest, historians are not short of opportunities to reach out beyond the university. But, apart from being popular, it is not at all obvious what function the study of history now serves. There is a desire and a demand for us to entertain and inform, but how historical debate can or should resonate beyond its own discipline—how it should seek to contribute to wider debate within the public sphere—is not clear.

In one sense, there ought to be no urgency about the issue. Given that the role of the historian has existed for over two millennia, the case for seeing a basic continuity to the task is strong. This is the sense of 'historian' that rests upon an antique notion of the *histor* as one who arbitrates between differing claims, and thus, more broadly, as one who works to present a coherent account of the past, treating the available evidence with fidelity and seeking to communicate this account to a reasonably broad audience. This more or less describes the task as understood by every history writer, from Thucydides, Orderic Vitalis, and Edward Gibbon to Leopold von Ranke and all modern historians. But in another sense it is quite clear that the role has altered in a variety of ways, as contexts and societal needs have changed and as different societies have had different predominant understandings of their relationship to past time. We would note here, for example, the differences between historians who were predominantly civic or monastic creatures and historians as professionals overwhelmingly supported by and subject to state-sponsored academe; or between historians whose obvious object of study was the institution to which they belonged and historians who wrote about the glorious trajectory of their 'nation-state', down to the great efflorescence of social and cultural history in the latter half of the twentieth century (where *who* gets to be an historian also played a major factor, as women began to enter the profession in much greater numbers). And in reality this of course reflects only the trajectories of *western* historiography in medieval and modern times; the historical practices of other cultures provide further variants and contrasts.[1] How historians have

---

[1] Jörn Rüsen, ed., *Western Historical Thinking: An Inter-Cultural Debate* (New York, 2002).

understood their task, their tools, their role, and their value in society has undergone considerable change, not only across the centuries but within the last century in particular.

This book does not aim to cover all possibilities with regard to the future of history writing in the twenty-first century. We are not principally concerned with defending the discipline against a perceived 'crisis in the humanities'—though we do hope that the kind of history explored by the contributors to this volume does help to make the case for the importance of historical study.[2] Our task is both more specific and somewhat broader. We have asked of our contributors what being an historian *should* mean in their particular fields of study—partly in terms of methods, questions, topics, and themes, but with an underlying sense of what *best* role an historian might seek to play, in attempting to help twenty-first-century society understand 'how we got here'. The chapters in this book therefore cover a wide range of subjects and periods. They present new work in their field but also pointers as to how their specialisms are developing, how they might further grow in the future, and how different areas of focus might speak to the larger challenges of history—both for the discipline itself and for its relationship to other fields of inquiry.

In asking these sorts of questions, our prompt and exemplar is the late Eric Hobsbawm. Hobsbawm's work is known to millions of readers. He has been described as one of the greatest historians of the twentieth century, drawing plaudits even from those who sat very clearly on the other side of the political spectrum. A number of things contributed to that reputation: a sustained and substantial output that spanned monographs, journal articles, reviews, and contributions to the wider press; a prose style that was accessible and witty, embracing narrative without patronizing his audience or overly simplifying his analysis; an extraordinary range of reference across modern European history in particular, but frequently drawing upon an even greater chronological and geographical canvas. But perhaps most important of all was his sense of engagement. History, for Hobsbawm—and, via Hobsbawm, for his readers—was not just a story of past times. It was a hugely important debate about *now*, about how we had come to 'now', and about where we might be heading next. It was about both 'past' and 'present', to borrow the title of the journal to which Hobsbawm was most closely associated throughout his career.[3] One could not be in any doubt, when reading his books, that history really mattered—and that what one thought about it thus mattered too. In his 1979 inaugural lecture at Birkbeck, Hobsbawm claimed (perhaps a little disingenuously): 'I used to think that the profession of history, unlike that of, say, nuclear physics, could at least do no

    [2] See Peter Mandler, 'The Rise of the Humanities', at https://aeon.co/essays/the-humanities-are-booming-only-the-professors-can-t-see-it (accessed 12 December 2016).
    [3] Hobsbawm was one of the founding editors of *Past & Present* in 1952, became vice-president of the Past & Present Society in 1987 and its president in 2003. He published a series of influential articles in the journal, the first in 1952, the last in 2002. For an appreciation of his role, see Roy Foster, 'Eric Hobsbawm', *Past & Present* 218 (2013), 3–15.

harm. Now I know it can.'[4] The particular harm against which he warned was the propensity for historians to provide the raw materials that facilitated the false narratives of nationalism, even when they had not wittingly intended to write in the service of a national identity. For this reason, if no other, historians *must* think about the implications of what they write, the wider societal and political frames within which their stories will be received and understood. And, Hobsbawm counselled his fellow practitioners, historians ought to be active in challenging misrepresentations of the past, from the outright lies upon which demagogues built populist movements to the nihilistic rejection of all historical truth claims. History, for Hobsbawm, thus always presented a challenge—in the sense of a political and moral demand—that could not truly be avoided; because, if one avoided it, one was then in fact meekly passing the debate into the hands of one's political opponents.

This challenge, the challenge over the control, in the present, of the terrain of the past, is another constant factor in the doing of history. How the struggles of the early Christian church were to be remembered was an abiding concern for Orosius. How the past feuds and factionalism of the Florentine city-state should be understood was, similarly, an abiding concern for the fourteenth-century chronicler Gregorio Dati. One could multiply the examples for each subsequent century. This, we might say, is the first challenge for the historian: the intertwined task of not letting an account of the past fall prey to misinterpretation or misappropriation, while building a sufficiently robust platform to render persuasive the claims one makes about that past.

But, as we move into the twenty-first century, other challenges present themselves. First, as professional history has developed across the modern age, it has, if not 'fragmented', then at least subdivided much of its effort into a large number of specialist areas. For much of the time we are now mostly required to be 'truffle hunters'—nose to the ground, burrowing down into a particular field—rather than 'parachutists' (ranging across and mapping a whole landscape).[5] Undoubtedly this has led to the production of some quite extraordinary works. It is not difficult for the student today to find excellent new books and articles on any period and covering almost every geographical region. The professionalization and expansion of history as a discipline has also meant that there are more opportunities for students to engage with such specialisms. But with the increase in the number of modular courses it is not always apparent what are the core issues, themes, and topics that students today might be expected to take from the past. To be sure, there are the perpetual debates about truth, facts, and the nature of history that concern all of us in all our fields, and these are taught in dedicated, sometimes compulsory, courses.

---

[4] Eric Hobsbawm, 'Outside and Inside History', in idem, *On History* (London, 1997), 5 (here taken from a 1993 address to the CEU in Budapest; the line is absent from the published version of his inaugural—'Has History Made Progress', in the same volume—but is present in the typescript held at Birkbeck).

[5] Emmanuel Le Roy Ladurie, *Paris-Montpellier P.C.-P.S.U., 1945–1963* (Paris, 1982), 207–8; see J. H. Elliott, *History in the Making* (New Haven, CT, 2012), 197.

But there are fewer central narratives, debates, or issues that all can feel they are contributing towards through either their research or their study.

The second challenge, then, is how best to bring into a wider setting the treasures that we uncover; a challenge that involves recognizing the potential importance and broader implications of a particular finding in a particular subfield, then being sufficiently empowered and inspired to step out from our comfortable niche onto a more expansive and more broadly visible stage, and then taking these larger debates back into one's own subfield, to try to ensure that history remains an intertwined (if variegated) conversation. If we cannot maintain such a conversation across our own specialisms, then how is history as a whole to engage in fruitful dialogue with other disciplines across the humanities and social sciences? For instance, the explanation of causation—why change happens—was once the issue that would prompt other scholars to turn towards history when seeking to understand the various presents that they were themselves examining. But does history still have such an important part in broader cross-disciplinary debates? Does it provide the interpretive frameworks to which other disciplines feel obliged to listen? We entertain, to be sure; but do we explain?

Following from this, there is a third challenge arising from the times in which we write. There are pressing questions that society asks, about 'how we got here' and the historian's role, if any, in helping to decide 'where we go next'. For Hobsbawm, member of the Communist Party (though not an orthodox believer) and a key member of the influential group of postwar British Marxist historians, there was a particular political and intellectual inheritance that helped to answer that challenge. While the detailed analysis of 'how we got here' was open to considerable discussion, the underlying factors could be related to economic structures and political practices; 'where shall we go?' was oriented towards some form of revolutionary transformation that would make a more equal society, on the basis of a reorganization of fundamental socioeconomic structures. For the members of the Communist Party Historians' Group—including those who, unlike Hobsbawm, left the party in 1956, after the Soviet suppression of the Hungarian uprising—the project of producing history that focused on socioeconomic forces and social experience rather than on the political decisions of 'great men' continued to present itself very clearly as the best answer to both questions. It was this generation of historians and the one immediately following (those who, for example, established *Past & Present* and later created the History Workshop series and the accompanying journal) who set the tone for social history in Britain in the latter part of the twentieth century. And, while few of their subsequent students and intellectual inheritors would subscribe as explicitly and wholeheartedly to quite the same politics as their tutors, the interpretive framework and project they created largely persisted, and continued for some long while to present a sense of what the historiographical task at hand was and should be. The great methodological arguments of the 1970s and 1980s, while hugely important in shifting some of the scope and content of historiography, were at heart discussions, first, of what should rightly be *included* in a meaningful social history (the experiences and changes, or lack thereof, of women, people of colour, those marginalized by social norms) and, second, of how one should best *conceptualize* the interplay of power and experience that constituted the terrain of social history (discourse, culture, practice, the construction of social reality, and so forth).

Hobsbawm, it should be noted, was not best pleased with these latter developments. In his autobiography he wrote of how it seemed to him that around 1970 historiography had satisfactorily established a 'comprehensive project', broad in its ambition—which for him was to understand 'how and why *Homo sapiens* got from the palaeolithic to the nuclear era'—and clearly committed to understanding the past within the present. In a few years, however, this had 'changed utterly': there was, first, a shift from an interest in structure to that of culture, a shift that brought with it an ever-increasing focus (as he saw it) on 'trivialities'; and, second, a move from 'recovering fact to recovering feeling'.[6] The close-focus, microhistorical approach and the cultural interests of something like Carlo Ginzburg's *The Cheese and the Worms* (1976) was, for Hobsbawm, a turn away from the necessary breadth of the field. How could one satisfactorily present an account of 'how we got here' when stuck in the middle of the sixteenth century with just one rather odd individual? How could one make robust claims about the underlying structure of historical change if distracted by the details of premodern culture? Of course, for many younger historians in the latter decades of the twentieth century, these elements were precisely what made microhistory, the new cultural history, the linguistic turn, and so forth exciting and productive. But one can demur at Hobsbawm's somewhat grumpy rejection of the cultural turn that historiography took, and still recognize that the move away from the relative certainties of the older framework left something of a gap. If one was to focus on the particular, the individual, the marginal, and the cultural, who tended to the general, the collective, the 'mainstream', and the socioeconomic?

Of course, in the 1980s and early 1990s in particular, much of the work being done in the 'new' vein was precisely reacting against the certitudes of its inheritance and was at the same time able to take some of the wider context or narrative for granted as part of that inheritance. And further questions have returned to the debate over the role of the historian—both older questions regarding the broad sweep of historical change and new questions framed in particular by scholars who started to grapple with a widened geographical perspective. Much of the work done roughly between 1975 and 1995 sought to point out what the inherited social history accounts had 'left out' and how their basic periodizations might need to be taken apart and reconsidered—as, for example, in Joan Kelly's classic 1977 essay 'Did Women Have a Renaissance?', which begins: 'One of the tasks of women's history is to call into question the accepted schemes of periodization.'[7] Calling things into question is a very powerful tool, and one that historians in particular can use adeptly in wider debates; but it is a tool of critique for what already exists rather than a tool that can, by itself, build new structures and movements.

---

[6] Eric Hobsbawm, *Interesting Times* (London, 2002), 293–4.
[7] Originally published in R. Bridenthal and C. Koonz, eds, *Becoming Visible: Women in European History* (New York, 1977); reprinted in J. Kelly, *Women, History and Theory* (Chicago, IL, 1984), 9–50.

Joan Scott—not only a key figure for gender history but someone who, as importantly, has taught us how to incorporate poststructuralist analysis into historiographical practice—has recently renewed the sense of the importance of critique. Channelling to some extent Michel Foucault's earlier insistence on the need for 'critical and effective histories', she writes:

> Critique ought to make us uncomfortable by asking what the sources of those values [that we hold] are, how they have come into being, what relationship they have constituted, what power they have secured. . . . to make visible the premises upon which the organising categories of our identities (personal, social, national) are based, and to give them a history so placing them in time and subject to review. This kind of history-writing takes up topics not usually considered 'historical' because they are either objects taken to be self-evident in their meaning (women, work, fever, incest) or categories of analysis outside time (gender, race, class, even postcolonial). The object of critical history-writing is the present, though its materials come from the archives of the past; its aim is neither to justify nor to discredit but to illuminate those blind spots. . . that keep social systems intact and make seeing how to change them so difficult.[8]

Critique here is not an end in itself, but a tool that one provides for society more widely; in this sense, for Scott it would appear that the role of the historian is both important and essentially ancillary. But how can the work of critique be done if the topics it takes up *have* now been considered historically—given that we now do have a plethora of works on topics that were not previously considered historically (for example sexual repression, rape, childhood, domesticity), and that categories of analysis *have* increasingly been historicized? And can the historian trust that her or his critique will in itself perform some necessary change to the wider landscape, in which the narratives of values, power, nation, and society seem so persistent? Is the role of the historian as critic still sufficient, or do we need to be challenged to move beyond critique to some further account, 'reconstructive', no matter how epistemologically problematic that conception may be?

There is a wider sense in which the direction of travel in sociocultural history echoed the wider fortunes of the political left: providing powerful areas of critique (although, it should be noted, with expanses of relative complacency), but being unwilling or unable to forge any persuasive 'big story' of its own, and thus tending always to be liable, at the very least, to having to work to a backdrop of the narratives proffered by others. This was a concern repeatedly returned to in the writings of the New Left, which are particularly inspired by the focus on culture undertaken by Stuart Hall and others. The effects on history were seen in the embrace of the radical potential of cultural critique, but also in the subsequent heated divisions provoked when the latter came into conflict with more traditional social historical analyses. This sense of crisis within the discipline towards the end of the twentieth century has been set out extremely evocatively by Geoff Eley in *The Crooked Line*

---

[8] Joan Scott, 'History-Writing as Critique', in K. Jenkins, Sue Morgan, and Alun Munslow, eds, *Manifestos for History* (Abingdon, 2007), 34–5. This book was launched with a roundtable debate at Birkbeck, with Eric in the audience; he and Scott amicably demurred (one of the editors writes here from his personal memory, as he was sat on the panel beside Scott).

(2005). He, however, chose to end that book with a more optimistic synthesis of the present. He felt that the challenging questions raised by cultural history were, at that moment, being integrated with the historian's concerns with empiricism and experience, and he pointed to a number of works produced by a younger generation that he believed to be exemplars of this new moment. A decade on, questions remain, though, as to whether the accomplishments in method, practice, and presentation that have been achieved have still prompted the same level of engagement between history, other disciplines, and the challenges of the present.

For historians writing in the twenty-first century, the analytical and political frameworks of the mid- to late twentieth century no longer appear quite so automatically persuasive, nor do they come so readily to hand. The critique of which Joan Scott talks, and the arguments that followed among historians, brought to the fore some of the assumptions—about gender, race, sexuality, and in some ways about class itself—embedded in the progressive views of the founders of modern social history. By the start of the twenty-first century, as Eley suggested, a number of scholars were happy to adopt the label of 'sociocultural historian' or to talk of 'cultural and social history' in a combined sense, as a way of recognizing the conjunction of focus.[9] While this represented a move beyond an earlier sense of sub-disciplinary conflict, the move to détente has rather allowed us to continue to dodge the question of the fundamental relationship between the social and the cultural and what each should be understood to contain. The 'we' in the question 'how did we get here?' is no longer taken for granted and prompts a further challenge: if 'we' no longer assume that we are a unity by dint of a shared history, what kinds of accounts of the past might nonetheless allow individuals to find commonality? On the other hand, for a newer generation of historians, there is a longing to make the history they write have some wider purpose, be certain that in some way they *matter*—and within this longing there is perhaps an element of nostalgia for the collective project and certitudes of the earlier vanguard.[10]

To ask 'how did we get here?' in the second half of the twentieth century, the implied 'here' was strongly marked by the political ideologies of nationalism, the traumatic legacy of two world wars, an increase in consumption and living standards accompanied by a rise in capitalism and the diminution of labour movements internationally. For Hobsbawm in particular, perhaps the most pressing issue was to provide histories that could effectively challenge the claims of nationalism; and hence the need that historians provide narratives that were in themselves sufficiently broad and compelling to be able to tackle nationalism not only over the details, but in the very size and pull of the story that was told. As we (no longer quite so unthinkingly assumed to be a western 'we') move on within the twenty-first century, what 'here' looks like has also changed somewhat, and with it the nature of the challenge it presents to historians. Nationalism continues to be a

---

[9] The journal of the Social History Society, launched in 2004 under the title *Cultural and Social History* and with an editorial gloss that emphasized the importance of both elements.

[10] It is interesting to note the appearance of books by scholars who began their work in the 1970s, responding to this perceived lack: John Tosh, *Why History Matters* (Basingstoke, 2008); Judith M. Bennett, *History Matters: Patriarchy and the Challenge of Feminism* (Manchester, 2006).

major and deeply problematic ideology, but one as often framed by the failures and relative impotence of nation-states in an era of global capital as by the inheritances of late nineteenth-century triumphalism. Nationalist identities now often stand in uneasy tension with other claims of religion, ethnicity, and culture, some of which—one thinks of certain claims regarding religion in particular—are themselves politically freighted and intimately connected to violence and coercion. The vast inequalities of individual and collective wealth, both on a global scale and within western societies, have started a rather different debate about socioeconomic structures, where 'class' no longer captures the fractured experiences of those whom some commentators have dubbed 'the precariat' and where the global disjunctures have become so much more apparent—and pressingly disruptive to the comforts of the West—than in earlier times. While China, India, and some other countries have economies that are experiencing rapid and sustained expansion, it no longer feels safe to assume that living standards will continue to rise across the world—and thus that one of the core seductions of capitalism will continue on the path it took in the second half of the twentieth century. And, intimately connected to past and present industrialization, the massive challenge of climate change has, among many other effects, thrown into stark relief the inability of politicians to operate other than in the shortest term—prompting a rather different sense of how the ways in which we think temporally matter hugely. Ethnicity, culture, religion, gender, sexuality, and a host of other 'identity' factors are proving stubbornly persistent and cannot be dismissed as passing distractions from the 'realities' of class, even when they clearly are entangled with persistent socioeconomic inequalities.

Within the more limited sphere of historiographical practice, aspects of the 'postmodernism' that Hobsbawm denounced in some of his methodological essays have been more or less happily incorporated into standard historiographical practice, and most of us have learned to live with the epistemological weaknesses inevitable in historical enquiry (which were for the most part perfectly obvious, albeit equally intractable, to all historians throughout time). Historians have undergone a variety of further 'turns' since the linguistic turn associated with that postmodernism, among them a turn towards an interest in the materiality of history, which involves an appreciation of objects and things rather than texts alone as fruitful sources for understanding history, and with this appreciation a greater sense of past people in their embodied existences. Likewise, a turn to transnational history has prompted an incredibly rich literature, from the 'global middle ages' through to the present, which has pointed to the often unexpected transfers of people, goods, institutions, and ideas across boundaries and borders that historians operating with a comparative approach have not always discovered.

The period in which Hobsbawm was most active as an historian saw a sustained engagement of the profession with cognate disciplines, particularly anthropology. But it was an engagement that paid attention to the quantitative as much as to the qualitative. Hobsbawm's career saw the rise and fall of cliometrics, the application of econometrics to historical enquiry, assisted in particular by the use of computers. More recently computers have assisted historical enquiry by modelling spatial aspects of data (particularly through the use of geographic information systems), by making available vast digital archives, and by developing much more nuanced database tools.[11] This has, in turn, prompted new challenges for historians: methodological but also political, as 'big data' have been heralded as creating the opportunity to return to some of the larger questions facing global society. Some have gone as far as to issue a new manifesto, calling on historians to rise to the challenge of addressing major global concerns.[12] In itself, such a call to arms ought to be welcome. There is nothing wrong with a discipline that reflects on its purposes. But there is a danger that such manifestos succumb to nostalgia for a particular, former methodological authority (cliometrics in the case of the proponents of big data) and ignore too much of what has been lost in the turn to culture, meaning, and identity. If critique is forgotten, then history can too easily follow the questions set by others. Rather, history is better served by a more open exchange with scholars in other disciplines and by the political conditions in which we work. History therefore does not become a tool for policy prescription but another mode of thinking about pressing global challenges, helping to reset the terms of the debate within which we trade off cultural, social, economic, political, and material priorities when choices have to be made.

The chapters in this volume assess the state of the field in areas that broadly represent Hobsbawm's sizable interests. They are not meant to be a prescriptive account of what historians should offer or of why history matters. Instead they are overviews, mixed with primary research, of some of the most exciting recent historiographical developments that explicitly aim to understand the past within the present. These interventions fall into three areas that highlight Hobsbawm's lasting influence, while also featuring robust revisions of some of his interpretations: the history of nations and empires; the history of economies; and the history of popular politics. In engaging with discussions that are specific to these fields, the authors assembled here reflect about broader questions that concern current debate.

Catherine Hall's opening chapter in the section 'Nation and Empire' exemplifies this approach. Bringing together the history of race and gender with one of Hobsbawm's central subjects—the development of capitalism—she provides a powerful analysis of nineteenth-century slavery. Gender and race, she argues, played a part in both cementing and dissolving the system of slavery, with its particular forms of wealth creation. The legacy of this interdependence is all too obvious: 'The trauma of slavery is not over. It lives on in the structural inequalities that disfigure both Jamaican and British society.'

The links between histories that used to be studied in isolation are also at the heart of Jan Rüger's essay on the European and imperial dimensions of British history. Drawing on Hobsbawm's understanding of the relationship between continental Europe and the British empire, Rüger puts forward a critique of imperial history. It is a fallacy, he argues, to suggest that the empire allowed Britain to isolate

---

[11] But see caveats and reflections in Tim Hitchcock, 'Confronting the Digital', *Cultural and Social History* 10 (2013), 9–23.
[12] J. Guldi and D. Armitage, *The History Manifesto* (Cambridge, 2014).

itself from the continent. Europe and the 'English-speaking world' were not and are not two separate spheres, with Britain in a position to prioritize one over the other.

While Hobsbawm rarely shied away from large-scale comparisons, the theoretical implications in his comparative work remained implicit rather than explicit. What are the purposes and uses of comparison? What is the heuristic value of comparing countries, cultures, and societies in the past? Renaud Morieux follows these questions in his analysis of eighteenth-century France and Britain, an analysis in which a group of actors caught in between the two national stories play a key role, allowing us to understand the politics of comparison in past and present debates.

Following on from the question of comparison, John Breuilly historicizes Hobsbawm's work on nationalism. Benedict Anderson's 'imagined communities' and the concept of the 'invention of tradition', established by Hobsbawm and Terence Ranger, were key parts of a hugely influential phase in the study of nationalism which now seems to yield diminishing returns. Three promising new avenues have since opened up which treat nationalism as a force in its own right without taking the nationalist self-image for granted.

Bill Schwarz concludes the section 'Nation and Empire' with an assessment of the end of empire after the Second World War. 'Decolonization', he argues, cannot be understood merely as the dismantling of colonialism. Focusing on the way in which the end of colonial rule was articulated with the shift to the neoliberal age, he explores the tensions between nationalism and protectionist economics on the one hand and the evolving pattern of a new world order on the other, in which neoliberal capitalism, the openness of borders, and various attempts to close down flows of migration went hand in hand.

'Material Economies', the volume's second section of essays, can be read as a collective attempt to decentre the history of world economies. Hobsbawm was unapologetic about the European focus of much of his work. As he wrote in 1996:

> Everything that distinguishes the world of today from the world of the Ming and Mughal emperors and the Mamelukes originated in Europe—whether in science and technology, in the economy, in ideology and politics, or in the institutions and practices of public and private life. Even the concept of the 'world' as a system of human communication embracing the entire globe could not exist before the European conquest of the western hemisphere and the emergence of a capitalist economy. This is what fixes the situation of Europe in world history, what defines the problems of European history and indeed what makes a specific history of Europe necessary.[13]

This interpretation will seem problematic to many of those who write history in the twenty-first century, but what are the alternative frameworks in which one is to explain the economic transformation of the world? Chris Wickham, Maxine Berg, and Frank Trentmann suggest some answers in their chapters on global economies in the medieval, early modern, and modern period. Their essays have in common that they stress the need to investigate transnational connections while at the same

---

[13] Eric Hobsbawm, 'The Curious History of Europe', in idem, *On History* (London, 1997), 287–301, here 297. The essay was first published in German in *Die Zeit*, 4 October 1996.

time comparing economic structures in different parts of the world. By emphasizing the interconnectedness of economic development across the *longue durée*, they raise significant questions about the way in which we should approach the global nature of the modern capitalist economy.

While the essays by Wickham, Berg, and Trentmann operate on the macro level of global economic history, Pat Hudson refracts this large-scale vision through a specific example: the woollen industry in South Wales in the late nineteenth century. Engaging with new debates about the history of objects, she shows that the specific materiality of industrial productions is essential for understanding the histories of labour and production and the unequal relationship between global economies and real lives in specific localities—issues that matter now more than ever.

In rewriting the history of capitalism, scholars in the twenty-first century will not be able to separate the economy from the environment, a field with which Hobsbawm was acutely engaged. How do we conceptualize the history of the 'anthropocene', the period during which we know that human activity has had a global effect on the environment? One answer, Paul Warde suggests in his contribution to the section 'Material Economies', is to study the idea of 'the environment' itself, a concept with a history that needs to be understood in specific social and political contexts.

Giving those who have been written out of history a voice was one of Eric Hobsbawm's key concerns. 'People and Politics', the third section of essays collected here, engages with this project in a number of ways. Andy Wood's chapter deals with popular politics in the premodern era. Drawing on material that is related to folklore and popular memory, he rejects the categories of 'protest' and 'rebellion', canonized by Hobsbawm, as too narrow. 'Class', he argues, continues to be an essential category for understanding the experience of social life, but how class manifests itself and is experienced is more complex than earlier social historians recognized.

Sonya Rose and Sean Brady, too, focus on 'class', though their concern is mostly with classic debates of labour history and the trade union movement. This historiography has left out large numbers of workers who were non-unionized; and it fails to address the demise of industrial labour. Drawing on a range of recent work, the two authors argue strongly for a global turn in labour history that attends to changes over the *longue durée* and to areas of persistence in gender identities.

Jon Lawrence follows this trajectory with an essay that analyses the decline of 'the working class' as a political identity. Focusing on the post-1945 period, he challenges accounts that see this decline as a consequence of structural changes in the economy combined with Thatcherite populism. He suggests instead that we need to pay greater attention to the gulf that emerged between the rhetoric of labour politics and what might be termed the politics of everyday life. Changes in working-class life and culture were less radical than is often assumed; yet nonetheless Labour fundamentally failed to align itself with the rising expectations of working people from the mid-1960s. Politicians' investment in unrealistic, idealized conceptions of the 'working class' ultimately led to the collapse of any coherent politics of class in Britain.

While Wood, Rose, Brady, and Lawrence revisit in different ways a field that was at the heart of Hobsbawm's work—the politics of class—Yasmin Khan takes as her starting point a category that features less prominently in his work: the subaltern. The narratives of war in modern British history have tended to centre on Europe and have obscured decolonization. Yet both world wars were imperial wars, involving global inequalities and hierarchies that accompanied the fighting. The history of twentieth-century conflict was also a subaltern history of the British empire.

Alison Light rounds off the section 'People and Politics' by engaging with a genre that is conspicuously absent in Hobsbawm's work and most other academic writing: family history. Like 'history from below' and 'people's history', family historians bring their own experiences and memories to bear on their work. Light explores the potential that their work has, not only to revitalize working-class histories, but to make us think about the limits, forms, and purposes of writing history.

History after Hobsbawm closes with a wide-ranging intervention by Geoff Eley. Eley engages with Hobsbawm's legacy directly, in order to ask important questions about the political nature of the historian's task. By contrasting Hobsbawm's own political formation with that of a later generation—principally the one that was influenced by 1968 and its legacies—Eley calls for a renewed political engagement within the profession. In surveying the major conceptual and theoretical developments over the last forty years, he finds much to be optimistic about in a variety of approaches that can still be embraced to rejuvenate historical analysis and to make it speak to present-day politics. As he puts it in his concluding remarks: 'It was never just Hobsbawm's remarkable qualities as a historian that made him so inspiring as a model, but the consistency of his stance as a politically engaged intellectual.' Such consistency is perhaps harder to imagine in a more plural political present. So, too, is a consistent approach to the past, when history itself flourishes through its diversity. Nevertheless, it is hoped that the essays in this volume share in that consistency of commitment which, for Hobsbawm, made history matter.

I

NATION AND EMPIRE

2

Gendering Property, Racing Capital

Catherine Hall

In his autobiography *Interesting Times: A Twentieth-Century Life*, published in 2002, Eric Hobsbawm reflected on the shifts in the historical discipline in his lifetime. Perhaps his greatest regret, he reflected, despite the development of global history, was 'the almost total failure, largely for institutional and linguistic reasons, of history to emancipate itself from the framework of the nation-state. Looking back, this provincialism was probably the major weakness of the subject in my lifetime.'[1] Hobsbawm inspired us to think about the international and the comparative; he insisted on asking the *why* questions, convinced of the need for historians to be able to generalize and to explain, to focus on 'the big picture'. Rooted in European cosmopolitanism and in a particular version of Marxism, he had scant sympathy for some of the new approaches of historians. He was critical of the cultural turn. The emphasis had moved, he argued, from analysis to description, from fact to feeling, from the macro to the micro, and he made clear how much he thought had been lost in this shifting of the gaze. Feminist history, in his view, was at best interested in 'winning collective recognition' rather than in interpreting the world; postcolonial approaches were not on his radar beyond the work of subaltern studies.[2] In recent decades, however, such approaches have been influential, sometimes to the point of provoking anxieties about too exclusive a focus on questions of culture and identity at the expense of economic and political structures. As a protagonist of feminist and postcolonial work, far from abandoning the *why* questions or the significance of the macro, I want to make an argument about the value of connecting these insights with older Marxist traditions, particularly in relation to the debates over slavery and capitalism. The absence of grand narratives is a weakness of these new approaches in some respects, but the more elaborate understandings that we are developing of the complexity of the social formations we aim to understand offer novel and significant perspectives on the evolution and character of modern capitalism. As we struggle politically in a neoliberal world in which the clear battle lines that once seemed to be in place no longer work, as critical historians we need new maps, which fully engage with the differentiated understandings of class, labour, gender, and 'race' that help us to understand both

[1] Eric Hobsbawm, *Interesting Times: A Twentieth-Century Life* (London, 2002), 293.
[2] Ibid., 296.

the past that is not past and the present. Slavery and the plantation stand at the centre of these alternative analytical paradigms. My aim is to explore the ways in which gender and 'race' structured the organization of slavery, were embedded in the social formation, and were historically dynamic forces and axes of change in the nexus formed by metropole and colony.

Hobsbawm was well aware of the significance of plantation economies for the development of industrial capitalism. 'The major achievement of the seventeenth-century crisis', he wrote in 1954, 'is the creation of a new form of colonialism.'[3] In *Industry and Empire*, probably one of the most influential history textbooks ever written, he argued:

> This book is about the history of Britain. However... an insular history of Britain (and there have been too many such) is quite inadequate... Britain developed as an essential part of a global economy, and more particularly as the centre of that vast formal or informal 'empire' on which its fortunes have so largely rested.[4]

But his object of study was not the world economy or the British imperial sector; rather it was the transformation of Britain into an industrial capitalist economy. That preoccupation came from the concern of the group of Communist Party historians—in the wake of their struggle against fascism and of their commitment to communism—to rewrite the history of Britain, to challenge the dominant Whig narratives of a peaceful transition from feudalism to democracy, and to insist on the place of class, radicalism, revolution, and conflict in the history of these islands. Hobsbawm recognized that the origins of the Industrial Revolution lay in the new centres of expansion and in the commercial developments that had occurred—the rise of a market for overseas products for everyday use in Europe, the 'overseas creation of economic systems for producing such goods (e.g. slave-operated plantations) and the conquest of colonies designed to serve the economic advantage of their European owners'. Alongside this went the expansion of that 'most inhuman traffic, the slave trade'. 'Behind our Industrial Revolution', he argued, 'there lies this concentration on the colonial and "underdeveloped" markets overseas, the successful battle to deny them to anyone else.'[5] He might have cited the classic passage from Volume 1 of *Capital*: 'the veiled slavery of the wage-workers in Europe needed, for its pedestal, slavery pure and simple in the new world.... capital comes dripping from head to foot, from every pore, with blood and dirt'.[6] But his concern, and that of his fellow-Marxist historians, was not with 'race', slavery, and the Caribbean. C. L. R. James and Eric Williams did not appear in their pantheon. Confronted with their struggle against racism and colonialism, James and Williams insisted on the linkage between metropole and colony, on the intimate connections between the French Revolution and San Domingo, and between capitalism and slavery. It has been the work of later generations to attempt

---

[3] Eric J. Hobsbawm, 'The Crisis of the Seventeenth Century', *Past & Present*, 5 & 6 (1954); reprinted in Trevor H. Aston, ed., *Crisis in Europe, 1560–1660* (London, 1965), 50–3.

[4] Eric J. Hobsbawm, *Industry and Empire: An Economic History of Britain since 1750* (London, 1968), 7.

[5] Ibid, 36.   [6] Karl Marx, *Capital*, 3 vols (Moscow, 1961), vol. 1, 759–60.

not only to put together these different traditions and trajectories but to ask new questions, not least about the place of gender in these debates.

Just as Hobsbawm's preoccupations were formed by the conjuncture in which he matured as an historian, so the generations who have followed him to write 'history after Hobsbawm' have been shaped by the altered conditions in which we have lived and live, to which we have needed and need to respond. While class was the key historical dynamic in his analytical work, gender and 'race' have become key analytics for our 'interesting times'—the times shaped by the recognition of the unfinished work of anticolonialism, of culture as a material and symbolic force, of the reconfiguration of British society in the face of migration and globalization, of the triumph of neoliberalism, and of the ever deepening inequalities that mark our contemporary world.

The initial work detailing the links between capitalism and slavery came from the Caribbean. It was the Trinidadian historian Eric Williams who propounded the thesis that has caused such controversy over the generations. Williams never argued that slavery 'caused' the Industrial Revolution: 'It must not be inferred that the triangular trade was solely and entirely responsible for the economic development. The growth of the internal market in England played an important part in the accumulation of capital, but so too did the triangular trade.'[7] His arguments have been attacked on varied grounds, but—as Nicholas Draper, Keith McClelland, and I suggest in the co-authored book that documented the results of the first phase of our project on the legacies of British slave ownership—there is a move to a modified version of Williams's thesis among economic historians.[8] Recent scholarship has adopted a broader conception of the slave economy; Pomeranz sees the Atlantic slave economy, with its capacity to add 'phantom-land' together with the availability of coal, as the two key factors that allowed Britain to expand. Inikori sees Atlantic slavery, along with the commercialization of agriculture, as key to industrialization. His central thesis on the importance of overseas trade and, within it, on the slave economy has been broadly accepted by Pat Hudson and Nuala Zahediah.[9] At the micro level, local and regional studies consistently point to the flow of slave wealth into new institutions and industries—many concentrated in centres of commercial and financial power that were crucial to financing trade and industrialization. At the same time Williams's insight into the importance of slave-derived wealth to eighteenth-century society and culture has been greatly

---

[7] Eric Williams, *Capitalism and Slavery* (Richmond, VA, 1944), 105–6.

[8] Catherine Hall, Nicholas Draper, Keith McClelland, Rachel Lang, and Kate Donington, *Legacies of British Slave-Ownership: Colonial Slavery and the Formation of Victorian Britain* (Cambridge, 2014).

[9] Kenneth Pomeranz, *The Great Divergence: China, Europe, and the Making of the Modern World Economy* (Princeton, NJ, 2000); Joseph Inikori, *Africans and the Industrial Revolution in England: A Study in International Trade and Economic Development* (Cambridge, 2002); Pat Hudson, 'Slavery, the Slave Trade and Economic Growth: A Contribution to the Debate', in Catherine Hall, Nicholas Draper, and Keith McClelland, eds, *Emancipation and the Remaking of the British Imperial World* (Manchester, 2014), 36–59; Nuala Zahediah, *The Capital and the Colonies* (Cambridge, 2010). In the years since the crash of 2008 there has been a marked renewal of interest in questions about the development of capitalism and its relation to slavery among US historians. See, for example, Sven Beckert, *Empire of Cotton: A New History of Global Capitalism* (London, 2014).

expanded, by literary scholars in particular. Simon Gikandi, to take one example, has explored the introjections of slavery into manners, civility, sense, sensibility, and the culture of taste. Slavery and the culture of taste, he argues, were both fundamental to the shaping of modern identity.[10]

Since 2009 a team of historians at University College London, of whom I am one, have been investigating slave owners. The work of forgetting slavery—and remembering abolition—has been going on since the abolition of the slave trade. It continues unabated, despite myriad efforts—most notably around the bicentenary, in 2007, of the abolition of the trade—to put it back where it belongs, as an integral part of Britain's history. Disavowal and distantiation have been crucial mechanisms facilitating avoidance and evasion; 'it didn't happen here', 'not our responsibility'. Research on both the enslavers and the enslaved is essential; for at the heart of both metropolitan and colonial societies was the dichotomy of freedom and slavery. In recent decades, for very good reasons, much work has focused on the enslaved. But British slave owners provide one way of placing slavery back in the heartlands of the metropolis and of problematizing whiteness as an identity that carried privilege and power. Slave owners, their families, their properties, their plantations and merchant houses, their wealth, their homes and gardens, their writings, and their politics are the lens through which we are engaging in the work of remembering.

The West India Interest was a powerful grouping in the eighteenth and early nineteenth centuries, critical to holding back the abolition of the slave trade and to delaying the ending of colonial slavery in parts of the British empire for fifty years. Yet West Indian slave owners have not been systematically investigated, despite important work in the form of case studies of particular families. There is nothing equivalent to the body of work produced by Eugene Genovese and Elizabeth Fox-Genovese on the American South. The Genoveses' work has been highly controversial and their account of Southern paternalism—which, as they see it, combined with an anticapitalist politics—finds few echoes in our study of British slave owners, who were remarkable for their brutality and their commitment to mercantile capitalism. These owners' position among the British elite is one way of demonstrating that, although relatively few enslaved Africans lived in Britain, slavery was integral to the British economy, society, and culture—and was understood at the time to be so. As Edward Long, the famed historian of Jamaica, argued in 1774:

> If, upon the whole, we revolve in our minds, what an amazing variety of trades receive their daily support, as many of them did originally their being, from the calls of the Africa and West India markets; if we reflect on the numerous families of those mechanics and artisans which are thus maintained, and contemplate that ease and plenty, which is the constant as well as just reward of their incessant labours; if we combine

---

[10] Simon Gikandi, *Slavery and the Culture of Taste* (Princeton, NJ, 2011). There is a substantial literature on the significance of empire, 'race', and slavery to early modern and eighteenth-century British culture. See, for example, Kim F. Hall, *Things of Darkness: Economies of Race and Gender in Early Modern England* (Ithaca, NY, 1995); Felicity A. Nussbaum, *The Limits of the Human: Fictions of Anomaly, Race and Gender in the Long Eighteenth Century* (Cambridge, 2003); Catherine Molineux, *Faces of Perfect Ebony: Encountering Atlantic Slavery in Imperial Britain* (Cambridge, MA, 2012).

with these the several tribes of active and busy people, who are continually employed in the building of ships...we may from thence form a competent idea of the prodigious value of our sugar colonies, and a just conception of their immense importance to the grandeur and prosperity of their mother country.[11]

British wealth owed much to slavery, as the pro-slavers trumpeted for decades and as Sidney Mintz has long maintained, because 'the slave plantation, producing some basic commodity for the mother country, was a special emergent form of capitalist organization'.[12] But the slavery business was never just about the economy: values associated with it permeated the culture and politics of both metropolitan and colonial societies. In this essay I outline a few of the ways in which attention to this repressed history of capitalism both challenges and enriches our understanding of the genealogy of the modern.

Using Nicholas Draper's study of the compensation records, published under the title *The Price of Emancipation*, as the starting point for the first phase of our project, we documented all the claims to compensation at the time of emancipation; for £20 million was paid to the slave owners to secure their agreement to the loss of 'their property'.[13] Nearly half that money stayed in Britain; for the absentees—that is, those whose primary residence was in Britain—dominated the ownership of the enslaved: indeed 80 per cent of the enslaved were 'owned' by 20 per cent of the planters and merchants. Our biographical work has focused on the absentees and on exploring their economic, political, and cultural significance and the contribution they made to the development of modern Britain. Of these absentees, 21 per cent were women—but few of them owned large numbers of enslaved people. Our project has necessarily been the work of a team, both because of the scale of the research and because we needed the skills of economic, political, and cultural historians to document and analyse the legacies of these men and women. We have created an online encyclopaedia with the fruits of our labour (see www.ucl.ac.uk/lbs).

The material from the first phase of our project suggests that, at the microeconomic level, the flow of human and financial capital from the British colonial slave economy was a significant contributor to the remaking of Britain's commercial and, to a lesser extent, industrial fabric throughout the first half of the nineteenth century. Wealth derived from slave ownership went into the railways, marine insurance, merchant banking, and urban property development. It was redeployed into the new colonies of white settlement and into multiple forms of consumption, from country-house building to connoisseurship. The planters continued to have political success on some fronts—the securement of compensation and apprenticeship, delays on the abolition of the sugar duties, and the introduction of

[11] Edward Long, *The History of Jamaica: Or, General Survey of the Ancient and Modern State of That Island, with Reflections on Its Situation, Settlements, Inhabitants, Climate, Products, Commerce, Laws, and Government* (3 vols, London, 1774), vol. 1, 493–4.

[12] Sidney W. Mintz, 'Slavery and Emergent Capitalisms', in Laura Foner and Eugene D. Genovese, eds, *Slavery in the New World: A Reader in Comparative History* (Englewood Cliffs, NJ, 1969), 33.

[13] Nicholas Draper, *The Price of Emancipation: Slave-Ownership, Compensation and British Society at the End of Slavery* (Cambridge, 2010).

indentured labour. Furthermore, the slave owners and their descendants were active agents in the remaking of 'race' as a hierarchical category. Once slavery no longer fixed the African as inferior, other legitimations for his/her subordination had to be found. In the debates over 'race' in the mid-nineteenth century and in the shift from the ascendancy of abolitionist humanitarian discourse to a harsher version of stadial theory, which envisioned the civilizational process as glacially slow, historians, novelists, and travel writers with slave-owning origins played a significant part. They used their eyewitness experience to make claims as to the veracity of their characterizations of racial difference.[14]

The second phase of our project—entitled 'The Structure and Significance of British Caribbean Slave-Ownership 1763–1833'—has begun the task of analysing slave ownership and its consequences for Britain across the designated period. We are establishing patterns of ownership across more than 8,000 estates. This time the sources we are using have enabled us to collect material on the lives of the enslaved—clearly a vital part of any study of slave ownership, which must necessarily be embedded in an examination of the master–slave relationship. Some of these new data are now publicly available and offer a formidable research tool. Our particular focus as a research team is once again on the absentees and their legacies. We concentrate on tracing their commercial, political, and cultural presence and impact on Britain, which in turn allow us to re-examine the relationship between slavery, empire, and the early imperial nation. My own research is focused on the writings of the slave owners—at this stage, particularly those based in Jamaica; I am trying to grasp how they understood the world they were making and how it was organized through the marking of racial and gendered difference.

Slavery was an accepted part of British culture in the eighteenth century. There were always critics, but the slave-trading business was considered ordinary, although the details were repressed. James Thomson's immensely popular *Rule Britannia*, first performed in 1740, celebrated the freedom that was the antithesis of the slaves' condition, while—as Suvir Kaul notes—repressing and disavowing knowledge of what that business entailed.[15] Free traders had successfully challenged the Royal Africa Company's monopoly on the lucrative slave trade and argued that freedom to trade was a natural right, part of a distinctively British conception of freedom. By the 1750s the 'Guinea trade' was dominated by the British and 'enslaved labour became embedded in the very fabric of democratic freedom and economic liberalism'.[16]

In the classic accounts of the development of industrial capitalism, factory workers were waged labourers—exploited, but in possession of their own labouring bodies. In the colonies, however, workers were enslaved. At the time of emancipation there were approximately 670,000 enslaved people working on the plantations, pens, and houses of slave owners. In the planters' parlance, these men, women, and

---

[14] For a full development of these arguments see Hall et al., *Legacies*.

[15] Suvir Kaul, *Poems of Nation, Anthems of Empire: English Verse in the Long Eighteenth Century* (London, 2000).

[16] William A. Pettigrew, *Freedom's Debt: The Royal African Company and the Politics of the Atlantic Slave Trade, 1672–1752* (Williamsburg, VA, 2013), 218.

children were 'stock': commodities like any other. 'As our trade esteemed Negroe labourers merely a commodity, or *chose* in merchandize,' wrote Edward Long in his outraged *Candid Reflections* on Lord Mansfield's judgement in the celebrated *Somerset* v. *Stewart* (1772) case,

> so the parliament of Great Britain has uniformly adhered to the same idea; and hence the planters were naturally induced to frame their colony acts and customs agreeable to this, which may be termed the *national sense*, and deemed their negroes to be fit objects of purchase and sale, transferrable like any other goods and chattels: they conceived their right of property *to have and to hold*, acquired by purchase, inheritance, or grant, to be as strong, just, legal, indefeasible, and compleat, as that of any other British merchant over the goods in his warehouse.[17]

The slave was not regarded as a subject but as a property, albeit a special kind of property. First of all s/he was merchandise when bought and sold in the slave trade, quantified in the double-entry account books in terms of price and value.[18] This was the beginning of the processes through which captive human beings were turned from men and women into 'things'. Then came the terrible Middle Passage, when the work of commoditization, of 'producing' slaves, continued the deprivation of personhood, of language, and of community.[19] Once acquired by a planter, a person became private property, being regarded partly as chattel, partly as real property, and counted alongside cattle and sugar mills. 'The idea of slaves as property was as firmly accepted in the law of England as it was in that of the colonies.'[20] It was always clear, however, that a slave was not simply a 'thing'—s/he was not a commodity like any other. Slaves were both property and persons—persons who could be prosecuted for theft or rebellion; and, if they were executed, their owners received compensation. The black body was commodified and, when a slave died, the owner lost capital; yet enslaved people refused commodification, resisted dehumanization in multiple ways. While labour may be treated as abstract at some level, in life it was embodied—gendered, raced, and aged. The price of an enslaved man was significantly higher than that of a woman, particularly if the man was skilled, despite women's centrality in reproduction. Not all Africans were enslaved, but virtually all slaves were of colour. Racial otherness came to justify subordinate status. Law was not the original basis of slavery but, as Elsa Goveia has argued, the slave codes of the British Caribbean were essential for its continuance. A whole system of laws was built up on the first slave code, that of Barbados of 1661, which provided the model for other British colonies and used racial justifications to establish a separate system of trial and punishment for those who were enslaved.

---

[17] Edward Long, *Candid Reflections upon the Judgement Lately Awarded by the Court of King's Bench in Westminster Hall on What Is Commonly Called the Negroe Cause by a Planter* (London, 1772), 4.

[18] Stephanie E. Smallwood, *Saltwater Slavery: A Middle Passage from Africa to American Diaspora* (Cambridge, MA, 2007).

[19] Emma Christopher, *Slave Ship Sailors and Their Captive Cargoes, 1730–1807* (Cambridge, 2006); Marcus Rediker, *The Slave Ship: A Human History* (London, 2008).

[20] Elsa V. Goveia, 'The West Indian Slave Laws of the Eighteenth Century', in Laura Foner and Eugene D. Genovese, eds, *Slavery in the New World: A Reader in Comparative History* (Englewood Cliffs, NJ, 1969), 119.

Negroes were described as 'heathenish, brutish and an uncertain dangerous kind of people' and were subjected to the authority of their owners. In cases of rebellion or criminality they were defined as unfit to be tried according to English law and passed on to special magistrates' courts with no jury, no appeal, and a range of brutal penalties. The judicial practice of the West Indian colonies 'emphasized the difference between slave and free, and valorized the slaveholder's private power'.[21] White men, meanwhile, enjoyed the protection of English common law.

Slavery was distinguished from other forms of servitude by its permanence and by its degree of commodification; it was perpetual and inheritable. In Orlando Patterson's formulation, slavery was a form of 'natal alienation', of being alienated from all rights or claims of birth and denied any claims or obligations to one's parents. The enslaved had no right to any legitimate social order. They were born and lived under the domination of their masters. For men, the loss of manhood was central to their subordination. For women, sexual subjection to their masters and the absence of rights over the children they had born encapsulated total lack of control over their own bodies. The destruction of familial roles through denial of paternal authority and through the mother's ever present fear of losing her daughter to the predatory desires of the master has been, in Patterson's view, 'the single most destructive feature of slavery and the one that has had the most lasting effect on black life'.[22] As servants came to be distinguished from slaves and increasing emphasis was placed on origins and bodies, the differences between white people and those of African descent 'were most clearly marked in women's bodies'.[23] The breasts of the African woman were seen as confirming her fundamental difference. Edward Long in his *History* claimed that, in Africa:

> The women are delivered with little or no labour; they have therefore no more occasion for midwives than the female oran-outang, or any other wild animall. A woman brings forth her child in a quarter of an hour…Thus they seem exempted from the course [sic] inflicted upon Eve and her daughters, 'I will greatly multiply thy sorrow; in sorrow shalt thou bring forth children.'[24]

In appropriating the reproductive power of women, slave owners were attempting to ensure their labour force across generations and 'defining a biologically driven perpetual racial slavery'.[25] 'Capital comes dripping from head to foot, from every pore, with blood and dirt,' wrote Marx in *Capital*. The blood was not only the blood shed by workers; blood ties were critical to the forging of colonial slavery and to the formation of planter capital.

[21] Diana Paton, 'Punishment, Crime and the Bodies of Slaves in Eighteenth-Century Jamaica', *Journal of Social History*, 34.4 (2001), 923–54.

[22] David Scott, 'The Paradox of Freedom: An Interview with Orlando Patterson', in idem, *Small Axe: A Caribbean Journal of Criticism* 40 (2013), 96–243, here 186; Orlando Patterson, *Slavery and Social Death: A Comparative Study* (Cambridge, MA, 1982).

[23] Susan Dwyer Amussen, *Caribbean Exchanges: Slavery and the Transformation of English Society, 1640–1700* (Chapel Hill, NC, 2007), 64.

[24] Long, *History of Jamaica*, vol. 2, 380.

[25] Jennifer L. Morgan, *Laboring Women: Reproduction and Gender in New World Slavery* (Philadelphia, PA, 2004), 1.

The delineation of enslaved black men and women as property had as its counterpoint the naming of whiteness as a different kind of property, the property of freedom; for the idea of freedom generated by the colonists depended on the existence of slavery. Freedom, they maintained, meant access to public and private privileges, the mastery of their property, and the possibility of controlling critical aspects of one's own life rather than being the object of others' domination.[26] Drawing on Locke, white settlers articulated a notion of liberty that was intimately associated with the enjoyment and protection of property alongside the right to representative government, which could limit executive authority and set them free from 'political slavery'. At the same time, their legitimation of chattel slavery depended on an understanding of the enslaved as people who fell outside the social contract.[27] A set of assumptions, privileges, and benefits were attached to being white in colonial society that were affirmed and protected by law. Black racial identity marked those who were enslaved (though there were always free black people); white racial identity marked those who were free. As Bryan Edwards— slave owner, historian, and MP—wrote in his *History of the British Colonies in the West Indies*, there is

> something of a marked and predominant character common to all the White residents.... the leading feature is an independent spirit, and a display of conscious equality, throughout all ranks and conditions. The poorest White person seems to consider himself nearly on a level with the richest, and, emboldened by this idea, approaches his employer with extended hand, and a freedom, which, in the countries of Europe, is seldom displayed by men in the lower orders of life towards their superiors. It is not difficult to trace the origin of this principle. It arises, without doubt, from the pre-eminence and distinction which are necessarily attached even to the complexion of a White Man, in a country where the complexion, generally speaking, distinguishes freedom from slavery.[28]

Edwards capitalized White, just as he capitalized Negro: these were two 'classes' of people—not different species, as his friend and fellow historian Edward Long maintained, but 'classes' that could not be thought about or treated in the same way. Just as the usage of 'Negro' collapsed colour with status and defined slavery as a feature inherent in bodies rather than as a product of law and of the system of labour,[29] so the usage of 'White' collapsed colour with status too. To be white and male was to be free, to have ownership of oneself and one's labour. White men had the right to hold public office, to sit on juries, to vote (if they held sufficient property), to carry arms, to move freely, and to engage in economic activities. White women bore children who were proclaimed free. Just as slavery was passed through the mother, so was freedom. Hence the horror of white women associating with

[26] Cheryl I. Harris, *Whiteness as Property* (UCLA School of Law, Public Law and Legal Theory Research Series, Research Paper no. 06.35, 1993).
[27] For an interesting recent assessment of Locke's thinking on liberty and slavery, see Mary Nyquist, *Arbitrary Rule: Slavery, Tyranny, and the Power of Life and Death* (Chicago, IL, 2013).
[28] Bryan Edwards, *The History, Civil and Commercial, of the British Colonies in the West Indies* (3 vols, Dublin, 1793), vol. 2, 7.
[29] Amussen, *Caribbean Exchanges*.

black men: by the mid-eighteenth century such relations were strictly taboo. The juridical determinants of status, slave or free, which derived along the maternal line, were structured into the plantation system; and the work of attempting to maintain this binary between black and white could never be neglected. Yet the line was fractured by the sexual relations that characterized colonial society. Whiteness was a slippery concept. Was it a class or a species? How could it be secured? 'Race' was to be read off the body—but it was not consistently legible. The boundaries of this artificial categorization were difficult to hold in place. It was possible to become white, Matthew Lewis noted after the time he spent on his Jamaican plantations:

> The offspring of a white man and a black woman is a mulatto; the mulatto and black produce a sambo; from the mulatto and white comes a quadroon; from the quadroon and white the mustee; the child of a mustee by a white man is called a musteefino; while the children of a musteefino are free by law, and rank as white persons to all intents and purposes.[30]

The white fantasy was one of absolute power. In this society the masters were the laws—they were masters in 'the kingdom of *I*' as the abolitionist Ramsay described it.[31] Those masters relied on both physical and symbolic power: the whip was the icon of white domination and symbolic whips were woven from many areas of culture—naming, branding, and clothing. The fullest description we have of this mid-eighteenth-century period comes from Thomas Thistlewood, a relatively small slave owner who emigrated in 1750 and died in 1786. Over those years he kept an extraordinarily detailed diary, which has been transcribed and written about by Douglas Hall and Trevor Burnard.[32] In Thistlewood's world masters had complete licence to run their plantations and punish 'their' slaves as they chose. There were no restraints and the violence was terrible. Jamaican whites were notorious for the treatment of 'their' slaves, and in his years on the island Thistlewood recorded only one white man who was disciplined over ill treatment. Whites felt themselves to be living in a dangerous world, a society at war; they lived in fear and believed that this world could be controlled only through coercion. The enslaved were cowed with arbitrary and tyrannical actions, which were always supported by the full weight of the authority of the state. White Jamaicans celebrated their 'land of liberty', where they enjoyed the rights of freeborn English people; but that liberty was predicated on the infliction of terror, both real and symbolic, on the bodies and minds of the enslaved.[33] While British industrial capitalism has been associated with the disciplinary regimes of the factory and the prison, the plantation system

[30] Matthew Gregory Lewis, *Journal of a West Indian Proprietor, Kept during a Residence in Jamaica* (London, 1834), 63.

[31] Cited in Trevor Burnard, 'Evaluating Gender in Early Jamaica, 1674–1784', *The History of the Family* 12.2 (2007), 81.

[32] Douglas Hall, *In Miserable Slavery: Thomas Thistlewood in Jamaica, 1750–86* (Basingstoke, 1989); Trevor Burnard, *Mastery, Tyranny, and Desire: Thomas Thistlewood and His Slaves in the Anglo-Jamaican World* (Chapel Hill, NC, 2004).

[33] Jack P. Greene, 'Liberty, Slavery, and the Transformation of British Identity in the Eighteenth-Century West Indies', *Slavery & Abolition* 21.1 (2000), 1–31.

forcibly reminds us that other disciplinary regimes that operated directly and brutally on labourers' bodies were integral to the operation of capital.

White colonists went to Jamaica to make money: if they were successful, they were likely to return to England, which was always defined as 'home'. Their plantations would then be managed by attorneys, a phenomenon that weakened the white presence. Although himself an absentee, Long was seriously worried by the scale of absenteeism and by the fragility (as he saw it) of the white family, which put the survival of colonial society at risk. European societies were built on family and kin and systematically privileged men. These patterns were carried across the Atlantic and adapted to another place. Businesses were built on kin connections; marriage and inheritance were central to the transmission of property. As David Sabean and others have established in relation to continental Europe and Leonore Davidoff in relation to Britain, alliances between families, systematically repeated over many generations, established tight bonds of reciprocity with large networks of kin.[34] Cousin and brother–sister marriages were among the many strategies employed. This provided a form of security, since groups were bound together in dense networks. Capital was not anonymous—it had 'blood' coursing through its veins, and this had implications for how it functioned on both sides of the Atlantic. Given the dearth of commercial, professional, and financial infrastructures and the vulnerability to disease and early death, familial relations became a touchstone of commercial as well as professional trustworthiness, limiting risk at a time of huge risks. The strength of these networks was particularly crucial in places like Jamaica, where death and disease were rife and white mortality was staggeringly high. The status of the white family, with its extended elite connections, was critical to the survival of white patriarchal domination.

The Long family was part of this elite white world that crossed England and Jamaica, cementing colonial power. The family had been in Jamaica since this colony was first conquered by Oliver Cromwell's forces led by Penn and Venables, in 1655. Samuel Long was on the original expedition, acting as secretary to the four commissioners appointed by Cromwell. The expedition was planned and resourced badly and it took a few years to beat off the Spanish, who had been in occupation; but by 1657 the advantages that the island offered had become clear. Land grants were awarded to the soldiers and many became 'red-hot planters'. Thirty-acre lots were being sold by 1660 and Samuel Long patented and purchased great tracts of land, accumulating between 16,000 and 18,000 acres. His principal settlement was in Clarendon, where he had seven plantations that had already been established by the Spanish and had been used for growing provisions, indigo, and sugar. He became a highly significant political figure, speaker of the House of Assembly, successfully challenging the Crown's effort to limit the colony's rights to representative government. His son Charles returned to England around 1700 and bought an estate in Suffolk. Samuel had married twice; both women were daughters

---

[34] David Warren Sabean, Simon Teuscher, and Jon Mathieu, eds, *Kinship in Europe: Approaches to Long-Term Development, 1300–1900* (Oxford, 2007); Leonore Davidoff, *Thicker than Water: Siblings and Their Relations, 1780–1920* (Oxford, 2012).

of West Indian governors, and his second wife was heiress to Sir William Beeston.[35] The Long and the Beeston families became intimately connected. Beeston Long (named of course after his mother's connection) married into the Drake family and together they established a West Indian merchant house based in Fenchurch Street that was doing business with the East Indies too, as Clare Taylor has documented.[36] Around 1758 they were joined by Henry Dawkins, heir to huge Jamaican estates, and for decades Drake, Long, and Dawkins traded in the West Indian and American markets.

Charles Long lost his own and other people's fortunes in the South Sea Bubble and left his son Samuel, Edward Long's father, severely indebted. Samuel married Mary Tate, a woman with little dowry. Facing a serious shortage of money to support his growing family, he was impelled to return to Jamaica to try and save the family estates, Lucky Valley and Longville, from the maladministration of his attorney. When he died in 1757, Edward, his second son, set sail for Jamaica. The following year Edward married Mary Ballard, widow of John Palmer, second daughter and eventually heir of Thomas Beckford, one of the Beckford clan. They, too, had been in Jamaica from early settlement and had extensive metropolitan and colonial business and political connections. Around 1750 the Beckfords, Ballards, and Palmers between them owned nearly half of the cultivated land in Jamaica. The Longs were thus connected with key Jamaican planter families. One of Edward Long's daughter's married a son of Henry Dawkins (a marriage that Dawkins strongly objected to on the grounds of money) and another married into the English aristocracy, extending further their web of connection. These families all operated transatlantically—they were neither residents nor absentees on a permanent basis. But metropole and colony were different localities with very different sexual economies. For the most part the men aimed to live in England but, when family finances required it, they would return to Jamaica, knowing that slave-produced sugar was their surest route to riches. 'Uncle Beeston' was 'the kindly man of business' for the Longs, heading the merchant firm, always ready to give advice and act as trustee or executor;[37] kind to his own family but running a slaving business that was anything but kind. The men in these networks did business and politics together, took one another's sons into their households, gave advice on education and training, and kept one another informed on metropolitan and colonial affairs. They were active in the defence of West Indian interests in London, serving on the committee of the West India Merchants and Planters, organizing meetings, lobbying men of influence, and providing evidence to the parliamentary inquiries that threatened them once the movement for abolition had gained strength in the 1780s.

The control of their wives' property and their capacity to manage the distribution of their own after death were critical tools in the maintenance of patriarchal

---

[35] On the Long family history, see R. Mowbray Howard, *Record and Letters of the Family of the Longs of Longville, Jamaica, and Hampton Lodge, Surrey* (2 vols, London, 1925).

[36] Clare Taylor, unpublished manuscript. Thanks to Dr Taylor for sharing this material with me.

[37] Howard, *Record and Letters*, vol. 1, 132.

power. Strict settlement and entail were employed to keep control over family property. Sons were always privileged over daughters. Henry Dawkins's will distributed his landed properties among his sons, while his daughters received marriage portions in money.[38] In cases of intestacy there were clear regulations over dower, all land went to the eldest son, and personal property was divided between the children. Sometimes first sons were left all the property; sometimes it was divided between brothers. There may have been particular reluctance to leave Jamaican property to daughters: running a plantation was difficult work for a woman. Trevor Burnard has found that female inheritance was severely restricted up to the mid-eighteenth-century at least, and there was no provision in Jamaica's Court of Chancery for marriage settlements for women.[39] Daughters were more likely to be left money, usually paid on marriage, and marrying a West Indian heiress became a well-known route to riches in the late eighteenth century. White women were critical to the transmission of property through marriage, widowhood, and the bearing of children. Their subordinate legal status secured men's dominance. William Beckford had no scruples about taking advantage of his brother's early death to seize his properties, effectively disinheriting his mother and instigating a long legal battle.[40]

Families were full of tensions and rivalries that could weaken and fragment familial power. A wife who displeased her husband could find herself cast out on a meagre annuity—as Edward Long's mother Mary Tate did. The art of growing rich, went a saying in Jamaica, was to marry and bury. Women's mortality was marginally better than men's; they were frequently widowed and married again. Male relatives could not be relied on for support. Edward Long's sister Charlotte, for example, was locked in conflict with her brother-in-law after the death of her husband. She was pregnant when her husband, George Ellis, an extensive plantation owner, died. He had made a will in which he bequeathed her a dower of £1,200 but no provision had been made for the child. His brother John immediately claimed the whole property, bar the annuity. Their friends and relations were divided, but eventually a settlement was made that secured provision in case the child was a boy—but only for his lifetime. The son, George, had to tread very carefully with his uncle and pursued a profession, since he had no confidence that he would be able to secure any of his father's land. He wrote bitterly to his uncle Long of that 'deepest of all masks—that of apparent generosity'.[41] Familial belonging did not always secure dividends.

Edward Long was right that the white family was a fragile formation, not only because of mortality rates and familial conflicts but also because of the prevalence of concubinage and the relative paucity of white women on the islands. Initially white migration to Jamaica was heavily male, and the demographic imbalance

---

[38] Thanks to James Dawkins for this information.
[39] Trevor Burnard, 'Family Continuity and Female Independence in Jamaica, 1665–1734', *Continuity and Change*, 7.2 (1992), 181–98.
[40] Perry Gauci, *William Beckford, First Prime Minister of the London Empire* (London and New Haven, CT, 2013), 35–6.
[41] Howard, *Record and Letters*, vol. 2, 135.

remained a major issue. Planters who became absentees often left a mistress on the island and married in the mother country in order to secure legitimate heirs, as did William Beckford. The longing for 'exotic otherness' enthralled white men, and sexual desire cut across lines of racial belonging. Every white man had his 'house-keeper', as numerous contemporaries noted, and the children of these mixed relationships became the free population of colour, which increasingly peopled the island.[42] Edward Long was particularly condemnatory of this practice, hating the scale of miscegenation and its effects. In his mind, this is what prevented the development of an 'improved' and civilized society, one built on 'proper' familial relations. 'Intemperance and sensuality', he believed,

> are the fatal instruments which, in this island, have committed...havoc. It is a question easily answered, whether...it would be more for the interest of Britain, that Jamaica should be possessed and peopled by white inhabitants, or by Negroes and Mulattos?...it might be much better for Britain, and Jamaica too, if the white men in that colony would abate of their infatuated attachments to black women, and instead of being 'grac'd with a *yellow offspring not their own*' perform the duty incumbent on every good citizen, by raising in honourable wedlock a race of unadulterated beings.

He bemoaned the ways in which men became enslaved by their passions, abject in the face of the manipulations of their grasping lovers, producing 'a vast addition of spurious offsprings of different complexions' rather than legitimate white sons and daughters.[43] No shame was felt in this 'torrid clime', where, as Bryan Edwards wrote, many considered 'a family as an encumbrance' and marriage was held in 'but little estimation'.[44] Some men left their wives in England and lived with their mistresses in the colony. Rich bachelors were common—like Simon Taylor, one of the wealthiest of Jamaican planters in the late eighteenth century, who, as Lady Nugent noted, had 'a numerous family, some almost on every one of his estates'.[45] Taylor left the bulk of his property to his nephews in England, ensuring the continuity of the white male line. But he also left a large sum of money and an annuity to one of his mistresses, and his granddaughter received compensation for one enslaved person, willed to her by her grandfather after abolition. She was living in London in the 1830s and is recorded as having married a chemist in 1848—her life a far cry from that of her planter grandfather.[46] Like many others, Taylor's illegitimate children were the product of a power relationship. Yet that power, which was one of the cements of slave society, also presaged its dissolution.

Many of these white fathers clearly felt some responsibility or affection for their mixed-heritage children. They provided for them in their wills, albeit on a very

[42] Illegitimacy was a complicated question in the metropole, but its connotations were infinitely more complex in the colonies. On the metropole, see Margot Finn, Michael Lobban, and Jenny Bourne Taylor, eds, *Legitimacy and Illegitimacy in Nineteenth-century Law, Literature and History* (Basingstoke, 2010).

[43] Long, *History of Jamaica*, vol. 2, 327–8.

[44] Edwards, *The History, Civil and Commercial*, vol. 1, 217.

[45] *Lady Nugent's Journal of Her Residence in Jamaica from 1801 to 1805*, ed. by Philip Wright (Jamaica, 2002), 68.

[46] See http://www.ucl.ac.uk/lbs/person/view/12954 (accessed 19 May 2014).

different scale from that of provisions for the legitimate. This meant that familial property was fragmented and that people of colour became significant owners, posing a threat to white hegemony. By 1733 legislation had been passed preventing freemen of African heritage from political participation and limiting their rights in courts and on plantations. 'Privilege petitioning', however, was used to make individual exemptions in numerous cases. A very serious rebellion in 1760 provoked a sharp reaction against any further encroachments on white power, and a limit was set on the amount that free people of colour could inherit. This act was defended in the metropole on the grounds that it would check unauthorized 'fornication and concubinage' and encourage 'the legal propagation of Children by marriage' and the transmission 'of property and power to a pure and legitimate race'. The then agent for Jamaica, Lovell Stanhope, expressed his deep concern over 'the ascendancy which the Mulattoes, especially the females, have already in that Country over dissolute Minds, and of the necessity which there is of restraining them'.[47] The French Revolution and events in San Domingo were a further cause of terror to white Jamaicans, as people of colour claimed political rights. After 1802, as Daniel Livesay has documented, privilege petitions were no longer agreed upon and by 1816 the first lobby of people of colour was organized.[48] But the white population's refusal to share its privileges meant that it could not hope for the support of the 'browns' in the face of slave rebellion and abolition. As the white population failed to reproduce itself and shrank in relation to the 'browns' and the 'blacks', the project of white domination was doomed—albeit only in some respects. A white–black binary cannot capture the political complexities around emancipation and its aftermath any more than a class analysis can give us a full account of the development of industrial capitalism.

Women's property ownership and economic independence were severely restricted in eighteenth-century and early nineteenth-century England, as numerous studies have shown, the law of coverture that prevented married women from owning property in their own right being only the most obvious legal restriction. In Jamaica there were even greater difficulties, since running a plantation depended on white men's physical mastery. Edward Long conducted a survey of landownership in 1750, recording full names and acreage. Where it is possible, as James Dawkins has calculated, to establish gender, out of a total of 1,575 landholders 84 per cent were men, 11 per cent women. Yet 90 per cent of the land was held by men, only 4 per cent by women.[49] In other words, not only were men the vast majority of landowners—they also owned most of the land. The parish of St Catherine, in which Spanish Town, the capital, was situated, had the largest number of women owners—a phenomenon probably linked to urban ownership.[50]

[47] Cited in Brooke N. Newman, 'Gender, Sexuality and the Formation of Racial Identities in the C18 Anglo-Caribbean World', *Gender & History* 22.3 (2010), 586–7.

[48] Daniel Livesay, 'The Decline of Jamaica's Interracial Households and the Fall of the Planter Class, 1733–1823', *Atlantic Studies* 9.1 (2012), 107–23.

[49] Thanks to James Dawkins for his analysis of Long's statistics.

[50] Thanks to Kate Donington for her work on the Slave Registers of St Catherine, from which she has derived these figures.

This compares most interestingly with the figures we have established in relation to the compensation claims. Of the 47,000 individual claims registered after emancipation, approximately 41 per cent were made by women. Yet only 21 per cent of the absentee claimants were women. This points to the very large numbers of women in the Caribbean who owned property in the enslaved. The majority of these women, who were single or widowed, were small owners and were almost certainly women of colour (a fact that is rarely recorded). In Christer Petley's analysis of ownership in St James, a parish in Jamaica, in the early 1800s, he found that over 10 per cent of the registered land was owned by women, and two-thirds of these had fewer than five slaves.[51] Of course many men had small numbers of slaves too, but the vast majority of the enslaved were owned by large planters, virtually all of whom were men. In the unusual cases where there was a woman owner with large numbers of enslaved people, she would have to rely on a male attorney to manage the property for her. There is evidence that, in the transient world of the Southern Caribbean, the frontier colonies of Grenada, Trinidad, and Demerara may have provided more opportunities for women. Indeed some were able to amass wealth and enslaved property in the late eighteenth century.[52] Many of the small women owners were in the urban centres, perhaps with two or three enslaved women whom they hired out as domestics. Others were landladies with hotels, brothels, or eating places—service providers for the urban population. A typical example would be Ann Marryat, who successfully claimed compensation for thirteen enslaved men and women.[53]

Ann Marryat was the illegitimate daughter of Joseph Marryat, a key supporter of the West India Interest. He was one of the most articulate of the absentee slave owners and had properties in Trinidad, Grenada, Jamaica, and St Lucia and a merchant firm in London. In 1807 he petitioned Parliament against the abolition of the slave trade and, while an MP, spoke vociferously in defence of the trade and of slavery and against the equalization of East Indian and West Indian sugar duties.[54] He published numerous pamphlets—most notably his *Thoughts on the Abolition of the Slave Trade and Civilization of Africa* in 1816, which was part of a long-running controversy with the leading abolitionists James Stephen and Zachary Macaulay. At his death in 1824 he was said to be worth half a million. While he was living and working as a merchant in Grenada in the 1780s, his 'natural' daughter Ann was born and baptized. In 1790, before leaving the island, he manumitted 'my negroe woman slave...Fanny, together with her two mulatto children, Ann and Joseph'. Ann was able to establish herself independently and, like many women of colour, she did not marry, though she lived with a man, thus keeping control of her property. In 1815 Ann Marryat appeared in the will of a Demerara planter, Robert Kingston, named as his 'housekeeper' and left a £100 p.a. Kingston also willed £1,000 to each of his children by her, John, Joseph, and

[51] Christer Petley, *Slaveholders in Jamaica: Colonial Society and Culture during the Era of Abolition* (London, 2009), 20.

[52] Kit Candlin, *The Last Caribbean Frontier, 1795–1815* (Basingstoke, 2012).

[53] See http://www.ucl.ac.uk/lbs/claim/view/9138 (accessed 19 May 2014).

[54] See http://www.historyofparliamentonline.org/volume/1820-1832/member/marryat-joseph-1757-1824 (accessed 6 May 2017).

one unborn.[55] Ann Marryat became a slave owner herself and later appeared in the compensation records for Demerara, being awarded £567/4/6d for thirteen enslaved people.[56] In later years her father expostulated on the political dangers associated with the growing free population of colour. Such contradictions were at the heart of the slavery system.

It is not known whether Marryat's legitimate children were aware of Ann's existence. At his death Marryat's wealth was divided between his widow and his legitimate children: his sons received his property in Britain and the Caribbean; his daughters received £20,000 each.[57] Ann had fared very differently. Nevertheless, the scale of women's ownership in the Caribbean marks one of the ways in which the colony opened up possibilities for women, particularly if they were unmarried or widowed, as so many were in a society in which marriage was marginalized. This was of considerable significance in post-emancipation society—Jamaica has long had a tradition of single women, now married too, in business, commerce, and more recently government.

The failure of white society to reproduce itself meant that Jamaica could never become a settler society on the model of the North American colonies.[58] But, as Kathleen Wilson argues, Jamaica's motley population of whites rich and poor, free blacks and people of colour, Maroons and Jews could never be permanently dragooned into the black–white binaries of the slave-owners' fantasies.[59] Rather it became a society with a majority population of black and brown people, who ensured that Jamaica would never be the place that Long desired—one dominated by white men of taste who would take care that order and hierarchy were properly maintained. At the same time the denial and destruction of the black family has had profound and long-term effects, shaping the patterns of Jamaican society into the present and with destructive echoes in the metropole. Gender and 'race' structured the organization of property and power in slave society. But they did more than this; they were historically dynamic—axes of change. Gender and 'race' both cemented and dissolved the slave system. White men's power was secured in part through the subordination of white women and the control that could be exercised over their property. White men's use of sexuality as a form of power and control over the black population acted towards emasculating black men and terrorizing black women. But at the same time it dissolved those controls, since the brown population, the product of desire for otherness, gradually came to exceed the white, and the claims by people of colour, alongside those of the black majority, disrupted

---

[55] Personal communication from Paul Roper, a descendant of the Marryats, who has done extensive research on the family. Many thanks to him for the help he has given to the Legacies of British Slave-ownership.

[56] T71/885 British Guiana (Werken Rust estate); see http://www.ucl.ac.uk/lbs/person/view/9216 (accessed 6 May 2017).

[57] Will of Joseph Marryat, TNA PROB 11/1681/288, 16/2/1824.

[58] Trevor Burnard, 'A Failed Settler Society: Marriage and Demographic Failure in Early Jamaica', *Journal of Social History* 28.1 (1994), 63–82.

[59] Kathleen Wilson, *The Island Race: Englishness, Empire and Gender in the Eighteenth Century* (London, 2003); Kathleen Wilson, 'The Performance of Freedom: Maroons and the Colonial Order in C18 Jamaica and the Atlantic Sound', *William and Mary Quarterly* 66.1 (2009), 45–86.

efforts at white domination. Furthermore, the figure of the lascivious and immoral slave owner was used by humanitarians as one of the rallying cries for the abolition of slavery. Women activists in particular highlighted the immorality of slavery, drawing attention to the predatory sexuality of corrupted white men, the enforced separation of mothers from children, and the lack of support for the family.

*   *   *

'Capital comes dripping from head to foot, from every pore, with blood and dirt,' wrote Marx; the blood we could associate with the bloodlines of familial capitalism and with women's bodies—as objects of desire, as workers in the cane fields, as bearers of children, as transmitters of capital—whether the capital of the heiress or the capital of labour reproduced. The dirt carries connotations with the plantation as much as with the cotton factories. This compels us to rethink the classical accounts of industrial capitalism, dominated by the mill and the emaciated body of the factory worker. The clues are there for us to follow—the task of critical historians is to make out what has been forgotten.

The trauma of slavery is not over. It lives on in the structural inequalities that disfigure both Jamaican and British society, in the gun culture of the inner cities, in the crises of black masculinity, in the appalling figures of ill health and illiteracy that are characteristic of the contemporary Caribbean and are mirrored in the figures of black underachievement and mental illness in this society. The memory work that we seek to facilitate though our project—the critical appraisal of the past as 'a time that is not yet past and which continues to disfigure the present and fore-close the future'—involves recognition of the persistent privileges that have belonged to whiteness, the persistent poverty of the Caribbean that has been, as David Scott argues, 'a constituting condition for ill-gotten European prosperity'.[60] Such work requires attention to the organization of capital and labour, to systems of distribution and consumption, to the issues that Hobsbawm did so much to help us understand, alongside a recognition of the centrality of cultural practices, of reproduction, of gender and 'race' as axes of power. The movement for reparations is growing apace in the Caribbean. Reparation will need to take many forms. A necessary precondition for this is remembering: forgetting took work; remembering takes work too. There is much work to be done.

ACKNOWLEDGEMENTS

This paper originated as a plenary lecture at the conference 'History after Hobsbawm: A Conference on the Current Trajectories of History', organized by Birkbeck and *Past and Present* in April 2014. I would like to thank Nick Draper, Margot Finn, Mark Harvey, and Keith McClelland for their very helpful comments. A shorter version was published in *History Workshop Journal* 78 (2014), 22–38. The Legacies of British Slave-Ownership project has been generously supported by the ESRC, the AHRC and UCL.

---

[60] The term is David Scott's; see his 'Preface: Debt, Redress', *Small Axe* 43 (2014), x.

3

Writing Europe into the History of the British Empire

Jan Rüger

What effect did the empire have on Britain's relationship with Europe? Historians have tended to give a deceptively simple answer: the empire pulled the British away from the continent; it enabled them to disengage from Europe. From the Napoleonic Wars to the Cold War and beyond, this idea has proved attractive not only to scholars, but also to politicians and commentators. Empire and Europe, they have suggested, amounted to alternative choices, the one, in Hugo Young's words, 'necessarily imperilling the other'.[1] The continent, plagued with revolution and tyranny, was something Britain would do well to stay away from. The empire, intimately connected as it was to the role of the Royal Navy, allowed it to do just that. As long as the fleet dominated the world's maritime thoroughfares, Britain would not need to meddle in continental politics. It could concentrate on extending its empire and worldwide trade. So, in building their empire, the British distanced themselves from the continent. Only after the Second World War, as Britain's strategic influence was rapidly contracting, did this alleged effect of the empire come to an end. As A. G. Hopkins has put it with more than a hint of regret, by the end of the twentieth century the British had become 'drawn, less willingly, into Europe—a fate forestalled for centuries by the possession of the empire'.[2]

Hopkins's depiction can be seen as paradigmatic for a tradition that continues to be prominent in the writing of British history. The underlying assumption—namely that empire and Europe constitute opposing historical dynamics—has obvious political implications (on which, more further below). It also mirrors the functional differentiation of history as a profession into subdisciplines, a

---

[1] Hugo Young, *This Blessed Plot: Britain and Europe from Churchill to Blair* (London, 1998), 2. The new currency that the 'Europe vs Empire' dichotomy has acquired through the British referendum on EU membership has been commented on extensively. See only Linda Colley, 'Brexiters Are Nostalgics in Search of a Lost Empire', *Financial Times*, 22 April 2016; Sally Tomlinson and Danny Dorling, 'Brexit Has Its Roots in the British Empire', *New Statesman*, 9 May 2016; Ben Judah, 'England's Last Gasp of Empire', *New York Times*, 12 July 2016.

[2] A. G. Hopkins, 'Back to the Future: From National History to Imperial History', *Past & Present* 164 (1999), 198–243, here 239. For an appreciation of Hopkins's influence on the writing of imperial and global history, see Toyin Falola and Emily Brownell, 'The Intellectual Universe of Professor Antony Gerald Hopkins', in Toyin Falola and Emily Brownell, eds, *Africa, Empire and Globalization: Essays in Honor of A. G. Hopkins* (Durham, NC, 2011), 3–50.

differentiation that was the product of the age of empire itself. Imperial history rose in the late nineteenth and early twentieth century as an endeavour that was meant to be distinct from British history, developing its own institutions, professorial chairs, and academic journals.[3] In the early 1970s it was, in Linda Colley's words, still 'thoroughly compartmentalized' (as well as 'comprehensively masculine').[4] Historians of modern Britain, in turn, showed comparably little interest in the empire. If they looked beyond the shores of the British Isles, they were most likely to explore the historical connections between Britain and its European neighbours—so much so that in the mid-1970s John Pocock felt compelled to warn them not to fall for the supposedly hegemonic perspective of 'Europe', 'that tendentious and aggressive term'.[5] British history, he argued, ought to be actively distanced from the European context and redirected into the imperial and global arena inhabited by 'Greater Britons'.[6]

Much has changed since those days. After the 'imperial turn', which gathered momentum from the 1990s onwards, few historians will need reminding about the need to study Britain and its colonies in one context.[7] As Dane Kennedy put it recently, it 'has become all but impossible for historians who study modern Britain to ignore its empire'.[8] The rethinking of the relationship between Britain and its empire has been broadened out by the rise of world history, prompting historians to 'write the British empire into world history' (Antoinette Burton) or to 'rewrite the British themselves, so that they may be put more accurately in their place in global history' (Linda Colley).[9] As fruitful and welcome as these trends

---

[3] Dane Kennedy, 'Imperial History and Post-Colonial History', *Journal of Imperial and Commonwealth History* 24 (1996), 345–63; David Armitage, *The Ideological Origins of the British Empire* (Cambridge, 2000), esp. ch. 1; Linda Colley, 'What Is Imperial History Now?', in David Cannadine, ed., *What Is History Now?* (Basingstoke, 2002), 132–47.

[4] Colley, 'What Is Imperial History Now?', 132.

[5] J. G. A. Pocock, *The Discovery of Islands: Essays in British History* (Cambridge, 2005), 78. For the original article, see J. G. A. Pocock, 'British History: A Plea for a New Subject', *Journal of Modern History* 47 (1975), 601–24. See also J. G. A. Pocock, 'The New British History in Atlantic Perspective: An Antipodean Commentary', *American Historical Review* 104 (1999), 490–500, esp. 492–5.

[6] On Pocock, see David Armitage, 'Greater Britain: A Useful Category of Historical Analysis?' *American Historical Review* 104 (1999), 427–45 and Richard Bourke, 'Pocock and the Presuppositions of the New British History', *Historical Journal* 53 (2010), 747–70.

[7] Ann Laura Stoler and Fredrick Cooper, eds, *Tensions of Empire: Colonial Cultures in a Bourgeois World* (Berkeley, CA, 1997); Catherine Hall, *Civilising Subjects: Colony and Metropole in the English Imagination, 1830–1867* (Chicago, IL, and London, 2002); Antoinette Burton, ed., *After the Imperial Turn: Thinking With and Through the Nation* (Durham, NC, 2003); Kathleen Wilson, ed., *A New Imperial History: Culture, Identity and Modernity in Britain and the Empire 1660–1840* (Cambridge, 2004); Catherine Hall and Sonya O. Rose, eds, *At Home with the Empire: Metropolitan Culture and the Imperial World* (Cambridge and New York, 2006); Kathleen Wilson, 'Old Imperialisms and New Imperial Histories: Rethinking the History of the Present', *Radical History Review* 95 (2006), 211–34; Catherine Hall and Keith McClellan, eds, *Race, Nation and Empire: Making Histories, 1750 to the Present* (Manchester, 2010); Antoinette Burton, *Empire in Question: Reading, Writing, and Teaching British Imperialism* (Durham, NC, and London, 2011).

[8] Dane Kennedy, 'The Imperial History Wars', *Journal of British Studies* 54 (2015), 5–22, here 5.

[9] Antoinette Burton, 'Re-Positioning British Imperialism in World History', in Catherine Hall and Keith McClelland, eds, *Race, Nation and Empire: Making Histories, 1750 to the Present* (Manchester, 2010), 199–216, here 213; Linda Colley, *Captives: Britain, Empire and the World, 1600–1850* (London, 2002), 19.

have been, regrettably few historians have taken the opposite route: towards writing European history into the imperial British past, or indeed towards writing the British empire into European history. The two magisterial histories of the nineteenth century by Chris Bayly and Jürgen Osterhammel should be read as evidence that this is possible.[10] But Bayly's call for historians to study 'within one frame' how European and imperial experiences interacted 'in the creation of modern Britain' has yet to be answered by a broader historiography.[11] Most of the innovative work of the 'new imperial history' has moved outwards, from British to imperial and then to world history—but it has rarely sought to integrate a European perspective into this enlarged context.[12]

Anglophone historians of continental Europe have made a similar journey. Those who pioneered new approaches in the writing of European history after the Second World War worked on phenomena that they approached, first and foremost, within national frameworks.[13] From these they then extrapolated towards 'modern Europe'—which mostly excluded Britain. This was mirrored by the way in which the teaching of modern history became structured at most British universities. Survey courses on 'modern Europe' typically consisted of series of lectures on national topics: 'the French Revolution', 'Italian unification', 'German nationalism', 'the Russian Revolution', and so on.[14] Only rarely did continental Europe, this sum of national pasts, meet with modern Britain, taught in a separate series of lectures by a separate set of academics. The empire was a distinct subject yet again, taught by a third set of historians who, until the end of the Cold War, would have been unlikely to predict the remarkable rise of interest that their field has attracted since.

If the relationship between these three subject areas—Britain, Europe, empire—was discussed, it was (and continues to be) done mostly in terms of Britain's strategic priorities, as if 'empire' and 'continent' represented two distinct world-historical routes between which the British were in a position to choose. Thus one school of thought, represented by Paul Kennedy and Paul W. Schroeder, has argued that the empire mattered comparably little for Britain's role in the European concert.[15]

[10] C. A. Bayly, *The Birth of the Modern World 1780–1914* (Oxford, 2004); Jürgen Osterhammel, *Die Verwandlung der Welt: Eine Geschichte des 19. Jahrhunderts* (Munich, 2009), translated as *The Transformation of the World: A Global History of the Nineteenth Century* (Princeton, NJ, 2014).

[11] C. A. Bayly, 'Afterword', in Burton, *Empire in Question*, 300.

[12] Duncan Bell, 'Empire and International Relations in Victorian Political Thought', *Historical Journal* 49 (2005), 281–98, esp. 295, makes the same point for the history of political thought. There are obvious and important exceptions, especially with regard to the eighteenth and early nineteenth centuries. See especially Nick Harding, *Hanover and the British Empire, 1700–1837* (Woodbridge, 2007).

[13] For a recent critique of this approach, see Richard J. Evans, *The Pursuit of Power: Europe 1815–1914* (London, 2016), xvi–xvii. See also Richard J. Evans, *Cosmopolitan Islanders: British Historians and the European Continent* (Cambridge, 2005) and Geoff Eley, 'Crossing the North Sea: Is There a British Approach to German History?', in Jan Rüger and Nikolaus Wachsmann, eds, *Rewriting German History* (London, 2015), 1–25.

[14] Jan Rüger, 'OXO: Or, the Challenges of Transnational History', *European History Quarterly* 40 (2010), 656–68, here 660.

[15] Paul M. Kennedy, *The Rise of the Anglo-German Antagonism 1860–1914* (London, 1980); Paul W. Schroeder, *The Transformation of European Politics, 1763–1848* (Oxford, 1994). For a more detailed

Brendan Simms has pushed this line further recently. The history of Britain 'is primarily a continental story', he has declared.[16] In his picture the empire is merely a function of Europe: 'no Europe, no England, no United Kingdom, no British empire', he posits with a strong dose of historical determinism.[17] Another school of thought, of which Niall Ferguson is a prominent advocate, has suggested the opposite: the empire, not Europe, had priority as the most significant determinant of British foreign policy. Rather than continental rivals such as Germany, it was the threat posed by Britain's imperial antagonists Russia and France that motivated London to align itself, however hesitantly, with Paris and St Petersburg in the decades before 1914.[18]

Was Britain's entry into the First World War a logical decision, taken in order to defend the status quo in Europe, or should it be seen as a deeply misguided step, which should have been avoided for the sake of the empire? The controversy on this question has mostly focused on establishing which factor, empire or continent, dominated (or should have dominated) in British thinking. Rarely have the protagonists in this debate considered Britain's imperial and European challenges systematically in one context. With few exceptions, 'empire' and 'continent' continue to represent distinctly separate lenses through which historians interpret Britain's external affairs in the modern period. 'It was as though Britain was vaccinated from the contagious problems of Europe,' Peter Frankopan has recently asserted, neatly summing up a long tradition of historiographical stereotypes.[19] Never mind that such depictions repeat the tired cliché of Europe as ridden by disease and instability and contrast it with an equally clichéd picture of British prosperity—the caricature of a British *Sonderweg*.[20] What is of interest here is that such evocations of British exceptionalism claim the empire as an alternative to Europe that allowed Britain to disengage from the continent. But when exactly was this mythical period in which Britain could isolate itself from any of the challenges arising in continental Europe?

*   *   *

For Eric Hobsbawm, there never was any question of studying Britain and its empire in a context that excluded Europe. While Pocock and others were busy

---

survey, see Jan Rüger, 'Revisiting the Anglo-German Antagonism', *Journal of Modern History* 83 (2011), 579–617.

[16] Brendan Simms, *Britain's Europe: A Thousand Years of Conflict and Cooperation* (London, 2016), xiv.

[17] Ibid., 243.

[18] Niall Ferguson, *The Pity of War* (London, 1998); Keith Wilson, *Empire and Continent: Studies in British Foreign Policy from the 1880s to the First World War* (London, 1987); Keith Neilson, *Britain and the Last Tsar: British Policy and Russia, 1894–1917* (Oxford, 1995); Andreas Rose, *Zwischen Empire und Kontinent: Britische Außenpolitik vor dem Ersten Weltkrieg* (Munich, 2011).

[19] Peter Frankopan, *The Silk Roads: A New History of the World* (London, 2015), 271.

[20] Geoff Eley, 'The British Model and the German Road', in David Blackbourn and Geoff Eley, *The Peculiarities of German History: Bourgeois Society and Politics in Nineteenth-Century Germany* (Oxford, 1984), 39–155; Bernd Weisbrod, 'Der englische "Sonderweg" in der neueren Geschichte', *Geschiche und Gesellschaft* 16 (1990), 233–52; Jürgen Osterhammel, *Geschichtswissenschaft jenseits des Nationalstaats: Studien zu Beziehungsgeschichte und Zivilisationsvergleich* (Göttingen 2001), 122–40.

trying to extract the British past from the fate of being 'Europeanized', Hobsbawm wrote his trilogy of the nineteenth century, which explicitly transcends such categories. In *The Age of Revolution, The Age of Capital,* and *The Age of Empire,* published between 1962 and 1987, he established a narrative that continuously interweaves Britain, Europe, and the world.[21] In his account it is precisely the combination of European and global contexts that explains Britain's pivotal role in the long nineteenth century. Importantly, the approach he takes is not based on any clear-cut definition of Europe, be it geographical or political. In 'The Curious History of Europe', an essay first published in 1996, Hobsbawm is characteristic-ally dismissive about such definitions. 'Europe', he writes, is simply one of the various 'human names for parts of the global land-mass'.[22] It 'exists exclusively as an intellectual construct'.[23] With its focus on Europe as a 'shifting, divisible and flexible concept',[24] the essay reads like a retrospective explanation of the rationale that Hobsbawm followed in his trilogy. While he does not demonize Europe, he shares Pocock's fundamental scepticism about the European idea, which he debunks as a dangerous ideology aimed at continental hegemony. For Hobsbawm, the Cold War had produced the latest twist in this tradition, which had defined and redefined the continent as a single entity according to political aims. The historian's task, in contrast, was to explore Europe's 'economically, politically and culturally heterogeneous' character: 'There has never been a single Europe. Difference cannot be eliminated from our history.'[25]

As we go about writing history after Hobsbawm, it is worth recalling that 'empire' has been a similarly ill-defined and shifting concept. There was little of a 'project' or 'system', certainly until late in the nineteenth century, that would have united this staggeringly diverse patchwork of territories and claims held together by a thin layer of administration and representation.[26] Moreover, just as the European idea has been a political construct ('from Napoleon via the Pan-European movement of the 1920s and Goebbels to the European Economic Community', as Hobsbawm had it), the opposition between empire and Europe has been one, too.[27] Again and again, British politicians have found it advantageous to juxtapose the two as separate and inherently opposed spheres of influence. From the Napoleonic Wars to the Cold War, they have declared Britain's exceptional path to be founded on its global empire, allowing it to withhold from playing an active role 'in Europe'. Yet just as consistently has the claim of exceptionalism founded on imperial detachment come up against the messy reality of geopolitical inter-dependence. From Pitt to Churchill, British governments had to acknowledge

---

[21] Eric Hobsbawm, *The Age of Revolution: Europe, 1789–1848* (London, 1962); Eric Hobsbawm, *The Age of Capital: 1848–1875* (London, 1975); Eric Hobsbawm, *The Age of Empire: 1875–1914* (London, 1987).
[22] Eric Hobsbawm, *On History* (London, 1997), 287–301, here 287.
[23] Ibid., 289.   [24] Ibid., 290.   [25] Ibid., 293.
[26] John Darwin, *The Empire Project: The Rise and Fall of the British World-System, 1830–1970* (Cambridge, 2011); Duncan Bell, *The Idea of Greater Britain: Empire and the Future of World Order, 1860–1900* (Princeton, NJ, 2007).
[27] Hobsbawm, *On History*, 291.

that empire and Europe were bound up with one another strategically and economically, in a way that made it impossible to choose one over the other.

At the beginning of the nineteenth century, when Napoleon's army was rapidly advancing against its continental opponents, this was one of the most important lessons that consecutive British governments were forced to learn. Faced with the prospect of French dominance on the continent, important voices in the political establishment advocated a turn away from Europe. Henry Dundas, 1st Viscount Melville, secretary of war under Pitt from 1794 to 1801, was one of them. In March 1800 he penned a memorandum that has come to be seen as a classic formulation of the imperial argument for British disengagement from Europe. The struggle against Napoleon, Dundas argued, was not at the heart of Britain's long-term interests. Rather than dedicate what he saw as disproportionate resources to the struggle for Europe, Britain ought to invest in overseas expansion. Worldwide trade and the Royal Navy's command of the global maritime thoroughfares would define its future. Consequently, the communication with Britain's 'distant Possessions in every Part of the World' had to be strengthened and fewer resources dedicated to the fight against Napoleon on the continent.[28]

G. F. Leckie, the author the influential *Historical Survey of the Foreign Affairs of Great Britain*, published in 1808, advocated a similar strategy. In their fight against France, Leckie argued, the British would do best to use their 'insular empire' rather than try to take part directly in the struggle on the continent.[29] The empire and the Royal Navy's command of the sea would allow Britain to remain detached. For Leckie, this strategy was encapsulated by the string of islands along the continent that the British had acquired in response to French expansion: Corsica (1794–6), Elba (1796), Malta (1800), Sicily (1806), and Heligoland (1807).[30] Together with Gibraltar, acquired in the early eighteenth century and vigorously defended during the Napoleonic Wars, these outposts were catalogued as Britain's 'European possessions'. They would, Leckie argued, ensure Britain's maritime supremacy, while allowing it to refrain from too much engagement with the continent.

[28] Memorandum by Henry Dundas, Secretary for War, for the consideration of his Majesty's ministers, 31 March 1800, in John B. Hattendorf, R. J. B. Knight, A. W. H. Pearsall, N. A. M. Rodger, and Geoffrey Till, eds, *British Naval Documents, 1204–1960* (Aldershot, 1993), 344–50, here 345. For a more detailed discussion, see John Ehrman, *The Younger Pitt: The Consuming Struggle* (London, 1996), 353–8.

[29] Gould Francis Leckie, *An Historical Survey of the Foreign Affairs of Great Britain* (London, 1808). On Leckie, see Diletta d'Andrea, 'The "Insular" Strategy of Gould Francis Leckie in the Mediterranean during the Napoleonic Wars', *Journal of Mediterranean Studies* 16 (2006), 79–89.

[30] Manuel Borutta and Sakis Gekas, eds, 'A Colonial Sea: The Mediterranean, 1798–1956', *European Review of History* 19 (2012), 1–13; Robert Holland, *Blue-Water Empire: The British in the Mediterranean since 1800* (London, 2012); Stephen Constantine, *Community and Identity: The Making of Modern Gibraltar since 1704* (Manchester, 2009); E. G. Archer, *Gibraltar: Identity and Empire* (New York and London, 2006); Desmond Gregory, *Sicily, the Insecure Base: A History of the British Occupation of Sicily, 1806–1815* (London and Toronto, 1988); Lucy Riall, *Under the Volcano: Revolution in a Sicilian Town* (Oxford, 2013); Desmond Gregory, *The Ungovernable Rock: A History of the Anglo-Corsican Kingdom and Its Role in Britain's Mediterranean Strategy during the Revolutionary Wars* (London and Toronto, 1985); Desmond Gregory, *Malta, Britain and the European Powers, 1793–1815* (London, 1996); Jan Rüger, *Heligoland: Britain, Germany and the Struggle for the North Sea* (Oxford, 2017).

But Leckie's idea of an 'insular empire' and the broader 'blue water' strategy it reflected were based on a false dichotomy. As the Napoleonic Wars showed all too clearly, empire and Europe were not opposites, nor was Britain in a position to choose one over the other. Both economically and strategically, its shifting imperial project (if it ever was that) was bound up with continental Europe. Economically, there was no such thing as a distinct imperial zone that would have operated in isolation from continental commerce. Already at the end of the eighteenth century Britain's trade was rarely exclusively with either Europe or the colonies and the rest of the world. Rather the movement of goods and capital was typically triangular, involving European as much as overseas locations.[31] Napoleon's Continental System was meant to sever this link and create a French-dominated economic bloc on the mainland. Britain's counter-blockade aimed to cut the continent off from crucial overseas supplies. But few merchants in London, Manchester, or Edinburgh had an interest in withdrawing from Europe. Their counterparts in the port cities along the shores of Europe were prepared to pay highly inflated prices for colonial produce. So a lucrative smuggling trade ensued that continued to link Europe and the empire in Britain's economy.

Two British colonies, Malta and Heligoland, both acquired in order to counter the French threat, were the lynchpins of this trade. Its scale was staggering. Between 1809 and 1811 goods valued at roughly £86 million went to Heligoland alone, more than Britain's annual public budget for 1811. As the island's chamber of commerce explained to the underwriters at Lloyd's, Heligoland was 'the only medium through which the North of Germany and the countries upon the Rhine can receive their supplies'.[32] Malta, the smuggling centre of the Mediterranean, played a similar role for Southern Europe.[33] Between January 1808 and April 1812, the authorities there issued 2,180 commercial licences to merchants who shipped goods from Malta to the mainland. Through their 'ingenuity, put in motion by a real interest, the decrees of the French Government are constantly eluded', reported the British commissioners in 1812.[34] The smuggling trade was made possible by 'adventurers from all nations', wrote Lieutenant-General Sir George Cockburn, who visited Malta in 1810 and 1811:[35]

> Here you see Turks, Greeks, Algerines, Jews, Germans, Maltese, Spaniards, Swiss, Morocco men, English, Italians, Albanians etc., in short persons from almost every nation on earth, and all dressed in their proper costume.[36]

---

[31] Stephen Conway, 'British Governments, Colonial Consumers, and Continental European Goods in the British Atlantic Empire, 1763–1775', *Historical Journal* 58 (2015), 711–32.

[32] TNA, CO 118/1, Minutes, Chamber of Commerce, 20 November 1808.

[33] Michela D'Angelo, *Mercanti inglesi a Malta 1800–1825* (Milan, 1990), esp. ch. 4; Gregory, *Malta*, ch. 14.

[34] Report of H.M.'s Commissioners for Enquiring into the Affairs of Malta (1812), printed in D'Angelo, *Mercanti inglesi a Malta*, 261–3, here 262.

[35] George Cockburn, *A Voyage to Cadiz and Gibraltar up the Mediterranean to Sicily and Malta in 1810 and 1811* (London, 1815), vol. 2, 114.

[36] Ibid., vol. 1, 60.

This diverse network of merchants linked the empire with Europe through their illicit trade, facilitated by the British and fought by the French. The same applied to Heligoland, where a multilingual chamber of commerce organized the smuggling trade. The majority of merchants operating on the island had British or Hanseatic–German backgrounds, though there were also Danish, Swedish, Dutch, and French traders. What they had in common was an overriding commercial interest and a cosmopolitan outlook—many among them had ties to both the British empire and Europe.[37]

The goods that the smugglers ferried from these colonial outposts to the continent showed how closely intertwined empire and Europe were in British trade. Produce shipped from India, East Asia, the Caribbean, and the Americas was particularly prominent. 'Immense importations of Colonial Produce, more particularly of Coffee, are constantly received and instantly disposed of at Malta,' reported the government's commissioners in 1812.[38] The goods that arrived in Heligoland from Britain provided a similar picture. The most important items traded (in descending order of value) were coffee, sugar, tobacco, cotton wool, pimiento, pepper, cocoa, ginger, indigo, nutmeg, cinnamon, cardamom, treacle, gum, shellac, currents, raisins, rum, tea, rice.[39] Coffee was consistently at the top of the lists of smuggled goods. In 1813 more than 11 million pounds of coffee were shipped via Heligoland, about a third of what Britain's colonies produced.[40] There was, as the Scottish merchant Patrick Colquhoun wrote, 'a universal taste for coffee on the continent, which pervaded all ranks of the people'.[41] It was colonial products such as coffee, followed by sugar and tobacco in traded volumes, that broke the Continental System—leading Marx and Engels to declare later that Napoleon had lost the war because of the continental love of sugar and coffee.[42]

The example of the trade that linked Britain's colonies and the European continent at the height of the Napoleonic Wars alone shows how erroneous it is to think of the British empire as a distinct economic zone that somehow stood in opposition to, or was isolated from, the continent. Even during the conflict that was aimed at cutting the ties between Britain's overseas empire and continental Europe, the economic activity on the ground continued to link the two—a dynamic that was to intensify in the course of the nineteenth century.

Strategically, too, empire and Europe were bound up with each other. Most London governments in the late eighteenth and early nineteenth century were all

---

[37] Rüger, *Heligoland*, ch. 1.

[38] Report of H.M.'s Commissioners for Enquiring into the Affairs of Malta (1812), printed in D'Angelo, *Mercanti inglesi a Malta*, 261–3, here 262.

[39] TNA, CO 118/6, Return of quantity and description of colonial produce and British manufacture, 20 July 1812. See also NMM, HNL/56/10 and HNL/56/11, Accounts, Captain James Hillary of *The Fame*, 1810–1811 and LA Schleswig, Abt. 174, 166, Rechnungsbuch der Firma Geller & Co, Helgoland, 1809–1811.

[40] TNA, CO 118/9, Total of Goods Exported and Imported from and to this Island from 1 Jan. 1813 to 1 Jan. 1814. The precise figure was 11,595,176 pounds of coffee, followed by 9,616,946 pounds of sugar and 588,347 pounds of tobacco. Compare TNA, CO 118/7, Statement of the Articles Exported and Imported from and to this Island, 11 May 1813 and Patrick Colquhoun, *A Treatise on the Wealth, Power, and Resources of the British Empire* (London, 1814), 378.

[41] Ibid., 331.   [42] Karl Marx and Friedrich Engels, *Werke* (Berlin, 1969), vol. 3, 46.

too aware that overseas expansion hinged on European stability, just as European instability typically resulted in overseas conflict. Playing a strong role in Europe and expanding the empire were intrinsically linked rather than opposed interests. This interdependence was encapsulated by Britain's 'European possessions', scattered as they were around the shores of the continent. Leckie and others thought of these outposts as part of an 'insular empire' that would allow Britain to refrain from too much engagement with the continent while ensuring British maritime supremacy. Yet, rather than symbols of withdrawal, George III's 'European possessions' became hinges between empire and continent, much like the royal family seat of Hanover itself.[43] Their occupation was aimed at supporting the fight against Napoleon— they were testament to the expressed British will to tilt back the balance of power in Europe. The consequence of these acquisitions was that the British empire became more rather than less enmeshed with European affairs.[44] The government in London learned this particularly with regard to the various forms of nationalism that it had to contend with in its 'European possessions'. In the Ionian Islands and, later, in Cyprus, it promoted Greek nationalism and its irredentist claims.[45] In Malta and Gibraltar, by contrast, London actively encouraged local forms of identity—which it hoped would resist the irredentism promoted by Italian and Spanish nationalists.[46] In Heligoland it depended on the influx of German capital, yet became increasingly suspicious of German nationalism, claiming the island as part of the fatherland.[47] Both strategies, enlisting and resisting European nationalisms, involved Britain with rather than kept it aloof from continental politics.

* * *

The economic and strategic interdependence between empire and Europe continued through the nineteenth century. The point here is not to posit some form of linear dynamic that would have expanded from the Congress of Vienna to the outbreak of the First World War. Clearly, economic and political developments fluctuated hugely over the course of the century. There were periods when British governments felt that, strategically speaking, continental Europe needed less active involvement, though this was never elevated to a foreign policy doctrine. And

---

[43] Torsten Riotte, *Hannover in der britischen Politik 1792–1815: Dynastische Verbindung als Element außenpolitischer Entscheidungsprozesse* (Münster, 2005); Nick Harding, *Hanover and the British Empire 1700–1837* (Woodbridge, 2007); Brendan Simms and Torsten Riotte, eds, *The Hanoverian Dimension in British History, 1714–1837* (Cambridge, 2007).

[44] Manuel Borutta and Sakis Gekas, 'A Colonial Sea: The Mediterranean, 1798–1956', *European Review of History*, 19 (2012), 1–13; Robert Holland, *Blue-Water Empire: The British in the Mediterranean since 1800* (London, 2012).

[45] Thomas Gallant, *Experiencing Dominion: Culture, Identity and Power in the British Mediterranean* (Notre Dame, IN, 2002); Robert Holland and Diana Markides, *The British and the Hellenes: Struggles for Mastery in the Eastern Mediterranean 1850–1960* (Oxford, 2006); Andrekos Varnava, *British Imperialism in Cyprus, 1878–1915* (Manchester, 2009).

[46] Henry Frendo, 'Italy and Britain in Maltese Colonial Nationalism', *History of European Ideas* 15 (1992), 733–9; Stephen Constantine, *Community and Identity: The Making of Modern Gibraltar since 1704* (Manchester, 2009); E. G. Archer, *Gibraltar: Identity and Empire* (New York and London, 2006).

[47] Jan Rüger, 'Sovereignty and Empire in the North Sea, 1807–1918', *American Historical Review* 119 (2014), 313–38.

there were periods when trade barriers and tariffs suggested that in some sectors continental and British economies were becoming less rather than more permeable. Yet, by and large, the interdependence between empire and Europe remained a strong underlying reality.[48]

Even when longer periods of non-intervention suggested to some that Britain had entered an era in which it could 'endeavour not to interfere needlessly and vexatiously with the internal affairs of any foreign country', as the earl of Derby, the foreign secretary, famously put it in 1866, the explanation lay as much in Europe as in the empire.[49] Neutrality was a route the British took when it was politically advantageous, but rarely when it was bound to directly harm their interests. Nationalist movements and revolutions on the continent were seen with scepticism but, as long as there was no clear indication that they would lead to a serious threat either to the balance of power or to Britain's imperial position, they could be tolerated.[50] This did not, however, mean that Britain had abandoned Europe for the empire. As Disraeli put it in 1866, Britain had a 'greater sphere of action than any other European Power' but could not 'look with indifference upon what takes place on the Continent'.[51] Conservative and liberal politicians disagreed over the extent to which Britain should directly interfere in continental conflicts, but no prime minister, be it Disraeli, Gladstone, or Salisbury, suggested that Britain take a course of actively isolating itself from the continent.

It was only at the turn of the century that the idea of 'splendid isolation' gained traction, especially among colonialists and navalists. Yet this was a retrospective label that romanticized a period of detachment that had arguably never existed—or, if it had, then it had been forced onto Britain, most prominently during the Napoleonic Wars, rather than sought by imperially minded governments in London. Similarly, colonial agreements between Britain and other European powers were never only about rearranging spheres of influence overseas, just as it is short-sighted to explain them simply as a function of the European balance of power. Empire and Europe were intrinsically linked, whether in Africa, India, or the Middle East. Few international treaties of the decades before the First World War show this more clearly than the Anglo-French agreement of 1904. This was, on paper, nothing more than the regulation of a number of colonial conflicts that had plagued the two countries' relations. Yet no one in London and Paris could have been under any illusion about the effect the agreement would have on

[48] Frank Trentmann, *Free Trade Nation: Commerce, Consumption, and Civil Society in Modern Britain* (Oxford and New York, 2009); Paul Bairoch, 'European Trade Policy, 1815–1914', in Peter Mathias and Sydney Pollard, eds, *The Cambridge Economic History of Europe* (Cambridge, 1989), vol. 8, 1–160; Peter Marsh, *Bargaining on Europe: Britain and the First Common Market, 1860–92*; Martin Daunton, 'Britain and Globalisation since 1850, Part 1: Creating a Global Order, 1850–1914', *Transactions of the Royal Historical Society*, Sixth Series, 16 (2006), 1–38; John R. Davis, 'The British *Sonderweg*: The Peculiarities of British Free Trade, 1845–80', *Diplomacy & Statecraft* 8 (1997), 68–90.
[49] Hansard, House of Lords, 9 July 1866, vol. 184, 726–51, here 736.
[50] For the German example, see Frank Lorenz Müller, *Britain and the German Question: Perceptions of Nationalism and Political Reform, 1830–63* (Basingstoke, 2002); Klaus Hildebrand, *No Intervention: Die Pax Britannica und Preußen, 1865/66–1869/70* (Munich, 1997).
[51] William Flavelle Moneypenny and George Earle Buckle, eds, *Life of Benjamin Disraeli*, rev. edn (London, 1929), vol. 2, 201.

European politics. Just as in 1890, when a similar Anglo-German treaty had been seen as the beginning of an alliance between London and Berlin, the Franco-British agreement of 1904 became symbolic of a broader rapprochement. Whether that rapprochement, celebrated as the *Entente Cordiale*, amounted to anything more substantial than the stated but non-binding intention to cooperate is not the question here. The point is that an agreement about aspects that concerned first and foremost the empire took on a strong European function—the two sides were inseparable in diplomacy and foreign policy, all the way until 1914.[52]

Economically, too, the European continent and the British empire continued to be bound up with each other. The combination of free trade and imperial expansion meant that the empire was never a closed economic sphere separating Britain and its colonies from the rest of Europe. To be sure, there were debates and conflicts about the limits of free trade. Moreover, in a number of sectors, especially agriculture and heavy industry, tariffs and subsidies persisted. Yet the overall picture was one in which trade rarely stopped at national or colonial boundaries.[53] At the very time when the red on British maps of the world suggested that there was a homogeneous empire that could be defined in national terms, the opposite dynamic defined the reality on the ground. The porous and varied patchwork that was the empire had no clear boundaries that would have allowed for a separation between British and continental influences. As Gary Magee and Andrew Thompson have shown, early forms of globalization relied 'on a plethora of dense, everyday social networks that straddled national borders'.[54] Throughout the nineteenth century Europe was the most important market in which colonial exports and British products based on colonial raw materials were sold. Coffee continued to be one of the most prominent examples. While the British were much less enthusiastic about drinking it than their continental neighbours, they dominated the global trade in coffee beans. Until 1914 Northern Europe remained by far the biggest consumer and Britain its main supplier.[55] And when continental merchants were increasingly importing coffee directly, thus beginning to sideline British traders, the City continued to profit directly: most coffee was shipped in British vessels, insured by British underwriters and, most of all, paid for through British banks.[56]

[52] T. G. Otte, *The China Question: Great Power Rivalry and British Isolation, 1894–1905* (Oxford, 2007); T. G. Otte, 'The Fragmenting of the Old World Order: Britain, the Great Powers and the War', in Rotem Kowner, ed., *The Impact of the Russo-Japanese War* (London, 2007), 91–108; T. G. Otte, 'Grey Ambassadors: The Dreadnought Revolution and British Diplomacy, 1906–1914', in Robert Blyth, Andrew Lambert, and Jan Rüger, eds, *The Dreadnought and the Edwardian Age* (Aldershot, 2011), 51–78; T. G. Otte, *The Foreign Office Mind: The Making of British Foreign Policy, 1865–1914* (Cambridge, 2013).

[53] Daunton, 'Britain and Globalisation since 1850, Part 1'; Gary Magee and Andrew Thompson, *Empire and Globalisation: Networks of People, Goods and Capital in the British World, c.1850–1914* (Cambridge, 2010), 239–41; Frank Trentmann, *Empire of Things: How We Became a World of Consumers, from the Fifteenth Century to the Twenty-First* (London, 2016), esp. ch. 3.

[54] Magee and Thompson, *Empire and Globalisation*, 243.

[55] William G. Clarence-Smith and Steven Topik, eds, *The Global Coffee Economy in Africa, Asia and Latin America, 1500–1989* (Cambridge, 2003), 443 (Appendix).

[56] Steven Topik, 'The Integration of the World Coffee Market', in Clarence-Smith and Topik, eds, *The Global Coffee Economy*, 21–49; Julia Laura Rischbieter, *Mikro-Ökonomie der Globalisierung: Kaffee, Kaufleute und Konsumenten im Kaiserreich, 1870–1914* (Cologne, 2011), esp. 41.

Countless other examples illustrate the triangular patterns of trade, finance, and consumption that linked Britain with both the empire and Europe. You could discern this interdependence not only at the ports and financial markets, but also in the department stores that sprang up in the urban centres of late nineteenth-century Europe. A vast range of products were on offer here, which bore witness to the links between Europe, Britain, and the empire.[57] After 1914 many of these ties were severed: the First World War ushered in a period of 'insular capitalism' during which free trade was abandoned.[58] The world became divided into regional economic blocs, each, in John Darwin's words, 'aiming to shrink its trade with the others'.[59] The Second World War accelerated this dynamic, which suggested now that the empire was a distinct economic zone that stood in opposition to or was isolated from continental Europe. From a British postwar perspective, it was thus tempting to think of empire and Europe as separate economic entities. Decolonization and EEC membership reinforced this perception, suggesting that, with regard to its economic future, Britain had opted for Europe. Yet in the nineteenth century there had never been a distinct European economic sphere; nor would the British, at the zenith of their imperial influence, have allowed the empire to be isolated from such a zone. Before 1914 the prosperity of Europe's industrialized powers was interlinked: it was by trading with one another and by cooperating in global markets that they flourished.

A number of other factors require that we engage analytically with the interconnections between Britain, empire, and Europe. An obvious one is migration. In the course of the nineteenth century an estimated 100 million people crossed oceans to find work in other parts of the globe. If we add the number of people seeking refuge from conflict and persecution, the number is significantly higher. This movement of people not only defies national categories; it also complicates our understanding of 'Europe' and 'empire'. How British was the British empire? English, Scottish, Welsh, and Irish backgrounds formed only a part of the mix of people who acted as agents of empire. The merchants and missionaries, explorers and scientists, engineers and administrators, officers and mercenaries who spun the imperial web did not come from the British Isles alone. The empire offered a home to the colonial fantasies of continental Europeans, especially to those from countries that had no or few colonies themselves, among them Scandinavians, Swiss, Germans, and Italians.[60] What was more, the empire actively encouraged their collaboration. This symbiosis ranged from the supply of goods and commodities to the provision of expertise and skills. It was facilitated, as David Arnold has shown

---

[57] Trentmann, *Empire of Things*, ch. 3; Gerhard Pfeisinger and Stefan Schennach, eds, *Kolonialwaren: Die Schaffung der ungleichen Welt* (Göttingen, 1989); Magee and Thompson, *Empire and Globalisation*, 239–41; Rüger, 'OXO'.

[58] Martin Daunton, 'Britain and Globalisation since 1850, Part 2: The Rise of Insular Capitalism, 1914–1939', *Transactions of the Royal Historical Society* 17 (2007), 1–30.

[59] John Darwin, *After Tamerlane: The Global History of Empire* (London, 2007), 503.

[60] Susanne Zantop, *Colonial Fantasies: Conquest, Family, and Nation in Precolonial Germany, 1770–1870* (Durham, NC, 1997); Bernhard C. Schär, 'On the Tropical Origins of the Alps: Science and the Colonial Imagination of Switzerland, 1700–1900', in Patricia Purtschert and Harald Fischer-Tiné, eds, *Colonial Switzerland: Rethinking Colonialism from the Margins* (Basingstoke, 2015), 29–49.

in the case of India, 'by a prevailing doctrine of laissez-faire and by the inadequacy or backwardness of the British in certain technical and commercial fields'.[61] The making of 'British' India thus had a strong European dimension, to the degree that colonial governance itself was directly influenced by continental actors.[62] Elsewhere in the empire, too, British and European contexts were bound up with each other. While continental experts and administrators routinely acted as agents of British colonialism, they simultaneously wrote Europe into the empire.[63] In the twentieth century this transnational character of colonialism was downplayed—the image of the empire as homogeneous and British became enshrined at the very time when it declined.

* * *

On 9 October 1948 Winston Churchill gave a speech in which he coined one of his most influential metaphors, still used today by politicians and commentators who try to make sense of Britain's position in the world. Churchill received the 'cheers of the massed Conservatives who welcomed him so movingly' as he arrived in Llandudno, the Welsh town at the edge of the Irish Sea, for the last day of the Conservative Party Conference.[64] There was a 'fine fervour of confidence' among the audience, noted the *Times* correspondent, as Churchill (in his third year as leader of the opposition) laid out his vision of Britain's international role:[65]

> As I look out upon the future of our country in the changing scene of human destiny I feel the existence of three great circles among the free nations and democracies. I almost wish I had a blackboard. I would make a picture for you. I don't suppose it would get hung in the Royal Academy, but it would illustrate the point I am anxious for you to hold in your minds. The first circle for us is naturally the British Commonwealth and Empire, with all that that comprises. Then there is also the English-speaking world in which we, Canada, and the other British Dominions and the United States play so important a part. And finally there is United Europe.

The relationship between the three circles, Churchill was sure, would decide Britain's future in the world. So far these had been separate, distinct geopolitical

---

[61] David Arnold, 'Globalization and Contingent Colonialism: Towards a Transnational History of "British" India', *Journal of Colonialism and Colonial History*, 16.2 (2015), doi: 10.1353/cch.2015.0019.

[62] Ibid. See also David Arnold, 'Plant Capitalism and Company Science: The Indian Career of Nathaniel Wallich', *Modern Asian Studies* 42 (2008), 899–928; Ray Desmond, *The European Discovery of the Indian Flora* (Oxford, 1992); Zaheer Baber, *The Science of Empire: Scientific Knowledge, Civilization and Colonial Rule in India* (Albany, NY, 1996); Mahesh Rangarajan, *Fencing the Forest: Conservation and Ecological Change in India's Central Provinces, 1860–1914* (Oxford, 1999).

[63] Stephen Conway, 'Continental European Involvement in the Eighteenth-Century British Empire', in Arnd Reitemeier, ed., *Kommunikation und Kulturtransfer im Zeitalter der Personalunion zwischen Großbritannien und Hannover* (Göttingen, 2014), 123–41; Brett M. Bennett and Joseph P. Hodge, *Science and Empire: Knowledge and Networks of Science across the British Empire* (Basingstoke, 2011); Ulrike Kirchberger, *Aspekte deutsch-britischer Expansion: Die Überseeinteressen der deutschen Migranten in Großbritannien in der Mitte des 19. Jahrhunderts* (Stuttgart, 1999); Shalini Randeria, 'Colonial Complicities and Imperial Entanglements', in Patricia Purtschert and Harald Fischer-Tiné, eds, *Colonial Switzerland: Rethinking Colonialism from the Margins* (Basingstoke, 2015), 296–306; Rüger, *Heligoland*, ch. 2.

[64] *Times*, 11 October 1948, p. 5.   [65] Ibid.

spheres, but in the postwar settlement they ought to be interlinked, stabilizing one another and thus Britain's global position:

> We stand, in fact, at the very point of junction, and here in this Island at the centre of the seaways and perhaps of the airways also, we have the opportunity of joining them all together. If we rise to the occasion in the years that are to come it may be found that once again we hold the key to opening a safe and happy future to humanity, and will gain for ourselves gratitude and fame.

Churchill left open how exactly the three circles ought to be joined. What would Britain do to link them? The question remained unanswered in the years that followed, during which he cultivated the image of the 'three circles'. In April 1949 he gave a speech that was meant to signal Britain's support for the European Movement. 'There are three circles which are linked together,' he exclaimed, 'the circle of the British Empire and Commonwealth, the circle of the English-speaking world, and the circle of united Europe.' Yet despite the close links between Britain and its empire, he was certain

> that it is not impossible for Britain to draw closer to Europe, and to enter more force-fully into European life, without abandoning the ties with our Dominions which to us are paramount and sacred, and comprise the ideal of the British Empire and Commonwealth of Nations.[66]

Again, he left it open how exactly the different circles related to one another and how Britain would link them. The phrase about Britain 'drawing closer to Europe' mirrored the tension that was to remain at the heart of Churchill's geopolitical vision. Britain, he suggested, would promote European reconciliation while remaining an outsider, as defined by its position in between empire and Europe.

The neatly separated geopolitical spheres that Churchill offered his audiences as an instructive metaphor for Britain's place in the world made sense in the context of the mid-twentieth century, after two world wars and a series of geopolitical shifts had radically altered the international order. But, as much as Churchill felt compelled to posit empire and Europe as separate circles, he was in no doubt about the underlying interdependence of the two. Not only was it not wise for Britain to try to choose one over the other—it was impossible: Britain's European and imperial roles were inherently linked.

In the early twenty-first century, the idea of 'the three circles' is less convincing than ever before, notwithstanding the fact that it is still routinely evoked by those who wish to rebuild some illusionary miniature empire.[67] It would be wrong to deny that the social, cultural, and economic legacies of empire continue to shape Britain. Yet they do so in a context in which they are inseparable from European influences. 'Europe' in the meantime remains, as Hobsbawm suggested, a changing

[66] Winston S. Churchill, *Complete Speeches*, ed. by Robert Rhodes James (London, 1974), vol. 7, 7810–11 (speech at the Economic Conference of the European Movement, London, 20 April 1949).
[67] For a particularly striking example, see Andrew Roberts, 'CANZUK: After Brexit, Canada, Australia, New Zealand and Britain Can Unite as a Pillar of Western Civilisation', *The Daily Telegraph*, 13 September 2016.

ideological construct as much as a socioeconomic and strategic reality from which there is no escaping. Writing Europe into the history of the British empire does not imply that the one ought to be subsumed in the other, but rather that we should account for the many ways in which European, imperial, and global dynamics are bound up with one another in Britain's past. We ought to be able to acknowledge that neither of the two key terms that the British employed in order to define their role in the world can be understood in isolation. Europe and empire were not two distinct spheres between which Britain was somehow in a position to choose. It is a fallacy to argue that the empire allowed Britain to isolate itself from the continent and that more isolation 'from Europe' would have preserved the empire for longer. But it is just as misleading to suggest that modern Britain was 'made' first and foremost by Europe. In the minds of those who ran Britain's affairs in the nineteenth century there was no need to choose.

4

Indigenous Comparisons

Renaud Morieux

One advantage of comparative history is that it forces historians to think in terms that are not familiar to them. Turning the telescope around to point it towards the observer rather than the observed, to question the observer's own society, is a practice that cultural anthropologists or sociologists of everyday life are familiar with,[1] historians less so. Common-sense shared assumptions, which are seen as unproblematic because they are so deeply imbedded in a culture, come to the fore when one is looking at them as if at a distance, from the outside. This way of using comparison is hardly new: eighteenth-century writers drew on the perspectives of outsiders in order to shake off the prejudices of Europeans or to demonstrate their shared features despite their internal strife. Historians, too, have resorted to similar rhetorical strategies. In the striking incipit of *Nations and Nationalism*, Eric Hobsbawm playfully distanced himself in space as well as in time, by taking on the clothes of an 'intergalactic historian' from the future, who travelled back to Earth after humanity had been wiped out by a nuclear war. In order to show that categories of thought do not apply to every time and society, Hobsbawm described the puzzlement of this historian from the future, who would try to make sense of what was an alien concept to him: the concept of nation.[2]

But besides these rhetorical uses comparative history, as a subfield of the historical discipline, has gone out of fashion since the 1980s. The initial period of enthusiasm, shown for instance in the founding of the *Comparative Studies in Society and History* journal in 1968, and the appeal of historical sociology, led by Theda Skocpol and Charles Tilly, and of their comparative study of social movements and revolutions have been left behind somewhat with the move away from 'history as science'. Worries about the legitimate and coherent frame of comparison, about the specificity of 'contexts' and 'cases' that imply their incommensurability, about oversimplification and teleology, which arise from the need to isolate comparable

[1] Richard Handler, 'The Uses of Incommensurability in Anthropology', *New Literary History* 40 (2009), 627–47; Erving Goffman, *Asylums: Essay on the Social Situation of Mental Patients and Other Inmates* (Garden City, NY, 1961); Erving Goffman, *Stigma: Notes on the Management of a Spoiled Identity* (New York, 1963).

[2] Eric Hobsbawm, *Nations and Nationalism since 1780: Programmes, Myth, Reality* (Cambridge, 1992), 1. On the use of distance between the historian and his/her object of study and on the power of puzzlement that can emerge from it, see Carlo Ginzburg, *Wooden Eyes: Nine Reflections on Distance* (New York, 2001); Mark Salber Philipps, *On Historical Distance* (New Haven, CT, 2013).

'variables', or, more prosaically, about the ability of one scholar to master two or more terrains have all played a part in this phenomenon.[3] Recent interest in trans-national, world, global, or connected history, while offering a myriad of exciting new perspectives on the discipline, has tended to bypass comparative history altogether. To give only one example (which is based on my own work), the focus on entangled spaces and contact zones as 'common grounds' finds in part its rationale in the desire to avoid adopting arbitrarily constructed units of compari-son as the building blocks of analysis.[4] However, the comparative method is not dead yet. In part as a necessary counterpoint to the 'global turn', recent work has sought to revive comparison in a variety of ways, without returning to social scien-tific 'structural' comparisons.[5] One fruitful avenue of research, I want to suggest, is to reinvigorate subjective and empirical comparisons—those used by the historian as well as by the actors he/she studies.

For the historian, stepping back provides a way of justifying the selection of those kinds of units of comparison that would show that, seen from a distance, they share many distinctive characteristics. In order to qualify the idea that France and England were fundamentally dissimilar, the French philosopher and historian of British Methodism and liberalism Élie Halévy set this binary comparison within a broader frame. As seen by someone crossing the Channel, he wrote, the differences between Calais and Dover appear huge, but from another perspective, that of someone going from India or China, the distinction might seem much less signifi-cant. Likewise, for a Brahmin, the theological differences between Catholicism and Anglicanism are mere variations of a monochrome pattern.[6] This comparison is a warning against the most basic ethnocentrism.

So far I have focused on comparative history as a self-conscious way of writing history. However, it could be argued that any history is inherently comparative. Just like the bourgeois gentleman in Molière's eponymous 1670 play who is told,

---

[3] Simona Cerutti and Isabelle Grangaud, 'Comparer par cas: Esquisse d'un projet comparatiste' and Jean-Frédéric Schaub, 'Survivre aux asymétries', in Antoine Lilti, Sabina Loriga, Jean-Frédéric Schaub, and Silvia Sebastiani, eds, *L'Expérience historiographique: Autour de Jacques Revel* (Paris, 2016), 151–62 and 165–79; J. H. Elliott, 'Comparative History', in Carlos Barros, ed., *Historia a debate*, vol. 3: *Otros enfoques* (Santiago de Compostela, 1995), 9–19; William H. Sewell, *Logics of History: Social Theory and Social Transformation* (Chicago, IL, 2005), 81–123.

[4] Renaud Morieux, *The Channel: England, France and the Construction of a Maritime Border in the Eighteenth Century* (Cambridge, 2016). See also Richard White, *The Middle Ground: Indians, Empires, and Republics in the Great Lake Region, 1650–1815* (Cambridge, 2011).

[5] See, for instance, Deborah Cohen and Maura O'Connor, eds, *Comparison and History: Europe in Cross-National Perspectives* (Baltimore, MD, 2004).

[6] Élie Halévy, *A History of the English People in the Nineteenth Century*, vol. 1: *England in 1815* (New York, 1924 [1913]), Preface, xiii. There is more than this in Halévy's remark, which is also allud-ing to another type of comparison: changing the scale of analysis makes us see things differently; the study of England's representative institutions becomes a European problem, since all 'European nations' have borrowed ideas and institutions from one another throughout history. I will leave aside this problem in the present essay. In the same way, other historians have taken a perspective from the 'periphery' in order to illuminate features of the 'core' that hitherto had been left in obscurity. To jus-tify their choice to take a global and comparative approach to Britain and France in the age of revolu-tion, Jones and Wahrman borrow the voice of an imaginary Caribbean slave, for whom these two distant countries 'must have looked pretty much alike': Colin Jones and Dror Wahrman, 'Introduction: An Age of Cultural Revolutions?', in eidem, eds, *The Age of Cultural Revolutions: Britain and France, 1750–1820* (Berkeley, CA, 2002), 7.

to his delight, that all his life he had been speaking in prose without knowing it, one could argue that all historians write comparatively without always being aware of it. Indeed, as every textbook on the epistemology of history makes clear, historians must eschew 'anachronism'; as in L. P. Hartley's famous dictum, 'The past is a foreign country: they do things differently there.' One cannot comprehend that strange land with present-day notions and values.[7] The fear of anachronism is based on an implicit comparison and contrast between the past and the present. According to this view, historians must cultivate and be aware of the chronological distance that separates them from the period they study.[8] Objections have been raised against this statement: is it at all possible to abstract ourselves from the present we live in? And is it possible to abstract ourselves from the subject position from which we, as researchers (and as women or men, as racialized beings, embodied creatures, etc.), are asking these questions?[9] Are not all the questions we ask of the past fuelled by present-day problems? Can we even understand the past without empathizing with and understanding people's thoughts, actions, and desires?[10]

Comparison matters for another reason, often not mentioned by historians. It matters because it is how the people we study made sense of the world they lived in: from a cognitivist perspective, it has been argued that comparisons, analogies, and metaphors are 'natural' ways to look at the world.[11] All people, not just historians, think comparatively. For this reason, their comparisons are worth studying in their own right. Furthermore, 'indigenous comparisons' can also help us enrich what we mean by doing historical comparisons.[12] Focusing on the comparisons used by historical actors gives us a way to sidestep some of the classic issues associated with comparative history, and especially cross-national comparisons.[13]

---

[7] L. P. Hartley, *The Go-Between* (London, 1953).

[8] This raises epistemological questions about the way in which history as a discipline has evolved since the Enlightenment and the impact of the 'cultural turn' on concepts of change over time, from the notion that there are constants in history to the idea that 'things change dramatically': Peter Baldwin, 'Comparing and Generalizing: Why All History Is Comparative, Yet No History Is Sociology', in Cohen and O'Connor, *Comparison and History*, 7.

[9] These questions are dealt with by the 'standpoint theory' school within feminist epistemology: Sandra Harding, 'Rethinking Standpoint Epistemology: What Is "Strong Objectivity"?', in Ann E. Cudd and Robin O. Andreasen, eds, *Feminist Theory: A Philosophical Anthology* (Oxford, 2005), 218–36.

[10] There might also be virtues in anachronism and in the adoption of a genealogical perspective. Gadamer's version of hermeneutics has a vocabulary for this, conceptualizing the interpretive analysis of the past through a 'fusion of horizons'—that of the researchers and that of the subjects studied—rather than through (one-way) empathy alone, as older versions of hermeneutics argued. See Antoine Lilti, 'Rabelais est-il notre contemporain? Histoire intellectuelle et herméneutique critique', *Revue d'Histoire Moderne et Contemporaine* 5 (2012), 65–84.

[11] Rita Felski and Susan Stanford Friedman, 'Introduction', in *Comparison*, special issue of *New Literary History* 40 (2009), v–ix; George Lakoff and Mark Johnson, *Metaphors We Live By* (Chicago, IL, 2003).

[12] I am using 'indigenous comparisons' here in the same sense as that of Brubaker and Cooper's 'categories of practice', which they define, following Pierre Bourdieu, as 'categories of everyday social experience, developed and deployed by ordinary social actors, as distinguished from the experience-distant categories used by social analysts': Rogers Brubaker and Frederick Cooper, 'Beyond "Identity"', *Theory and Society* 29 (2000), 1–47, here 4.

[13] On the risks and rewards of this kind of comparative history, see Deborah Cohen, 'Comparative History: Buyer Beware', Susan Pedersen, 'Comparative History and Women's History: Explaining

In particular, justifying the choice of a comparative framework and, within it, the focus on specific units, scope, scale, and categories of comparison is often challenging; the most convincing comparative studies are those that explicitly confront these problems instead of sweeping them under the carpet and show their awareness of the biases at work in the crafting of historical units of comparison and categories of analysis. Starting with the actors' own comparisons provides a way to approach this discussion from a different perspective. I am not concerned here with defining what comparative history is in general, nor do I want to offer a general essay on comparison and the comparative method.[14] Instead, I propose to choose, as a starting point, the comparisons made by the actors themselves,[15] in other words to place the emphasis on comparison in practice or comparison in action, without presupposing the superiority of social scientists vis-à-vis the actors they are studying.

This approach builds on the work of many anthropologists, sociologists, and cultural historians who have tried, since the 1970s, to adopt the perspective of the 'native' or the 'popular'.[16] Objections have indeed been raised against the tendency to 'ventriloquize' the peoples that are studied.[17] It is in those terms that the anthropologist Marshall Sahlins responded to Gananath Obeyesekere's attack on his analysis of the death of Captain Cook in Hawaii by accusing Obeyesekere of depriving Hawaiians 'of their own voices'.[18] Instead of 'subsuming their lives' under universalisms or ethnocentrisms,[19] Sahlins argued, scholars should pay heed to the Hawaiians' ability to give meaning to their world by using the tools at their disposal in their own culture. For historians, this entails trying to understand the

Convergence and Divergence', and Michael Miller, 'Comparative and Cross-National History: Approaches, Differences, Problems', all three in Cohen and O'Connor, *Comparison and History*, 57–70, 85–102, and 115–32.

[14] There is no consensus among historians about it. It has been defined as a method, as a 'mode of analysis', and as a 'tool to provoke thought' and to ask new questions. Some historians are interested in highlighting differences and causation, others in emphasizing similarities and local contexts: Deborah Cohen and Maura O'Connor, 'Introduction', in eaedem, *Comparison and History*, xii–xiii. Contemporary societies can be compared across space (synchronically) and distant societies across time (diachronically). See in particular the stimulating reflections in Elliott, 'Comparative History', and in Natalie Zemon Davis, 'Beyond Evolution: Comparative History and Its Goals', in Wojciecha Wrzoska, ed., *Swiat Historii* (Poznan, 1998), 149–58.

[15] Historians and classicists, in dialogue with other disciplines, have recently started to consider the forms and roles that comparison could take in different periods: see the ambitious project led by Renaud Gagné, Simon Goldhill, and Geoffrey Lloyd at CRASSH in Cambridge (http://www.crassh.cam.ac.uk/programmes/the-history-of-cross-cultural-comparatism).

[16] To focus only on historical studies, various 'schools' of thought, besides their important differences, have shared the same goals: the history from below, microhistory, and subaltern studies are just a few examples.

[17] Marshall David Sahlins, *How 'Natives' Think: About Captain Cook, for Example* (Chicago, IL, 1995), 116.

[18] Ibid., 6. The book is a response to Gananath Obeyesekere, *The Apotheosis of Captain Cook: European Mythmaking in the Pacific* (Princeton, NJ, 1992), which was an unbridled attack on Sahlins's *Islands of History* (Chicago, IL, 1985). Sahlins rebukes Obeyesekere's method as 'a pidgin anthropology—which is at the same time a pseudohistory', one that subsistutes 'a folkoric sense of "native" beliefs for the relevant Hawaiian ethnography' and interprets 'the historical events by notions concocted out of commonsense realism and a kind of pop nativism': Sahlins, *How 'Natives' Think*, 60.

[19] Ibid., 6.

historical actors' own concepts and categories of analysis.[20] Particularly stimulating from my perspective is the sociology of Luc Boltanski and Laurent Thévenot, which focuses on 'situated' social interactions. Rather than starting from the assumption that situations and actions are determined by pre-existing structures, these sociologists argue that disputes, controversies, and crises themselves reproduce the social order but can also redefine it. Central to their methodology, which draws on ethnomethodology, is the attempt to 'take seriously' the actors' different registers of argumentation and justification and their attempts to evaluate the actions of others.[21] Simona Cerutti showed how fruitful this programme can be for social historians by applying Boltanski and Thévenot's theoretical framework to the early modern Italian justice system.[22] According to Cerutti, by adopting 'the actors' point of view', what interpretive anthropologists call the 'internal' or *emic* perspective,[23] historians can gain a great deal of hindsight. Thus, in eighteenth-century Turin, those brought to trial were not simply 'responding' or 'adapting' to legal norms predefined by legal theorists or twentieth-century legal historians. In specific contexts, the actors drew upon their own cultural resources, namely their own ideas of justice, to undertake original legal procedures, which contributed in turn to the making of legal norms 'higher up', by central authorities.[24]

The main focus of this article is on the practical use of categories of comparison in everyday negotiations. By using Anglo-French comparisons as they were practiced in the eighteenth century in case studies, I want to propose a different

[20] A similar discussion, but a much more urbane one, opposed cultural historians Robert Darnton and Roger Chartier. While Darnton claimed to be trying 'to see things from the native's point of view' in his study of the culture of eighteenth-century Parisian print workers, Roger Chartier criticized him for artificially pinning on them codified and 'external' cultural references, drawn from western folklore and Geertzian anthropology. Chartier suggested adopting an internal mode of analysis, which would pay greater attention to the creativity of these actors, which materialized in the texts they produced: Robert Darnton, *Great Cat Massacre: And Other Episodes in French Cultural History* (New York, 1984), 260; Roger Chartier, 'Texts, Symbols, and Frenchness', *Journal of Modern History* 57 (1985), 682–95, here 694.
[21] Luc Boltanski and Laurent Thévenot, *On Justification: Economies of Worth* (Princeton, NJ, 2006); Étienne Anheim, Jean-Yves Grenier, and Antoine Lilti, 'Reinterpreting Social Status', *Annales HSS* 4 (2013), 609–13; Cyril Lemieux, 'De la théorie de l'habitus à la sociologie des épreuves: Relire *L'Expérience concentrationnaire*', in Liora Israël and Daniel Voldman, eds, *Michaël Pollak: De l'identité blessée à une sociologie des possibles* (Paris, 2008), 179–205.
[22] Cerutti has also pointed out some caveats to this sociology, in particular the notion that the models of justification are theoretical and external to the experience of the actors, whereas she (rightly) points out that legal practices are often not very formalized: see her review of *On Justification* in Simona Cerutti, 'Pragmatique et histoire: Ce dont les sociologues sont capables (note critique), *Annales ESC* 46 (1991), 1437–45, here 1440–3; Simona Cerutti, 'Normes et pratiques, ou de la légitimité de leur opposition', in Bernard Lepetit, ed., *Les Formes de l'expérience: Une Autre Histoire sociale* (Paris, 1995), 127–49, here 132–3.
[23] Simona Cerutti, 'Microhistory: Social Relations versus Cultural Models?', in Anna-Maija Castrén, Markku Lonkila, and Matti Peltonen, eds, *Between Sociology and History: Essays on Microhistory, Collective Action, and Nation-Building* (Helsinki, 2004), 17–40, here 26, 32. See, however, Carlo Ginzburg's warning against the risk of uncritically conflating *etic* and *emic* categories of analysis: Carlo Ginzburg, 'Our Words, and Theirs: A Reflection on the Historian's Craft, Today', in Susanna Fellman and Marjatta Rahikainen, eds, *Historical Knowledge: In Quest of Theory, Method and Evidence* (Cambridge, 2012), 97–119.
[24] Cerutti, 'Normes et pratiques'; Simona Cerutti, *Giustizia sommaria: Pratiche e ideali di giustizia in una società di Ancien Régime (Torino, XVIII secolo)* (Milan, 2003).

analytical and methodological framework for writing comparative history, an approach that can in turn help us define new objects of research. Studying comparisons *in the making* entails looking at attempts, including failed ones, at establishing equivalences and establishing commensurability. Rather than theory, it is the very practical problems posed by comparison that will be the focus, highlighting the difficulties, approximations, and pragmatism that are always present in any comparative endeavour. In particular, one can look at the interaction between two levels of comparisons: (1) the production of categories and classifications by institutional discourses, especially legal discourses; and (2) their practical use in communicative interactions, especially letters to and from state administrators. Among the questions that then come to the fore are the following: in specific transactions, how did protagonists who belonged to different societies, with different histories and sometimes conflicting aims, manage to iron out their differences and invent working equivalences? Conversely, when was it that a comparison did not work or failed to convince, and why? Was it simply a problem of misunderstanding or mistranslation? Or was the search for alternative comparisons and classifications a form of discursive resistance to 'official' discourses?

Because these comparisons were the result of circumstances and power relations, they warn us against the danger, pointed out by others, of reifying cultural 'systems' and of seeing historical actors merely as expressing rather than adapting, resisting, and sometimes modifying social and cultural norms. The fact that these Anglo-French comparisons were framed in a transnational arena raises another set of problems. The example of prisoners of war in the eighteenth century will provide a test case. A classic comparison would choose France and England as two distinctive and well-identified units of comparison that provide the 'setting' of the comparison and would list, for instance, differences and similitudes in the way prisoners were perceived and treated in both countries. I propose instead to reframe the question of war imprisonment by starting with the comparisons made by prisoners, prison administrators, diplomats, and prison observers and to follow them where they lead us. This requires focusing on the concrete situations of social interactions in which these comparisons were produced. If we do so, new questions might emerge while others might lose their salience. Thus the question of the relevance of the 'nation' to understanding war captivity, instead of being taken for granted, is left open. The categories of comparison used in the eighteenth century to classify prisoners might use the idiom of the nation, but the nation might also be sidelined in these 'indigenous' comparisons, which often worked at a transnational scale.

THE COMPARATIVE WORLD VIEW

Traditionally, the most common reason for comparing two or more societies has been to contrast them in order to show how superior one of them is to the other. This characterized the so-called 'comparative method', with its tendency to see all human civilizations as 'so many deviations from the true norms of civilization, that of Great Britain'.[25] Such comparisons were favoured for example by Victorian jurists, historians, and anthropologists. Their main purpose was essentially to uncover laws by arbitrarily isolating cultural traits and rearranging them according to universal criteria, without paying much attention to historical context. Comparison as a hierarchy-making tool was also commonly used in the eighteenth century.[26] Arguing for the universality of moral norms and legal values that transcended cultures and borders enabled drawing new hierarchies and showing the superiority of one civilisation, nation, religion, or race over others. For instance, according to Montesquieu, 'savages' were deemed to follow *ius gentium*; but he described their practice of torturing or eating their prisoners of war as 'more barbaric' and 'less civilized' than those adopted by Europeans.[27] Another example is the language of 'humanitarian patriotism', which was increasingly used from the second half of the eighteenth century onwards in France and Britain and was rooted in the idea of human invariants, which made it possible to assess the merits and virtues of different people, countries, or nations comparatively and was deployed in debates about the abolition of slavery or the treatment of prisoners of war.[28]

But making comparisons was not a monopoly of philosophers, legal theorists, and travellers. A much broader variety of people resorted to comparison. In specific contexts, the language of comparison could be employed in order to make claims or legitimize one's cause or behaviour. A good example is the letters and petitions of prisoners of war to political and administrative authorities. In these documents, the comparative and superlative were very commonly used. The reference to the universality of moral norms that had been violated could make a powerful argument. Many prisoners complained about their gaolers, describing them as the cruellest they had encountered and asking for the removal of the culprits. Other prisoners used more general comparisons, in which the *tertium comparationis* was the humanity or Christianity of the prisoners, which had been denied: 'your petitioners are in great want of being released out of what bondage we now lyeth under',[29] 'that we may be treated as prisoners of war and not as slaves',[30] 'under most unchristian usage that their lives are more like beasts, then men'.[31] One

---

[25] Halévy, *England in 1815*, Preface, xii–xiii.

[26] Melvin Richter, 'The Comparative Study of Regimes and Societies', in Mark Goldie and Robert Wokler, eds, *The Cambridge History of Eighteenth-Century Political Thought* (Cambridge, 2006), 145–71.

[27] David Armitage, 'Is There a Prehistory of Globalization?', in Cohen and O'Connor, *Comparison and History*, 170. See also Anthony Pagden, *The Fall of Natural Man: The American Indians and the Origins of Comparative Ethnology* (Cambridge, 1982); Sahlins, *How 'Natives' Think*, 10–13.

[28] Renaud Morieux, 'Patriotisme humanitaire et prisonniers de guerre en France et en Angleterre pendant la Révolution française et l'Empire', in Laurent Bourquin, Philippe Hamon, Alain Hugon, and Yann Lagadec, eds, *La Politique par les armes: Conflits internationaux et politisation, XVe-XIXe siècles* (Rennes, 2014), 301–16.

[29] Petition of the crew of HMS Hampton Court and [Goaflor], detained at Abbeville, 8 October 1707; British Library (BL), Add MS61592, fo. 7.

[30] Petition of 'the Prisoners at Kinsale' to lords commissioners of the admiralty, 17/6 August 1747; National Maritime Museum (Greenwich), ADM M399, document 264/1.

[31] Peter Lamie and John Pais, French prisoners of war, petition to the earl of Sunderland, 1706, in letter from commissioners for the sick and wounded seamen, 28 December 1706; BL, Add MS 61591, fo. 84.

comparison they particularly favoured was that with common criminals: 'I have been put, despite being a prisoner of war, in a prison for criminals.'[32] 'We find ourselves in the prisons of Plymouth (where we are unfortunate enough to moan for innocent causes [*sic*], destitute and in the condition of criminals.'[33]

Instead of immediately rejecting this language as groundless or treating it as mere rhetorical strategy, one might take seriously the actors' own comparisons. Thus, instead of considering war imprisonment as inherently different from other forms of internment, one can try to understand why these comparisons made sense to those who used them. Was there anything specific to the context of imprisonment and to the state of being a prisoner that led these people to resort to comparisons? Did they make such comparisons because they thought the comparisons would be understood and acted upon by the addressees? Were these comparators chosen arbitrarily? Were comparisons between war captivity and other forms of detention shared collective representations at that time? And, if so, what does this tell us about the notion of captivity in war during this period? And is it substantially different from the corresponding notion at the present time?

One psychological consequence of imprisonment, in the eighteenth as in the twenty-first century, is the propensity to compare across time and space, to contrast life inside the walls with life 'out there', but also to fantasize about a future after prison or to remember fondly a time before prison. Captivity is a transitory space, a hiatus or a limbo,[34] prone to feeding such diachronic comparisons. A comparative world view is inherent in the state of being a prisoner. Since Gresham Sykes's pioneering study, prison sociologists have documented the 'pains of imprisonment' and their attendant effects on the prisoner's changing sense of time, sexuality, relationships with authority and fellow inmates.[35] Depersonalization and alienation often come together with imprisonment, especially as months and years go by. In their letters to the administration, prisoners are a kind of participant observers who describe their surroundings, ask for an improvement in their situation, plead to be released, or complain about favours that are granted to others and refused to them. A chief area of demand or protest is not so much detention itself as the shifting categories that are imposed on the prisoners and that entail different rights, privileges, or punishments: in prison, the politics of comparison revolves around a discussion of categories. This applies to contemporary imprisonment, for instance in the United Kingdom, where male penal prisoners are distributed according to four 'security categories' and can ask for a review of their categorization

---

[32] Saujon, French Catholic priest, from Petersfield, 27 November 1707; BL, Add MS61594, fo. 62. In fact Saujon was detained in a bridewell with prostitutes. In his long litany of grievances, he added: *ils ne me donnent pas un pauvre liard ni un morceau de pain pour manger, ce qu'ils ne refusent a leurs chiens* (Saujon, from Winchester, 11 March 1708, ibid., fo. 66).

[33] French officers in Plymouth to Duke of Newcastle, 3 July 1744; BL, Add MS32804, fo. 129.

[34] Michael Walzer, 'Prisoners of War: Does the Fight Continue after the Battle?' *American Political Science Review* 63 (1969), 777–86.

[35] Gresham Sykes, *The Society of Captives: A Study of a Maximum Security Prison* (Princeton, NJ, 1958).

after a varying period of time.[36] In their prison memoirs, former Guantanamo inmates also contest their labelling as 'unlawful enemy combatants', which deprived them of the rights they were entitled to under the 1949 Geneva Convention regarding the treatment of prisoners of war.[37] This is not to say that the experiences of prisoners, in whatever time and space, are all similar, but simply to highlight the fact that, in the context of imprisonment, self-categorization and categorization from outside are crucial for determining the way in which people are treated, which makes the use of comparisons by government, prison authorities, and prisoners all the more important.

To choose a specific example, what was at stake in the analogy that prisoners of war drew between the evil treatment they said they were subjected to and that of common criminals? First, in the eighteenth century it was widely understood, and not just present in the writings of jurists, that a prisoner of war was to be detained but must not be punished. On the contrary, he was to be protected. Second, the prisoners of war's refusal to be punished and tortured like imprisoned criminals revealed their awareness of the numerous abuses committed against detainees awaiting trial, a knowledge that resonated with the public calls for reforming the prisons, which become more vocal in Europe from the middle of the century onwards, under the influence of Cesare Beccaria's *On Crimes and Punishments* (1764).[38] In legal theory, although neither criminals nor prisoners of war were

---

[36] On entering a British penal prison, detainees are subject to a process of 'categorisation' as a result of which they are allocated to a specific category, according to different criteria, such as their likelihood to escape, the security of the public should they abscond, their history, or their personal circumstances; subsequently they can undergo a 'recategorisation': Ministry of Justice, National Offender Management Service, 'National Security Framework: Categorisation function: Categorisation and recategorisation of adult male prisoners', 2011 (at https://www.justice.gov.uk/downloads/offenders/psipso/psi-2011/psi-40-2011-categorisation-adult-males.doc, accessed 18 May 2017).

[37] Murat Kurnaz, a Turkish citizen and legal resident in Germany, was arrested in Pakistan and detained in Kandahar and Guantanamo for five years. He describes how he was sold by the Pakistani army to the Americans for a bounty of $3,000, 'as if we were slaves', and then how he was photographed in Kandahar before boarding the plane to Guantanamo, shackled and hooded: 'they were taking photos to depict us as terrorists to the world... The photos were to be used as "evidence" that we had been captured in the war zone in Afghanistan by American soldiers—even though we had all been taken prisoner in Pakistan by Pakistani police' (Murat Kurnaz, *Five Years of My Life: An Innocent Man in Guantanamo*, New York, 2008, 47–8). A prison guard remarked to him, with shame, that the US government was treating its prisoners just as the Vietcong had treated its American prisoners (ibid., 193). After three years of captivity, the US Combatant Status Review Tribunal determined in October 2004 that Kurnaz was an 'enemy combatant', categorized as dangerous' (ibid., 195, 198). Moazzam Begg, a Briton captured in Pakistan, sold to the United States and interned for four years in Afghanistan and Guantanamo, noted the refusal of his American and British interrogators to consider him a Briton; they preferred to see him as a 'Paki': Moazzam Begg, *Enemy Combatant: A British Muslim's Journey to Guantanamo and Back* (London, 2007), 10. Begg compared his treatment to the treatment of US prisoners by the Nazis during the Second World War or to that administered by the Taliban to their prisoners (ibid., 115, 121). The justification for treating these prisoners as exceptions to the laws of war was that they were 'the worst of the worst' (Donald Rumsfeld) and 'could not be compared to other prisoners' (George W. Bush, quoted in Kurnaz, *Five Years of My Life*, 206).

[38] 'In our current criminal system... the accused and the convicted are thrown together into the same dungeon; because prison is more a punishment than a place of custody of the accused': Cesare Beccaria, *On Crimes and Punishments and Other Writings*, ed. by Richard Bellamy, trans. Richard Davies (Cambridge, 1995), 74 (in chapter 29, 'Of Detention Awaiting Trial'). The book was first published in Italian in 1764, then translated into French in 1765, and into English in 1767. This mode of

to be punished by imprisonment, a clear distinction was made between the two categories: the former were awaiting a trial; the latter were detained for the duration of the war or until exchanged. But these complaints also show that we need to go beyond normative discourses to look at practices and at what went on inside the prisons.

How much truth was there in the allegations of prisoners, and was there any basis for their analogies? The experience of prisoners of war was not structurally different from that of common detainees. For instance, for most of the eighteenth century, prisoners of war were not physically separated from civil inmates. In France, as in Britain and in their empires, the same places were used, at different times or simultaneously, to detain common prisoners and prisoners of war, as well as other categories of detainees. Moreover, labelling someone a prisoner of war or a common detainee was never neutral, because it carried with it specific legal expectations. In February 1708, during the War of the Spanish Succession, a French ship, the *Salisbury*, part of a squadron that endeavoured to land the Pretender (James II) and his troops in Scotland, was captured in a naval battle off the Firth of Forth. The 400 English and Irish Jacobite soldiers on board were made prisoners. The question of how to class those men immediately became contentious. Captain Edmund Fitzgerald, who was imprisoned at Newgate, the famous London prison, wrote a long petition detailing his conditions of detention, in which he complained about the corruption of gaolers, the price of beer, and the quality of the bedding. He remonstrated that he was handled 'like ye most infamous of common malefactors', without due consideration for his status as a prisoner of war.[39] The keeper of Newgate replied that Fitzgerald and his fellow officers were treated exactly like normal criminals:

> As soon as an apartment was prepared for them they were put into it paying the customary dues which amounted to three and six pence a week for each man, and is what all criminals are obliged to pay. [They were told that] if they would like [to live] on the common side of the prison they might without paying any thing.[40]

A 'disagreement about the state of worth of the persons' involved in the dispute was at stake.[41] There was often a discrepancy between the ways in which prisoners assessed their own worth and status and the equivalences that were imposed on them by state administrators. What matters in this discussion is the choice of the

---

distancing oneself from criminals was also the standard way for debtors to present their case. English reformers took up the cause of debtors by using the same language: Margot Finn, *The Character of Credit: Personal Debt in English Culture, 1740–1914* (Cambridge, 2003), 157–8.

[39] Letter to [Lord Sunderland?], 25 August 1708; BL, Add MS61595, fo. 52v. A memorandum sent by an anonymous writer ('Anglicus') used the same analogy when he complained about the ill treatment of French prisoners at Bristol by the sword bearer: 'Your Lordship will think that man a villain that takes three pence half penny a day out of six pence, that the king grants to those whom the fortune of war throws into our hands, besides treating them in such a manner as the jaylor of Newgate would blush at' (copy of the letter, 10 October 1747, NMM, ADM M399, document 318/1).

[40] Unsigned and undated; BL, Add MS61595, fo. 54.

[41] Luc Boltanski and Laurent Thévenot, 'The Sociology of Critical Capacity', *European Journal of Social Theory* 2 (1999), 359–77, here 367.

comparator: when compared to the condition of detention of other prisoners of war, that of Fitzgerald was shocking; but, in comparison to that of 'all criminals', there was nothing anomalous in his situation. If the terms of the comparison varied and different measuring sticks were used, a complaint could be seen as legitimate or not. Thus, in 1757, the British commissioners for the sick and wounded prisoners wrote to their French counterparts to demand that the English prisoners in France

> would be treated in the same manner as French prisoners were treated in England, that orders would be given that those of their prisoners who would be ill in hospital would each have a bed, whatever might be customary in French hospitals in such cases for the sick of that nation [French], since French prisoners were so treated in England.[42]

According to the British officials, the standard of treatment of prisoners of war should not be determined by the local context of their captivity. Thus comparisons with the host population were not relevant. What mattered was the principle of reciprocity: prisoners of war should all be treated the same.

Of course, the same commissioners reversed the terms of the comparison whenever they needed to win an argument. The logic of reprisals, what an English commissioner called *lex talionis*,[43] was also based on the same idea of a strict reciprocity in the treatment of prisoners of war.

The inquiries that the English prison reformer John Howard (1726?–90) conducted in the 1770s and 1780s provide a perfect illustration of the need not to draw too neat a distinction between categories of captives, which in practice continued to overlap to a great extent, and well after the eighteenth century. Himself a former prisoner of war in France, where he had been briefly detained during the Seven Years War, Howard published in 1777 the first edition of *The State of the Prisons*. Howard did not invent prison inspections, and there was a long tradition of empirical social inquiries in England since the late seventeenth century.[44] Howard's investigations stand out because of the sheer breadth and the 'doggedly empirical character' of his inquiries.[45] He regretted the general disorder and confusion in the way different categories of prisoners were mixed with one another and lamented that legislation to improve the conditions of detention remained a dead letter. In order to remedy what he saw as a great national evil, John Howard resorted to the comparative method.[46]

---

[42] 'Mémoire sur la correspondance du Ministre de la Marine avec les Commissaires anglois au sujet de l'échange des prisonniers respectifs', [11] November 1757; AN, Marine B4/97, fo. 179.

[43] 'Mémoire sur la correspondance du Ministre de la Marine avec les Commissaires anglois au sujet de l'échange des prisonniers respectifs', 3 January 1758; AN, Marine B4/97, fo. 181.

[44] Joanna Innes, 'Power and Happiness: Empirical Social Enquiry in Britain, from "political arithmetic" to "moral statistics"', in eadem, *Inferior Politics: Social Problems and Social Policies in Eighteenth-Century Britain* (Oxford, 2009), 109–75 (and, specifically on Howard, 161–3).

[45] Ibid., 162.

[46] Howard is seen by comparative criminologists as a precursor of their discipline, but in these assessments his work is not grounded in its eighteenth-century context: see Francis Pakes, 'Howard, Pratt and beyond: Assessing the Value of Carceral Tours as Comparative Method', *Howard Journal* 54 (2015), 265–76 (272–3 on Howard's comparisons).

Howard's quest for models that could be emulated in England led him incrementally to broaden the scope and scale of his comparisons. Starting in the county of Bedfordshire, where he had been appointed High Sheriff in 1773, Howard then extended his research by geographical contiguity to 'neighbouring counties'[47] and then to the rest of England and Wales in 1774. In 1775, 'conjecturing that something useful to [his] purpose might be collected abroad', he visited prisons and gaols in Scotland and Ireland as well as in continental Europe, voyaging to 'France, Flanders, Holland and Germany',[48] then visiting again the same countries and Switzerland too, in 1776. He extended his travels further in 1778, going to the United Provinces, Flanders, Austrian and German territories, Italy, Switzerland, and France.[49] In 1781, following his now customary procedure, he 'revisited Holland, and some cities in Germany', as well as 'the capitals of Denmark, Sweden, Russia and Poland', and in 1783 'some cities in Portugal and Spain, and returned through France, Flanders and Holland'.[50] The same pattern was repeated until his death at Kherson in southern Russia in 1790.[51]

The content and scale of Howard's comparisons expanded as his research progressed. The interconnection between different spaces of incarceration led him to 'laterally' extend his research to new institutions: starting with county gaols, he went on to study bridewells, houses of correction, city and town gaols, hospitals, prison hulks, and lazarettos. Howard pleaded for a 'total separation'[52] between categories of prisoners, in order to avoid both physical and moral contagions: 'what is pernicious... is, the confining all sorts of prisoners together: debtors and felons; men and women; the young beginner and the old offender... the lunatics with the sane'.[53] This led him to compare these different categories of detainees with one another as well as with prisoners of war or the sick in hospitals. Whereas all prisoners suffered in England, one class of prisoners, according to Howard, was handled 'with tenderness and generosity'; therefore prisoners of war should be a model for the rest, and he asked that 'the same humanity [be] shewn to our own countrymen in distress'.[54] Howard used this example to make a more general point about the arbitrary distinctions between types of inmates, which were simply the outcome of specific contexts and history, not an illustration of structural variations in human nature. Thus, he argued, despite obvious differences 'in the circumstances of foreign and domestic prisoners... there is none in their nature: debtors and felons, as well as hostile foreigners, are *men*, and by men they ought to be treated as men'.[55] The *tertium comparationis* here was the prisoners' common humanity.

---

[47] John Howard, *The State of the Prisons in England and Wales, with Preliminary Observations, and an Account of some Foreign Prisons* (Warrington, 1777), 2 (Introduction).
[48] Ibid., 78.
[49] John Howard, *The State of the Prisons*, 2nd edn (Warrington, 1780), 52.
[50] John Howard, *The State of the Prisons*, 3rd edn (Warrington, 1784), 44.
[51] Rod Morgan, 'Howard, John (1726?–1790)', in *Oxford Dictionary of National Biography* (Oxford, 2004), http://www.oxforddnb.com/view/article/13922.
[52] Howard, *State of the Prisons* (1777), 46.   [53] Ibid., 15–16.
[54] Ibid., 21–2.   [55] Ibid., 23.

Howard's comparisons also worked within a single category of detainees, but his units of comparison were flexible and adapted to changes of circumstances. Howard started to work on the second edition of his *State of the Prisons* at the beginning of the War of American Independence and added a whole section on prisoners of war, as well as a substantial appendix, in the 1780 edition. There he compared the treatment of English prisoners in France with that of the French, Spanish, and Americans in England, Ireland, and Scotland.[56] As the United Provinces entered the war against Britain in 1780, Dutch prisoners were added to the comparison in the third edition (1784).[57] Methodologically, a characteristic feature of Howard's work was its emphasis on the empirical gathering of quantitative evidence. He described his modus operandi as follows:

> I have described no Prison but from my own examination at the several dates set down before the number of Prisoners. I entered every room, cell, and dungeon with a memorandum-book in my hand, in which I noted particulars upon the spot. My descriptions will to some readers appear too minute; but I chose rather to relate circumstances, than to characterize in general terms.[58]

At first sight, Howard's way of presenting his results and of ordering his empirical data (the information was listed prison after prison) did not provide the reader with the means to consider synthetically such diverse information.[59] But he repeated the same procedure from place to place, measuring and numbering, assessing the quantity and quality of beef, beer, or bread, the size of wards, and the fees of wardens. And the search for good practices always remained on the horizon: wards were more spacious at the Bristol prison than at Plymouth, while the bread at Bristol was better than at Winchester.[60]

Howard's comparative framework was based on the premise that it made no sense to consider spaces of captivity, categories of inmates, and practices of punishment and detention separately in order to understand what he saw as a political, philosophical, and 'humanitarian' problem that England shared with the rest of Europe. Comparability was never an issue for him, because comparison served a clear purpose throughout his work: looking abroad to draw useful lessons at home. Howard explicitly wrote from the perspective of an Englishman, on the assumption that things were different elsewhere and consequently worth examining, 'to imitate or avoid'.[61] This was conveyed stylistically when Howard narrated his

---

[56] Howard, *State of the Prisons* (1780), 152–61.

[57] Howard, *State of the Prisons* (1784), 190–1.

[58] Howard, *State of the Prisons* (1777), 149.

[59] Moreover, because his totals were based on ever-changing figures, they are 'meaningless': Innes, 'Power and Happiness', 162.

[60] Howard, *State of the Prisons* (1780), 156. On Howard's travels to European prisons, see Michael Ignatieff, *A Just Measure of Pain: The Penintentiary in the Industrial Revolution, 1750–1850* (London, 1978), 47–53, 94.

[61] Howard, *State of the Prisons* (1777), 94.

encounters with prison keepers ('I was surprized', 'he expressed his surprize').[62] The comparison was driven by the search for models, which explains Howard's often laudatory tone, for instance in writing about the Bruges prison: 'two things are remarkable in this prison, and well worth imitating', 'the other exemplary practice'.[63] Because the comparison was written with a practical aim in mind, that of reforming English prisons, Howard felt compelled to defend himself against the charge of being partial towards foreign examples:

> I hope [the Reader] will do me the justice to think that neither an indiscriminate admiration of every thing foreign, nor a fondness of censuring every thing at home, has influenced me to adopt the language of a Panegyrist in this part of my work, or that of a Complainant in the rest.[64]

In fact, as his works demonstrate, good models were to be found everywhere, and his section on English prisons was also comparative and 'intra-national'.

In a critical assessment of Erving Goffman's work on 'total institutions', fellow sociologist Howard Becker took issue with Goffman's choice of applying the term 'inmate' to very different groups—from patients in mental hospitals to soldiers and sailors, from schools to concentration camps. According to Becker, lumping together these different groups might be morally and intellectually problematic:

> This creates what seems to be a moral confusion at the heart of his method, for we are confronted with a classification that combines and treats as equivalent things that, as morally competent members of our society, class, and profession, we 'know' are morally quite disparate. We may be antimilitarist, but most of us do not think that army camps are concentration camps.[65]

Although Becker ultimately sided with Goffman and lauded the way he used comparison to disorient his readers and to challenge their unquestioned assumptions, Becker's remark is also problematic: why should we even assume that these different institutions are 'morally' different? As we saw in the case of Howard's prison tours, if we turn the problem on its head and take the perspective of the inmates and prison 'practitioners' instead of that of the social scientist, the comparison is not illegitimate: analogies and comparisons were generated in everyday practice. There is value in taking seriously 'indigenous' world views, which can help us refine and reframe our own categories of analysis.

---

[62] 'I was surprized': ibid., 80 and 190 (respectively on visiting Paris prisons and Whitechapel prison); 'he expressed his surprize': ibid., 99 (Lausanne keeper on hearing about gaol fever).
[63] Ibid., 137–8. Likewise he commended the 'exemplary provision' of the French court towards its prisoners of war in England and the 'exemplary benevolence' of the Liverpool gentry: John Howard, *The State of the Prisons in England and Wales, with Preliminary Observations, and an Account of some Foreign Prisons and Hospitals*, 4th edn (London, 1792), 190, 314.
[64] Howard, *State of the Prisons* (1777), 145.
[65] Howard Becker, 'The Politics of Presentation: Goffman and Total Institutions', *Symbolic Interaction* 26 (2003), 659–69, here 667. See Erving Goffman, 'On the Characteristics of Total Institutions', in idem, *Asylums: Essays on the Social Situation of Mental Patients and Other Inmates* (New York, 1961), 3–124.

HOW MUCH IS A BISHOP WORTH?
DRAWING EQUIVALENCES

In the context of war, the status of the prisoners was always understood to be relational and situational. For the same reason, the French and English commissioners for the exchange of prisoners adopted analogies and equivalences that helped to make the labels they assigned to them 'stick', in spite of a constantly changing social landscape. The social categories that would provide the basis for individual or general exchanges (the so-called 'exchange cartels') were the result of years of correspondence across the Channel.[66] At stake was the construction of a 'transnational knowledge space'[67] in which equivalences between English and French social categories were drawn. Intellectual and political spaces of equivalence were produced through discussions on the comparability of social statuses. This is another example of the politics of comparison in practice.[68] Negotiators had to find a way to establish commensurability between their units of comparison. These men had to find a common ground, a terrain of mutual understanding, in order to achieve the repatriation of as many of their compatriots as possible without weakening the war effort by striking an inequitable deal.

The problems that these negotiators faced when drawing such comparisons are different from those of the social scientist who tries to justify his/her units or criteria of comparison.[69] Negotiators were, so to speak, 'given' their sample from the outset; and they did not select their cases. The 'cases' were all the prisoners of war captured and detained at a given time. Therefore negotiators must find and invent comparisons that 'worked'—that made sense and were understandable to their counterparts across the Channel. In the language of the sociology of science, these men were translators of knowledge. For them, action was impossible unless comparability was first established. Both sides had to explain why 'this group is more like that one than this one'[70] and to justify the claim that certain individual or groups simply did not have any equivalent. By focusing on comparatists at work, I will highlight the ambivalence of any act of comparing—which was already tangible in eighteenth-century definitions. Thus, in 1755, Samuel Johnson defined 'comparable' as follows: 'worthy to be compared; of equal regard'. The question of estimation, of worth and value, is central in this definition.

Likewise, commissioners for exchange had to grapple with the knotty problem of the worth of prisoners and of how to assess it. According to the economic

---

[66] These exchange cartels have been studied by diplomatic and military historians, who have above all been interested in the number of prisoners who were exchanged during conflicts and the impact of these exchanges on the balance of power. My approach is different.

[67] I borrow the notion from David Turnbull, *Masons, Tricksters and Cartographers: Comparative Studies in the Sociology of Scientific and Indigenous Knowledge* (Amsterdam, 2000), 120.

[68] See Ann Laura Stoler, 'Tense and Tender Ties: The Politics of Comparison in North American History and (Post) Colonial Studies', *Journal of American History* 88 (2001), 829–65.

[69] D. Berg-Schlosser, 'Comparative Studies: Method and Design', in N. J. Smelser and P. B. Baltes, eds, *International Encyclopedia of Social and Behavioral Sciences*, 2nd edn (Amsterdam, 2015), 2427–33.

[70] Ibid., 2429.

anthropologist Jane Guyer in her work on Atlantic Africa, worth is not conceived of here solely in quantitative and objectively measurable terms, determined by the market and by fixed monetary prices. Value is a relational and situational notion: by focusing on economic transactions, Guyer shows that different 'standards of valuation' can coexist and compete among themselves. It is by maintaining what she calls a 'value disjuncture' and by crossing the threshold between multiple 'scales of valuation' that African merchants make an economic gain. Thus defining value is a political, social, and cultural process.[71] The definition of worth as contingent is very useful from our perspective: in their search for equivalences and units of comparison, actors can perform at different levels simultaneously and combine various definitions of worth. Moreover, Guyer's emphasis on the process of construction of value as a subject of enquiry also offers us a useful model. Does the fact that the categories and social statuses that were discussed by commissioners were flexible mean that the very aim of comparing was meaningless, since the units that were compared were permanently changing? Not quite, as can be seen if we focus our analysis on the moment of the transaction, when comparability was actualized.

Following sociologists Luc Boltanski and Laurent Thévenot, I will examine the 'pragmatic conditions of attribution of worth' and the 'qualification process' that sees the attribution of a case to a category.[72] The discussion of the 'worth' or 'size' of specific persons is particularly interesting from my perspective. In this kind of practical comparison, taxonomy is the condition of possibility of comparing: 'the background of comparability was established by the *per genus et differentiam* mode of analysis, i.e. by a taxonomical treatment. In this context, 'comparable' means something which belongs to the same genus, species, or subspecies—in short, to the same class.'[73] One problem—which occurs, of course, in any comparison—is what to do with those cases for which no equivalent can be found. This raises the issue of incommensurability, 'the situation of phenomena that are, ostensibly, impossible to measure or compare in terms of the same metric'.[74] Why is it that some individual or groups cannot be translated from one culture to another? Should we simply ignore the exceptions that do not fit into our models? Or could we not, on the contrary, use them as the basis for redefining these theoretical models, or even invent new ones?[75] If we find multiple exceptions, what does this tell us about the general categories we use? One needs to interrogate the relationship between the individual case and the general structures of reference. Exceptions, exemptions, and anomalies can help the historian to delineate, by induction, the spaces of comparability that were thinkable during a specific period. They can also provide the basis for reframing the historian's own comparisons so as to make room

[71] Jane I. Guyer, *Marginal Gains: Monetary Transactions in Atlantic Africa* (Chicago, IL, 2004), 9–19. I would like to thank Bronwen Everill for drawing my attention to this book.

[72] Boltanski and Thévenot, 'Sociology of Critical Capacity', 366–7.

[73] Giovanni Sartori, 'Concept Misformation in Comparative Politics', *American Political Science Review* 64 (1970), 1033–53, here 1036.

[74] Handler, 'Uses of Incommensurability', 627.

[75] See Jean-Claude Passeron and Jacques Revel, 'Raisonner à partir de singularités', and Pierre Livet, 'Les Diverses Formes de raisonnement par cas', both in Jean-Claude Passeron and Jacques Revel, eds, *Penser par cas* (Paris, 2005), 9–44, and 229–63.

for these supposedly exceptional cases by pushing the limits of the frame outward. Exceptions are a useful reminder that our units of comparison must be redefined as we discover counterexamples.

Many principles could justify the evaluation of a prisoner's worth in the context of transactions about his/her exchange. Measuring the worth of prisoners was a complex matter. Individual prisoners could be converted into monetary equivalents, but also commodified and turned into goods, or 'converted from one condition to another'.[76] When a negotiation took place about the 'exchangeability' of specific prisoners, the situation for their commodification existed.[77] In 1708 the French secretary for foreign affairs asked his English counterpart that the marquis de Levy, prisoner of war in England, be sent back to France on his parole: 'We do not have in France any prisoner of his rank taken at sea, but we could, if you think it fit, give you an equivalent in other prisoners…let me know what you consider this equivalent might be.'[78]

The choice of vocabulary exposes the reification of the prisoners, who were categorized and exchanged like things. The language used in this correspondence was that of trade.[79] The rhetoric shows how the state was hard at work to standardize social categories and commodify people.[80] In the eighteenth century, this conversion of military officers into a precise number of rank-and-file soldiers and sailors became standardized and generally took the following form: when someone from a similar rank or grade in the army or navy could not be found, 'so one captain of a ship of the line will count against ten men'.[81] Common sailors or soldiers were thus converted into units of valuation. This principle of calculating the exchange rates of prisoners survived throughout the eighteenth century and beyond. In the cartel of exchange for prisoners of war taken in the Indian Ocean, signed between France and Britain in 1805, the unit of measure was that of 'simple sailors'; for instance a *capitaine de frégate* was the equivalent of a 'master and commander', or eight men, and so on.[82] The process of commodification did not stop

[76] Karin Barber, 'When People Cross Thresholds', *African Studies Review* 50.2 (2007), 111–23, here 114. The notion of the prisoner as a commodity is inspired by Arjun Appadurai, 'Introduction: Commodities and the Politics of Value', in idem, ed., *The Social Life of Things: Commodities in Cultural Perspective* (Cambridge, 1986), 3–63.

[77] On 'exchangeability', see ibid., 13 and Michel Foucault, *The Order of Things: An Archeology of the Human Sciences* (London, 2002 [1966]), 206–12.

[78] Pontchartrain to Sunderland, 16 May 1708; BL, MS61594, fo. 27v.

[79] As in these instructions from the French minister to the French commissary for the exchange of prisoners, Lempereur: *Les commissaires anglois…comptent le tarif de 20 hommes proposes pour chaque cap.ne de v.au [capitaine de vaisseau] pris de part et d'autre.* The British government must *reponde a nos manieres honnestes, parce que jusques icy nous avons fait toutes les avances sans aucun retour.* We must *consommer l'eschange de ces hommes,* 18 September 1709; Archives Nationales (Paris) (AN), Marine B2/216, fos. 1444–5.

[80] On the standardization, classification, and codification of social categories by modern states, see Alain Desrosières, *The Politics of Large Numbers: A History of Statistical Reasoning*, trans. Camille Naish (Cambridge, MA, 2002).

[81] French proposal of a cartel, with English comments, [December 1744], Article 10; The National Archives, Kew (TNA), ADM 98/2, fo. 70v. The same agreements were reached in December 1702: commissioners for sick and wounded seamen to the earl of Sunderland, 24 July 1707; BL, Add MS61591, fo. 155.

[82] Cartel of exchange for the prisoners of war taken in the Indian Ocean, signed by the French and the British commanders, 18 July 1805, Article 1; Mauritius Archives, GB 10G/1, n.f.

here and, if needed, one common sailor could be converted into one monetary unit.[83] These conventions ensured commensurability between classes of people who did not have an exact equivalent. Such exchanges also revealed conceptions of society in which only people of a certain rank or class were worthy of being exchanged as individuals; the others were interchangeable and were only 'considered...with regard to their number'.[84]

Another fruitful avenue of research, which, to my knowledge, has escaped the attention of historians, is how comparisons were drawn materially and how the way to present this material could constrain the intellect. From basic local accounts through tallies computed by marine administrators and parole agents all over the world to receipts or lists of expenditures, the paper trail left by war imprisonment in the archives is long. One tool that commissaries for exchange often used was the 'list of exchanges', which presented the name of the prisoner in the first column, the number of men the French wanted for their exchange in the second column, and the English exchange rate in the third column.[85] According to Michel Foucault, 'the centre of knowledge, in the seventeenth and eighteenth centuries, is the *table*'.[86] Drawing on Foucault's intuition, Alain Desrosières has shown, in his prehistory of statistics, how the very shape of the table 'required the construction of spaces of comparison, common referents, and *criteria*' and created a 'space of equivalence'.[87]

How a particular equivalence could be achieved depended on the local context of negotiation as well as on general principles. Certainly the laws of supply and demand could determine the attribution of value to prisoners. There was a political economy of the prisoner of war: the regular calculation of the stocks of prisoners could increase the desirability or need for prisoners or, on the contrary, force the enemy to bear the cost of their detention. The cost of their transport and of their subsistence and the corruption of the commodity also impacted the market for prisoners (when prisoners were sick or old, their value was depreciated and they were liberated 'for free'). But social factors were also important. Privileges, whim, or personal relationships were vital too. Thus the place of prisoners on the ladder of exchange did not simply depend on the duration of their captivity. To the French commissioners who contested a specific exchange between two captains proposed

[83] 'By the 2d article of the Convention with Spain signed the 25th June 1782 for a general exchange of all prisoners taken at sea, it was agreed, in case of a deficiency of prisoners on either side to give in exchange, one guinea shall be accepted as an equivalent for every private man, and the officers to bear the same value in guineas, as by the Convention of July 1781 they were to bear in men' (commissioners for sick and wounded seamen to Philip Stephens Esq., 28 November 1783; TNA, ADM 98/14, p. 406).

[84] 'We must also think about the Gardes de la Marine, for whom nothing has been decided so far; since they are not officers, they must only be considered...with regard to their number, not as officers to be exchanged' (letter from Guillot, 28 November 1746; AN, Marine B2/329, fo. 250). Officers of merchant navy or privateers should not be exchanged individually, unlike officers of Royal and Navy. Likewise for the surgeons of merchants and corsairs: AN, Marine B2/331, fo. 233.

[85] 'Liste d'eschange', from Lempereur to the commissioners for the sick and wounded seamen, 12 June 1709; BL, Add MS61593, fo. 97 sq.

[86] Michel Foucault, *Order of Things*, 82.   [87] Desrosières, *Politics of Large Numbers*, 21.

by the British on the grounds that there were in Britain 'more ancient prisoners than Mr Martet', the British commissioners put forward their discretionary right to select specific prisoners, the so-called 'exchange by preference which has taken place on both sides in all the wars'.[88] Cultivating goodwill between negotiators could also ensure the success of transactions. Commissioners could step out of their way and accept an asymmetrical exchange, in order to guarantee the furtherance of exchanges, if proof of the trustworthiness of their partners could be found in past transactions.[89]

State administrators constructed spaces of equivalence but did not express a vision of society as a whole; nor did they invent new categories, which would have represented a compromise between French and British conceptions of society. However, *ancien régime* societies were based on corporatist ideologies, according to which individuals did not exist in isolation. This had important epistemological consequences, as pointed out by Michel Foucault: the criteria for the definition and classification of individuals (plants, animals, humans) were furnished by comparisons with others.[90] A social status could never be defined by itself, but was necessarily relational and comparative, positively or negatively. Long discussions took place over the rightful 'placing' of particular groups in the exchange system.

Women are a case in point. During the War of the Austrian Succession, the French and British commissioners debated the status of women, the former considering that women should be entered into the balance of exchange, the latter that they should be exempted. The matter was sensitive because France detained over 200 British women in 1744. Different principles of justification clashed. The British listed the (bad) reasons that the French had for detaining and exchanging women as prisoners: the discrepancy between their pretentions to be a civilized nation and their attitude to the *beau sexe* ('very unbecoming the politess [*sic*], which that nation is so apt to boast, for subjecting the sex to the hardships attendant on prisoners of war'); the lack of coherence of this policy, which classed women as prisoners but exempted boys under the age of 12; economic rationality, based on the French assumption that English women travelled more often by water; hence more would be taken and exchanged for French men. By contrast, a high moral ground dictated the British policy:

> It is already a rule in England, to set at liberty, without any consideration, all female prisoners, as well as the boys abovementioned. It is to be hoped, the French, upon second thoughts, will not give occasion even to a bare suspension of these acts of generosity.[91]

[88] Translation of a letter from the commissioners for the sick and wounded seamen and the exchange of prisoners of war, 26 September 1759; AN, Marine B4/97, fo. 209.
[89] On this phenomenon, see Sarah Berry, 'Marginal Gains, Market Values, and History', *African Studies Review* 50.2 (2007), 57–70, here 61–2.
[90] 'To know what properly appertains to one individual is to have before one the classification—or the possibility of classifying—all others' (Foucault, *Order of Things*, 157–8).
[91] 'Some observations & reflexions upon the report of a conference, which Mr. Abraham Hume, had with Mons. De Givry at the Castle of Wattignies the 28th August 1744. N.S., upon the subject of a cartel between Great Brittain & France. Office &c', 4 September 1744; TNA, ADM 98/2, fo. 10.

'As they cannot have any part in acts of hostility in the war,' the British commissioner added, women were not to be considered as prisoners of war but 'as *neutres*' [neutrals].[92] The onus to discontinue such a moral policy was placed on France. The French negotiator used a different set of arguments: first, precedent (in previous wars, women passengers were included, just like men, in the balance of exchanges); and, second, the idea of an unfair comparative advantage, which transgressed 'the principles of equality' and reciprocity (the cost of the subsistence of these women, while imprisoned in France, had to be compensated by the British).[93] Women passengers, as he had argued before, were not to be given a special status: they must be 'exchanged on the same footing as the rest of the crews'.[94] The French eventually yielded and the British view was entered in the general cartel of exchange of 1745. Women were exempted from war imprisonment in subsequent conflicts.[95] In this discussion two registers of value were opposed, that of military value and that of economic value, and the former won. Women were worth nothing as far as the exchange of prisoners was concerned.

Race constituted another exception. In the already mentioned 1805 cartel for the prisoners captured in the Indian Ocean, non-Europeans were not placed on the same comparative scale as Europeans. Article 2 specified that lascars (sailors), 'cypahis [i.e. soldiers, *spahis*] and other men of colour...can only be exchanged against each other and man for man'.[96] Distributing them on the same measuring scale would have been a recognition of the commensurability between European and 'indigenous' societies. Moreover, one notes the refusal to take into account the internal social hierarchies of non-Europeans: unlike in the case of cartels for Europeans, there was no attempt here to devise fine-grained social taxonomies. Race erased all other criteria of social categorization. Once again, one finds impositions of inequality and power in the administrative definition of equivalences. Those at the bottom of *ancien régime* social hierarchies, who were incapacitated in law—such as servants, children, women—were simply excluded from the exchange system as minors or dependants. But other logics of comparative hierarchy, such as utility in war and racial prejudice, were also at work.

While women and non-Europeans were simply excluded from spaces of equivalence due to prevailing prejudices, there were also anomalous cases. The example of the bishop of Quebec, who was imprisoned in England and whose exchange dragged on for six years between 1704 and 1709, illustrates how the assessment of an individual's value was highly contextual and how the categorization of prisoners

---

[92] 'Observations of the Commissioners for taking care of the sick and wounded seamen, and for exchanging prisoners of war, upon the project of cartel transmitted to His Grace the Duke of Newcastle, by Mr. Van Hoy, the Dutch Ambassador at Paris', 27 November 1744; TNA, ADM 98/2, fo. 78.

[93] French proposal of a cartel, with English comments, [December 1744], Article 12; TNA, ADM 98/2, fo. 71v.

[94] 'Observations sur le projet de cartel que m'a remis à Wattignies le 28 de ce mois, Mons. Hume, de la part de son excellence Mons.r le Marechal Wade.' [August 1744]; TNA, ADM 98/2, fo. 20.

[95] 'Articles du Projet de Cartel changé conformément aux Observations', [June 1745]; TNA, ADM 98/2, fo. 162.

[96] Article 2, Mauritius Archives, GB 10G/1, n.f.

was politicized.[97] The English first proposed to exchange this clergyman, who had been captured at sea in 1704, for French Protestant priests who had been sent to the galleys. To this France objected that juridical conditions were very different, since the Huguenots were 'criminals', not prisoners of war.[98] Then the British offered to exchange him for the grand dean of Liège, another cleric, who had been arrested for treason by the elector of Cologne, an ally of Louis XIV.[99] In their reply, the French insisted on 'the different conditions of those two Ecclesiastics':

> you cannot detain that Prelate [the bishop of Quebec] with any colour of Justice... having been taken on the sea, he is in the same case with others that are Prisoners of War, whereas the Dean of Liege being neither a Prisoner of War nor of the King's, but of his own Sovereigns, there can be no resemblance between them.[100]

International law was thus opposed to domestic law and the status of the prisoner of war was opposed to that of the prisoner of state. In fact the distinction between these categories was not always clear-cut, as shown by the endless discussions about the labelling of combatants involved in civil wars or in non-conventional forms of warfare. In reality, the similarities between the situations of these two Catholic prelates were striking, and the reasons for the French reluctance to release the dean of Liège had nothing to do with his condition but everything to do with international relations.[101] The French reiterated their stance for years, contending that the dean of Liège 'was not taken at sea [*prisonnier de mer*]...and cannot be included in this exchange for any sort of reason, since there is here no issue of birth or dignity'.[102]

War, and specifically the context of the capture, prevailed over the equivalence between traditional social hierarchies. Moreover, the value of an individual could change drastically once that person was imprisoned. The French commissioners proposed to exchange the retinue of the bishop of Quebec for army officers, thus consenting to an asymmetrical exchange:

> I know Gent.^m very well at what value among men so respectful for Religion as we are, the Ecclesiasticall state ought to be rated, but you will confess again on your parts, that one days service of an officer of war is of more value to the politicall state, than one

[97] James H. Thomas, 'Quebec's Bishop as Pawn: Saint-Vallier's Imprisonment in England, 1704–1709', *CCHA, Historical Studies* 64 (1998), 151–60.

[98] [Duke of Pontchartrain] to Mr Brilac, 24 June 1705; AN, Marine B2/215, fo. 791–v.

[99] Paul Harsin, *Les Relations extérieures de la principauté de Liège sous Jean Louis d'Elderen et Joseph Clément de Bavière (1688–1718)* (Liège, 1927), 181–210. I am grateful to Catherine Denys for this reference and for the exchanges about this.

[100] Extract of the translation of a letter from Monsieur Lempereur, commissioner for the Marine at Saint-Malo, to the commissioners for the sick and wounded seamen, 25 January 1707, [with S&W commissioners 24 Jan./4 Feb. 1706/7]; BL, Add MS61591, no. 103.

[101] He was a partisan of the Anglo-Dutch alliance, and very influential within the chapter of the principality of Liège. To prevent a revolt of the *Liégeois* against the French occupation, it was better to keep him in prison for as long as possible.

[102] Duke of Pontchartrain, 28 March 1708; AN, Marine B2/206, fo. 1036. Lempereur expressed the same view in April 1708: *Le caractere de pretre ou de prelast n'y la condition ne peuvent etablir entre ces Messieurs aucun raport n'y aucune egalité, puisqu'il s'agit dans nos eschanges de prisonniers faits sur mer et que Mons. L'Evesque de Quebec se trouvant dans ce cas il est constamment et necessairement dans celuy du cartell et de l'eschange qui est la loy des deux nations* (extract of a letter from Mons. Lempereur, Saint-Malo, 18 April 1708 [with S&W 17/28 Apr. 1708]; BL, Add MS61592, fo. 58).

hundred years service of the most zealous devotee can be to the ecclesiasticall one, wherefore all the disproportion that can be in the exchange I propose to you, falls on our side, because you will have that service of your officers that we cannot expect of our ecclesiaticks.[103]

The state of war profoundly unsettled traditional conceptions of social hierarchy and social worth. In the spiritual and civil world a bishop was highly ranked. In wartime his value was much more contested and subject to fluctuations.[104] One cannot help thinking that this difficulty in agreeing on an exchange for this personage also had something to do with a lack of motivation to reach an agreement. Leaving him in a legal vacuum was somehow convenient for the French monarchy, and the bishop of Quebec described his own devaluation in his letters to the French and British ministers and administrators. He deplored that his many appeals to the comte de Pontchartrain had been left unanswered, which he interpreted as a sign of 'estrangement [*raffroidissement*] of the French Court from us', in other words, of his depreciation. He described how the British strategy of raising the stakes by demanding higher-ranked officers such as *lieutenants de vaisseaux* for his exchange and that of his retinue had been counterproductive, and spoke of his fear that 'we will in effect be forgotten by France'. The future looked grim, and the bishop predicted

> that the King will prefer to remove his officers, who can be of service to him in war, rather than a bishop and clergymen who are no use to him in his armies... There was readiness to do a great deal for us at another time, but now things are very different.[105]

The value of a prisoner of war, just like that of any commodity, could swing upwards or downwards and depended on a number of factors. The bishop of Quebec was eventually exchanged in August 1709 for the dean of Liège.[106]

Prisoners of war also participated in this process of attribution of worth by resisting commodification or by claiming other labels than those ascribed to them, in order to modify their value.[107] For instance, in their petitions to be released, they often employed the rhetoric of 'self-aggrandizement', which by definition was based on a comparison with collectives.[108] They asked to be moved up the ladder

---

[103] Extract of the translation of a letter from Monsieur Lempereur, commissioner for the *Marine* at Saint-Malo, to the commissioners for the sick and wounded seamen, 25 January 1707, [with S&W commissioners 24 Jan./4 Feb. 1706/7]; BL, Add MS61591, fo. 104.

[104] See Foucault, *Order of Things*, 180–232 (chapter 6, 'Exchanging'); Igor Kopytoff, 'The Cultural Biography of Things: Commodification as Process', in Arjun Appadurai, ed., *The Social Life of Things: Commodities in Cultural Perspective* (Cambridge, 1986), 64–92.

[105] Copy of a letter from the Bishop of Quebec to commissioners for sick and wounded seamen [with S&W 12/23 Oct. 1708], from Petersfield, 4 October 1708; BL, Add MS61592, fo. 160–1.

[106] B2/216, f987.

[107] On how labelling modifies value, see Berry, 'Marginal Gains', 60.

[108] Cultural anthropologist Karin Barber analyses 'self-making' in West African praise poetry, a genre that reveals the extreme fluidity of social representations and the 'competitive self-aggrandizement of individuals' (Barber, 'When People Cross Thresholds', 115). Boltanski analyses these 'techniques of aggrandizement' in the context of public denunciations (Luc Boltanski, *Love and Justice as Competences: Three Essays on the Sociology of Action*, trans. Catherine Porter, Cambridge, 2012, 207–19).

of priorities for release, putting forward their merits, honours, or good behaviour. Others chose to emphasize, in their self-presentations, qualities and circumstances that they knew would be regarded favourably by state authorities. In May 1707, Peter Drake, an Irish-born Catholic, was captured on board a French privateer. His parents had emigrated to France legally, according to the Treaty of Limerick of 1691, when he was 10 years old.[109] How to categorize Drake was not straightforward. In his defence, he argued that he had been serving on the French ship in order to prepare his escape to England and was 'getting home into his new country'. And he presented attestations on his behalf 'from several persons...of good repute tho Roman Catholicks'. The English commissioners for the exchange of prisoners were not sure what to do with him and asked the Attorney General for his guidance, 'whether he ought to be tried as a traytor, or whether we may exchange him as a subject of France, but if neither, that he may give good security for his peacable behavior in England'.[110] All of these labels were potentially legitimate, and the decision to favour one criterion or another was political.

National labels themselves were reversible in the context of prisoners' exchange, and the nationality of the ship could get precedence over the place of birth of the combatant. Thus foreign prisoners taken on board French ships 'shall be reputed French', and those taken on board English ships 'shall be reckon'd as English',[111] while Frenchmen taken in the Spanish fleet 'could not be considered otherwise than as Spanish prisoners'.[112] One sees the verbs denoting the process of social estimation at work in these designations. Such examples serve as a useful reminder that 'nationality' was a largely anachronistic notion for most of the eighteenth century, not simply because people constantly shifted their allegiances and played with the language of the nation, but also because states themselves blurred the legal distinctions between subjecthood, foreignness, and state of enmity.

Despite state attempts to control the assignation of identities to prisoners and to monitor their movements, there were structural loopholes in this system. Although the practice was illegal, many prisoners changed sides, enlisting in the army and navy of their captors. Others completely turned the logic of the system on its head by posing as prisoners of war in order to get a free journey home. In October 1783, nine passengers landed in Calais from a Dover ship. The *rôle de débarquement* of the ship illustrates the gap between the identities claimed by these passengers in their statements and the identities that were attributed to them by state agents: 'claiming to be from Corsica coming from Martinique', 'Id. from Cadix coming from the coast of Guinee', 'Id. Basque coming from Antigua', 'S. Jean de Luz coming from Jamaica', and so on (*se disant de Corse venant de la Martinique; Id. de Cadix venant de la cote de Guinée; Id. Basque venant d'Antigue; St. Jean de Luz*

---

[109] This treaty allowed Jacobite soldiers and their families to leave for France accompanied by their families and to continue to serve James II in the Irish Brigade.

[110] R. Adams and W. Churchill to the earl of Sunderland, 3 May 1707; BL, Add MS61591, fo. 127v.

[111] Robert Hunter, 17/23 December 1708; BL, Add MS61595, fo. 58.

[112] Commissioners for the sick and wounded seamen to Philip Stephens Esq., 3 July 1780; TNA, ADM 98/13, fo. 5v.

venant de la Jamaique). The admiralty agent at Calais noted, as an aside, that he had refused to pay for these prisoners' expenses:

> Because in the course of the interrogations to which they were submitted in this harbour, it was discovered that they had betrayed the good faith of Mr. the ambassador, and during the war had not served on any French vessel, he had simply given the order that they be returned home. Some of these sailors are Italian and Spanish.[113]

The relative fluidity of social statuses in the context of war captivity made these itineraries possible.

* * *

Who could be a prisoner of war in the eighteenth century? Someone who was in the military profession? This is impugned by the case of bishops. Someone who was clearly differentiated from criminals? The distinction lost its meaning in practice. Someone who travelled on an enemy ship? This did not always apply, for example to passengers or neutrals. Someone who was the subject of a prince at war with another sovereign? But what, then, of French Huguenots fighting alongside Britain and of Irish Catholics fighting alongside France? None of these criteria was sufficient to determine how a particular individual would be treated in practice.

The categorization of prisoners and the drawing of equivalences were situational and depended on power relations; thus, as today, normative categories did not adequately describe the reality of war imprisonment. This is not to argue that such categories were interchangeable and equivalent: different labels provided justifications for radically different treatments. But we need to question the rigidity and social utility of these classifications. The same people, depending on the moments and the places of their captivity, could be categorized and, accordingly, treated as prisoners of war, as criminals, as rebels, as penal prisoners, or as enemies of the state. Because of the legal uncertainty regarding the status of prisoners of war, it therefore remains of crucial importance to pay attention to indigenous comparisons instead of limiting ourselves to a purely institutional approach.

What does the story of prisoners in the eighteenth century tell us about comparison more generally? Studying comparison as a historian means looking at the politics of taxonomy in order to analyse the classificatory schemes and material instruments of knowledge mobilized by the state. State bureaucrats and administrators commodified people and built specialist tools of measurement and quantification. They thus devised a language that allowed them to draw comparisons that could travel across state borders, relying on notions such as 'equivalence' or 'worth'.[114] I have shown how arbitrary some of these equivalences were, but also how vital it was to reach an agreement, even a messy and temporary one, and fix a picture of the social world in order to act upon it. More broadly, the production of social categories always took place through a dialogue involving different social

---

[113] Passengers landed in Calais on 23 October 1783 from the English packet boat *The Courier*; AN, Marine F2/101, n.f.

[114] Willibald Steinmetz is currently engaged on a vast project of mapping out the uses of comparisons by the states in nineteenth and twentieth-century Europe, through law or statistics.

groups and cultures. Comparisons in practice involved constant negotiations, which mobilized official classifications, drew social, racial, or sexual hierarchies, and sometimes failed to find working equivalences. Instead of eliminating from our purview the cases that did not fit, I have tried to show that a focus on exceptions can help us delineate what the norm was.[115]

This chapter has focused less on comparison as a method than on comparison as a historical object. Who compares, how, what, and why people resort to comparison are questions worth studying in themselves. Indeed, comparison has a history. Just as comparison, as it is used by social scientists and historians, can serve many purposes—such as decentring the gaze, breaking with common sense and inherited preconceptions, or helping us particularize our objects of research—so the indigenous comparisons were also used with specific aims in mind.[116] Writing about Enlightenment thought, Melvin Richter rightly asked 'whether comparison meant the same thing in the eighteenth century as it means to us now'.[117] In the same way, I have suggested that we need to pay attention to the political meaning of comparisons and take into account the social context in which they were mobilized.

Future work would be desirable at the conjunction of cultural approaches to comparison with more cliometrically driven approaches. In this we might once again follow Eric Hobsbawm's lead. While social structure and domination were always part of his framework, he never forgot what he called 'the multidimensionality of human beings in society' and underlined the many ways in which an individual subjectively defines him-/herself in different contexts.[118] Similarly, studying comparisons from below allows one to bypass what is often a forced opposition between structure and agency. The focus on situated comparisons could thus provide a way of answering the growing calls for bridging the global and microhistory. The search for robust comparators, which work across long periods and across large spaces, has produced some of the most exciting works in global economic history at the macro level, which has opened the way to reciprocal comparisons.[119] At a micro level, undertaking a reciprocal comparison would mean placing at the centre of the analysis the mutual perceptions of historical actors, as they were trying to reach an understanding of 'the other side' in different contexts and in

[115] Edoardo Grendi, 'Microanalasi e storia sociale', *Quaderni Storici* 35 (1977), 506–20.
[116] Pierre Bourdieu, 'The Practice of Reflexive Sociology (the Paris Workshop)', in Pierre Bourdieu and Loïc Wacquant, *An Invitation to Reflexive Sociology* (Chicago, IL, 1992), 218–60, here 234–5.
[117] Vicente Oieni and Melvin Richter, 'Conceptual History and Translation: An Interview with Melvin Richter', *Contributions to the History of Concepts* 4 (2008), 226–38, here 236; Richter, 'Comparative Study', 145.
[118] Eric Hobsbawm, 'Working-Class Internationalism', in Frits L. van Holthoon and Marcel van der Linden, eds, *Internationalism in the Labour Movement, 1830–1940* (Leiden, 1988), 3–16, here 14.
[119] By 'reciprocal comparison' Pomeranz means 'viewing both sides of the comparison as "deviations" when seen through the expectations of the other, rather than leaving one as always the norm' (Kenneth Pomeranz, *The Great Divergence: China, Europe, and the Making of a Modern World Economy*, Princeton, NJ, 2000, 8). See also R. Bin Wong, *Before and Beyond Divergence: The Politics of Economic Change in China and Europe* (Cambridge, MA, 2011); Gareth Austin, 'Reciprocal Comparison and African History: Tackling Conceptual Euro-Centrism in the Study of Africa's Economic Past', *African Studies Review* 50 (2007), 1–28.

different ways, through the exchange of insults, objects, or gestures.[120] The search for intelligible and effective equivalences often proceeded haphazardly and did not always succeed; often, indeed, it ended in mistranslation or miscommunication. These very failures, which are intrinsic to any comparative endeavour, are worth studying in themselves.[121]

ACKNOWLEDGEMENTS

I would like to thank Joel Isaac, Véronique Mottier, Filippo de Vivo, and Charles Walton for commenting on previous drafts of this article, as well as John Arnold, Peter Garnsey, Joanna Innes, and Sam James for their critical suggestions.

---

[120] See for instance Natalie Zemon Davis, 'Decentering History: Local Stories and Cultural Crossings in a Global World', *History and Theory* 50 (2011), 188–202.

[121] Handler, 'Uses of Incommensurability', 637; Sanjay Subrahmanyam, 'Par-delà l'incommensurabilité: Pour une histoire connectée des empires aux temps modernes', *Revue d'histoire moderne et contemporaine* 54 (2007), 34–53.

5

Hobsbawm and Researching
the History of Nationalism

John Breuilly

INTRODUCTION

I will begin with a consideration of recent debates in nationalism studies and then relate these to Hobsbawm's changing interpretations of nationalism. Then I will consider how Hobsbawm's work can inform innovative historical research that goes beyond those debates.

DEBATES IN NATIONALISM STUDIES

The view that not only is nationalism modern chronologically, but modernity is the necessary and sufficient condition for nationalism predates the rise of the 'modernist paradigm'[1] in the 1980s. Karl Deutsch anticipated arguments about mass media in *Nationalism and Social Communication* (1953). Elie Kedourie began *Nationalism* (1960) by asserting: 'Nationalism is a doctrine invented in Europe at the beginning of the 19th century'; and he presented it as an ideology of huge (for him pernicious) significance. In the 1980s this modernism was elaborated upon for different aspects of nationalism and became central to social science interpretations.

Yet it remained marginal for historians.[2] Modern social and political history (less so economic and intellectual history), especially for the West, is national history.[3] Such 'methodological nationalism' essentializes the national framework as politics (nation-state) and as society and culture (nation). Nationalism is located within a national history of long duration and the concept of nation is made chronologically and causally prior to that of nationalism. The key claims of modernism—that nationalism is modern and shapes the nation—are thereby undermined.

---

[1] This is the title of the introductory section in Anthony Smith, *Nationalism and Modernism* (Abingdon, 1988).

[2] On the impact of different concepts of nationalism on historians, see Stefan Berger and Eric Storm, eds, *Writing the History of Nationalism* (forthcoming).

[3] Modern diplomatic history, nowadays usually called 'international' history, takes the powerful nation-state as its key unit of action.

The modernist paradigm accompanied a renewed interest in nationalism that had languished after the defeat of the 'nationalist' Axis powers and subsequent bipolar supranational cleavage imposed by the Cold War. Colonial nationalisms were seen as civic movements aiming for national self-determination within the territories mapped out by European empires. Only the 'failure' of new states—a failure of modernity—revived interest in ethnic nationalism and secessionism. In the developed world, nationalism remained of marginal interest. This changed with the collapse of the Soviet Union and Eastern European communism, a wave of nation-state formations, and ethnic cleansing; but these phenomena also modified the perspective. There was scepticism about theories of modernization. Nationalism was equated with ethnonationalism and ethnic cleansing. Instead of distinctions between developed and less developed regions, attention was drawn to commonalities of ethnic cleansing and genocide, to continuities between the era of the world wars and the contemporary period.

In mature capitalist societies that appeared stable until 2007, a new interest was in 'identity politics', which included race, ethnic, feminist, and gay rights movements, all set within the overarching framework of multiculturalism. This contrasted with the study of national identity as 'everyday' identity.[4] Political instability since the economic crisis of 2007–8 has extended the interest in ethnonationalism to Western Europe.

Another expanding field of research is globalization. In relation to nationalism, it is associated with questions of identity (cosmopolitanism, diasporas, regionalism, religious fundamentalism, postnationalism) and politics (NGOs, multinational corporations, supranational bodies such as the European Union or the International Monetary Fund).

These research fields tend to be present- or near future-oriented and dominated by non-historical social science. How can they be linked to innovative historical research concerned with the issues that preoccupied Hobsbawm?

HOBSBAWM'S CHANGING VIEWS OF NATIONALISM

Hobsbawm was a lifelong communist, happy to accept the tag 'Marxist historian'.[5] As a cosmopolitan, multilingual European whose formative political experience was Hitler's rise to power, Hobsbawm regarded nationalism with political hostility and personal indifference. His 'sentimental' politics was oriented to a socialist, Soviet-led world revolution; his 'pragmatic' politics looked to popular front-line antifascist and, later, broad centre-left movements.[6] For Hobsbawm as an historian, class was 'real', while nation was something contrived and artificial.

---

[4] Seminal was Michael Billig's *Banal Nationalism* (London, 1995).
[5] For details, see John Breuilly, 'Eric Hobsbawm: Nationalism and Revolution', *Nations and Nationalism* 21.3 (2015), 630–57.
[6] The distinction is Hobsbawm's own: see Eric Hobsbawm, *Interesting Times* (London, 2007), 218.

Thus Hobsbawm used the concept of an 'aristocracy of labour' with sectional interests in explaining cooperation between labour organizations and the Liberal Party in mid-Victorian Britain.[7] *The Age of Revolution* (1962) and *The Age of Capital* (1975) presented nationalism as a progressive politics of bourgeois liberals, supported by organized workers and establishing large, constitutional states within which capitalism could mature—a necessary condition for socialism. Nationalism that was romantic and anticapitalist, often that of 'small' nations, was regarded as reactionary, elaborated by intellectuals in exile and appealing to pre-industrial popular strata.

His approach shifted with the final crisis and collapse of the Soviet Union. This can be seen in *The Age of Empire* (1987), *The Invention of Tradition* (1983, co-edited with Terry Ranger), and *Nations and Nationalism since 1780* (1990, especially the 1992 edition). Hobsbawm was losing confidence in socialism and in the labour movement as progressive forces while coming to see nationalism as a powerful impetus, something more than a function of class interests.

This shift coincided with new interpretations of nationalism, which regarded it as modern but stressed aspects of modernity other than capitalism and class.[8] Most influential for Hobsbawm was Benedict Anderson's *Imagined Communities: Reflections on the Origins and Spread of Nationalism* (1983).[9] Imagined communities and invented traditions are not the same; imagining does not have the manipulative connotations of invention. Nevertheless, they are closer to each other than understanding nationalism as class ideology would be to either of them. Both approaches stimulated new research—on political entrepreneurs who invent symbols and ceremonies and on writers in the era of 'print capitalism' who enable mass readerships to 'imagine' themselves as national. Nationalism was not class ideology but sentiments produced by elites in order to gain popular support. That could include left-wing elites, which fitted with Hobsbawm's contributions towards constructing centre-left popular movements to combat forces such as Thatcherism.[10]

In Hobsbawm's last works I discern another shift towards seeing nationalism as irrational expressions of psychological states. He had anticipated this in harsh judgements of student movements during the days of 1968. His world history volume *Age of Extremes: The Short Twentieth Century, 1914–1991* (1994), his autobiography *Interesting Times: A Twentieth-Century Life* (2002), and the essays in the posthumous publication *Fractured Times: Culture and Society in the 20th Century* (2013) trace the rise of 'identity politics' that has no class or elite rationale.

---

[7] The relevant works are reprinted in two collections of Hobsbawm's essays: *Labouring Men* (New York, 1965) and *Worlds of Labour* (London, 1984).

[8] Apart from Anderson, see Ernest Gellner, *Nations and Nationalism* (Ithaca, NY, 1983), John Breuilly, *Nationalism and the State* (Chicago, IL, 1982), and Anthony Smith, *The Ethnic Origins of Nations* (Oxford, 1986).

[9] On Anderson's influence in a range of disciplines, including history, see John Breuilly, Thomas Hyland Eriksen, John Sidel, Jonathan Hearn, Joep Leerssen, and Elliott Green, 'Benedict Anderson's Imagined Communities: A Symposium', *Nations and Nationalism* 22.4 (2016), 625–59.

[10] In 1982–3 Hobsbawm still stressed costs and benefits and did not follow those like Stuart Hall, who saw Thatcherism as a hegemonic ideological force.

This was of a piece with Hobsbawm's growing pessimism after the collapse of the Soviet Union and the ascendancy of neoliberalism in a US-dominated world.

I think the most fruitful aspects of Hobsbawm's writing on nationalism are in his 'Marxist' phase, and insights from his later work are of value when set in that first phase.[11] For its bearing on promising lines of historical research, I select four themes:

1. Transnational approaches that distinguish the global history of nationalism from national history. Here Hobsbawm's work as a world historian is relevant.

2. Nationalism as political ideology and its implications for successful political action. More important than the 'invention of tradition' is Hobsbawm's writing on 'primitive rebels' when he was perhaps the first historian to draw on Gramsci's thought.

3. The distinction between ethnic and civic has been central to nationalism studies but its historical assumptions need investigation. These assumptions draw upon Hobsbawm's distinction between progressive and reactionary nationalism.

4. Nationalism studies have been dominated by top-down approaches. We need more history from below, something Hobsbawm strongly advocated and of which he was a pioneer.

TRANSNATIONAL APPROACHES TO THE HISTORY OF NATIONALISM

In the debates of the 1980s there was agreement that nationalists aimed to establish nation-states, in opposition to non-national states or 'alien' nation-states.[12] Once nation-states existed, historians could trace how they extended and consolidated national identity and used nationalism in international conflicts. Long-run national history focused on key agents (states, nationalists) was the characteristic form of such accounts.

By contrast, globalization is usually treated as a recent development after the formation of a world order of nation-states. A central question has been whether globalization will undermine the nation-state, national sentiment, and nationalism as the key power container, political identity, and ideology of the modern world. Study of general processes (communications, transportation, economic and financial flows, etc.) in the present or, at best, in the very recent past, with little

---

[11] I use inverted commas because Hobsbawm avoided theoretical discussions of Marxist history, did not explicitly use Marxist concepts, and insisted that good historical writing did not come labelled with an 'ism'.

[12] The subdirectory 'What Is Nationalism?', on the Nationalism Project website (www.nationalismproject.org) quotes definitions from writers involved in the debate. 'Non-national' is a deliberately open term, which may refer to multinational empires, national dynasties like Bourbon France, and polities such as city-states and small princely states.

concern for longer-term origins or specific agents, has been the characteristic form of such accounts. The different approaches to globalization and nationalism, characterized as they are by the dominance of non-historical social science in the former and of national history in the latter field, make it difficult to connect the two fields. Only by questioning these approaches can we open up fruitful historical research.

We must first question defining nationalism by the objective of a nation-state. For every 'successful' nationalism, there will be many 'failures'. Research into 'nationalism without states' is valuable, but still defines the nationalist objective as the sovereign nation-state and focuses on the 'national' pathway to that objective. Yet this objective only became central with the dominance of the idea of the international community as consisting of nation-states. It is also misleading to use some notion of a non-political 'early stage' of nationalism if that makes the objective of sovereignty into a key standard. The problem is how to move from the narrow teleological definition without ending up with something too general.

Before 1918–19 a world of sovereign 'nation-states' was scarcely imaginable. At best one could envisage a world order of imperial powers with national cores—Britain, France, the United States, Germany, Japan—and with some zones where imperial stand-offs enabled the formation of small states that called themselves national, as in the Balkans.[13] Nationalism adapted to rather than opposed this imperial world, which, as Hobsbawm showed in his first three world history volumes, was equated with large, powerful, 'civilized' states. Placing nationalism in this global perspective rather than portraying it as a series of national movements that pursue sovereign states enables innovative research.

This begins by noting that nationalism was not generated within, but across, national and state boundaries and that the relationship between assertions of cultural nationality and political demands is more complex than the conventional definition of nationalism allows. We can see this in recent research on nineteenth-century European nationalism and on pan-nationalism around 1900.

Nineteenth-century European nationalism is closely associated with language. Hroch's 'stage A' of nationalist movements documents elite cultural renewal centred upon language: compiling dictionaries and grammars, collecting and publishing 'folk' songs and stories, promoting creative writing (poetry, novels, opera libretti).[14] The problem arises when this is placed in a national framework linked to later nation-state formation.[15]

---

[13] Groups with a dominant high culture and elements of a non-sovereign political system could imagine transforming this system into a nation-state. Cases include the German, Italian, and Polish lands, Imperial China and Siam/Thailand, the Ganda and Zulu polities, Persia, and Egypt.

[14] Miroslav Hroch, *Social Preconditions of National Revival in Europe* (Columbia, NY, 1985) and, most recently, Miroslav Hroch, 'National Movements in the Habsburg and Ottoman Empires', in John Breuilly, ed., *The Oxford Handbook of the History of Nationalism* (Oxford, 2013), 175–98.

[15] For example, the work of Alberto Banti on a Risorgimento canon, which has been a major influence on Italian historical writing. See the various articles authored by Alex Körner, Lucy Riall, David Laven, Maurizio Isabella, Catherine Brice, and John Breuilly in the section titled 'Alberto Banti's Interpretation of Risorgimento Nationalism: A Debate' (396–454) in vol. 15, issue 3 of the journal *Nations and Nationalism*, which appeared in 2009.

A different perspective starts with two observations. First, reformers concentrated upon *written* language, while claiming that a written version of the 'national' language was based upon the existence of a spoken one.[16] This claim changed the perception of linguistic diversity. In a world where a literate minority communicated in a written language distanced from the diversity of spoken languages, there could be no conception of a plurality of distinct and equally worthwhile national languages competing with one another for status and power. This became the common ground on which defenders of elite literary languages and advocates of culturally subordinate languages carried out their disputes. If one is to translate from the domain of language to that of nationality, spokesmen for the dominant culture contrasted the historical nation with the non-historical nation, while their opponents denounced this asymmetric dualism.[17]

Second, such debates were not confined to individual national cultures or to multinational states. The SPIN research centre in Amsterdam has shown that this was a pan-European process. The 'discovery' of national epics was achieved by a small, widely distributed network of scholars. A European perspective was essential to generating the concept of a national epic and to using it on order to bring to light 'unique' national epics.[18]

For the different but related formation of nationalist political ideology we can turn to the role played by political exiles. It was in Paris and London that identity stories about Poles and Italians, Hungarians and Germans were constructed.[19] These stories of dominant cultural groups generated an equivalent amount of opposition from subordinate cultural groups, though one must go further afield, to cities such as Vienna and St Petersburg. Insofar as the national identity stories of dominant cultures were placed within a 'full' ideology such as liberalism or radical democracy, these were taken from the two dominant polities—monarchical Britain and republican France.[20] By contrast, stories of Slav identities worked out in Vienna and St Petersburg were informed by the political values of those two imperial dynasties.

Why were these transnational connections important? I would suggest two reasons; but more research is needed to sustain this view. First, national identity claims, being novel and modern, must initially be constructed in supranational contexts that enable contrast. Heinrich Heine claimed that he had to be exiled from the German lands to become conscious of being German. He could have

---

[16] Efforts to reform *spoken* language were made in languages that already had a standardized written form. Elocution schools in late eighteenth-century London and German nationalist efforts at 'purification' are examples of such efforts.

[17] Marx and Engels shared the dualist assumption with liberal and conservative writers; see Roman Rodolsky, *Engels and the 'Non-Historic' Peoples: The National Question in the Revolutions of 1848* (Glasgow, 1986).

[18] *The Encyclopedia of Romantic Nationalism in Europe* is the flagship project of the Study Platform on Interlocking Nationalisms (SPIN, for which, see www.spinnet.eu). The director of SPIN, Joep Leerssen, has sketched out the approach in Joep Leerssen, *When Was Romantic Nationalism? The Onset, the Long Tail, the Banal* (Antwerp, 2014).

[19] We know a good deal about these circles, but not from the perspective of a transnational interpretation of nationalism.

[20] I deal with nationalism and 'full' ideologies in the next section.

added that this was helped by the company of would-be Italian, Polish, Hungarian, and other exiles, who worked out their national identities together. Second, the political and intellectual dominance enjoyed by constitutional Britain and republican France enabled these exiles to relate national identities to broader political claims. More instrumentally, awareness that support from those states imparted to their movements a sense of importance they could not otherwise have enjoyed encouraged exiles to present their politics so as appeal to their hosts.

Similar lines of research at a global level are being pursued for the era of global imperialism around 1900. Weak British global hegemony was replaced by multilateral imperialism, pursued in cooperative as well as competitive ways. Imperial powers 'nationalized' their metropolitian cores while drawing ever sharper distinctions between that core and colonial peripheries. This generated three distinct kinds of nationalism: dominant core nationalism, defensive reactions from minority cultures within the core, and responses from the peripheries.[21]

The first two are well-researched topics within modern European history because they operate within the nation-state framework. Less well researched is the periphery response, except as anticipation of 'full' nationalism at a later stage. This is because the main responses either were not nationalist or took a form unlike that of 'successful' nationalism later on. The non-nationalist response involved efforts to import metropolitan values and practices into the periphery.[22] I will not consider it further.

The nationalist periphery's response is pan-nationalism. It is remarkable how many pan-national ideologies and movements formed around 1900: pan-Africanism, pan-Slavism, pan-Turkism, pan-Arabism, pan-Islamism, pan-Asianism, even less well-known movements such as pan-Celtism and pan-Americanism. This widespread and simultaneous development can be explained if we see them as responses to the most powerful and successful 'pan-' movement—the one we might call 'pan-whiteism' or 'pan-westernism'—just as the cooperative global imperialism practised by the major European powers and by the United States reached its zenith.[23]

This imperialism constructed a hierarchical view of the world, whether racial, religious or civilizational, which was communicated to its 'own' populations through popular writings, cartoons and exhibitions, fairs and popular science. It was also communicated, more forcibly and effectively, to those deemed inferior. Pan-nationalism was a set of countermovements that opposed this hierachical vision. Pan-nationalists shared with imperialism the assumption of a world of a few large blocs—civilizations, races, or cultures—but they converted hierarchy into plurality.[24] This conversion parallels the earlier one whereby representatives of

[21] A stimulating study is Jörn Leonhard and Ulrike von Hirschhausen, *Empires und Nationalstaaten im 19. Jahrhundert* (Göttingen, 2009).

[22] A good recent study is C. A. Bayly, *Recovering Liberties: Indian Thought in the Age of Liberalism and Empire* (Cambridge, 2012).

[23] Marilyn Lake and Henry Reynolds, *Drawing the Global Colour Line: White Men's Countries and the International Challenge of Racial Equality* (Cambridge, 2008).

[24] There were some, including certain kinds of 'orientalist' westerners, who inverted the hierarchy in one way or another; but this was not common.

'subordinate' nationalities in Europe opposed a vision of equal nations to the hierarchical vision of 'historical' nations.[25]

Another parallel is with transnational networks of political exiles in imperial cities. Different versions of pan-Africanism were elaborated in Paris and London and by black Americans in New York and Washington. Dramatic was the impact of the Japanese defeat of Russia in 1904–5, which undermined the claim to superiority of white over non-white and provided pan-nationalists with an intellectual model and a place of refuge. Tokyo in the first three decades of the twentieth century enabled the development of 'pan-' movements, especially (but not only) pan-Asianism.[26]

From this perspective, the vision of a world of nation-states presaged by Woodrow Wilson's Fourteen Points and by Lenin's near-simultaneous call for national liberation—declarations with a global impact[27]—was not a continuation of earlier nationalist trends but a rupture produced by a war of unparalleled destruction, by the collapse of dynastic empires, and by the unwillingness of the western empires to extend direct rulership to the territories of the defeated. Earlier visions of cultural autonomy and limited federalism were transformed into multiple demands for sovereign nation-states, demands that took the national cores of the triumphant empires as models and appealed for support from those powers. Only a transnational framework can explain this transformation of nationalism into what became the familiar demand for 'national self-determination'. That claim, notoriously vague and ambiguous, would go through characteristic changes in the interwar period, after 1945, and following the collapse of the Soviet bloc, each change only to be understood within a global historical perspective.[28]

NATIONALISM AS POLITICAL IDEOLOGY

Another transnational but distinct task is to research nationalism as political ideology. Hobsbawm viewed ideology in relation to class. There is, then, a temptation to contrast ideology with truth. The exploiting classes—feudal landowners or capitalist employers—promote views of the world that suggest that current arrangements serve not only these classes but those they rule and exploit; they argue that there is no practical alternative and (mis)represent such arrangements in

[25] For an introduction to this rapidly developing research field, see Cemil Aydin, 'Pan-Nationalism of Pan-Islamic, Pan-Asian, and Pan-African Thought', in John Breuilly, ed., *The Oxford Handbook of the History of Nationalism*, 672–3.

[26] The best known figure was Sun Yat Sen. One story yet untold should explain why the two rival and leading Polish nationalists of the day—Jósef Pisuldski and Roman Dmowski—were in Tokyo at the same time in 1905.

[27] Erez Manela, *The Wilsonian Moment: Self-Determination and the International Origins of Anti-Colonial Nationalism* (Oxford, 2007).

[28] The changes from the perspective of US policy are traced in Liliana Riga and James Kennedy, 'To Build a Notion: US State Department Nation Building Expertise and Postwar Settlements in 20th Century [*sic*] East Central Europe', *Sociological Research Online* 18.2 (2013), doi: 10.5153/sro.3097. For a transnational history into the interwar period, see Adam Tooze, *The Deluge: The Great War and the Remaking of the Global Order, 1916–1931* (London, 2014).

an idealized way. It is easy to understand why a ruling class should believe this (though how such a belief helps it to rule is less clear), but not why those it exploits should. Hobsbawm in his studies of archaic social movements in Italy used the work of Gramsci, who was preoccupied with this problem.

Hobsbawm's work on the invention of tradition opened up another line of research, shifting as it did from class ideology to popular discourse, though mainly as elite production rather than popular reception. However, that is not adequate to the task of researching the history of nationalism as political ideology.

First, the history of political ideology is a field distinct from those of the history of ideas, political theory, and political history.[29] Ideology should not be treated as an expression—clear or masked, genuine or instrumental—of interests, including ones of class. Instead it should be defined as any set of interlinked political concepts that claim to describe how politics does and should work and to prescribe how to act. Ideas are researched as concepts that grasp the political world in order to enable effective action.[30] Political theory is researched insofar as such concepts make assumptions about human nature, society, and politics but are considered for their bearing on political action, not for a theoretical critique. Political history is researched insofar as we need to see how ideology enables political action.

Subsumed under political ideology, nationalism presents problems. Anderson suggested it has more affinities with concepts such as religion and kinship than with liberalism, conservatism, or socialism.[31] It makes assertions about identity, loyalty, and commitment that are particular, not universal; yet it has proved to be the most widespread and significant modern political ideology. This puzzle holds a key to researching its emergence, spread, and triumph.

Freeden argues that nationalism is either a 'thin' ideology or a component of a 'full' ideology. As a thin ideology, nationalism is a bare assertion of collective identity and loyalty. It does not work by presenting concepts about human nature, how society works, and what policies a state should pursue but by arbitrary imposition, as when the government of a nation-state justifies universal conscription with the cry 'nation in danger'. The popular response involves fuller conceptions of what makes the nation worth defending, but there will be many such conceptions, often contradicting each other and accumulated through the habits that are consequent upon living in a nation-state.

As component of a full ideology, nationalism couples an assertion of identity and loyalty with a more elaborate ideology of the society and polity in which the nation is embodied. Carlton Hayes organized his pioneering history of nationalism around this idea, tracing a sequence from Jacobin nationalism through liberal

---

[29] I am indebted to Michael Freeden for the argument that follows. See Michael Freeden, *Ideology: A Very Short Introduction* (Oxford, 2003); Michael Freeden, *Ideologies and Political Theory: A Conceptual Approach* (Oxford, 1996); and Michael Freeden, 'Is Nationalism a Distinct Ideology?' *Political Studies* 46.4 (1998), 748–65.

[30] The key thinker for this view of political concepts is Reinhart Koselleck. The German word for concept is *Begriff*, a cognate of the verb *begreifen*, 'to grasp'. Koselleck led a multivolume enterprise that analysed a large number of *Geschichtliche Grundbegriffe*—'key historical concepts'.

[31] Benedict Anderson, *Imagined Communities* (London, 1991), 5; as quoted in Freeden, 'Is Nationalism a Distinct Ideology?', n. 12.

nationalism to conservative nationalism and finishing with integral nationalism in post-1918 Europe, or what we could call fascism. It was the ideologies of radical democracy, liberalism, conservatism, and fascism that gave meaning to nationalism.

In 1931 Hayes could not take account of the global breakdown of an imperial world order of empires and its replacement by one of the nation-states—a global success for nationalism that changed its nature and complicated how one could trace its diffusion as an ideology. This major task for nationalism research is being pursued in various ways. One is by means of global intellectual history, which ranges from studies of global diffusion to considering how one individual becomes a nationalist in the context of global interactions.[32] Another possibility is an intraregional approach into the emergence and spread of nationalism, which should combine detailed historical research and knowledge with a framework that extends beyond any particular national history.[33]

I have outlined a framework to relate the diffusion of nationalist ideology to global relationships of coercive power.[34] Building on the earlier point that the transnational diffusion of nationalist political ideas takes its cue from the dominant polities of the day even when opposing those polities, I distinguish between hegemonic, challenger, and peripheral polities and argue that diffusion proceeds down the power hierarchy.[35] As this hierarchy of power changes, so does nationalist ideology take on a great variety of forms.

As Freeden has also argued, political ideology is 'essentially contested'. (Totalitarian regimes can prevent the public appearance of any but the orthodox view, but that is never more than arbitrary imposition.) Ideologies include value assertions (what worthwhile ends are, what human nature is like) and contain more potential meanings than any one particular instance of the ideology can accommodate. This provides another key to how to pursue historical research, because the diffusion of an ideology is always accompanied by *political argument*. By following the traces left by such arguments, historians can show how and why a political ideology with a nationalist component spreads. An exemplary study (from which, interestingly, a nationalism component is absent) is Bernard Bailyn's *The Ideological Origins of the American Revolution* (1967). More research along such lines needs to be undertaken.

One must also show why political ideology matters. For political elites, ideology provides long-term goals and values essential for coordinating collective action in

---

[32] Samuel Moyn and Andrew Sartori, eds, *Global Intellectual History* (New York, 2013). There are by now many fine studies of such interactions, either at a local or at a biographical level. See, for example, Rebecca E. Karl, *Staging the World: Chinese Nationalism at the Turn of the Twentieth Century* (Durham, NC, 2002).

[33] See the chapters in Parts 2 and 3 of John Breuilly, ed., *The Oxford Handbook of the History of Nationalism* (Oxford, 2013).

[34] I follow Michael Mann's approach in his four-volume *Sources of Social Power* (New York, 1986), which distinguishes between military, political, ideological, and economic power, modifying 'power' by combining the first two under the concept of coercive power.

[35] See John Breuilly, 'Nationalism as Global History', in Daphne Halikiopoulou and Sofia Vasilopoulou, eds, *Nationalism and Globalisation: Conflicting or Complementary?* (Basingstoke, 2011), 65–83.

uncertain and unstable situations.[36] Once such movements achieve power, the role of ideology changes, the latter serving as a rationalization for opportunists and providing emotionally charged guidance at a popular level. These two aspects have been more fully researched, but usually in order to argue for an 'instrumental' or an 'emotional' interpretation of nationalism. Attention to the ideological function helps create a framework within which these other functions can be placed.

THE CIVIC VERSUS ETHNIC DISTINCTION

Much writing on nationalism concerns the distinction between civic and ethnic. This resembles Hobsbawm's argument about progressive and reactionary nationalism. However, whereas Hobsbawm framed this distinction in terms of class interests and ideologies, current debates consider its empirical content and normative validity. I leave aside the normative work of political theorists,[37] except where they make assumptions about the history of nationalist norms that need questioning through research.

This assumed history is the agreed ground on which theorists dispute. It often starts with a contrast between Ernst Renan and Friedrich Meinecke after the Franco-Prussian War of 1870–1.[38] Renan is best known for his striking claim that the nation is a twenty-four-hour-a-day plebiscite—the 'civic' view of the nation as subjective commitment to a common set of democratic and republican values. Meinecke's distinction between *Staatsnation* and *Kulturnation* is conflated with the civic–ethnic distinction.[39]

However, Renan advanced a second argument, to the effect that a nation was constituted by a shared stock of memories (and forgetting): an argument reminiscent of how scholars have understood the ethnic roots of nations. Renan knew that defining the nation in purely subjective terms was meaningless. Meinecke's *Staat–Kultur* distinction hinges on whether a national high culture formed within or before the construction of a national polity. After 1918 German historians who were disciples of Meinecke devised a third concept, *Volksnation*, to be applied to the 'small' nations that achieved national self-determination. This concept resembles that of the non-historical nation, which was used during the 1848 revolutions. For Meinecke, *Staatsnation* and *Kulturnation* belonged to the historical nation category. Radical right nationalists and race theorists in Europe and the United States appropriated the *Volk* concept and the Third Reich used it to claim power

---

[36] See Stephen E. Hanson, *Post-Imperial Democracies: Ideology and Party Formation in Third Republic France, Weimar Germany, and Post-Soviet Russia* (Cambridge, 2010).

[37] A key debate is how far the civic–ethnic dualism should be aligned with that of liberal–illiberal nationalism. A major recent study with details on the previous literature is Bernard Yack, *Nationalism and the Moral Psychology of Community* (Chicago, IL, 2012).

[38] One line of continuation is Kohn's distinction between 'western' and 'eastern' nationalism: see Hans Kohn, *The Idea of Nationalism* (New York, 1944). There is no space here for a detailed critique, so I will just take the Renan–Meinecke and France–Germany distinctions as exemplary.

[39] Ernst Renan, *Qu'est-ce qu'une nation?* (Paris, 1882); Friedrich Meinecke, *Weltbürgertum und Nationalstaat* (Munich, 1907).

over other nations and races. In 1945, confronted by the barbarism and ruin this project had brought about, the elderly Meinecke invoked *Kultur* as the path to national salvation and expiation, calling for Goethe societies to be established throughout Germany. Projecting back our contemporary dualism effaces a complex history that tells us much more about nationalism. Research is needed to recover this complexity.[40]

The problem deepens when a misleading history of national concepts is aligned with arguments about national identity and citizenship practices. So, to return to Renan and Meinecke, the distinction is widened from two individuals to two states and nations.[41] The state distinction focuses on the criteria for the automatic acquisition of citizenship. In France, the law of 1889 conferred citizenhip on all those born on the territory of France: *ius soli*, 'the law/right of the soil'.[42] In Germany, practically after 1871 and enshrined in a law of 1913, the criterion was parental citizenship: *ius sanguinis*, 'the law/right of blood'. The final step is to project the values supposedly expressed by Renan and Meinecke and the contrasting citizenship laws onto the 'civic' French and 'ethnic' German nations.

Research on citizenship law casts doubt on such connections. Citizenship is not the same as nationality, although in a world of nation-states the two are frequently equated. There is nothing civic about the involuntary act of birth; nothing ethnic about parentage. Most people acquire citizenship by both routes. A third route, that of naturalization, tells one more about the connection between national values and citizenship. Citizenship is a complex concept with different qualities, as any woman in either France or Germany after 1871 could testify, so we need to know just what is at stake when someone acquires or loses citizenship.

The contrasting laws can be explained independently of nationalist discourse or national values. Unless some special concern was raised, these usually drew on legal traditions. There was such a concern in France, where the Third Republic abandoned *ius sanguinis* because its elites were anxious about demographic decline and wished to revenge the defeat of 1870–1. *Ius soli* could encourage immigrants and make their sons liable to conscription. In the German lands there was less incentive to alter traditions rooted in the small states of pre-unification Germany, where acquiring citizenship by parentage and residence was normal. Nevertheless, in western regions local administrators wishing to encourage immigration from Belgium, France, and Holland advocated *ius soli*. Their counterparts in the east, who sought to ensure that Slav and Jewish seasonal workers could not gain citizenship for children they might bear in Germany, defended *ius sanguinis*.

Citizenship law constantly changed to address specific problems, such as how to exclude children born to Muslim Algerians in France or to German men and their Herero wives in German South West Africa. As such modifications accumulated,

---

[40] I have sketched out some of these points in more detail in John Breuilly, 'Nation-States Matter More Than Nationalism', *Quaderni di Scienza Politica* 6.3 (2012), 443–68.

[41] The key work is Rogers Brubaker, *Citizenship and Nationhood in France and Germany* (Cambridge, MA, 1992).

[42] I leave aside the complication that men are treated differently from women when it comes to both the acquisition and the meaning of citizenship.

they resulted in ever more complex legal provisions. Citizenship law became what it is today: an arcane field that only experts understand.

In relation to nationalist discourse, it is easy to find significant groups of French nationalists who fall under the ethnic label and of German nationalists who propound civic values. As for national values, this is a vague concept and, if it refers to the subjective states of minds of millions of people, one impossible to research historically; it is difficult to do so even today, with the aid of mass surveys.

There are situations when it is valid to make connections between nationalist values, citizenship law, and national sentiment. When citizenship law becomes a matter of political debate, we can observe conflicts between different kinds of nationalists. As the nation-state consolidates and such debates are attended by a mass public, they relate to widespread values. A good example is the parliamentary and public debates that preceded the enactment of the 1913 German citizenship law. Finally, insofar as a nation-state—deliberately or inadvertently—shapes a political culture, it becomes meaningful to investigate something called 'national values'. However, one must expect to find here cleavages, conflicts, and constant shifts.

Yet, while historical research complicates the dualist distinction at the levels of norms, citizenship law, and national values and shows that one cannot align these histories with one another, while political scientists critique the distinction in contemporary politics, and while political theorists expose its logical problems, why does the distinction stubbornly persist in academic, political, and popular language?

To answer this question, we need to return to the argument about nationalism as thin or non-ideology. Critiques of the civic–ethnic distinction point out that a minimal (thin) definition of the two concepts excludes almost every actual nation-alist discourse, ideology, or sentiment that draws upon religion, language, history, and culture. Any thicker definition arbitrarily extends one or another of the concepts to include such elements. The concepts cannot work as two ideal types at opposite ends of a continuum because it is impossible to see how religion, language, history, or culture can be positioned 'between' the civic and the ethnic. Not only that; the concepts, in their minimal forms, are *different types of concept*. Ethnicity is an identity concept answering the question 'Who am I/we?', while civicness is a value concept answering the question 'What do I/we stand for?'.

This contrast points the way forward for research. Zimmer has distinguished between 'symbolic resources' and 'boundary mechanisms'.[43] The first consist of political discourses of nationalism and the second tell us who is included in or excluded from the nation. Zimmer's point is that the relationship between these two categories is contingent. For example, one can make language a symbol of national identity but use language either to exclude or to assimilate newcomers.

Any full political ideology must answer both the identity and the value ques-tions. The value question must be answered not just in general terms (freedom, justice, communal solidarity, etc.) but by specifying institutional features of the

---

[43] Oliver Zimmer, 'Boundary Mechanisms and Symbolic Resources: Towards a Process-Oriented Approach to National Identity', *Nations and Nationalism* 9.2 (2003), 173–93.

ideal polity. A 'thin' ideology cannot do this, whether it is nationalism, ecology, or feminism. By contrast, a 'full' ideology such as liberalism cannot answer the question 'Who am I/we?' *precisely because it is universalist.* Liberalism and nationalism are effectively combined by assuming a nation-state and then evaluating that state according to liberal criteria. Only by implicitly accepting the boundaries of this polity and its minimal identity claims can liberalism can go on to specify the institutional forms and policies of that polity.

This suggests two lines of research. First, one needs to investigate the history of concepts of the nation that I have sketched, how these concepts relate to fuller political ideologies, and what their implications are for political action. However, one needs also to recognize that concepts of the nation extend beyond issues of identity and political institutions and values and encompass concepts of sovereignty and territoriality. These concepts have been fruitfully explored by geographers and political theorists but neglected by historians.[44]

The second task is to research how these identity and value concepts are combined in particular forms of nationalism. Thus, to return to post-1871 France and Germany, we can look at how nationalists committed to values of hierarchy and continuity used symbolic resources to defend monarchy, privilege, and church establishment, while nationalists drawing on the revolutionary tradition deployed other resources to advocate republican and secular nationalism. There will be much overlap in the resources deployed but the key is the conflicting values to which they were attached. As these different kinds of nationalists came to accept the sovereign, territorial, and national state as the 'natural' frame for their contending politics, so was the ground laid for common action in the face of external threat.

Historical research can thus help explain the persistence of the civic–ethnic distinction. A full ideology must include value and identity concepts. However, at times of political conflict, one rather than the other will be highlighted. An ethnic identity claim will be discredited in the name of liberal values, which in turn will lead those making such claims to rephrase them in value terms, just as those advocating liberal values will seek to attach a national identity to them. Seeing how this happens historically can illuminate contemporary debates. Right-wing populism in Europe has shifted from attacking Muslims to attacking Islam, precisely so it can occupy the liberal ground of its opponents.[45] British conservatives seeking to defend values like free speech, tolerance, and rule of law label these 'national' values. Currently any focus on the thin identity claim is labelled 'ethnic', while the elaboration of a liberal set of values is labelled 'civic'. In fact the two elements can never survive for long without combining among themselves, but one-sided awareness of their distinct qualities leads to their being constantly opposed as two essential types.

---

[44] An exception is Charles Maier's pioneering work, for example Charles Maier, 'Leviathan 2: Inventing Modern Statehood', in Emily S. Rosenberg, ed., *A World Connecting, 1870–1945* (Cambridge, MA, 2012), 27–282.

[45] D. Halikiopoulou, S. Mock, and S. Vasilopoulou, 'The Civic Zeitgeist: Nationalism and Liberal Values in the European Radical Right', *Nations and Nationalism* 19.1 (2013), 107–27.

NATIONALISM AND HISTORY FROM BELOW

In the 1960s to the 1980s there was a boom in Western Europe and the USA in 'social history' or 'history from below'. This was associated with radical and left-wing values. For many historians in the United Kingdom—including myself—who were choosing a research topic, the book that made the most impact was *The Making of the English Working Class* (1963) by E. P. Thompson, one of the key members, along with Hobsbawm, of the Communist Party Historians' Group. Hobsbawm's early work as a British labour historian was more about labour organizations and standards of living than about social history. Nevertheless, his writing on 'primitive rebels', 'bandits', and 'archaic social movements' expanded the focus from industrializing or industrial society and its labour movements to pre-industrial societies and to what one might call 'history from the margins'.

Even if written in a supranational and comparative way (*Primitive Rebels*, published in 1954, spanned Spain, Italy, and South America), such work was framed nationally, concerned with subordinate social groups, and, when considering relationships between these groups and the state or the ruling classes, focused on domination and containment, opposition and resistance. Just occasionally, the problem of nationalism was raised—and, for left-wing historians, nationalism almost always was a problem—but usually in order to explain (away) specific episodes, such as the support that socialist and labour organizations gave to their respective national governments at the outbreak of war in 1914.

Such work, including Hobsbawm's on the labour aristocracy and his deployment of Gramsci's concept of hegemony, provides valuable insights for anyone seeking to write a social history of nationalism. Yet almost all the methods and sources used by social historians were abandoned or forgotten as the field of 'nationalism studies' burgeoned in the wake of the Soviet collapse.[46]

In part this was because the field was dominated by sociology, social psychology, and political science, concentrating on the recent past and on current events, and often venturing disciplined guesses about the near future in order to inform policymakers. Longer-term historical perspective privileged elite actions and sources. Historical 'discourse' studies use published sources that are normally elite-produced. Billig's pioneer work on 'banal nationalism' analysed elite products like newspapers and radio and television broadcasts. Reception studies in the fields of sociology and social psychology that extend beyond such material are limited to the present and generate data by methods such as interviews and questionnaire surveys. Political scientists study mass political action—for example in what has become a veritable academic industry, namely ethnic conflict studies—but with elite-produced data such as censuses or surveys.[47]

---

[46] Here is not the place to pursue this argument. In addition to Breuilly, 'Eric Hobsbawm', see John Breuilly, 'What Does It Mean to Say that Nationalism Is Popular?', in Maarten van Ginderachter and Marnix Beyen, eds, *Nationhood from Below: Continental Europe in the Long Nineteenth Century* (Basingstoke, 2012), 23–43.
[47] Daniel Posner has produced some of the best work in this field. On the types of data and methods of analysis, see Daniel Posner, 'Measuring Ethnic Fractionalization in Africa', *American Journal of Political Science* 48.4 (2004), 849–63.

Work with a longer-run historical perspective is also usually elite-focused. Much involves trawling through secondary sources in order to piece together a general argument about the modernity or otherwise of 'nationalism'. Research on nationalism as history of ideas focuses on the writings of 'intellectuals', even if it extends beyond major thinkers to journalists and others who simplify and popularize political ideas. The study of nationalism as politics looks at movements and organizations, often small and oppositional, and, even when these achieve mass support or state power, continues to be concerned with an activist minority.

For many periods and places it is not possible to do more. Sources are scarce and often have been destroyed or lost. Oral history becomes speculative the further one goes back in time. Largely non-literate societies provide little direct written testimony 'from below'. There are difficulties about inferring values and attitudes from the everyday artefacts that archaeology researches. More cautious scholars are aware of these problems and do not prematurely leap from what may be established about nationalist ideas, politics, and sentiments at elite levels to claims that these 'reflect' popular attitudes.[48]

Yet that earlier wave of social history, focused on the first stages of industrial development, demonstrated that one *can* research the attitudes, values, and actions of non-elite groups or individuals. It is difficult and there are problems about representativeness and typicality, but it can be done. I will mention a few projects and possible lines of research.

First, one can relate existing social and labour history to subsequent nationalism debates. The early history of nationalism as a component of a fuller ideology included research into its radical, oppositional forms.[49] Thompson, who defended and personified a 'radical Englishness', understood this, though that deep sense of a radical English tradition led him to resist attempts to generalize and compare.[50]

This radical yet national legacy was largely forgotten when attention turned to nationalism as a thin ideology linked to state formation, authoritarian regimes, and populism. Often it was explicitly marginalized, with the claim that nationalism had shifted from left to right. Yet arguably it informed the values of organized labour and socialist movements within consolidating nation-states. Combined with the way in which that consolidation gave the labour movement a stake in the nation-state, one can account for 'labour nationalism' without treating it as betrayal or false consciousness.

Such nationally framed radicalism underpinned the antifascist, popular-front politics that Hobsbawm supported in the 1930s. It was a component of resistance movements in occupied Europe during the Second World War. Its myths were central to the 'socialist patriotism' of Eastern European communist states during

---

[48] Walter Pohl, 'Conceptions of Ethnicity in Early Medieval Studies', in Lester K. Little and Barbara H. Rosenwein, eds, *Debating the Middle Ages: Issues and Readings* (Oxford, 1998), 13–24.

[49] Werner Conze and Dieter Groh, *Die Arbeiterbewegung in der nationalen Bewegung* (Stuttgart, 1966) was a pioneering work. For England, see Margot Finn, *After Chartism: Class and Nation in English Radical Politics, 1848–1884* (Cambridge, 1993).

[50] See his marvellous polemic against Perry Anderson and Tom Nairn, whom he takes to task for engaging in precisely such a generalizing analysis: E. P. Thompson, 'The Peculiarities of the English', in Ralph Miliband and John Saville, eds, *The Socialist Register* (London, 1965), 311–62.

the Cold War. Much of this history could only be properly researched after the collapse of those regimes.[51]

The perspective can be widened. After 1918, the Leninist moment endured longer than the Wilsonian one, the new Bolshevik regime linking the call for national liberation to progress towards socialism. Anticolonial movements across the world responded and, in the form of communist parties affiliated to the Third International and COMINTERN, gave this link an organized political expression. Such parties became junior partners of more powerful nationalist parties. Most notable was China in the 1920s, until the Kuomintang under the leadership of Chiang Kai-shek massacred the communists. That forced the surviving cadres into the Long March and the construction of a new strategy focused on the country-side, peasant mobilization, and guerilla warfare. Yet that transformed communist movement fought in alliance with the Kuomintang against the Japanese invasion between 1937 and 1945.[52]

Most of this research—on socialist movements in Europe or on communist ones in European overseas empires—is focused on minorities of activists, even when they gain mass support in elections or insurgent armies. One might call this 'elite history from below'. Even if there is popular support, it cannot be taken to mean values and interests shared between leaders and followers. For example, a high level of British volunteering for military service during the Boer War is better explained by levels of unemployment than by patriotic enthusiasm.[53]

We need other ways to research popular responses to nationalism more directly. Leaving aside the patient social historical work that pieces together disparate sources on a few individuals—a cache of correspondence, diaries, even autobiographies—I take up briefly three lines of research.

Social historians have long been alert to the opportunities that moments of social and political breakdown or transformation—in particular those associated with revolutions and civil wars—offered for glimpsing below the elite surface of societies. For example, the collapse of regimes across continental Europe in early 1848 was accompanied by an unprecedented expansion of writing, speaking, meeting, and organizing. This was a transformative moment, though how far these new voices were saying old things that could only now be heard or were indeed saying new things is a big question. Nevertheless, given that the 'national question' assumed major importance during that short revolutionary period,

[51] See Pavel Kolár and Milos Rezník, eds, *Historische Nationsforschung im geteilten Europa, 1945–1989* (Cologne, 2012). An attempt to trace the continuity of nationalism across the communist–postcommunist divide was made by Sabine Rutar, 'Nationalism in Southeastern Europe, 1970–2000', in John Breuilly, ed., *The Oxford Handbook of the History of Nationalism*, 515–34.

[52] Whether Mao can be regarded as a Chinese nationalist is a matter of debate. The positive argument advanced by Chalmers Johnson in a pioneering study, *Peasant Nationalism and Communist Power* (Stanford, CA, 1963), has been robustly criticized. The complexity of peasant responses during the war against Japan comes out in Rana Mitter, *China's War with Japan, 1939–1945: The Struggle for Survival* (London, 2013).

[53] Richard Price, *An Imperial War and the British Working Class: Working-Class Attitudes and Reactions to the Boer War, 1899–1902* (London, 1972).

historians can explore popular views on that question. Darkness returned with the counter-revolution.

Political elites become interested in popular attitudes and sentiments during such times, and this generates new sources that the social historian can exploit. For example, during the First World War, the military high commands wanted to track the morale of soldiers. One way to do this was through sophisticated sampling and analysis of the letters soldiers sent home. Martyn Lyons looked at such material from French soldiers who occupied part of Alsace during the war. This was interesting because of the nationalist obsession with recovering this sacred part of France and with revenging the humiliating defeat of 1870–1. Were these concerns shared by soldiers of largely peasant origins drawn from across France? If so, how had these soldiers come to know and care about this unknown land? How did they react when they discovered that these fellow Frenchmen sounded German? The source allows detailed answers.[54]

Such research takes us away from structured classes like workers or peasants to 'situational groups'. The combination of crisis and situation—in this case, French soldiers serving in Alsace—allows us to explore the relationship between popular attitudes and national values in new ways. Sometimes sentiments can be explored with the help of evidence on popular views or on the official treatment of minorities such as Jews, Roma, 'enemy aliens', or immigrant workers. This is also where much valuable research on the history of women can be undertaken.[55]

Another line of research starts with scepticism about the popular resonance of nationalism, treating nationalism as an elite preoccupation that encounters popular indifference. Jeremy King's argument is summarized in the title of his book: *Budweisers into Czechs and Germans*.[56] Nationalism penetrates popular levels with difficulty and through the efforts of competing nationalist elites. The argument is given a pointed form in Zahra's study of national indifference.[57] There is now a cluster of such studies, and they extend beyond the original focus on German–Czech relationships in the late Habsburg empire.[58]

This research has been on multinational states and territories with mixed language and confessional populations, along with rival nationalist movements. It is no accident that the most innovative efforts to integrate Marxist history with a positive view of national identity before 1914 came from the late Habsburg empire, notably from Otto Bauer and Karl Renner. Subsequently a disproportionately large number

---

[54] Martyn Lyons, 'France: National Identity from Below and the Discovery of the "Lost Provinces", 1914–1919', in idem, *The Writing Culture of Ordinary People in Europe, c.1860–1920* (Cambridge, 2013), 91–112.

[55] All these groups are considered in Maarten van Ginderachter and Marnix Beyen, eds, *Nationhood from Below: Continental Europe in the Long Nineteenth Century* (Basingstoke, 2012).

[56] Jeremy King, *Budweisers into Czechs and Germans: A Local History of Bohemian Politics, 1848–1948* (Princeton, NJ, 2002).

[57] Tara Zahra, *Kidnapped Souls: National Indifference and the Battle for Children in the Bohemian Lands, 1900–1948* (Ithaca, NY, 2008).

[58] See, for example, Sener Aktürk, *Regimes of Ethnicity and Nationhood in Germany, Russia, and Turkey* (Cambridge, 2012); James E. Bjork, *Neither German nor Pole: Catholicism and National Indifference in a Central European Borderland* (Ann Arbor, MI, 2008); Pieter M. Judson, *Guardians of the Nation: Activists on the Language Frontiers of Imperial Austria* (Cambridge, MA, 2006).

of major scholars investigating why nationalism became popular—such as Karl Deutsch, Hans Kohn, Ernest Gellner, and Eugen Lemberg—came from this region. One desideratum of such research is to extend it to nation-states. Could a similar story be told for Britanny or Wales?

One last research possibility, still in its infancy, concerns how the state—national or multinational—inadvertently shapes national identity. In the second edition of *Imagined Communities*, Benedict Anderson looked at maps, censuses, and museums as 'nation-making' instruments. Research on these subjects has since burgeoned.[59] However, it is usually confined to the elite production of such material. The studies on national indifference have taken the subject further, researching how nationalist elites in the Habsburg empire mobilized themselves to influence drawing up language censuses and putting pressure on those surveyed to respond in the 'right' way. Once results were announced, those same elites selectively interpreted them so as to push their own agenda. Issues such as language in elementary schools became politically relevant for future disputes, and competing nationalist elites sought to influence parental choices and decisions taken by local authorities. Yet it is the multinational state concerned to combat nationalist challenges that creates national identity categories that promote such nationalism. This raises the least well-understood question of all, namely whether the modern state—through popular participation, sharply defined territoriality, claims to unmediated sovereignty—cannot avoid creating national categories and consciousness among its subjects.[60]

CONCLUDING REMARKS

Each of these possible lines of research connects to various of Hobsbawm's interests. Transnational perspectives on nationalism connect to his work as a world historian. Nationalism as political ideology connects to his Marxist approach to ideology, modified by the idea of 'invented traditions'. It also connects to his interest in why subordinate classes accept the values projected by the dominant order, an interest stimulated by his pioneering reception of Gramsci. More specifically, explaining why organized labour movements could support nationalism was something Hobsbawm had explored through his work on the labour aristocracy. The implications of the changing titles of the first three *Ages* volumes—*Revolution* to *Capital* to *Empire*—signalled the increasing containment of oppositional politics, first by a new economic and then by a new political order.

The danger was that continued radical and oppositional tendencies at popular level could be neglected. In his active politics Hobsbawm never accepted this possibility as he campaigned against fascism and then against Thatcherism, even

---

[59] To take an example at random, a very recent study with good references to much earlier work is Jason D. Hansen, *Mapping the Germans: Statistical Science, Cartography and the Visualisation of the German Nation, 1848–1914* (Oxford, 2015). An Asian study is Thongchai Winichakul, *Siam Mapped: A History of the Geo-Body of a Nation* (Honolulu, 1994).

[60] Leonhard and Hirschhausen, *Empires und Nationalstaaten* and Maier, 'Leviathan 2' consider this issue.

while he became more pessimistic after the collapse of the Soviet Union. His awareness that nationalism could have a progressive as well as a reactionary face can be linked to exploring how different concepts of the nation fit into broader ideologies, an issue raised in the debates over civic and ethnic nationalism.

Finally, exploring the meanings of nationalism at a popular level and how that related to the political and economic order within which subordinate classes were contained rather than writing of self-enclosed subaltern cultures and politics can be related to Hobsbawm's efforts to write history from below and from the margins. By bringing the insights and methods of social history, to which he contributed so much, we can enlarge our understanding of the history of nationalism.

6

Decolonization as Tragedy?

Bill Schwarz

We have lost the twentieth century; are we bent on seeing our children also lose the twenty-first? God forbid.

Chinua Achebe[1]

I can open with an iconic moment in the history of decolonization. Jawaharlal Nehru speaks to the Indian nation, late on 14 August 1947, broadcasting words that have entered the lexicon of twentieth-century history.

> Long years ago we made a tryst with destiny, and now the time comes when we shall redeem our pledge, not wholly or in full measure, but very substantially. At the stroke of the midnight hour, when the world sleeps, India will awake to life and freedom. A moment comes, which comes but rarely in history, when we step out from the old to the new, when an age ends, and when the soul of a nation, long suppressed, finds utterance.[2]

As the hands of the clock turned, they signalled the countdown to independence for India and, also, the creation of the new state of Pakistan. Despite the deep-seated political contradictions of the occasion, which were apparent not only to historians retrospectively but to many at the time, the sentiments expressed by Nehru nonetheless still move me. They can properly be understood as historic, in that they identified an emergent historical force on the very point of its realization. Word and deed were one. As Nehru acknowledged, such moments in the collective self-consciousness of the workings of history seldom happen. Or they seldom happen with a comparable degree of resonance and transparency.

Throughout the first half of the twentieth century the hopes invested in the breaking of colonial rule ran deep. It was commonly imagined that the eviction of the colonial masters would inaugurate qualitatively new societies in which the fruits of the nation's collective labours would be retained by the masses, the domination of racial whiteness would be annulled, and more democratic, convivial modes of social life would be created. 'Life and freedom', in Nehru's crystalline

---

[1] Chinua Achebe, *The Trouble with Nigeria* (Enugu, Nigeria, 1983), 4.
[2] Cited in Michael Edwardes, *Nehru: A Political Biography* (Harmondsworth, 1971), 214. It is revealing to listen to the words (at http://audio.theguardian.tv/sys-audio/Guardian/Correspondents/2007/04/30/jawaharlalnehru.mp3).

formulation. The conviction that the non-white masses of the globe were mobilizing represented a sea change in the collective mentalities of the colonial period, presaging its demise. There occurred many set-piece occasions when these convictions were politically codified. They moved into the line of vision on the national stage when movements committed to independence gained a measure of political authority, as was the case in India with Gandhi and Nehru. In the international arena, they were perhaps at their most rhetorically potent at the great congresses that publicly declared the epoch of the white man to be over: the Fifth Pan-African Congress of October 1945 in Manchester, the Asian–African Congress in Bandung in April 1955, and the First Congress of Negro Writers and Artists held in Paris in September 1956, exactly as the French, the British, and the Israelis were secretly coordinating their assault on Nasser's Egypt.

But, as we know, these hopes were hard to sustain. Within months of Nehru's broadcast regions of the subcontinent were aflame with murderous religious and ethnic outrages, which accounted for hundreds of thousands put to death, violated, or driven from their homes. Almost contemporaneously, nationalists in Vietnam embarked upon a long march designed to overcome first the French, then the military might of the United States. In the Dutch territories, the reimposition of colonial authority after the defeat of Japan proved long and bloody. The Emergency in Malaya, installed in 1948, was to continue for another twelve years, unleashing systematic counter-insurgency.[3] In Africa and the Middle East the precipitous dismantling of anticolonial dreams proliferated. Decolonization itself, for all its promises, activated brutal ethnic rivalries. Its characteristic zone of operation was the nation-state. The nationalist project espoused by the new states, far from containing such divisions, seemed only to animate them, bringing to the surface unforeseen species of 'morbid symptoms', to borrow from Gramsci. 'The crisis consists precisely in the fact that the old is dying and the new cannot be born,' wrote Gramsci with the prospects of international socialism in the forefront of his mind; 'in this interregnum a great variety of morbid symptoms appear'.[4] States subsumed the nations that they had been designed to represent. Citizenship and the imperatives for civic life came to function as pretexts for the imposition of brutal external disciplines and—*in extremis*—for state-inspired terror that, once its job looked done, turned and consumed its perpetrators.[5] Susan Buck-Morss argues that 'every state that claims sovereign power' carries inside it the potential for the makings of an 'unlimited, unmonitored wild zone of power'.[6] The corrosive presence of such 'wild zones of power' has been all too evident in the evolution of the postcolonial world.

[3] Christopher Bayly and Tim Harper, *Forgotten Armies: Britain's Asian Empire and the War with Japan* (London, 2005); and the sequel, Christopher Bayly and Tim Harper, *Forgotten Wars: The End of Britain's Asian Empire* (Harmondsworth, 2008).

[4] Antonio Gramsci, *Selection from the Prison Notebooks*, trans. Quintin Hoare and Geoffrey Nowell Smith (London, 1973), 275–6.

[5] For a stunning evocation of the postcolonial in these terms, Chinua Achebe's 1987 novel *Anthills of the Savannah* is unsurpassed. Achebe also locates, with great care, where in human sociability the countervailing tendencies to terror are to be found.

[6] Susan Buck-Morss, *Thinking past Terror: Islamism and Critical Theory on the Left* (London, 2006), 31.

Notwithstanding the aspirations that drew the scores of delegates to Bandung, the emergent independent nations found themselves subject to the overriding imperatives of the Cold War. New strategies for maintaining the economic subordination of the erstwhile colonies were devised, which obviated the need for formal political rule. The traditional insignia of the metropole, its hidebound judges and senior military officers, gave way to corporate functionaries in Brooks Brothers shirts and with a disarming air of easy informality, behind which the new, unforgiving balance of forces was partially or momentarily obscured. The colonial world transmuted into the Third World but, as it did, the depredations of the colonial epoch were reproduced in new forms. This was never universally so: pockets of considerable wealth coexisted with—but were walled off from—the shanty towns of the dispossessed, attesting to the inexorable logics of capital's uneven development. The dark arts of neocolonialism transformed struggling postcolonial nations into laboratories for the refinement of what would later be termed neoliberalism, which in due course journeyed from the peripheries to the one-time metropoles. In Eric Hobsbawm's words, in this social upheaval the reserve army of labour was globalized, driven by a geographical mobility that undid the customary spatial divide between colony and metropole, leading to the desperate, perilous migrations from the South to the North that have come to dominate our own times.[7] In the metropoles the imperative to colonize the racialized and the dispossessed takes new forms but continues apace. Capital itself has come to be militarized.[8] Images of famine, pestilence, ecological collapse, wars, and terror speed past us on the computer screen, tangible but inhabiting a far-off world, even though it is one that presses in ever closer.

Decolonization is a continuing story, its afterlives active in the present.[9] Ours are dangerous times. Human collapse accumulates. The metaphysics of the war on terror seeps ever more deeply into the psychic organization of our everyday lives, given justification by the remorseless progression of daily barbarism inflicted on women, children, and men as they go about the otherwise uneventful business of their private routines. It is difficult to comprehend the enormity of the catastrophes that tear into human lives and to grasp the escalating violence that has come to shadow our age. We gasp out loud at the latest outrage, particularly when it breaks into the metropolitan tranquillity of the boulevards and cafes of known neighbourhoods. The very speed by which one newsflash follows the next allows little scope for reflection, inviting in its place a chaotic clamour in which the mainspring of human agency itself seems to slip away and move beyond our reach.[10]

---

[7] Eric Hobsbawm, *On Empire: America, War, and Global Supremacy* (New York, 2008), xi.

[8] David Theo Goldberg and Susan Searls Giroux, *Sites of Race* (Cambridge, 2014), 109–10.

[9] This history runs through countless press reports each day. They concentrate the mind. For one that has stayed with me, tracking the story since the collapse of the Soviet Union and focusing on the replacement of socialism or secular nationalism by new religious forces, see Patrick Cockburn, 'Somalia and the Extinction of Nation-States', *London Review of Books*, 2 June 2016.

[10] I draw here on Bill Schwarz, 'After Decolonization, after Civil Rights: Chinua Achebe and James Baldwin', *James Baldwin Review* 1 (2015), 41–66.

It is difficult, in these circumstances, to place the end of European colonialism in historical focus. This phenomenon is properly taken to be one of the defining currents in the history of the twentieth century. But the further we move away from the moment of the independence of the colonial world, the more telling the contradictions and ambiguities become: the doubling back, the wrong turns, the detours, all of which lead us to unexpected and unwilled destinations. The persistence of colonial domination and its capacity to assume new forms are unnerving. The divides between the colonial and the postcolonial epochs slip further from our grasp. As a consequence, the historical imagination itself needs to be placed under greater scrutiny. After all, the discipline of history possessed, and maybe still possesses, a close intellectual intimacy with the expansion of Europe.

Yet it was not as if these developments, in the early days of decolonization, had never been anticipated. They were. In this respect the views of Richard Wright, the esteemed black American writer and courageous 'race man', were luminous and should be better remembered. In the 1940s Wright quit the United States for Paris, becoming a significant figure in the making of *Paris noir.* He was close to a generation of Antillean intellectuals, both francophone and anglophone, on which, more in a moment. His initial political commitments, while he was still in the United States, had been Garveyite, and for a significant portion of his subsequent political life he was devoted to the Communist Party. In Europe his politics was dedicated above all to the cause of anticolonialism. He attended the Bandung Conference. He travelled to the Gold Coast, then in its last days as a British colony before it assumed the new name of Ghana, and for a while he was close to the new nation's first leader, Kwame Nkrumah. He was an active progenitor of the 1956 Paris Congress of Negro Writers and Artists. Wherever his political commitments took him, he held true to what he considered to be the founding precepts of the American enlightenment—which accounts for his long-standing hostility toward any perceived manifestation of primitivism, tribalism, or irrationalism that he espied on the horizon.

In 1957—the year in which independent Ghana was founded and the political investments in a pan-African future were riding high—he identified the emergence of a phenomenon he called, scandalously, 'Post-Mortem Terror'. This he explained as:

> a state of mind of newly freed colonial peoples who feel that they will be resubjugated, that they are abandoned, that no new house of the heart is as yet made for them to enter.[11]

Such reflections proved harshly prescient. 'Resubjugation' has to be acknowleged as a powerful countervailing force that lies at the heart of the postcolonial dynamic. There was no decolonization free from the collateral impress of its 'morbid

---

[11] Richard Wright, *White Man, Listen!*, in idem, *Black Power: Three Books from Exile: Black Power; The Color Curtain; and White Man, Listen!* (New York, 2008), 683. I have discussed Wright more fully in Bill Schwarz, 'Black America and the Overthrow of the European Colonial Order: The Tragic Voice of Richard Wright', in Ruth Craggs and Claire Wintle, eds, *Cultures of Decolonisation: Transnational Productions and Practices, 1945–1970* (Manchester, 2016), 29–50.

symptoms' or from its 'wild zones of power'. Decolonization could never operate in its own unsullied state, free from contrary, intersecting historical times. From the beginning, this is what decolonization entailed. In the complexity of its configurations, it was—always—already overdetermined.

This is a story told in large brushstrokes. In daily life the slow-motion collapse it describes can be overwhelming. We reel from one apocalypse to the next. This state of affairs does not encourage *thought*. How can we think these historical transformations, which have made our contemporary world?

DECOLONIZATION, POSTCOLONIALISM, GLOBALIZATION

Before I turn to substantive matters, there is a preliminary point that needs to be considered. It concerns the contending methodological approaches that organize the study of the end of empire into its conceptually distinct variants. These can be reviewed as decolonization, postcolonialism, and globalization.

Decolonization takes for its object the transfer of political authority from the metropole to the colony and is concerned mostly with the shifting patterns of the political, economic, and social structures that initially enabled decolonization to occur and subsequently followed the transfer of authority.[12]

Postcolonial history is more contentious. It continues to drive a sharp divide between professional historians. To their cost, postcolonial histories have too frequently taken the material transformations that underwrite decolonization as a given, and have been content to leave the decisive, deeper social processes analytically buried. Even so, postcolonial perspectives are preoccupied with the necessary task of revealing the epistemic properties of colonial thought and with the consequent matter of how it is possible, in our own times 'after' colonialism, to think beyond the mental horizons of the colonial order. Such a venture works from the premise that there is no stable, foundational divide between the colonial and the postcolonial. As the prefix indicates, the colonial exists inside the postcolonial. The 'post-' and the 'colonial' exist in a contradictory conjunction.

Stuart Hall, in what is now an old intervention in the field, found that he was drawn to the idea of the postcolonial precisely on account of its endeavour to free itself from the inherited foundational categories of mainstream theorizations. We are obliged, he attested,

> to re-read the very binary form in which the colonial encounter has for so long itself been represented. It obliges us re-read the binaries as forms of transculturation, of cultural translation, destined to trouble the here/there cultural binaries for ever.

---

[12] Stuart Ward's recovery of the etymology is gratifyingly surprising; see Stuart Ward, 'The European Provenance of Decolonization', *Past & Present* 230 (2016), 227–60.

The term 'postcolonial', Hall continued,

re-reads 'colonisation' as part of an essentially transnational and transcultural 'global' process—and it produces a decentred, diasporic or 'global' rewriting of earlier, nation-centred imperial grand narratives. Its theoretical value therefore lies precisely in its refusal of this 'here' and 'there', 'then' and 'now', 'home' and 'abroad' perspectives... In this scenario, 'the colonial' is not dead, since it lives on in its 'after-effects'.[13]

This slide away from the organizing categories of the social sciences, classical Marxism included, generates divergent responses. For its critics, it represents a capitulation to the prevailing zeitgeist, where the law of value predominates, surrendering and debasing hard-fought intellectual gains that allowed a critical purchase on the historical world. For those sympathetic to postcolonial reasonings, of whom I am one, the argument is exactly the reverse. It is only by loosening our organizing conceptual categories and by dismantling their totalizing ambition that we can grasp the complexities of historical developments in all their extreme and contrary forms, which I sketched above. To put this strategically, postcolonialism represents an approach that is itself recast by placing at the centre of things the vagaries of *actual* decolonization: that is, through the contradictory histories that I have been describing.

Lastly, there are theories of globalization which accompanied the historical intensification of the global financialization of social life since the late twentieth century and which reconceptualize colonialism as a determining, but single, instance of the broader tendential capacity of capital to conquer space and time. In this reading, histories of empire cease to be regarded as exceptions to an unstated norm and are located as a constitutive component of a longer, more complex process, in which the transnational takes precedence over the national. This signals a paradigmatic shift. It represents a renewed intellectual sensitivity to the global properties of our times that has proved itself equally alluring to proponents of decolonization and to proponents of postcolonialism.[14]

These three problematics mark, roughly, different phases in formulating how the end, or ends, of European colonial rule might be theorized. But this sequence, so far as it holds, should not be understood as progressive, such that the latest instalment would qualify as the most persuasive. The virtue of each approach also signals what each cannot say, or what it too quickly dismisses or fails to see.

---

[13] Stuart Hall, 'When Was "The Post-Colonial"? Thinking at the Limit', in Lidia Curti and Iain Chambers, eds, *The Post-Colonial Question: Common Skies, Divided Horizons* (London, 1996), 242–59, here 247–8. In the same essay Hall addresses the overdetermined properties of the postcolonial. Of the Gulf War of 1990–1 he asks whether it was not 'characteristic of a certain kind of political event of our "new times" in which *both* the crisis of the uncompleted struggle for "decolonisation" *and* the crisis of the "post-independence" state are deeply inscribed' (244).

[14] As I hinted in my comments on Wright, I believe there is analytical value in placing in the single conceptual frame the histories of Civil Rights and Black Power movements in North America and the histories of decolonization, which a transnational reading of the end of European colonialism encourages. See, for example, W. Louis Rogers, 'The Dissolution of the British Empire in the Era of Vietnam' *American Historical Review* 107.1 (2002), 1–25; Antony Gerald Hopkins, 'Rethinking Decolonization', *Past & Present* 200 (2008), 211–47; and Rob Waters, 'Imagining Britain through Radical Blackness: Race, America and the End of Empire', unpublished PhD thesis, Queen Mary University of London, 2014.

TRAGEDY

Yet all this still leaves open an important question. How should we organize conceptually our narratives of the end of European colonialism? In part, this is simply a particular example of the more general question of the relations between metahistory and narrative. All the time historians contend with the problem of how best to arrange and plot the story they are telling. The case of colonialism, however, demonstrates how much the emplotment matters, and also to what degree it is imbricated in the hopes and desires of the historical participants themselves.

There is an entire library of works devoted to the issue. There is one argument, however, that stays in my mind, troubling me when I navigate the requirements of everyday life and when, by rights, I should be getting on with other things. Its proponent is David Scott, the Jamaican anthropologist, the spiritual force behind the founding of *Small Axe*, the Caribbean's premier journal of politics and letters, and the author of a series of fine monographs.[15] Scott argues that current histories of decolonization still remain indebted to a mode of telling that is given form by 'romance'—that is, by a narrative drive to 'closure', in which the wrongs of the past are righted and harmony reigns—and that, given the depredations of postcolonial histories, the time has come for our accounts to be conceived, in their very structures, through narratives that conform to the tragic mode. This addresses the darkness inside the postcolonial; and it is this element that draws me to Scott's centring of tragedy.

In *Conscripts of Modernity* Scott explores C. L. R. James's great historical epic, *The Black Jacobins*, first published in 1938, which charted the history of the slave revolt in San Domingo in the 1790s that was to result, in 1804, in the formation of the independent republic of Haiti. He compares the first edition with the second, which appeared in 1963. Among other, seemingly inconsequential amendments, James added seven paragraphs to the new edition that, until Scott, no one had much heeded. In these interpolations James reflected on the tragedy of Toussaint L'Ouverture's predicament, which destroyed him in the closing phases of the slave insurrection, his death—the death of this extraordinary black Jacobin—coming in the frozen depths of a dungeon in metropolitan France. For James in 1963, if Toussaint

> was convinced that San Domingo would decay without the benefits of the French connection, he was equally certain that slavery could never be restored. Between these two certainties, he, in whom penetrating vision and prompt decision had become second nature, became the embodiment of vacillation. His allegiance to the French Revolution and all it opened out for mankind in general and the people of San Domingo in particular, this had made him what he was. But this in the end ruined him.

[15] The monographs include David Scott, *Refashioning Futures: Criticism after Postcoloniality* (Princeton, NJ, 1999); David Scott, *Conscripts of Modernity: The Tragedy of Colonial Enlightenment* (Durham, NC, 2004); and David Scott, *Omens of Adversity: Tragedy, Time, Memory, Justice* (Durham, NC, 2014).

Central to James's interpretation, as it is to Scott's sharp-eyed recuperation, was to draw to the fore the 'truly tragic character of his [Toussaint's] dilemma'.[16]

For Scott, these few paragraphs were decisive, both in James's intellectual and political life and, by implication, in the larger intellectual history of decolonization. Whereas according to Scott the narrative structure of the original manuscript had been organized under the banner of the revolutionary romance, deriving both from Marxism (indeed, from Trotskyism) and from the protocols of an insurgent pan-Africanism, the recognition of the tragic element interrupted the narrative of romance, unobtrusively detonating the theoretical precepts that had organized the first edition.[17] As Scott explains, drawing from Hayden White's *Tropics of Discourse*, his own argument is pitched within narratology. It is about how the practice of narrative gives shape and form to the past. It is an exercise in metahistory.

Scott, born in Jamaica in 1958, is not—as he himself acknowledges—of the generation to be touched by what he takes to be the romance of decolonization.[18] He is emphatic about the 'virtual closure of the Bandung project'; he is disheartened by the damage wreaked by the fallout from a politics in thrall to 'the old utopian futures' (in a telling, paradoxical phrase); and he finds that 'the longing for anticolonial revolution' generates not only a disastrous politics but a mode of thought inimical to historical explanation. Looking back to the long duration of anticolonial struggles his verdict is unequivocal: 'What I doubt is the normative usefulness of continuing to understand these upheavals in terms of the modern conception of revolution.' Even more, he concludes that 'the modern is confronted *as* a tragic condition'.[19]

He reads James as saying that Toussaint's predicament derived neither from darkness nor from the operations of some manifestation of primitivism, but from the aspirations embodied in the spirit of colonial enlightenment. In a Foucauldian manoeuvre, Scott comes to situate enlightenment and tragedy in a single, entangled embrace.

Scott's intellectual affiliations are close to the variant traditions of postcolonialism. There is a tough deconstructive temper to his work, in which the reigning foundational categories are insistently called into question. His work overlapped for a moment with the subaltern studies grouping in South Asia, which, as I see things, represents a singularly powerful moment in the creation of a postcolonial— or deconstructive—historiography.[20] In *Conscripts of Modernity* Scott determines,

---

[16] C. L. R. James, *The Black Jacobins: Toussaint L'Ouverture and the San Domingo Revolution* (London, 1991), 290.

[17] While this is right, I think the body of the text is less secure than this assertion supposes. I give greater credence to its deconstructive attachments: Bill Schwarz, 'Haiti and History', in Charles Forsdick and Christian Høgsbjerg, eds, *The Black Jacobins Reader* (Durham, NC, 2017). In this respect we can recognize the import of Gramsci's realization that 'The history of subaltern groups is necessarily fragmented and episodic' (Gramsci, *Prison Notebooks*, 54–5).

[18] David Scott, 'In Conversation with Stuart Hall', *Bomb* 90 (2005), 54–9, here 56.

[19] Scott, *Conscripts of Modernity*, 30, 1, 7, 65, and 164 (quotations in this order).

[20] The core of the venture can be tracked in the twelve volumes of *Subaltern Studies*, published between 1982 and 2005. The first six volumes were edited by Ranajit Guha, and all but the last two published by Oxford University Press in Delhi. Volume 11 appeared from Columbia University Press in New York and volume 12 from Permanent Black in Delhi. There were numerous accompanying

among other things, to dismantle the concept of revolution—or, perhaps more exactly, the concept of 'the' revolution, which for long had been a constituent of anticolonial practice—by removing it from the discursive frame of romance and rethinking it in terms of tragedy. As a consequence, the idea of revolution is increasingly eliminated from Scott's field of vision. As this occurs, he seeks to reformulate the terms in which the relations between past and present, between the colonial and the postcolonial are to be imagined.

This is an ambitious project, with which I have an immediate empathy. Scott's is a wonderful book. There is no doubt in my mind that the diminishing cadres of anticolonial activists, wedded to the logos of 'the revolution', for long have faced political extinction. Indeed, history does not offer transcendent salvation as much as a perpetual succession of contingencies, which—when they arrive—present new impossibilities. The invocation of romance and tragedy works to deliver a means to think this through. Line by line, it is a book steeped in the imponderable ethics of thought. I have long found Scott's argumentation productive. Decolonization, or the postcolonial, looks properly different as a result.

However, my interests are distinct from Scott's. My project is not his, and I am looking for different things. In *Conscripts of Modernity* much of his analysis occupies a high level of abstraction, inspired by his engagement with literary form. By placing questions of narrative structure at the centre he seeks to pinpoint an epistemic shift in the work of C. L. R. James, which offers him a vantage point for meditating more generally on the variant readings of the postcolonial. I am interested in pursuing a more concrete, more conventionally historical exploration and in asking how—or if—Scott's use of the romance–tragedy couplet could be fruitfully employed at a lower level of thought, face to face with the historically concrete. How can we traverse the paths between the metahistorical and the historical?

Once one leaves the field of narrative theory and enters the more familiar historical world, the formal distinctions between romance and tragedy never quite stay in their allotted places.[21] Form, the organizing principle of modern narratology, gives way to successive, perpetual instabilities. The borders between romance and tragedy move back and forth, as circumstance or temperament demands. James's seven paragraphs added to the second edition of *The Black Jacobins* do indeed introduce a sharp tragic tone which is absent from the initial publication. Yet his afterword 'From Toussaint L'Ouverture to Fidel Castro', which was composed at the same time, can be read in opposite terms, as exemplifying the rudiments of romance. We should not expect an epistemological rupture between one and the other. Theoretical reflection rarely moves like this.

From his writings in the period leading up to and during the October Revolution, Lenin would appear to qualify as an exemplary militant who adhered to the

essays and monographs. For my purposes the most compelling of these is Dipesh Chakrabarty, *Habitations of Modernity: Essays in the Wake of* Subaltern Studies (Chicago, IL, 2002).

[21] And surprises follow. Of the United States, James Baldwin observed: 'No other country has made so successful and glamorous romance out of genocide and slavery' (James Baldwin, 'Here Be Dragons', in idem, *The Price of the Ticket: Collected Non-Fiction, 1948–1985*, London, 1985, 677–90, here 678).

romance of politics at its most intoxicating. Yet read him six months after the Revolution, in *The Immediate Tasks of the Soviet Government*, where he insists—at length, despairingly—on the need urgently to introduce proper accountancy procedures in the factories and on the farms across the new nation, and he appears to inhabit an entirely different mentality. This is a historical point, not one of form or epistemology. History had moved and the requirements changed.[22] At the level of the conjuncture, discrimination of this kind is needed.

At this concrete level binaries keep collapsing. As Roland Barthes put it long ago, 'a little formalism turns one away from History, but...a lot brings one back to it'.[23] The revolutionary romance that stands as Scott's principal object of censure has long been discredited. His own concern is how, in contemporary criticism, the rhetorics of the postcolonial should be organized. Within this purview, the jettisoning of romance has much to commend it. But on the terrain of lived history there is reason to be more circumspect. A popular 'longing for anticolonial revolution', *in itself,* is no bad thing. It can carry its own persuasive rationality. Down the road, of course, the intricacies of what comprises the idea of 'revolution' need to be confronted. It is a question, not a solution. There are many potential outcomes, not all of which are governed by a heavily accentuated sense of romance in the tropological sense. Scott quotes from Northrop Frye's reading of romance as 'the nearest of all literary forms to the wish-fulfilment dream'.[24] Yet is it possible to imagine a popular politics of any value that, by a swift act of pre-emption, forbids all 'wish-fulfilment dreams'?[25] Do we inexorably subscribe to the closures of romance if we seek—in the beautiful phrase James claims for Toussaint—'bare freedom'?[26] At the lower reaches of historical analysis the category of romance conflates too many things.

For Scott, tragedy is a means that allows for 'a more respectful attitude to the past' to emerge.[27] This must be right. In the revolutionary romance the past is infinitely plastic, requiring only faith—or only *greater* faith, as exemplified by Boxer in Orwell's *Animal Farm*—in order for history to be surpassed. In the tragic vision the gravity of the past lies heavily on the living, infiltrating the historical present. But this is not the only intellectual means to acknowledge a 'more respectful' conception of the past. Can we, in Derrida's terms, discover productive subjective

---

[22] Or, in a rather different register, Scott cedes Fanon's *The Wretched of the Earth* as the paradigmatic text announcing the romance of decolonization; others see it principally as an engagement with the tragedy of the colonial order. Scott, *Refashioning Futures*; Scott, 'In Conversation with Stuart Hall', 56; and Robert J. C. Young, 'World Literature and Postcolonialism', in Theo D'haen, David Damrosch, and Djelal Kadir, eds, *The Routledge Companion to World Literature* (Abingdon, 2011), 213–22, here 219.

[23] Roland Barthes, 'Myth Today', in idem, *Mythologies* (London, 2000), 109–59, here 112.

[24] Scott, *Conscripts of Modernity*, 70.

[25] I doubt Scott would disagree. At one point he declares that 'one of the great lessons of Romance is that we are masters and mistresses of our destiny, that our pasts can be left behind and new futures leaped into' (*Conscripts of Modernity*, 135). Quite properly he follows this with an all-important qualification. But, even with the necessary qualification, the point stands.

[26] James, *The Black Jacobins*, 290.   [27] Scott, *Conscripts of Modernity*, 135.

and social ways of being 'haunted' by the past?[28] I shall return to this question in a moment. In narratological terms, this approach may not even be the most helpful. 'For tragedy', Scott observes, 'history is not leading us anywhere in particular.'[29] Maybe. But, just as romance carries within it the impulse to one mode of closure, taking the literary conventions of the tragic as a virtue is not an innocent procedure. If we consider its classical articulations, we apprehend only too well where we will be taken. That is the point. We know exactly the destination—and in this lies the drama. We are heading for the fateful rendezvous with a prescribed doom.[30]

This is to suggest only that, if the conceptual space signified by romance is evicted from the radical imagination, the danger is that we are left with tragedy alone, unnourished by any counterpoint. The social itself becomes essentially tragic. And in such a scenario tragedy is on the road to establishing itself as a new, all-embracing foundational category.

THE GHANA REVOLUTION

At the end of the 1930s, James wrote *The Black Jacobins* as an explicit intervention in the politics of decolonization. It was the creation not only of his own expansive and searching historical imagination but of a larger diasporic pan-African politics.[31] It was, he claimed, a West Indian book conceived with Africa in mind. James's history of the rebellion of San Domingo's enslaved at the end of the eighteenth century closed with his portrayal of the millenarian vision of Central Africa's black miners in the 1930s—a portrayal that anticipated the history of Africa's decolonization, which was yet to be.

But, at the very moment when James was recasting the book he had authored a quarter of a century earlier, he was also alive to more contemporary and pressing issues raised by the unfolding dramas of decolonization. Just as Central Africa's proletariat appeared in *The Black Jacobins* as the momentous denouement of the story of the making of independent Haiti, so, in the 1963 interpolations, Ghana was active in his thought. For nearly twenty years he had shared a political intimacy with Nkrumah. On 6 March 1957 he had been in Accra to attend the independence celebrations. And at the time he was investing great mental labour in drafting his book *Nkrumah and the Ghana Revolution*, which can be read as a kind of sequel to, or update on, *The Black Jacobins*. The book is unacknowledged in Scott's account. Trinidad and Hungary receive a passing mention. Neither Ghana

---

[28] Jacques Derrida, *Specters of Marx: The State of the Debt, the Work of Mourning, and the New International* (New York, 1994). 'Haunting', writes Derrida, 'belongs to the structure of every hegemony' (37).

[29] Scott, *Conscripts of Modernity*, 166.

[30] I read James on tragedy in the section added to *The Black Jacobins* less emphatically than Scott. James suggests that Toussaint embodied 'authentic elements of the tragic' (289) and goes on to observe that 'in a deeper sense the life and death are not truly tragic' (291). Scott's conviction that 'we live in tragic times' is of a different order from James's view (*Conscripts of Modernity*, 2).

[31] For an initial assessment of the elements of London pan-Africanism, see Bill Schwarz, 'George Padmore', in idem, ed., *West Indian Intellectuals in Britain* (Manchester, 2003), 132–49.

nor Nkrumah appears. I, for one, think they need to be there, particularly if we are to understand how James imagined the retreat of Europe's colonial powers.

I also suspect that, in James's telling, Nkrumah functioned politically as a re-embodiment of Toussaint L'Ouverture. In the figure of Toussaint James had encountered Nkrumah's predicament, but in an earlier, previous history. They had met before, both literally and symbolically. Given the long mutual regard between James and Nkrumah, this would have been a psychically charged story for James to make his own. The Ghana Revolution did not turn out as its proponents hoped. If, in 1963, tragedy was in James's sights, there would be good reason to suppose that Nkrumah was the medium through which he lived it.

We need to take stock of *Nkrumah and the Ghana Revolution*; we should heed the circumstances of its creation, too.

After a spell of incarceration on Ellis Island as 'an illegal', James returned from the United States to Britain in July 1953. He had been away for fifteen years. His finances were shaky, his health poor, and he missed his political comrades, although his young American wife-to-be, Selma Weinstein, an activist of the utmost dedication, was shortly to join him. He could not call upon many immediate contacts in England. He deplored the state of English letters. Neither politically nor culturally was there much to excite him.

But this is to discount James's restive intelligence and political resolve. Intellectually, his first years in England were impressive, building on the laborious break from Trotskyism to which he and his group in the United States had devoted themselves.[32] He maintained a steady correspondence with his comrades, engaging from afar with his old political life. Very soon after his arrival he determined, against the odds, to make contact with F. R. Leavis, whom James judged to be an intellectual of impressive seriousness. He sent him a copy of his recently published book on Herman Melville, *Mariners, Renegades and Castaways*, which he had written while he was detained on Ellis Island. He asked whether Leavis would be interested in reviewing it for *Scrutiny*. (It seems that he was not.) James travelled to Cambridge in order to talk to Leavis, and his visit indeed occasioned a long discussion between them.

Alongside this new intellectual investment he returned to his writing on cricket, which he had abandoned in 1938, when he had left for the United States. He produced substantial drafts on George Headley, the black Jamaican batsman of mesmerizing talent, who carried within himself a quiet certainty of his own capacities. In June 1957 the West Indies team arrived for its tour in England, an event that triggered James's decision to pursue with renewed single-mindedness his study of cricket. This project came to be realized—after a succession of interruptions followed by further bursts of energy—as *Beyond a Boundary*, eventually published in 1963.[33]

[32] Bill Schwarz, 'C. L. R. James's *American Civilization*', *Atlantic Studies* 2.1 (2005), 15–43; and Bill Schwarz, 'Becoming Postcolonial', in Paul Gilroy, Lawrence Grossberg, and Angela McRobbie, eds, *Without Guarantees: Essays in Honour of Stuart Hall* (London, 2000), 268–81.

[33] I owe the information in these paragraphs to Robert Hill's magisterial lecture 'C. L. R. James and the Moment of *Beyond a Boundary*', delivered at the Glasgow conference '*Beyond a Boundary*: Fifty

James reckoned that these seemingly disparate preoccupations—Leavis, cricket—were necessary elements in his rethinking of politics. They were urgent and important. But they were not *of the moment*; and, as history turned, they had to be put aside.

The uprising against Soviet domination in Hungary in late October and November 1956 compelled James to drop everything and to reorder his theorizations of politics in the light of what he considered momentous historical developments in Budapest. In discussion with his US comrades, he set about formulating his ideas. The result was *Facing Reality*, published in Detroit early in 1958—a book that, in the vein of classical Marxism, announced the historical end of philosophy 'as such'.[34] It mounted an uncompromising attack on the Leninist idea of the vanguard party and promoted as an alternative a libertarian conception of council communism, which James was convinced the events in Hungary vindicated. The book was co-authored with Grace Lee, a comrade-in-arms from the 1940s, and with Pierre Chaulieu. James's alliance with Chaulieu—that is, Cornelius Castoriadis, also known as Paul Cardan and Jean-Marc Coudray—complicates the picture we may have of him as a castaway washed up in the early fifties on the uninviting shores of a declining metropole.

As a young man, Chaulieu had raced through the official communist movement and through Trotskyism before becoming affiliated with the group Socialisme ou Barbarie, in Paris, in 1948. This was a small but influential *groupuscule*, whose libertarianism was to provide one route to French postmodernism, as we can see in such figures as Jean-François Lyotard and Guy Debord. Chaulieu himself moved easily between the fields of politics, economics, philosophy, and (as a practitioner) psychoanalysis. After James's return to Britain he and Chaulieu would meet as brother agitators, in London or in Boulogne. Their alliance came to an end at almost exactly the point when *Facing Reality* was published; it was prompted by Chaulieu's determination to leap beyond Marxism, as he concluded that the time had come when true revolutionaries were obliged to make good Marx's own incomplete break with the capitalist imaginary.[35] On this James and Chaulieu differed; but they shared a recognition of the historical significance of those who defied the Soviet tanks in Budapest.

Hungary was one historical event that recomposed James's political landscape. The other, which followed after a few months only, was the coming into being of Ghana. For James, the making of Ghana realized the political hopes of a time, twenty years before, when a handful of West Indians and even fewer Africans had worked tirelessly, in London, for the cause of African freedom. Among these,

Years On' in May 2013. Hill was at pains to propose, persuasively to my mind, that James's *Beyond a Boundary* represents a Leavisite interpretation of cricket and that James himself at this moment—or part of him—can be understood as a 'Creole Leavisite'. This is supplemented by Hill's equally illuminating lecture 'Truth, the Whole Truth and Revolution-Making in *The Black Jacobins*', delivered at the conference '*The Black Jacobins* Revisited: Rewriting History' convened in Liverpool in October 2013.

[34] C. L. R. James, Grace C. Lee, and Pierre Chaulieu, *Facing Reality* (Detroit, MI, 1974), 65.
[35] Cornelius Castoriadis, 'C. L. R. James and the Fate of Marxism', in Selwyn Cudjoe and William E. Cain, eds, *C. L. R. James: His Intellectual Legacies* (Amherst, MA, 1995), 277–97.

James was closest to George Padmore, with whom his friendship was rekindled: between 1953 and 1957 they were in contact every day.³⁶ As the forces of what James interpreted as the Ghana Revolution advanced, in March 1957 it must truly have seemed that the dreams they had nursed were on the point of being realized. To James, this was a 'historical miracle'. 'I am fairly well read', he wrote with undue modesty, 'and I know nothing like it.'³⁷ Indeed, there was something miraculous about it. It looked as if a continental revolution was about to happen as a result of the cyclostyled call to arms that emanated from the threadbare lives of a scatter of dispossessed, lonely Londoners, most of whom had never even seen Africa. And in some respects it did, although not as they would have wished.³⁸

James had first encountered Nkrumah in Harlem in 1943 and, as he perceived things, it was he himself who tutored Nkrumah in the basics of politics. When Nkrumah travelled to London in May 1945, James effectively passed him on to his trusted co-worker and friend Padmore, whom he instructed to take Nkrumah in hand. When James arrived in Accra, he and Nkrumah had not seen each other for twelve years. When the rendezvous occurred, James faced a man who, as leader of a nation, had not only just wrested control from the colonial authorities but also trained his eye on the spread of freedom across the continent. It was a moment weighted with historical promise.

At the independence celebrations, assorted envoys of varying fame were engaged in the business of diplomacy and Vice President Richard Nixon happened to be one of them. Alongside them were fighters for the cause of black freedom who ranged from young militants to more seasoned veterans. Among the former was Martin Luther King. His path crossed momentarily with James's, but with no great significance. However, on his way home, King stopped in London, where he and James had the opportunity to talk. James wished to hear King explain the Montgomery bus boycott, which had ended the previous December after twelve months of sharp and bitter confrontation. He was enthused. A little while later he sent King a copy of *The Black Jacobins*, explaining its contemporary strategic significance.³⁹

³⁶ C. L. R. James, *Nkrumah and the Ghana Revolution* (London, 1977), 9.
³⁷ Ibid., 7.
³⁸ This perspective for considering the end of colonial rule in the British world needs to be supplemented with a more structural explanation. In the work of John Darwin, for example, the crucial period in which the British imperial system came apart is located in the global crisis of 1938–42, when the empire needed to be conscripted in order for Britain and its colonies to be defended from the advances of the Axis powers. See John Darwin, *After Tamerlane: The Rise and Fall of Global Empires, 1400–2000* (London, 2008); John Darwin, *The Empire Project: The Rise and Fall of the British World System, 1830–2000* (Cambridge, 2009); and John Darwin, *Unfinished Empire: The Global Expansion of Britain* (London, 2012). I have responded to these in Bill Schwarz, 'An Unsentimental Education: John Darwin's Empire', *Journal of Imperial and Commonwealth Empire* 43.1 (2015), 125–44. I find Darwin's geopolitical approach extremely helpful. Reading the story of Britain's decolonization from the point of view of the Soviet ambassador in the late 1930s and early 1940s has proved surprisingly illuminating: see Ivan Maisky, *The Maisky Diaries: The Wartime Revelations of Stalin's Ambassador in London*, ed. by Gabriel Gorodetsky, trans. Tatiana Sorokina and Oliver Ready (New Haven, CT, 2016).
³⁹ At the time when James was amending *The Black Jacobins*, King was thinking in terms of the tragic qualities of time. In his extraordinary 'Letter from Birmingham Jail' of 1963 he indicts the

This was the James who turned his attention to Ghana while in discussion with the unlikely pair of Leavis, the intellectual dean of English criticism, and Castoriadis (as Chaulieu is best known), who in May 1968 came to embody the situationist sensibilities of Parisian radicalism; the James who witnessed his protégé leading the pan-African revolution and to whom all manner of heads of state paid obeisance; and the James who, through the figure of King, extended his conspectus of revolution—and of anticolonial revolution in particular—so as to make it embrace US Civil Rights. *Nkrumah and the Ghana Revolution* had a lot of work to do.

The book opens with this dedication:

> To FRANCIS in never-to-be-forgotten memory. Like Cromwell and Lenin, he initiated the destruction of a regime in decay—a tremendous achievement; but like them, he failed to create the new society.[40]

Francis was the name coined by James for Nkrumah, a term of endearment for the younger man. This was not the only relationship of this kind in James's life. For much of the same time, James enjoyed the comparably warm friendship of Eric Williams, the chieftain of independent Trinidad and Tobago, whom he chose to call Bill.

Bill and Francis: there is a moving quality to these affections. The relations between these people were primarily intellectual and political, James acting as tutor to his promising young charges. However, Williams and Nkrumah were intent on entering a life that was not James's. They chose to be in government, deciding to bend the politics of decolonization to their own ends. As they first set their eyes on their careers, incomprehensibly so for men of their station in the colonial order, James was close by as a sagacious interlocutor, welcoming their ambition but endeavouring to keep his protégés true to their principles. Yet, at more or less the same time and in different circumstances, both Williams and Nkrumah found their paths diverging from that of their erstwhile master. There was hurt and recrimination. By the time Eric Williams placed James under house arrest, charges of bad faith were understandably rife. In these circumstances it must have been difficult for James to remain philosophical. How these subjective imperatives informed his understanding of the politics of decolonization remains to be seen.[41]

---

political moderates within the movement for succumbing to a 'tragic misconception of time': Martin Luther King Jnr, *Why We Can't Wait* (New York, 2000), 78 and 74.

[40] James, *Nkrumah*, 6.

[41] James was invited to Trinidad by Eric Williams in 1958, two years after the electoral victory of his People's National Movement, in order to edit the party's paper, *The Nation*. Williams's first loyalty was to the party, James's to the masses. According to Williams's most careful biographer, his first four years as the nation's leader were marked by political zigzagging. In 1960 there occurred a definite move to the right, which required the ruthless unloading of James: see chapter 20 in Selwyn Ryan, *Eric Williams: The Myth and the Man* (Kingston, Jamaica, 2009). James's most memorable depiction of Williams, on the cusp of this turn to the right, was C. L. R. James, *A Convention Appraisal: Dr Eric Williams, First Premier of Trinidad and Tobago* (Port of Spain, 1960); and, for his position after the break materialized, C. L. R. James, *Party Politics in the West Indies* (Port of Spain, 1962). There is a case for integrating more closely the Trinidad story into my own account here. The emergence of the People's National Movement (PNM) in 1956 closely echoed that of Nkrumah's Convention People's Party in the Gold Coast five years earlier. However, Williams and the PNM were never committed to *revolution* in the manner in which Nkrumah was, and James's expectations never ran so high.

Within a year of his return from Ghana, James had written the bulk of *Nkrumah*. For some reason, though, the final manuscript remained unpublished. When eventually it appeared in print in 1977, the first part contained the original material, as planned; a second section consisted of James's subsequent reflections, from 1960 to 1969. The published book thus spanned the years when James was recasting *The Black Jacobins* by introducing the vector of tragedy.

As the dedication to Nkrumah demonstrates, James imagined the Ghana Revolution as the contemporary instalment of the classic social revolutions of the past. Nkrumah is portrayed as a historical heir to Cromwell and Lenin. The precedents of France and Russia punctuate James's narrative. Jules Michelet and Georges Lefebvre rub shoulders with Isaac Deutscher and E. H. Carr, as historians able to explain the historic significance of Ghana. In July 1960 James declared to a local audience: 'the centre of the world revolutionary struggle is here in Accra, Ghana. [Loud applause.]'[42] Put like this, where Scott's scepticism rings true, one wonders whether either the exhortation or the applause was warranted.[43]

Heightened sentiments like these do indeed make 'failure' the most likely outcome. Nkrumah, we are told starkly, had 'failed to create the new society'. There can be no doubt that *Nkrumah and the Ghana Revolution* tells of the 'failure' of revolutionary dreams. But how is this story narrated?

The introduction—undated and certainly written after 1963, although in all likelihood conceived some while later—sets the scene. After a few pages James quietly leads the reader to the incendiary statement that 'Nkrumah prepared the population of Ghana for the morals of the Mafia'.[44] Notwithstanding the endearments to Francis, from this point the story darkens.

The pretext for James's condemnation was this. In 1958 Nkrumah had introduced the Preventive Detention Act, by which political malefactors could be arrested. Nkrumah's old comrades in the struggle, such as Dzenkle Dzequ, found themselves in jail. As the regime settled, in August 1962 Nkrumah was nearly killed in an assassination attempt. The Convention People's Party (CPP) dissidents grouped around Tawin Adamafio were arrested and placed on trial. Eventually, however, they were acquitted. Nkrumah responded by dismissing his Chief Justice, Sir Arku Korsah, by nullifying the court's proceedings, and by ordering the three putative plotters to be sent to prison, where they remained until the 1966 coup removed Nkrumah from power.

In December 1963 James wrote Nkrumah a warm letter (reproduced in the book), expressing his solidarity but asking for an explanation. None was forthcoming. Receiving no reply, James concluded: 'I suppose it brings to an end an association of twenty years that I have valued more than most.'[45]

---

[42] James, *Nkrumah*, 162.
[43] It is difficult picturing James in isolation. Hobsbawm's fifty-year engagement with revolutionary Latin America offers a nearly contemporaneous story that, notwithstanding their contrasting political temperaments, sometimes intersects with James's. Both attest to the defeat of a political generation. See Eric Hobsbawm, *Viva La Revolución: On Latin America*, ed. by Leslie Bethell (London, 2016).
[44] James, *Nkrumah*, 13.   [45] Ibid., 180.

To explain these developments, James turned to Marx's *Eighteenth Brumaire* and to the concept of Bonapartism. He cited Marx's analysis of the operation of the Bonapartist state, which 'enmeshes, controls, regulates, superintends and tutors civil society from its most comprehensive manifestations of life to its most insignificant stirrings, from its most general modes of being to the private existence of individuals'.[46] Informing James's critique of the new regime was his conviction that, in Ghana as in other newly independent nations, the state was working to engulf the citizen, undoing the mainsprings of civil society, and transposing the project of decolonization to the ultimate authority of the state. In James's account the antagonism between the state and the people moved to the centre of things.

When James was drafting *Nkrumah*, it was rare in the British world for the end of colonial rule to be thought of in terms of concerted mass political action. The transfer of authority was viewed by the colonial powers as essentially a passive affair, managed from above.[47] From this perspective, the Mau Mau groups were deranged and, like any formations that resorted to arms, beyond the horizon of reasoned action. There occurred, of course, incessant social unrest. But the combination of strategic–political manoeuvring and summoning of the masses to pursue more than sectional—namely, ethnic—interests was seldom either pursued or achieved by those who sought freedom. Perhaps Gandhi's politics represents a telling exception, particularly at the Congress meeting of August 1942, which sanctioned the Quit India resolution: there Nehru was cautious but Gandhi intransigent. And perhaps this was so in the Gold Coast, too. Certainly this was James's view; hence his determination to name the struggle a revolution.

Deep in his soul, James believed that the agency of the non-white masses was a key determinant in the fortunes of decolonization. Without decolonization from below, the colonial order would not be destroyed. Methodologically, this is how he alighted on Michelet and Lefebvre, who organized their histories on an understanding of the capacities of the masses to propel a revolution forward from below and to reorder world history. In this lies the conceptual link he strove to establish between *Nkrumah* and *The Black Jacobins*. The exigencies of popular life were of fundamental political significance for James. The popular signified the terrain where political identifications were fought out. And yet James realized that, analytically, this dimension of politics was difficult to reach. 'There are', he wrote, 'far greater deeps in the contemporary political psyche than were suspected even a generation ago.' Such phenomena, generated in vernacular domains, are 'utterly lost on the rationalists', recognized by them exclusively 'as a retreat from reason'. 'A revolution', James went on, 'is first and foremost a movement from the old to the new and needs above all new words, new verses, new passwords, all the symbols in which ideas and feelings are made tangible.'[48]

---

[46] Quoted ibid., 14.

[47] *Nkrumah* opens with a chapter that James entitled 'The Myth'. It is an exemplary demystification of the symbolic systems attendant upon colonialism, which serve to perpetuate colonial rule and to provide a moral justification for conquest and exploitation.

[48] Ibid., 98–9 and 107. This is followed by reflection on James's own relation to the 'irrational' elements of popular life in Ghana. It is in these terms that I read *Subaltern Studies*.

This is where the political weight of the book lies. By identifying the Bonapartist elements in the newly independent postcolonial state, James sought to determine how the opposite social forces were to be mobilized. The first part of his argument turned on what he had learned—alongside Grace Lee and Castoriadis—from Hungary: the virtues of collective self-management. Cultivating such virtues meant cherishing politics 'in the Greek-city sense of the word'.[49] It was a conception in which the civic and the political, rather than working as contraries, were brought into a single frame—one in which each coexisted inside the other.[50] From this perspective decolonization existed not as a forced march through the perils of history but as something rooted in the already existing conviviality of civic life. At the same time, notwithstanding his repudiation of the model of the vanguard party, James felt able to reconcile this idea of politics with a Leninist commitment to the power of organization.[51]

But this was only one part of James's argument. Looking back to his *The Black Jacobins*, he declared:

> The theoretical basis of the book...is that in a period of world-wide revolutionary change, such as that of 1789–1815 and our period which began in 1917, the revolutionary crisis lifts the backward peoples over centuries and projects them into the very forefront of the advanced movement of the day.[52]

This is decisive. James was striving to dismantle the conventional couplet advanced–backward, which worked as the epistemic foundation for the overriding justifications of colonialism. Refusing to understand historical time as linear and programmed—'an empty, indifferent flow which takes along with it a conglomerate of unconnected events'—he sought a more complex plotting, in which a multiplicity of historical times coexist and 'backwardness' can never be required to stipulate, by itself, a pre-given outcome.[53] Thus the paradox that James pursues in *Nkrumah* is that, through his understanding of combined and uneven development, backwardness *can*—in particular circumstances—confer historical privilege. Backwardness need not stand as a sentence from on high, banishing entire populations from history. A modern people in Ghana, moreover, does not necessarily resemble modern folk elsewhere, in Europe and North America.[54] For James, to engage in modern life was not the prerequisite of the metropolitan world. Colonized peoples, if the conditions are right, have the capacity to step 'over centuries'. Ghana

---

[49] James, *Nkrumah*, 84.

[50] James was close to Hannah Arendt's reformulations of politics, which had also been conducted in the wake of Hungary: see Richard H. King, *Civil Rights and the Idea of Freedom* (Athens, GA, 1996); and Richard H. King, *Race, Culture and the Intellectuals, 1940–1970* (Baltimore, MD, 2004).

[51] For Nkrumah's fiftieth birthday, James sent him a bound copy of Lenin's reflections on the state of the Russian Revolution in 1923, and included in *Nkrumah* his own 1964 article 'Lenin and the Problem'. James's emphasis falls on Lenin's invocation, in the underdeveloped world of Russia, of the political virtues of *teaching*.

[52] James, *Nkrumah*, 66; and Schwarz, 'Haiti and History'.

[53] Siegfried Kracauer, *History: The Last Things before the Last* (Princeton, NJ, 1995), 38.

[54] James acknowledges the modernizing role of the city, the market, the lorry, and war. On the role of the lorry in the social backlands of the twentieth century, see Eric J. Hobsbawm, *Primitive Rebels: Studies in Archaic Forms of Social Movement in the 19th and 20th Centuries* (Manchester, 1971).

could enter history as the 'vanguard of the twentieth century'.[55] Lenin, Gandhi, Mao Zedong, and Nkrumah were all testament to the possibility—in unpropitious material circumstances—for the colonial masses to meet the future and to make it theirs.[56]

I find *Nkrumah and the Ghana Revolution* to be the most Jamesian of James's books. In discussing the social insurgency of the Gold Coast he finds himself reflecting on the intellectual disposition of Pushkin and Dostoevsky. There occur asides on the traditions of Kierkegaard, Nietzsche, and Sartre. Aimé Césaire is a major presence. Even the BBC's *Goons* appear in a footnote. The significance he ascribes to intellectuals is that, if properly worldly, they are the means by which philosophies become material forces, entering the world of the people. In this he reveals a kind of practical Gramscianism. He is harsh about the habit of metro-politans to condemn African belief systems as throwbacks to a peculiarly primitive tribalism.[57] On the contrary, James's refrain is constant. Those fighting for colonial freedom are in the vanguard of modern life.

With this, James—his Marxian Hegelianism breaking through to the surface—establishes Nkrumah as the distillation of history at its most advanced. When, in December 1947, Nkrumah returned to the Gold Coast, he did so as a singularly historical being, carrying within himself active—if dissonant—social forces:

> In his elemental African consciousness of centuries of wrong and an unquenchable desire for freedom, there had met and fused... some of the most diverse, powerful and highly developed currents in the modern world... While they [the colonial author-ities] were meditating on how to restore order after the economic boycott and the shooting of the ex-servicemen, Nkrumah sat alone and wrote out his precise plans for what they would have considered stark insanity, their final and irrevocable ejection from Ghana.[58]

At this point in James's story Nkrumah inhabits the ghost of Toussaint.

AU BOUT DU PETIT MATIN

There are elements of romance in James's narrative, predictably so, particularly in the earlier sections, when hopes were high. Yet at the same time, from the materials

---

[55] James, *Nkrumah*, 84 and 91.

[56] Ibid., 187. It is instructive to recall the degree to which the major social transformations of the middle of the twentieth century, decolonization included, had at their heart peasant or rural mobiliza-tions—at the very moment when peasant populations were moving en masse to the cities. For the classic argument, see Eric R. Wolf, *Peasant Wars of the Twentieth Century* (London, 1973).

[57] Even James's closest comrades, Padmore and Wright, can be found expressing troubling senti-ments in this regard: Schwarz, 'Black America and the Overthrow', 44.

[58] James, *Nkrumah*, 78. He took 'all that he had absorbed during the years in Europe and America, and *translate[d]* it into the terms of the Gold Coast and for the struggle for the freedom of Africa' (112, emphasis added). By 1945 Nkrumah was thinking in terms of the arrival 'of a new phase of colonialism, which I call *neo-colonialism*': Kwame Nkrumah, *Towards Colonial Freedom: Africa in the Struggle against World Imperialism* (London, 1979 [1962]), x. This was written in 1945, although not published until 1962.

that James assembled, Nkrumah could have been construed as a tragic figure, as James had expressly portrayed Toussaint in 1963. And the historical moment itself could have been read as tragedy.

But James chose to make neither of these moves. Tragedy itself neither enters the story nor organizes its deep structure. Terrible things happen. There is, though, no predetermined, fateful end. This could be called 'tragedy' in colloquial terms. Or it could simply be called 'history'—unprogrammed in a deconstructive vocabulary—where the play of contingency is central. A set of social actors embarks upon one course of action and consequences of a radically different kind prevail, unwilled and unanticipated. When we distance ourselves from the idea of conjugating history as romance, this is what happens. It is not romance. But neither is it necessarily tragedy.

'Every revolution must attempt what by all logic and reason and previous experience is impossible. Like anything creative it extends the boundaries of the known.'[59] In saying this, James was drawing attention to the leaps in mental life that are integral to great historical transformations. Yet, by paying cognizance to the impossibilities that shadow human agency, he may also have been implying that underwriting history is the inevitable presentiment of *what cannot be*.[60] In an addition to the second edition of *The Black Jacobins* he emphatically follows this line of thought: 'Perhaps for [Toussaint] to have expected more than bare freedom was too much for the time.'[61]

What James claimed here is of the first importance. He acknowledged the moment when social expectations run deeper than historical circumstance can countenance—even though we can frequently be taken by surprise. This dilemma itself has a history, discernible from the June Days in 1848, from the destruction of the Commune in 1871, and from the upheavals unleashed in October 1917 and its aftermath. Hopes were high, social realities unforgiving, and the resultant bloodshed mortifying. In our own times collective expectation far exceeds what history is able to deliver.[62] *What cannot be* is a powerful current in the dynamics of modern subjectivity. James's 'bare freedom' and Nehru's 'life and freedom' continue to resonate.

David Scott followed *Conscripts of Modernity* with a book entitled *Omens of Adversity*.[63] While the crucial portions of the former were metahistorical, the mode of explanation in the latter is largely conjunctural; the book examines the desperate implosion of Grenada's New Jewel Movement in October 1983 and the swift

---

[59] James, *Nkrumah*, 129.

[60] I borrow this term from Stuart Hall, when he was trying to put into words his affinity with the music of Miles Davis: cited in Bill Schwarz, 'Stuart Hall', *Cultural Studies* 19.2 (2005), 176–202. The connections to a politics of decolonization may not be far-fetched. See Michael Denning, *Noise Uprising: The Audiopolitics of a World Musical Revolution* (New York, 2015), where he argues that the first expressions of a global decolonization were in vernacular musics.

[61] James, *The Black Jacobins*, 290.

[62] For a contemporary analysis, see Paul Mason, *Postcapitalism: A Guide to Our Future* (London, 2016).

[63] I am very grateful to Brian Meeks for sharing his thoughts on Scott's interpretation of Grenada in *Omens*.

intervention by US troops. The title and the subtitle—*Tragedy, Time, Memory, Justice*—suggest that tragedy works as the defining optic through which Scott's history is organized. There are two vectors along which the new directions evolve. First, tragedy is now located in the very operations of temporality. Historical time has given way to an apprehension that time is out of joint, in that the past can no longer guarantee the making of the future.[64] Second, tragedy is positioned in the very interstices of the political, as a founding impulse. Scott follows Arendt in arguing that the exercise of freedom is indeed an *invitation* to tragedy. Tragedy, in other words, is inscribed in the very dreams that animate political action.[65]

Insofar as these precepts work to loosen the categories of foundational thought and give scope to the contingent, there is no reason for reservation. Not only are they to be welcomed; they are also pertinent to the history of decolonization, which moves, in Brecht's formulation, by its 'bad' side. Yet, as the analytical framework tightens and when the connections between politics and tragedy deepen, politics itself threatens to *become* tragic. At that point I pull back. The ineliminability of contingency is what history is. At any moment the worst has to be expected. To call this 'tragedy' is to invite a new system of closure.

As I indicated above, one can follow lines of direction close to Scott's without having to resort to the idea of the tragic, which threatens to close down what has just been opened. James in *Nkrumah and the Ghana Revolution* was able to account for the comprehensive collapse of the democratic dream in Ghana without recourse to the concept (or trope) of tragedy. Heidegger—to whom James was much attracted at this point in his life—endeavoured to break out of the strictures of romance by imagining history to represent 'the quiet force of the possible'.[66] Psychoanalytical approaches to mental life explore the interplay between fantasy and the reality principle. Derrida, whom I have cited earlier, has many suggestive passages on the means by which the past exists inside the historical present. These, and many other readings, all turn on a 'respectfulness' towards the past.

But Scott is right to alert us to the political significance of specific structures of narration. They actively shape how we are able to imagine the complex temporal relations of past, present, and future.

I remain with Nehru's hope to step out 'from the old to the new'. And with Gramsci in identifying the generation of 'morbid symptoms' in that precise *durée*—in the 'interregnum'—between the old dying and the new being born. When James was drafting the first edition of *The Black Jacobins*, Aimé Césaire, with whom he later came to be close and whom he held in high regard, was simultaneously

---

[64] In a captivating formulation, Scott also proposes that the past used to be perceived as a *social* fact, while now it is understood as a *pathological* one, which is evident in the common emphasis on trauma and on the inability to free ourselves from the past: Scott, *Omens*, 13. This is a sharp, well-founded reflection. When I first encountered it, it drew me along. But now I am not so sure. Cannot *historical* time be manifest in 'pathological' ways? Are these necessarily contraries? Does not acknowledgement of the difficulty of freeing ourselves from the past indicate something important about the workings of history?

[65] Scott, *Omens*, 62. In n. 50 here I draw on a rather different reading of Arendt.

[66] Martin Heidegger, *Being and Time* (Oxford, 1962), 446; and C. L. R. James, *Wilson Harris: A Philosophical Approach* (St Augustine, Trinidad, 1965).

writing his long poem *Notebook of a Return to the Native Land*—a beautiful, epic succession of reflections on *négritude*. The poem was driven by as powerful an anticolonial conviction as James's *The Black Jacobins*. The opening verses repeat the refrain 'At the end of first light' (*Au bout du petit matin*).[67] The poem signals a dark, bleak reading of the colonial situation, where the social and psychic depredations that enmesh the colonized are visible to the naked eye. First light arrives. The day is beginning. The horrors accumulate. The old refuses to die. But, in the poem, 'first light', *le petit matin*, inaugurates not freedom but an interregnum from which new freedoms might emerge. The new is inscribed in the very writing of the poem. 'A revolution is first and foremost a movement from the old to the new and needs above all new words, new verses, new passwords, all the symbols in which ideas and feelings are made tangible.' It articulates *the possibility* of traversing 'from the old to the new'.

ACKNOWLEDGEMENT

I owe much to the editors, particularly to John Arnold, for their close reading of the chapter.

[67] I am using the bilingual A. James Arnold and Clayton Eshleman edition: Aimé Césaire, *The Original 1939 Notebook of a Return to the Native Land* (Middletown, CT, 2013).

II

MATERIAL ECONOMIES

7

Jiangnan Style
Doing Global Economic History in the Medieval Period

Chris Wickham

Eric Hobsbawm was not very interested in medieval history. Nor was his commitment to global history very great before the mid-nineteenth century—although of course he was fascinated by global difference. His *The Age of Revolution* focused explicitly on Europe; and, although *The Age of Capital* does not, it remarks: 'When we write the "world history" of earlier periods, we are in fact making an addition of the histories of the various parts of the globe'—because, he goes on to argue, they had so little contact with each other until the period of that book.[1] The captivating series of leaps from France to Macedonia to Egypt to China to Peru and back to Britain and Germany, which mark out that book series (and his personal style) so clearly, depended on their being part of a common, collective narrative—which, before 1850, for Eric, for the most part they were not.

Therefore, this chapter clearly has to move on from anything Eric wrote about its theme. All the same, if one wishes to approach medieval history from an after-Hobsbawm perspective, a global–historical analytical paradigm seems to me wholly appropriate, given Eric's interests. Inside that paradigm, which approach would he have used to understand the medieval global? Not a proto-transnational approach, clearly, given his views on pre-1850 international contacts (even if he might by now have revised the date of 1850 by pushing it earlier, given the wealth of analyses of global connectivity in the period 1500–1800 that have been published since);[2] still less an approach based on patterns of common development, such as the one now associated with Victor Lieberman.[3] Nor would he have gone for a teleological approach of the 'why Europe won' variety, not even in its Marxist version; he always opposed both triumphalism and assumptions of inevitability. He would probably have adopted a typological approach, for he was fond of

---

[1] E. J. Hobsbawm, *The Age of Capital, 1848–1875* (London, 1975), 48–9.
[2] Just to give a sense of the range of examples, see K. N. Chaudhuri, *Trade and Civilisation in the Indian Ocean* (Cambridge, 1985); J. Darwin, *After Tamerlane* (London, 2007); M. W. Mosca, 'The Qing Empire in the Fabric of Global History', in J. Belich, J. Darwin, M. Frenz, and C. Wickham, eds, *The Prospect of Global History* (Oxford, 2016), 108–23.
[3] V. Lieberman, *Strange Parallels*, vol. 2 (Cambridge, 2009).

typologies, particularly cross-cultural ones—types of land tenure, types of bandit.[4] He would certainly have adopted a bottom-up approach, attentive to how peasants adapted to the threats of the world as well as to the internal structuring of economic formations. And I am fairly sure that he would have been open to a comparative approach; for, although he seldom focused explicitly on a comparativist methodology, the latter is implicit in nearly all his writing. These last two are the directions I myself favour and want to develop here. I will focus on economic history, which presents comparable structures and processes everywhere, and I will compare economic patterns across the Eurasian continent in two regions, northern Italy and the Jiangnan region of China, both of them highly complex economies by the standards of the period. I shall focus on the central middle ages, the tenth century to the thirteenth, although I will sometimes stray later when looking for signs of change. This comparative process is not straightforward; it presents difficulties of all kinds—of evidence, of coherent model building, of incommensurability in the analyses of modern historians, and of the implicit grand narratives that underlie too many of these analyses and have to be recognized and corrected for before we can use their conclusions.[5] But it is a process worth undertaking; because, although medieval economic history has been a strong and active subdiscipline for a century or more, some of the comparisons that, it seems to me, we need to make have not been sufficiently confronted. This is therefore a sketch of how we might want to undertake future work as much as a survey of work already done.

This sort of discussion has been engaged in before, in particular by world-systems theorists; for our period, high-quality ones are Janet Abu-Lughod and K. N. Chaudhuri, to whom I would add, as among the best contributors to the debate about the relation between medieval and modern developments, Ronald Findley and Kevin O'Rourke.[6] All of these, however, have concentrated quite largely on the density and reach of international commerce. What its drivers are is less clearly articulated, even though such drivers are very simple concepts in economics: above all, the structures of production and consumption, not least at the local and regional level, where most economic relationships lay, and still lie today. Who produces, and how? Who buys, what do they buy, and on what scale? Above all, the socioeconomic framework inside which goods are produced—the social relations of production, in Marx's terms—is unclear in most comparative work.

The data on that framework are never good for the middle ages; but the issue is a key one. In particular, in the agricultural sector—which in every country, in every century before the nineteenth, was (usually overwhelmingly) the most substantial element of its economic structure—the distinction between tenants and wage labourers is economically central. Tenants were peasants, and peasants, however they held their land, from landlords or as independent landholders, grew

---

[4] E. J. Hobsbawm, *Bandits* (London, 1969).

[5] Compare the discussion of these issues for an earlier (and structurally different) period in C. Wickham, *Framing the Early Middle Ages* (Oxford, 2005), esp. 693–824.

[6] J. L. Abu-Lughod, *Before European Hegemony* (Oxford, 1989); K. N. Chaudhuri, *Trade and Civilisation*; R. Findlay and K. O'Rourke, *Power and Plenty* (Princeton, NJ, 2007). Lieberman, *Strange Parallels*, vol. 2 gives weight to economics but does not discuss the problematic as set out here.

the great bulk of their own subsistence; earners of a wage, if that was the only resource of a family, did not. The two therefore had radically different relationships to markets. For a peasant, the market was an optional extra: it might often have been necessary to engage with it, because rents or taxes were in money; but, in terms of acquisitions for the peasants themselves, the market was only significant if incoming goods were sufficiently low-cost to replace goods that could be made by the family, such as cloth, or by local specialists, as was usually the case for iron. In terms of rural commercial patterns in this context, mass markets for food are going to be marginal, and the appearance of a mass market for cheap artisanal products— in the central middle ages, above all cloth, ironwork, leather, and ceramics, in that order—will be the critical indicator of the complexity of an economic system. (Luxuries, I would add, were always and by definition marginal to the economic system taken as a whole.) For a wage labourer, by contrast, everything had to be bought, including food; and the only issue was whether or which goods were affordable. One would thus expect a considerably higher degree of commercialization of food if one was studying a society with a substantial proportion of families supported by wage labour; and one would expect also a greater market for cloth.

The consequence of these patterns is that one of the main variables in any medieval or early modern economy is going to be the percentage of people in any given region who were peasants as opposed to wage labourers (taking account, of course, of the grey area that consisted of people who were both). Of course, in any region there were also towns, large and small, in which work, whether artisanal or mercantile, was almost always done for wages, or at least for money. Many historians for this reason simply use levels of urbanism as a proxy for percentages of the waged, if they do this analysis at all. But the contrast between subsistence cultivation and wage labour by no means always and only mapped onto the rural–urban contrast, and we have to keep these two categories analytically separate. Empirically, there were rural artisans, who either worked for wages or survived by selling their own products (this difference means a different relation to production but has the same implications as far as the relation to the wider market is concerned); and, in some parts of Europe in particular, by the end of the middle ages there were growing numbers of agricultural wage labourers.[7]

This contrast therefore seems to me the most important one, if we want to understand how to get at the internal structuring of medieval economic systems. This is not least because our data are usually so partial that we have to have a particularly coherent economic model in order to know where to put the bits of the jigsaw puzzle on the otherwise empty table. I would add, however, that, although for an agricultural wage labourer the shift from agricultural to artisanal production (or, still more, to industrial production later on) was certainly a matter of acquiring a set of different skills, it was not a change in his or her relation to the market or to the means of production. For a peasant, however, whether a tenant or an owner-cultivator, moving to a dependence on wages meant a shift from one whole economic system to another. That is to say, the economic logic of a system

---

[7] See n. 16 here.

based on rent paying *by* primary producers is, structurally, entirely different from one based on wages paid *to* those producers in return for the employer's taking the entire product. The former is, in Marxist terms, the feudal as opposed to the capitalist mode of production. The labour process and the ways wealth is accumulated are quite distinct; the ways investment takes place and, more widely, the ways economic change occurs are different as well. If we want to understand how the central medieval economic system worked anywhere, we therefore need to understand this opposition and the analytical challenges it poses. My comparisons will therefore be used here to develop our understanding of it, quite as much as to develop the significance of the differences between my Italian and my Chinese examples; for, in this crucial respect at least, the economic systems analysed here were relatively analogous.

*   *   *

As I have implied, seen inside this framework, comparative work has mostly not even been attempted for the middle ages. But what would one look for if one wanted to understand how real economic systems actually worked and in what respects they were similar or different? To make this issue clearer, I will use two examples from northern Italy and build up my analysis as I compare them with China.

Let us therefore begin with Milan in Lombardy, which was far more important than any other centre of northern Italy throughout the central middle ages, and whose growth was visible in particular after 1050 or so—in its size (150,000 to 200,000 people by 1300), in its artisanal and commercial activity, and in its close relationship to the wide countryside around it. Above all, Milan made linen, woollen, and fustian cloth, both expensive and cheap; and it produced metalwork, not least armour and weapons. Iron was mined in the Brianza hills north of the city and then either worked locally or brought into Milan to be worked there. It seems, however, that the supply of primary materials for cloth weaving was more complex. Flax was always a Lombard crop, so linen was accessible in the city. Local wool production always existed too, in the foothills of the Alps (the word 'alp' originally meant 'upland pasture'), but it was substantially enlarged after the mid-twelfth century, when the transhumance of flocks increased greatly in scale; for moving them from summer pastures in the mountains to winter pastures in the lower Lombard plain meant that many more sheep could be fed. Beyond this, too, Milanese artisans imported wool, at first from north Africa but increasingly from Castile and southern Italy, as wool production became more specialized there, and even from England. And when it came to fustian cloth—a Milanese speciality, usually a cotton–linen mix—the import of cotton had to be systematic, this time from several centres in the Islamic world and southern Italy. Milan exported cloth and arms back. Its international connections were probably not the driver of its wealth—its economic hegemony inside northern Italy was more important in this respect—but, as can already be seen, it was tightly linked to that international commercial network. Its regional network extended to a hierarchy of other towns too. Cloth was also fulled and woven in a circle of smaller satellite towns up to 25 km away, such as Monza, Vimercate, or Cantù, and then finished in Milan.

Milan, as well as other cities, invested heavily in canals, especially in the thirteenth century, in order to move goods around. And, farther away, the cities nearest to Milan—Cremona, Bergamo, Piacenza—were its economic rivals as well as (mostly) its political enemies; but, despite this two-levelled rivalry, these cities bought Milanese products as well. By the thirteenth century the Lombard urban hierarchy had achieved a very substantial level of complexity and commercialization.[8]

The way these developments impacted on the countryside around Milan— and on the countryside around the urban hierarchy in other towns, too—was equally complex, but in some ways contradictory. It is quite common for us to see the expansion of money rents for medieval European peasants, generally an eleventh- to thirteenth-century development, as a sign that at least some elements of commercialization had extended properly into the countryside; and this inter-pretation is quite accurate. The need by lords for money with which they could buy things for themselves forced peasants to sell produce in order to 'buy' the coins, and also depended on the fact that they actually could sell it, usually to urban centres. But after 1100 we see in Italy, first around large towns, then around smaller ones, the opposite development: that of requiring rents in produce from peasants, to allow landlords to take advantage of market opportunities in the growing cities themselves. Peasants thus got cut out of the grain and wine market, even though in this case they lived around what was the largest city in Latin Europe (along with Paris); their buying power was presumably further depressed by the development of serious levels of taxation in the thirteenth century, which were higher in Italy than anywhere else in Latin Europe. There certainly was rural buying and selling: with an economy of this complexity, that could hardly not be. Among other things, peasants not only tended to consume different grains from those they handed over in rent, but on occasion actually bought some of the wheat that landowners wanted with their surplus of millet and other lower quality grains. All the same, there was a trend away from peasants benefiting from the fullness of the complexity of the wider economy.[9] Nor were there many wage labourers in Lombard agriculture in our period. They appear as occasional agricultural specialists or as temporary workers on some estates at high points in the year from the later thirteenth century onwards, and in most cases probably did this only during certain periods in the life cycle, for example as unmarried young adults earning

---

[8] On all this, see P. Grillo, *Milano in età comunale (1183–1276)* (Spoleto, 2001), 177–234; for an important recent contextualization, see P. Mainoni, 'Le produzioni non agricole', in *La crescita economica dell'occidente medievale: Un tema storico non ancora esaurito* (Rome, 2017), 221–54. For the eleventh-century roots of economic growth in the Milanese, see J. Norrie, 'Land and Cult', DPhil thesis, University of Oxford, 2016, ch. 2. On transhumance, see F. Menant, *Campagnes lombardes du moyen âge* (Rome, 1993), 249–87. For the wider context, see F. Menant, *L'Italie des communes (1100–1350)* (Paris, 2005), 267–77, 291–6; F. Franceschi and I. Taddei, *Le città italiane nel Medioevo, XII–XIV secolo* (Bologna, 2012), 48–52, 71–87. See further M. Fennell Mazzaoui, *The Italian Cotton Industry* (New York, 1981), 14–27, 28–32, 59–70; for a later period, S. R. Epstein, *Freedom and Growth* (London, 2000), 115–27; for North African wool via Genoa, G. Jehel, *Les Génois en Méditerrannée occidentale (fin XIème–début XIVème siècle)* (Amiens, 1993), 345–7; and, for Piacenza, Pierre Racine, *Plaisance du Xe à la fin du XIIIe siècle: Essai d'histoire urbaine* (Lille, 1979), vol. 1, 293–357, vol. 2, 705–13.

[9] Grillo, *Milano*, 186–98; for eastern Lombardy, see Menant, *Campagnes lombardes*, 236–49.

extra money for their peasant parents. This was the way rural wage labour began in most regions, but here it took a long time to become significant.[10]

Conversely, there were many rural artisans, smiths, weavers, and dyers, who were much more networked into the urban economies of Lombardy. Their existence indeed fed into the development of the small towns around Milan that had artisanal specializations, such as Monza. They represent the rural side of what can clearly be seen as a process of proto-industrialization in the region.[11] So the city did, so to speak, get into the countryside, even if rents were mostly in produce; and so did money and local exchange: first it reached rural artisans and local elites with buying power, then undoubtedly the peasant strata too. Exactly how far local exchange reached the peasant strata, however, is not illuminated by the sort of written documentation we have. Our sources do not provide exact figures for any of the statements made above; but they wholly fail us here. Our knowledge of peasant exchange will in the future depend on archaeology, which is as yet weak in Lombardy for this period: on what sorts of metal and ceramics were available in villages, and how sophisticated they were.

To develop this point, let us look briefly at a smaller but still important city: Lucca in Tuscany. In Lucca and its territory, after a period in which artisans are simply called *fabri*, a generic term that could mean anything, the range of identifiable trades widens from 1150 or so. We know of about thirty different ones in the later twelfth century: the most common are leatherworkers, then food vendors, then textile workers (especially dyers). Metallurgy is much less visible than around Milan. These artisans are mostly attested, in single-sheet parchment documents, as selling, buying, and renting pieces of land, normally at low prices; we do not have evidence for sales of goods in this period. To judge by this documentation, one could certainly conclude that leather was the most important artisanal product in the Lucchesia until 1200 or so; and I think that this conclusion would be largely correct.[12]

If we look, however, at the notarial registers of Lucca, which begin in the 1220s and document sales of goods, as well as commercial credit, the situation is quite different. At the time, inside the city, Lucca had a textile specialization both in

[10] E. Occhipinti, *Il contado milanese nel secolo XIII* (Bologna, 1982), 237–8; L. Chiappa Mauri, *Paesaggi rurali della Lombardia* (Bari, 1990), 289–306; F. Panero, 'Il lavoro salariato nelle campagne dell'Italia centro-settentrionale dal secolo XII all'inizio del Quattrocento', in A. Cortonesi, M. Montanari, and A. Nelli, eds, *Contratti agrari e rapporti di lavoro nell'Europa medievale* (Bologna, 2006), 179–202—a wide-ranging study, which stresses that rural wage labour in north-central Italy only took off—and, even then, very often in specific contexts, such as stock raising—after the Black Death.

[11] For this, see, above all, Epstein, *Freedom and Growth*, 106–40; more generally, P. Kriedte, H. Medick, and J. Schlumbohm, *Industrialization before Industrialization* (Cambridge, 1981) and S. C. Ogilvie and M. Cerman, eds, *European Proto-Industrialization* (Cambridge, 1996)—both, however, focused only on the early modern period.

[12] For the late twelfth century, see, above all, the documents in P. Guidi and O. Parenti, eds, *Regesto del Capitolo di Lucca*, 3 vols. (Rome, 1910–33). I discuss Lucchese developments in more detail in C. Wickham, 'Gli artigiani nei documenti italiani dei secoli XI e XII', in A. Molinari, R. Santangeli, and L. Spera, eds, *L'archeologia della produzione a Roma, secoli V–XV* (Rome, 2016), 429–38, here 432–4.

wool and in silk. This was originally based on imports of already woven fabrics: according to earlier Genoese registers, in the late twelfth century the Lucchese bought woollen cloth in Genoa 150 km away, dyed it 'Lucca scarlet', and sold the finished cloth, once again, through the market of Genoa.[13] This fits in with the importance of dyers in our twelfth-century documents. From 1200 or so, imported fabrics included raw silk, and in the thirteenth century Lucca owed much of its economic strength to an effective monopoly, within Italy, on the processing and, above all, the finishing of silk. This was a unique specialization for the period and transformed the Lucchese economy—but only inside the city itself. More important for Lucca and its territory, as a whole, was the start of rural wool production on a large scale, which, thanks again to the development of transhumance, was a very late twelfth- and thirteenth-century development. Once that began, woollen cloth was mostly woven in the countryside around Lucca, then bought by citizens and brought to the city for a finishing that was already a local speciality. In this way a more organic relationship between town and country developed, which could act as the basis for larger-scale production. That is to say, when the raw material for cloth making had all come from outside, as wool did in twelfth-century Lucca, the cloth produced from it was a luxury good, simply because transport costs were so high; and so was Lucca's ever more complex specialist silk production, even when, later in the middle ages, silk was grown locally. It would be the localization of the production of a non-luxury raw material—wool—and a consequent lowering of its cost that allowed a step change in the economy not only of Lucca but of its rural hinterland as well, around 1200.[14] As around Milan, however, the commercialization of the countryside was all in the rural artisanal sector. In this case, too, by 1200 rents were overwhelmingly in agricultural goods, and wage labour in Lucca is as little documented as it is around Milan. In the former there is, however, some archaeology, which shows rural access to ceramics from neighbouring Pisa and its territory: at least some people in the countryside could buy external artisanal goods.[15]

It is interesting and, in my view, significant that, despite the hyperdevelopment of Italian urban economies and their steadily greater linkage to at least some sectors of rural production, agriculture remained connected to the peasant family almost everywhere. Indeed, the only substantial region of medieval Europe where agricultural wage labour was really significant was—as it currently appears—late medieval England, where, although the size of towns and the scale of artisanal production in them did not remotely match those of Italy, capillary commercialization nonetheless steadily extended into the countryside of over half the kingdom through a

[13] A. Poloni, *Lucca nel Duecento* (Pisa, 2009), 36–60.

[14] For transhumance, see C. Wickham, *The Mountains and the City* (Oxford, 1988), 25; for the wool economy of the thirteenth century, see T. W. Blomquist, *Merchant Families, Banking and Money in Medieval Lucca* (Aldershot, 2005), article VI. For thirteenth-century silk, Poloni, *Lucca nel Duecento*, is basic.

[15] L. A. Kotel'nikova, *Mondo contadino e città in Italia dall'XI al XIV secolo* (Bologna, 1975), 26–64, 317–27; F. Cantini, 'Ritmi e forme della grande espansione economica dei secoli XI–XIII nei contesti ceramici della Toscana settentrionale', *Archeologia medievale* 37 (2010), 113–27, here 122.

network of local markets that may have matched even Italy in their density. Here large agricultural estates were for the most part exploited through labour service well into the thirteenth century, far later than in most of Europe, but this forced labour was steadily replaced by wage labour between 1150 and 1500. As a result, Chris Dyer has estimated that up to half of the rural population worked for wages for at least part of the year—or part of its members' lives—until the end of the middle ages. There is no space to work through the implications of this statement here (a statement rendered more complex by the unusually high quality of recent work on the economy of medieval England), but Dyer's conclusion puts into a wider perspective the much more substantial gap in the structures of production between city and country in Italy.[16]

What do these brief sketches of different economies tell us so far? Both the Italian cities I discussed had a similar development, even if Milan was so much larger than Lucca; the only major difference is that Lucca, unlike Milan, was not large enough for a network of small towns to develop around it—its interlocutors were instead cities of a similar size, such as Pisa and Pistoia, which were themselves not so far away. These two can thus stand for other similar cities, of which northern Italy had fifty-odd. We do not know everything about this network; far from it. The details of urban production escape us for this period;[17] we can hardly even dream of offering reliable statistics for anything; and a particular absence is a clear idea about what goods peasants had access to, which, as I have been stressing, only archaeology will be able to tell us about in the future. All the same, we can see the economy in its broad outlines. In the twelfth and especially thirteenth centuries, northern Italy showed an intense artisanal development in towns and a considerable division of labour, with (I must add) developed systems of credit that produced a banking system powerful enough to extend across much of the rest of Europe too. This development was based on a close relationship between town and country: not so much in terms of a peasant involvement in commercialization as in terms of a commercialization of peasant rents and an increasing density of rural artisans that contributed to the wider urban economy. Around Milan—and also around other particularly large cities, such as Florence—this stimulated the development of small-town artisanal centres in the countryside as well. I have used the term 'proto-industrialization' for this kind of process; and I do not think this terminology is controversial for what was a very highly developed economic region by medieval European standards. I would also add that, once Italy reached this point, some-time around 1300, it stayed there for a long time. The claimed decline of Italy's

[16] For wage labour, see C. Dyer, *An Age of Transition?* (Oxford, 2005), 194–232; J. Whittle, *The Development of Agrarian Capitalism* (Oxford, 2000), 226–47. For parts of the Netherlands that had the same development, see B. van Bavel, *Manors and Markets* (Oxford, 2010), 242–6; for parts of France that were more similar to Italy, see G. Bois, *The Crisis of Feudalism* (Cambridge, 1984), 97–117, 247–9. For recent surveys of England, see, among many, C. Dyer, *Making a Living in the Middle Ages* (London, 2002); R. Britnell, *Britain and Ireland, 1050–1530* (Oxford, 2004); and J. Masschaele, *Peasants, Merchants, and Markets* (New York, 1997). S. Ghosh, 'Rural Economies and Transitions to Capitalism', *Journal of Agrarian Change* 16 (2016), 255–90, develops the wage–labour argument, compares England to the very similar situation in parts of Germany, and convincingly argues for the stability of this high-equilibrium situation until after 1700.

[17] Except for Genoa, thanks to its remarkable notarial documentation: see D. Bezzina, *Artigiani a Genova nei secoli XII–XIII* (Florence, 2015).

urban artisanate in the wake of the Black Death has been comprehensively and convincingly thrown into doubt in recent work;[18] however, its urban economies always existed inside an agrarian economy with a different and more stable logic. Once the north Italian urban economy reached the notable sophistication that I have just been exploring, it established an economic equilibrium at a high level; and this equilibrium subsisted. European economic development from here on lay rather in the extension of this high-level equilibrium to ever more regions of the continent: from northern Italy and Flanders (Europe's other major commercial region) out to Sicily, eastern Spain, northern France, the northern Netherlands, southern Germany, eastern England.

*   *   *

Once we get outside Europe, comparison becomes rather harder, for the evidence base is so different and, except in a few regions, also far weaker. Evidence is, however, not lacking for China, which was almost certainly the world's major economic powerhouse during the central middle ages, more than anywhere in Europe and more even than Egypt, the most complex economy of the Mediterranean. People do tend these days to recognize that China's medieval economy was more complex than any other, but they do not always discuss exactly how this was so, so I will say more about it than about Italy. Here I will focus on the Song period (960–1276) in order to match my Italian evidence, although I shall stretch to later periods at the end.

China is, and was, the size of Europe. Even though I shall only deal with the China actually ruled by the Song dynasty, which was a smaller unit than in other periods (the Song emperors did not rule all of the north China plain, and after 1127 they controlled none of it), that China was made up of as many different socioeconomic regions as Europe was. I cannot consider them all here, obviously, even if work had been done on them; instead, as noted earlier, I will focus on one region, called by historians Jiangnan,[19] which consists of the southern delta of the river Yangzi in east-central China and is very roughly the same size as lowland northern Italy. During the Song period, Jiangnan was regarded—as, indeed, it still is now—as China's most economically developed region; and this is what historians tend to have in mind when they argue that China's economy was more complex than any other. (The north of China was for the most part both poorer and economically simpler; only Fujian down the coast south of Jiangnan, and Guangdong south of that, may have matched the Yangzi valley.) This much is common ground among western historians ever since Mark Elvin published *The Pattern of the Chinese Past* in 1973, although he in turn took his materials from two generations

[18] See recent summaries in Epstein, *Freedom and Growth*, 106–40; F. Franceschi and L. Molà, 'L'economia del Rinascimento', in M. Fantoni, ed., *Il Rinascimento italiano e l'Europa* (Treviso-Vicenza, 2006), vol. 1, 185–200; F. Franceschi and L. Molà, 'Regional states and economic development', in A. Gamberini and I. Lazzarini, eds, *The Italian Renaissance State* (Cambridge, 2012), 444–66.

[19] Note that this term is not wholly exact for the Song period. The word just means 'south of the river [Yangzi]', and in fact the Song provinces of Jiangnan were west of the delta, which was then the province of Liangzhe; to restrict 'Jiangnan' to the (southern half of the) delta is more of a Qing organizational decision—and also a standard, although less precise, modern usage. The region is divided between four provinces today, all with different names again.

of mostly Japanese historians, the early work of one of whom, Shiba Yoshinobu, Elvin translated into English in an abridged version.[20] (I should add that my expertise in Chinese and Japanese is zero, but English is the third scientific language in this field. This also means, however, that most of what I say here is, more than in Italy's case, perfectly well known to the experts.) During the Song period, China's economic heartland had become based in the Yangzi valley rather than in the dry plains of the north. Surviving registrations of Chinese households show a doubling in the empire's population between 742 and 1080; as important, however, was the fact that by 1080, inside China, the demographic weight of the middle and lower Yangzi valley plus the south-east had moved from 27 per cent to 50 per cent of the country's much larger population.[21]

This southern region was fed through the intensive cultivation of rice, which from then on became the most important staple crop in China, its yields far exceeding those of the wheat in the northern plains (and also in Western Europe). A major result was that high percentages of non-agriculturalists could be supported from rice agriculture—not only landowners, state officials, and soldiers but also artisans—and it became possible during the Song period to develop more specialist and also non-food-related rural crops: mulberry trees for silk and paper, bamboo for paper, too (both of them attested earlier but expanding in this period), hemp and eventually cotton for the clothing of the non-elite majority, as well as quasi-luxuries that soon became near staples, sugar, and especially tea.[22] The commercialization of rural crops, which was essential for this sort of economic system to be maintained, was made possible by good river connections, which, in the plains at least, were further extended through a complex canal system, more complex than anywhere in Europe until then. In addition, a hierarchy of village and small-town periodic markets was a normal feature of Song China, which allowed interagrarian exchange and the sale of artisanal goods. River and canal boats could be elaborate affairs, with a complex division of labour on the larger ones, and the merchants who used them had systems of joint-stock investment similar to that of contemporary Mediterranean shipping.[23] Peasants could often keep much of their surplus, for peasant owner-cultivators were very common in China. Even in the Yangzi valley, where landlords were stronger (in fact they reached their height during the Song period), a quarter of the land was peasant-owned; and state taxation under Song emperors (largely, unlike in other periods, on commercial transactions) ran at around 10–15 per cent of the average GDP—which was a lot, but not by comparison

[20] M. Elvin, *The Pattern of the Chinese Past* (London, 1973); Shiba Yoshinobu, *Commerce and Society in Sung China* (n.p., 1970). Shiba remains active as a Song historian; his long, co-authored article—J. P. McDermott and Shiba Yoshinobu, 'Economic Change in China, 960–1279', in J. W. Chaffe and D. Twitchett, eds, *Cambridge History of China* (Cambridge, 2015), vol. 5, part 2, 321–436—is now the most up-to-date survey of Chinese economic history for this period.
[21] McDermott and Shiba, 'Economic Change', 326–34.
[22] Shiba, *Commerce and Society*, 103–21.
[23] Ibid., 26–34; see also W. G. Liu, *The Chinese Market Economy, 1000–1500* (Albany, NY, 2015), 77–95.

with most medieval rents.[24] Therefore peasants could and did sell their produce to towns, either directly or via intermediaries, and (we assume, although the sources, as in Europe, say less about it) this means that urban artisanal goods were sold in the countryside. It was certainly possible for very large-scale productions of some artisanal goods to be developed, such as ceramics (which I will return to) or, further from Jiangnan, the major iron and steel productions in some parts of the north, lost to the Song in the 1120s, where forges were fired by coal: one could call much of this 'manufacturing'. Here we actually have a few rough figures. Robert Hartwell calculated in the 1960s that 125,000 tons of iron were produced each year in the late eleventh century; the evidence has been criticized, but the order of magnitude is generally accepted. We cannot give similar figures anywhere in medieval Europe, but it is highly unlikely that the Chinese figures were surpassed there before the eighteenth century.[25]

In contrast to Europe, however, cloth production in China, even when made for sale, was largely a rural handicraft. The cliché 'man ploughs, woman weaves' was widespread in traditional China; although exactly the same division of labour was standard in Europe too, here the weaving was very often for the market. This was perhaps not the case for hempen cloth, the standard clothing for Chinese peasants until the later middle ages, but the spinning and weaving of the silk that came from the mulberry trees of Jiangnan and other favoured regions was certainly for sale to urban and empire-wide elites, and also, on a smaller scale, to elites abroad. When cotton replaced hemp, by 1400 or so, cotton cloth was also produced not only for subsistence but for sale, and a large-scale rural cotton handicrafts specialism developed, first (in the thirteenth century) in Fujian, and then above all on Jiangnan peasant farms.[26] One result of this development was that levels of urbanism were never as great in China as in Western Europe; figures are here difficult to come by, but 10 per cent is a common figure canvassed for central medieval China as a whole, and perhaps only 15 per cent even in Jiangnan, setting aside the temporarily very large size of its major political centre, Hangzhou. (Hangzhou had well over a million inhabitants, which made it the largest city in the world in the later twelfth and thirteenth centuries, when it was the Song capital.)[27] European

[24] For landlords and tenants, see McDermott and Shiba, 'Economic Change', 348–52; Liu, *The Chinese Market Economy*, 155–9, argues that the percentage of landlords was rather lower. For the tax calculation, see P. J. Golas, 'The Sung Fiscal Administration', in J. W. Chaffe and D. Twitchett, eds, *Cambridge History of China* (Cambridge, 2015), vol. 5, part 2, 139–213, here 211n.

[25] R. M. Hartwell, 'A Cycle of Economic Change in Imperial China', *Journal of the Economic and Social History of the Orient* 10 (1967), 102–59; D. B. Wagner, 'The Administration of the Iron Industry in Eleventh-Century China', *Journal of the Economic and Social History of the Orient* 44 (2001), 175–97; D. B. Wagner, *Ferrous Metallurgy* (Science and Civilisation in China 5.11) (Cambridge, 2008), 278–320.

[26] For cotton, see B. K. L. So, *Prosperity, Region and Institutions in Maritime China* (Cambridge, MA, 2000), 73, 79, 96–7; H. T. Zurndorfer, 'Cotton Textile Manufacture and Marketing in Late Imperial China and the "Great Divergence"', *Journal of the Economic and Social History of the Orient*, 54 (2011), 701–38. For silk, a key point of reference is Li Bozhong, *Agricultural Development in Jiangnan, 1620–1850* (Basingstoke, 1998), here 143. For silk, cotton, and female labour, see F. Bray, *Technology and Gender* (Berkeley, CA, 1997), 191–236.

[27] For Hangzhou, Y. Shiba, 'Urbanization and the Development of Markets in the Lower Yangtze Valley', in J. W. Haeger, ed., *Crisis and Prosperity in Sung China* (Tucson, AZ, 1975), 13–48, here

urbanization percentages were generally rather higher: some 30 per cent could plausibly be canvassed for northern Italy by 1300, and 20 per cent even for England.[28] Chinese urbanization figures did not dramatically change later in the imperial period.

Song China was a single state, unlike Europe, and imperial intervention in the economy was far from unknown: again, rather more than was normal in the West. So, in the period 1069–85, the New Policies of chief minister Wang Anshih—who wanted to establish 'public authority over the ratios of exchange and the collection and disbursement of money and goods', although he never got as far as that[29]—led to a variety of specific economic interventions, such as the development of rural credit at low rates to farmers at planting season; this period also saw a wide range of water-control measures (it was only bad luck that the same period was one of widespread natural disasters, which voided many of these initiatives). Wang developed the tea industry of Sichuan in the upper Yangzi valley very substantially as well—indeed, overdeveloped it, Paul Smith reckons, to its long-term detriment—not only to furnish Chinese needs, but also to provide the government with a product that was particularly important and remunerative in trading with China's central Asian neighbours.[30] Throughout the Song period, as before and after, salt was a profitable government monopoly; the state evened out subsistence crises with public granaries and partly stabilized prices; the development of northern iron had considerable state backing; and later, in the Ming period (1368–1644), so would the expansion of cotton production. All the same, apart from the period when it was led by Wang Anshih, the Song government was not dramatically interventionist, and it would be hard to say that most of the economic effervescence that we have already seen was the result of the actions of the state, except in that its wealth made it a major buyer in every period. The state is likely most of all to have made a difference in inter-regional rather than intra-regional trade; this has parallels, for example, in the Roman empire.[31]

22–3. For urbanization percentages in Jiangnan as a whole, see Li, *Agricultural Development*, 20–2; Li Bozhong, 'Was There a "Fourteenth-Century Turning-Point"?', in P. J. Smith and R. von Glahn, eds, *The Song-Ming-Qing Transition in Chinese History* (Cambridge, MA, 2003), 135–75, here 144. These very tentative figures in fact claim only 10 per cent for the thirteenth century and 15 per cent for the seventeenth, but the former figure seems to exclude not only Hangzhou but two other large cities as well.

[28] For Italy, see the figures in Menant, *L'Italie des communes*, 133–9 and Epstein, *Freedom and Growth*, 90–1 (for *c.*1300). For England, C. Dyer, 'How Urbanized Was Medieval England?', in J.-M. Duvosquel and E. Thoen, eds, *Peasants and Townsmen in Medieval Europe* (Ghent, 1995), 169–83. The rather lower urban figures in S. Broadberry and B. Gupta, 'The Early Modern Great Divergence', *Economic History Review* 69 (2006), 2–31, here 20–1, are only for towns of over 10,000 inhabitants, but they show the same contrasts.

[29] P. J. Smith, 'Sheng-tsung's Reign and the New Policies of Wang An-shih, 1067–1085', in J. W. Chaffe and P. J. Smith, eds, *Cambridge History of China* (Cambridge, 2009), vol. 5, part 1, 347–483, here 390. The article as a whole is the best overall guide to the period in English to date.

[30] For Sichuan tea, see P. J. Smith, *Taxing Heaven's Storehouse* (Cambridge, 1991), 151–245.

[31] See, e.g., E. H. Worthy, 'Regional Control in the Southern Sung Salt Administration', in Haeger, *Crisis and Prosperity*, 101–41; for iron, see n. 25 here; for cotton, n. 26 here. For Ming interventionism, see now in the first place Liu, *The Chinese Market Economy*; for Rome, compare Wickham, *Framing the Early Middle Ages*, 708–20.

A good case study for these patterns is ceramic production, which is well attested in both documents and archaeology. Already before the Song period, Chinese pottery production had become very elaborate and often of high quality. By the tenth century the fine-glazed white wares of north China—Xing, then Ding wares—were fired at high temperatures in coal-fuelled kilns, which required considerable technical skill. In south China a development that was in some ways even more striking took place in the same period: the wide expansion of 'dragon kilns', so called because their length—up to 135 metres—resembled that of a (Chinese) dragon. We see this development at Changsha, on a tributary of the middle Yangzi before the Song period, in the eighth to early tenth centuries and, under the Song, at Jingdezhen near the Yangzi delta, at Yue and Fanchang in Jiangnan, and, from the late eleventh century on, at a range of kiln sites in Fujian. A dragon kiln did not fire at temperatures as high as those of northern coal kilns, but it had benefits on a huge scale: tens of thousands of vessels could be produced in a single firing. Large numbers of these kilns are known, with productive special-ization and full-time work forces. This was proto-industrialization, for sure; indeed, as a contribution to mass pottery production, the dragon kiln had—again—no parallels anywhere in the world until well into the British Industrial Revolution. It would be hard to imagine any purpose to producing on this scale except for a mass market. The Chinese court and government were certainly significant buyers of ceramics and exercised direct control at least over the overall organization of Jingdezhen (which was particularly rich and active, as it still is today).[32] But these kiln productions had a far wider distribution. They were often of such high quality that they could be considered elite products; lower-end and more localized (but still relatively good-quality) wares probably supplied the peasant majority most of the time, as some archaeological field surveys are beginning to show—although no such surveys have been done for Jiangnan, where I would guess that artisanal goods reached furthest to peasants.[33] All the same, no ceramics are really that expensive, and the major wares can be found in excavation, in different proportions, all over China: the complex commercial network that we assume existed, given the fore-going, can be shown to exist when we look at ceramic distributions. It must be added that many of these kilns are relatively remote; Changsha was far from the major Chinese political and demographic centres, the northern sites are some way from the Grand Canal routeways, and even Jingdezhen is not that central to the Chinese route network. The major kilns achieved success through quality and through a

---

[32] See in general R. Kerr and N. Wood, *Ceramic Technology* (Science and Civilisation in China, 5.12) (Cambridge, 2004), esp. 151–62 and 314–60; for the organization and imagery of Jingdezhen, see ibid., 184–239 and A. Gerritsen, 'Fragments of a Global Past', *Journal of the Economic and Social History of the Orient* 52 (2009), 117–52. Compare So, *Prosperity, Region and Institutions*, 186–201 and Ho Chuimei, 'The Ceramic Boom in Minnan during Song and Yuan Times', in A. Schottenhammer, ed., *The Emporium of the World* (Leiden, 2000), 237–79, for the organization of ceramic production in Fujian, seen through the archaeological record.

[33] Naomi Standen, personal communication, on the basis of her fieldwork in northern China and of parallels elsewhere. In her own area, on the edge of what is now Inner Mongolia, locally produced unglazed 'grey' wares dominate, with a tiny percentage of mass-produced glazed pottery made at a regional (dragon) kiln site.

distribution system that could cope with large quantities of breakable material. In
European history before 1800, only some ceramic types from the later Roman
empire matched this system, helped as they had been by the sea-based Mediterranean
trade routes; and the Chinese distribution system seems to have been more complex. This distribution was indeed highly complex, even though it was internal to
China; the Chinese economy was on such a large scale that international exchange
was even more marginal to it than it was in the West. (Those who lament the early
fifteenth-century Ming decision not to push on with voyages of discovery are
beside the point; China did not need them for wealth creation.)

It must be added, all the same, that Chinese pottery was very highly prized
abroad too, as the best wares were of a far higher quality than those of east and west
Asia and Europe. These wares, in varying distributions, can be found in every part
of the Pacific Rim (occasionally even in Australia), and well westwards. They
appear in considerable numbers in the Iraqi heartland of the 'Abbāsid caliphate,
and a set of striking excavations of wrecks off Indonesia show that they were
exported on a scale of tens of thousands of units at a time (the wrecks show that
the Arabs exported glass in return).[34] It has been argued that the coastal kilns, such
as those of Yue and in Fujian (Fujian is geographically cut off from the canal
network that connects the Yangzi valley with the north), were developed precisely
for this export trade.[35] Earlier and more surprisingly, this had almost certainly been
the case for Changsha, which, although over 1,000 km from the sea, saw a relatively restricted distribution of its products inside China itself, whereas they are
commonly found abroad (and 55,000 Changsha bowls were found in the Belitung
wreck off Sumatra, dating to 826–45). I do not think that it is an interpretative
stretch to see the hand of the state here, in this case under the Tang dynasty
(618–907), and indeed Changsha failed during the half-century period of political
division known as the Five Dynasties and Ten Kingdoms period in the early tenth
century, when states were more localized.[36]

This much is common ground, and, for comparative purposes, it is already a lot.
What is not is the direction of development in the Song period, with respect to
both before and after. Elvin, following one school of Japanese historians, as already

[34] See J. Stargardt, 'Indian Ocean Trade in the Ninth and Tenth Centuries', *South Asian Studies*
30 (2014), 35–55; for the organization of maritime trade from the Chinese side, see A. Schottenhammer,
'China's Emergence as a Maritime Power', in J. W. Chaffe and D. Twitchett, eds, *Cambridge History of
China* (Cambridge, 2015), vol. 5, part 2, 437–525 (493–507 for the main exports, ceramics, metals
and silk).

[35] e.g. So, *Prosperity, Region and Institutions*, a book that focuses on the export economy of the
Fujian region in general, and H. R. Clark, *Community, Trade and Networks* (Cambridge, 1991), 120–67,
shorter but holistic. For Quanzhou as the major Fujian exporting port, see A. Schottenhammer, *Das
songzeitliche Quanzhou im Spannungsfeld zwischen Zentralregierung und maritimen Handel* (Stuttgart,
2002); Schottenhammer, *The Emporium of the World*.

[36] T. S.-Y. Lam, *Tang Ceramics: Changsha Kilns* (Hong Kong, 1990), esp. 150–8, for their distribution inside China; for the Belitung wreck, see the Smithsonian Institution exhibition catalogue
Shipwrecked: Tang Treasures and Monsoon Winds (Washington DC, 2011); thanks to Anne Gerritsen
for making it available to me. For state involvement, see the silver ingots found in the Intan wreck
from the 930s, whose inscriptions show that they were connected to the Chinese salt tax: Stargardt,
'Indian Ocean Trade', 46–8.

noted, argued for a Song commercial and technological revolution followed by stagnation (or 'involution') for the rest of the imperial period; and some have been happy to agree, indeed presenting new data, perhaps most notably Philip Huang.[37] Others have doubted both parts of this view: Was change under the Song so dramatic? And was this the only period of change? An equally authoritative sequence of Chinese and Japanese, and now also US, historians have argued that the Ming–early Qing period (*c.*1400–1750) saw an equivalent—or perhaps greater—leap forward in production and commercialization, at least in the countryside, and, as in Europe, an extension of Jiangnan's economic complexity to more and more regions of China that had been left behind in earlier periods. In the case of Jiangnan itself, Li Bozhong in particular, a major expert on the region, has argued for a steady increase of rural productive specialization across the whole period 1100–1700 (and indeed later).[38] Some of the reasons for these quite stark differences in interpretation derive from the peculiarities of Chinese evidence, which, when dealing with regional economies, depends for the most part on official statistics, government reports, gazetteers, and advice manuals, rather than on documents of economic transactions themselves. Some quite basic information about rural productivity and household prosperity has to be deduced from careful extrapolations of sometimes not obviously reliable figures—although, to be fair, we must recognize that we could not even begin to construct this latter information anywhere in the medieval West. Other reasons derive from each author's underlying historical presuppositions about the period after 1300, which in many cases are affected by the grand narratives of Chinese 'failure' with respect to the West—a standard feature of the historiography since the mid-nineteenth century—or else by reactions to these narratives, which argue that China could perhaps have achieved an industrial breakthrough if England had not got there first. (The debate begins around 1300 because it is convenient from most traditional standpoints to blame the first break in Song prosperity and development on the invasion and conquest of south China by the Mongols in the 1270s.) These grand narratives do not interest me greatly, for I am very hostile to teleological arguments; but they do need some comment, because they contain some elements that are relevant here. In discussing them, one needs, again, to focus on Jiangnan, for the bulk of the historiography has done precisely that, and the evidence is anyway better for it than for most other regions.

We have seen that Jiangnan was a rich and complex region, with an exceptionally prosperous agriculture; Li has shown that double-cropping of rice with wheat and, later, of cotton with wheat, with mulberry trees for silk, was developing under the Song and fully developed by the early Qing period. For this reason Jiangnan was of interest to landlords, who wished to take its profits for themselves; and under the Song, as we have seen, they took over much of the region, even if they were never entirely dominant. Landlordship nonetheless dropped back afterwards

---

[37] Elvin, *The Pattern of the Chinese Past*, 203–316; P. C. Huang, *The Peasant Family and Rural Development in the Yangzi Delta, 1350–1988* (Stanford, CA, 1990).
[38] Li, *Agricultural Development*; Li, 'Was There a "Fourteenth-Century Turning-Point"?'.

and, although it expanded again under the later Ming (with a use of wage labour on larger estates), really large estates failed to extend into the Qing period (1644–1912). In the early twentieth century, the percentage of farms held by tenants rather than peasant owners has been calculated at 42 per cent, and this order of magnitude can probably be extended back to the early Qing: it is high by Chinese standards but very low by European ones. In all periods the basic productive unit was the family farm, and by 1700 or so over half of these farms were not beholden to any landlords—in fact to no one except tax collectors and creditors; and Qing taxation was not so high. It was on this basis that the silk and cotton weaving of the early modern period, which took place on such a large scale, developed. But what happened next? Was this family-based agriculture-cum-cloth production doomed to go nowhere, given the Malthusian trap that Jiangnan farmers never got out of (Huang)? Or was this productivity, which amounted to a widespread rural proto-industrialization, on the same trajectory as in Europe, before the Europeans—and especially the British—managed to make use of the resources of the Americas and of new technologies (Bin Wong, Kenneth Pomeranz)?[39]

I imagine that I am not alone in finding it hard to pick a winner in the rancorous debate between Huang and Pomeranz in 2002–3, given the recherché nature of their source base and rival calculations, although it seems to me that Pomeranz won on points. I would add that those later contributions to the debate that have focused on comparative wage rates between Jiangnan, parts of India, and parts of Europe do not seem to me to bite with respect to China: for, even though it has been straightforward to demonstrate that eighteenth-century Jiangnan wage rates did not compare with those of Britain or of the Netherlands (but rather with those of by then non-industrializing Italy, or Spain and Poland), this does not help our understanding of the Jiangnan economy, in which wage earners made up under 10 per cent of the rural population (and under 20 per cent of the combined urban–rural population) and, in the countryside at least, were taken from the lowest-status strata of society.[40] On the other hand, given the complexity of the rural economy,

[39] Huang, *The Peasant Family* (60–9 for the decline of wage labour after the Ming period; 42, 103 for the figure of 42 per cent); R. B. Wong, *China Transformed* (Ithaca, NY, 1997), esp. 9–52; K. Pomeranz, *The Great Divergence* (Princeton, NJ, 2000). For the flexibility of response to economic change in tea factories in districts just west of Jiangnan in the nineteenth century, see A. B. Liu, 'Incense and Industry', *Past & Present* 230 (2016), 161–95.

[40] For the Huang–Pomeranz debate, see *Journal of Asian Studies* 61 (2002), 501–90 and 62 (2003), 157–87. Concerning wage labour, Huang, *The Peasant Family*, 59–60, estimates 4–9 per cent in the early twentieth century for the Yangzi delta, where the percentage was lower than elsewhere; across China, wage labour was maybe 10 per cent in the early nineteenth century: see K. Pomeranz, 'Their Own Path to Crisis?', in D. Armitage and S. Subrahmanyan, eds, *The Age of Revolutions in Global Context, c.1760–1840* (London, 2011), 189–208, here 191–3; compare also Wong, *China Transformed*, 20, 43–6. For wage rates, see Broadberry and Gupta, 'The Early Modern Great Divergence'; R. C. Allen, J.-P. Bassino, D. Ma, C. Moll-Murata, and J. Luiten van Zanden, 'Wages, Prices and Living Standards in China, 1738–1925', *Economic History Review* 64.S1 (2011), 8–38. Allen recognized the point made here in an earlier article of 2006; see R. C. Allen, 'Agricultural Productivity and Rural Incomes in England and the Yangtze Delta, c.1620–c.1820', at http://www.nuffield.ox.ac.uk/users/allen/unpublished/yangtze.pdf; here he put the Yangzi–England divergence at around 1700 rather than at Pomeranz's 1800, which seems plausible to me. See also the sensible literature survey in Lieberman, *Strange Parallels*, vol. 2, 562–76. In the 2002 Pomeranz debate, the only contribution that

the low proportion of wage earners in Jiangnan seems to me significant in itself. I stressed earlier that it is a much bigger step for peasants than for rural wage labourers to go into factories, given that the former have not previously had to rely on the market for their subsistence; indeed, maybe such peasants are right to be cautious, for it is also a bigger step for the market to be able to provide subsistence for them, and it might well not manage it. This means that industrialization is much more of a step change for a peasant-based economy, and for this reason I am less surprised than Pomeranz that it took China two more centuries to achieve it fully; even Stalin found it impossible to achieve industrialization quickly under these circumstances without violence. Instead, China remained a high-level equilibrium system—it probably was, in 1700 as in 1300, the highest-functioning such system in the world—without needing to make that big step into something new, different, and not yet obviously advantageous.

* * *

To conclude: what does this East–West comparison tell us about the structures and possibilities of the richest central medieval economies? One thing should, I hope, be clear: the two economic systems that I have briefly characterized had many points in common. Northern Italy and the Yangzi delta both had complex urban and rural economies, with a considerable division of labour. Artisans were both urban and rural, and the structures of the urban economy linked city and country together. In neither of these regions can we be sure how far the large-scale demand for artisanal goods reached into the countryside; but it was at least beginning to. Neither region had significant levels of agricultural wage labour; all the same, both were regions where we can talk of proto-industrialization, both urban and rural, before 1300.

There were differences, too. Peasant-controlled agricultural commercialization was increasingly cut out from the major grain market of Italian cities, but in Jiangnan, thanks to a very active family-based handicraft sector, buying and selling involved the peasantry too, and this may very well have meant that peasants there could buy mass products early. Indeed, most indicators point to a rather higher level of commercialization and commercial complexity in the leading regions of China than in those of Europe in the central middle ages. Conversely, these peasant-based handicrafts meant lower levels of urbanization in Jiangnan and China as a whole, and the relative size of towns is not the proxy for economic complexity that it generally is in Europe. I do not think that this is a significant difference, but it is at least one that may be the sign of other differences, more hidden by the deficiencies in our evidence.

made points parallel to the ones made here—at a level of detail that cannot be matched within the compass of this article—was R. Brenner and C. Isett, 'England's Divergence from China's Yangzi Delta', *Journal of Asian Studies* 61 (2002), 609–62, although the authors wrapped up their argument into a general restatement of a 'triumph of the West' analysis that I do not follow; Pomeranz himself, however, stressed the peasant–labourer difference in a subsequent issue of the same journal: *Journal of Asian Studies* 62.1 (2003), 175–8 (Communications to the Editor).

What this comparison also shows, however, is not so much difference as the importance of comparabilities in structure, which are more significant than the simple statement, however true, that China was more 'developed' than Europe during the period I have been discussing. For all the deficiencies in our evidence, these were visibly high-level production and exchange systems, and the different sorts of documentation we have for each simply show different routes to a parallel complexity. They show how high-equilibrium systems worked and how proto-industry fitted into each separately, but in a comparable way. The word 'equilibrium' is important here. Each of these economies was capable of becoming more complex, often across a very long period, in a process of Smithian growth; this process radiated outwards too, in Europe and China alike, as more and more regions came to resemble northern Italy, Flanders, and Jiangnan, in at least versions of this complexity. But they did so in an overarching framework, which remained stable.

The point I wish to stress above all is this stability. Equilibrium systems were *normal* in global economic history up until very recent times; and this is as true for very high-level systems like these as it is for very simple ones. In constructing these comparisons, I could have used not dissimilar systems in earlier periods of Chinese history or, in the Mediterranean, in Roman imperial history—or, elsewhere in Eurasia, in Egyptian, Indian, or Iraqi history—and the point would have been much the same. Each of these systems shows us, inside a peasant-based feudal society, high levels of artisanal production and commercialization; highly complex economies indeed; but no trend to change their overarching structure. Mark Elvin popularized the phrase 'high-equilibrium *trap*' when characterizing the Chinese version of these economic systems; I think this is a mistaken formulation.[41] Rather we should ask why they *should* have changed. Each of them was fully functional to the possibilities of the logic of the economic system they were part of, which responded above all to what was by far the most widely diffused economic process in all of them: the subsistence strategies of the huge peasant majority—of course, inside the framework of the extraction of agrarian surpluses by elites from such primary producers, in whichever way this happened in each society.[42] That logic was therefore structured around two basic elements: the fact that elite demand—a fundamental motor for production and exchange and one capable of considerable growth—was always restricted by the fact that elites were a small minority; and the fact that peasant demand, even if it was not (as it usually was not) restricted by Malthusian constraints, was, given the peasantry's unmarketized subsistence base, finite. It is because these equilibria were so normal, not least but not only in my period, that the standard grand narratives of economic transformation interest me so little; they were more chancy, they happened in unexpected areas, and maybe they had unexpected reasons, too. Here, despite differences in approach, I find myself closer to Pomeranz than to his critics. I hope that Eric Hobsbawm would

---

[41] Elvin, *The Pattern of the Chinese Past*, 298–316. I have argued this point before, using different examples; see C. Wickham, 'Memories of Underdevelopment', in idem, ed., *Marxist History-Writing for the Twenty-First Century* (Oxford, 2007), 32–48, here 43–8.
[42] See Bois, *The Crisis of Feudalism*, 393–408, for one attempt at constructing a model here.

have agreed with me; but in any event this seems to me a useful direction for economic historians of what Europeans call 'the middle ages' to pursue in the future too.

ACKNOWLEDGEMENTS

I thank Naomi Standen for a detailed critique of this text; to audiences at the Catholic University of America and the Economic and Social History Seminar at Oxford for critical reactions; to Matthew Hilton and Leslie Brubaker for good advice; and to Leslie Brubaker for the title.

8

Global History and the Transformation
of Early Modern Europe

Maxine Berg

Eric Hobsbawm claimed an early interest in world and wide comparative history. This was largely because, when he was a young historian, economic and social history were frontier subjects. Challenging old paradigms, a younger generation of European historians quickly came to play an international role. An international association of economic history was founded in 1959, run by the Anglo-French partnership of Braudel and Postan. Hobsbawm lamented that, despite the international purpose of the association and its encouragement of comparative perspectives, it had no definitive impact on turning wider historians—or just economic historians—away from their national frameworks. Histories of Europe, of the United States, and of the rest of the world remained separate from one another:

> In my generation only a handful of historians has tried to integrate them in a compre-
> hensive world history. This was partly because of the almost total failure, largely for
> institutional and linguistic reasons, of history to emancipate itself from the framework
> of the nation-state. Looking back, this provincialism was probably the major weakness of
> the subject in my lifetime.[1]

The recent turn, among many historians, to including global and world history in their teaching and, where relevant, in their research has deeply affected perspectives in writing not only about the early modern world but about early modern Europe itself.

Encounters with exotic Asian manufactures, from lacquered cabinets and ivory carvings to silks and porcelain, turned into Europe's engagement with a major Asian export ware sector, especially in cotton textiles and porcelain.[2] Along with this, Europe's food and drink cultures witnessed, then integrated tea drinking. Tea was advertised in English coffee houses in the 1660s; but by that time it was already well established in the Dutch Republic as the drink of choice for small conversa-tion groups, the new 'private world of the tea table'. John Locke discovered it during his time there; he considered the teahouse a preferable alternative to the

---

[1] Eric Hobsbawm, *Interesting Times: A Twentieth-Century Life* (Harmondsworth, 2003), 293.
[2] Maxine Berg, 'Manufacturing the Orient: Asian Commodities and European Industry', in *Proceedings of the Istituto Internazionale di Storia Economica F. Datini, Prato*, vol. 29 (Paris, 1998), 385–419; Maxine Berg, 'In Pursuit of Luxury: Global Origins of British Consumer Goods', *Past & Present* 182 (2004), 85–142.

coffee house, and when he returned to England in 1688 privately shipped in consignments of good-quality tea.[3] By the later 1780s tea was so commonplace that Catherine Hutton could note in her diary that Joseph Priestley had knocked on the door to 'take tea' with her father, William Hutton, the Birmingham printer, 'without ceremony'.[4]

The China tea trade initiated great voyages—some from London that could take up to four years, such as that of the *Stretham* in 1703–7, others from Bombay, such as those of the *London* and *Worcester* in 1687 to Canton and Amoy. The latter two were sent to acquire 20,000 pounds of tea 'Extraordinary good and fresh, being for England'.[5]

How significant were these goods to Europe's future consumer and industrial cultures? I raised this question in the later 1990s. This chapter will look first at how historians, and especially economic historians in the past, looked at the part played by Asia in early modern Europe and at how we have written our histories since. These histories have changed, especially as historians have moved their interests out, to global history and to the history of consumer culture, and their sources and methodologies have been made to encompass objects, collections in museums, and the approaches of material culture and cultural history.

My chapter will then move on to summarize the new information that historians have gathered on the quantities and impact of the Asia–Europe trade. It will survey the estimates we now have on the quantities of goods traded, their contribution to European economies, and the histories of the trading companies that organized and carried out this trade. It will discuss the contributions that the trading companies made, their constraints as monopolies, and the great limitations they faced in providing the goods that the Europeans wanted.

The chapter will then set out the new part that cultural history can play in enriching our global history of the impact of Asia on Europe. For the key transition we see in the seventeenth and eighteenth centuries is a widespread shift in the desires and material culture of everyday life; this shift was to a degree initiated by the imports of Asian goods, but those desires had first to be created. Those desires had become so great and so widespread by the second half of the eighteenth century that Asian production systems and trade could no longer supply them. Developing industrial regions in Northern Europe were quick to imitate, compete, and initiate new consumer industries.

The chapter will conclude with a microhistorical analysis of a key global conjuncture of crisis in the manufacture of Bengal muslin and technological spurt in fine cotton spinning in the north of England in the 1780s and 1790s—a conjuncture that generated one of the central events that pushed Northern Europe towards the Industrial Revolution and 'divergence'.

---

[3] Markman Ellis, Richard Coulton, and Matthew Mauger, *The Empire of Tea: The Asian Leaf that Conquered the World* (London, 2015), 41–9.

[4] Maxine Berg, *Luxury and Pleasure in Eighteenth-Century Britain* (Oxford, 2005), 232.

[5] Ellis, Coulton, and Mauger, *Empire of Tea*, 54–5.

THE WORLD AND THE INDUSTRIAL REVOLUTION

What did historians of recent generations have to say about the impact of wider world trade on Europe's industry and consumption? We can look first to the best-known of Eric Hobsbawm's books, and certainly the one read by virtually all history students during the 1970s: his *Industry and Empire*, published in 1968.[6] The central point of his analysis of the origins of the Industrial Revolution was the impact of foreign and wider world trade. He argued that Britain's riches from early in the eighteenth century were based on its trade and enterprise, backed as these were by a strong navy and a powerful state—a state linked with trade and the middle class. All this was part of the 'world economy of the European maritime states'.[7] This is the book where he made his classic statement. 'Home demand increased—but foreign demand multiplied. If a spark was needed, this is where it came from.'[8]

Looking back on Hobsbawm's analysis, there is much in it that is similar to our current historical writing on the important role of foreign trade in economic change during the eighteenth century. Hobsbawm sought the historical foundations of Britain's relations with the underdeveloped world in the 'virtual elimination of the peasantry and the small-scale artisan producers'.[9] He described a 'nation of shopkeepers': 'it was the merchant rather than the industrialist who was its most characteristic citizen'.[10] He argued that Britain 'conquered other people's export markets by war and colonization'.[11] The state protected British producers from the effect of Indian textile imports. When the breakthrough came in the last quarter of the eighteenth century, Britain was part of a general 'world economy' of the 'advanced areas of mainly Western Europe' in relation to colonial and semi-colonial 'dependence economies'.[12]

Hobsbawm emphasized the role of the East India trade. It grew to 25 per cent of Dutch foreign commerce by the second half of the eighteenth century and to a third of the British trade by 1775. He cited Abbé Raynal (from a book first published in 1777) on the goods that brought new needs to Europe and on the stimulus to manufacture of foreign imports at home—Saxony's manufacture of fine porcelain, Valencia's manufacture of Pekins, Switzerland's imitations of muslins and calicoes like those of Bengal, English and French textile prints that employed the best artists: '[A]re we not indebted to India [and China] for all these advantages?' Repeating Raynal's question, Hobsbawm argued back in 1968 that the British industrial economy grew out of the country's commerce, and especially its commerce with the underdeveloped world.[13]

But his contentious statement on the strong impact of foreign trade had powerful detractors. David Landes published *The Unbound Prometheus* one year after *Industry and Empire*. He wrote that, 'while the large and growing home market might conceivably have been enough to elicit and sustain a revolution in the mode

---

[6] Eric J. Hobsbawm, *Industry and Empire: The Making of Modern English Society, 1750 to the Present Day* (Harmondsworth, 1968).

[7] Ibid., 35.   [8] Ibid., 48.   [9] Ibid, 21.   [10] Ibid., 25.
[11] Ibid., 49.   [12] Ibid., 51.   [13] Ibid., 53–4.

of production, the export trade (of which the colonial trade formed only a part) could not by itself have done so'.[14] Landes provided a compelling and indeed enthralling analysis of technological change, but he did not connect this change, as he might have done, to trade. Then a generation of economic historians collected extensive quantitative evidence to discount Hobsbawm's outward-looking position. Agricultural productivity, demographic change, and technological progress within national and small regional frameworks filled the diet of the next generations of students. The perspectives of this research are best summed up in E. A. (Tony) Wrigley's *Continuity, Chance and Change* (1988), which argued for England's peculiar transition from an 'advanced organic economy' to a 'mineral-based energy economy'. England experienced increasing agricultural productivity and increasing population; it escaped the constraints of a fixed supply of land through the use of mineral raw materials, but it still faced the limitations of supplies of these materials. Such constraints were only overcome through the discovery of extensive coal resources and their use in transforming other minerals as well as industrial processes, and above all in creating new forms of heat and mechanical energy, notably steam power. Power sources and the growth in industrial output and productivity appeared unlimited from here on.[15]

Hobsbawm's challenge to set our industrial revolution within a global framework disappeared from historical agendas and was not to re-emerge until the later 1990s. But what did emerge in the 1990s? There were two directions:

First, there was a new focus on the history of consumption and consumer culture on the part of social and cultural historians. This development did not engage many economic historians apart from Jan de Vries, who tried to confront the paradox of stable or even declining wages with the inventory evidence, gathered by social historians, of more and varied consumer and material goods in the possessions of ordinary people. His concept of the 'industrious revolution' connected shifts in consumer behaviour within the household with greater intensity of work in the market place. New goods, especially colonial groceries, stimulated greater industry and led to industrialization.[16] In recent reformulations of his concept, de Vries has incorporated the trade with Asia in fashionable textiles and fragile, breakable ceramics.[17]

Second, there was the turn to global economic history. This was first explored in the debate over the 'great divergence' by the California School. The California School, centred around Ken Pomeranz and his book *The Great Divergence*, which

---

[14] David Landes, *The Unbound Prometheus: Technological Change and Industrial Development in Western Europe from 1750 to the Present* (Cambridge, 1969), 38.

[15] E. A. Wrigley, *Continuity, Chance and Change: The Character of the Industrial Revolution in England* (Cambridge, 1988). For an updated and broader treatment of the argument, see E. A. Wrigley, *Energy and the English Industrial Revolution* (Cambridge, 2010).

[16] Jan de Vries, 'Between Purchasing Power and the World of Goods: Understanding the Household Economy in Early Modern Europe', in John Brewer and Roy Porter, eds, *Consumption and the World of Goods* (London, 1993), 85–132.

[17] Jan de Vries, *The Industrious Revolution: Consumer Behavior and the Household Economy, 1650 to the Present* (Cambridge, 2008). See also Jan de Vries, 'Understanding Eurasian Trade in the Era of the Trading Companies', in Maxine Berg, Felicia Gottmann, Hanna Hodacs, and Chris Nierstrasz, eds, *Goods from the East: Trading Eurasia, 1600–1800* (Basingstoke, 2015), 7–44.

compares the development paths of China and Europe, proposed instead that Europe and Asia faced common external conditions—environment, climate, and demography—and that their different solutions to these conditions created some 'broad similarities' between them, such as their being 'gunpowder empires', before a great divergence in the development paths of the two continents set in after 1800. Pomeranz accounted for this divergence by invoking Europe's greater ease of access to large volumes of coal resources and to further potential resources in the land and resources of wider world colonies. This was in reality an extension of E. A. Wrigley's environmental and resource-based explanation.[18]

But what significance did this research attribute to the impact of trade and of Asia on Europe's economic development? Not a lot. De Vries has recently pointed out a turn away from the interest in trade found in earlier historians of 'encounter', such as Braudel, to a global history that has not engaged with the trade that linked the societies of Eurasia.[19]

Indeed these historians—Kenneth Pomeranz, R. Bin Wong, and Robert Allen— took with little criticism the old questions and analyses of British and European economic history—agricultural productivity, demography and energy constraints— and wrote comparative, not connective global histories. The 'divergence debate' has not changed our pictures of Europe's and Britain's transition in the eighteenth century. The debate focused on what Europe had and Asia had not; it left entrenched a long-standing emphasis on the part played by Britain's superior coal reserves during its industrialization.[20]

Apart from resources, another major issue has been the 'divergence' in wages and prices; indeed this is another version of a much older debate on wages and the standard of living led by Hobsbawm in the 1960s.[21] An intensive and global historiographical effort has focused on demonstrating the higher wages in Britain (indeed just in England) over the rest of the world.[22] Robert Allen, leading this collection of data sets on wages, has used the evidence for higher wages in Britain than elsewhere to explain industrialization. His book *The British Industrial Revolution in Global Perspective* (2009) made this case in two key chapters: 'Why

[18] Kenneth Pomeranz, *The Great Divergence: China, Europe and the Making of the Modern World Economy* (Princeton, NJ, 2000); R. Bin Wong, *China Transformed: Historical Change and the Limits of European Experience* (Ithaca, NY, 1997). For surveys of the 'divergence debate', see Peer Vries, 'The California School and Beyond: How to Study the Great Divergence', *History Compass* 8 (2010), 730–51; Peer Vries, 'Assessing Kenneth Pomeranz's *The Great Divergence*: A Forum', *Historically Speaking* 4 (2011) 10–25; Shami Ghosh, '"The Great Divergence": Politics and Capitalism', *Journal of Early Modern History* 19 (2015), 1–43.

[19] De Vries, 'Understanding Eurasian Trade', 11.

[20] The case was made again in Paul Warde, *Energy Consumption in England and Wales, 1560–2000* (Rome, 2007), and in Robert C. Allen, *The British Industrial Revolution in Global Perspective* (Cambridge, 2010).

[21] Eric J. Hobsbawm, 'The Standard of Living during the Industrial Revolution: A Discussion', *Economic History Review* 16 (1963), 119–34.

[22] Robert C. Allen, 'The Great Divergence in European Wages and Prices from the Middle Ages to the First World War', *Explorations in Economic History* 38 (2001), 411–47; Robert C. Allen, Jean-Paul Bassino, Debin Ma, Christine Moll-Murata, and Jan Luiten van Zanden, 'Wages, Prices and Living Standards in China, 1738–1925: In Comparison with Europe, Japan, and India', in *Asia in the Great Divergence*, special issue of *Economic History Review* 64/S1 (2011), 8–38.

England Succeeded' and 'Why Was the Industrial Revolution British?'.[23] He argued there that Europe's ascent began in the century before the major impact of Atlantic and Asian commerce. High wages in England and the Low Countries continued from the seventeenth century, alongside population growth; the two countries' economies grew fast enough to sustain both. Especially Britain, he argued, was a 'high wage, cheap energy economy'. This combination was the key stimulus for the technological innovation that underpins the Industrial Revolution. High labour costs provided an incentive to replace labour with cheap fuel. Britain's high wages induced a technological change that substituted capital for labour.[24]

Allen has since refined his wage data by adding those of women and children. Now he argues that women's and children's wages rose over the eighteenth century and provided an inducement for the invention and innovation of the spinning jenny and spinning frame. In mid- to late eighteenth-century Britain, on Allen's estimates, women's wages were higher than they had been earlier; and overall wages were higher in Britain than in Italy, Austria, China, or India. This by itself, he believes, caused mechanization.[25] Such simplistic explanations raise many issues explored many years ago by historians of technology, from David Landes and Nathan Rosenberg to H. J. Habakkuk and Nicholas Von Tunzelmann. The economic historian Paul David, for example, contrasts this static explanation, which is based on prices of labour and capital, with a more dynamic explanation. Technologies changed, David argued, in response to 'learning by doing'. In David's hands, technologies were moving entities. Capital-intensive techniques might have been more amenable to further progress than labour-intensive manual techniques.[26]

Given the background of the 'great divergence' debate and the movement of the older questions of economic history into the collection of materials on Asia and Africa, it is easy to see the source of the re-emergence of the 'big data sets' that now dominate global history. This domination appears at its worst in Jo Guldi's and David Armitage's new polemic *The History Manifesto*.[27] At a level more confined to economic history, we find Robert Allen's global wage data. To his older project of collecting comparative estimates of wages across Europe—in an effort to show that Britain was the first country to industrialize because wages there were higher than elsewhere—he added data from India, China, and the Ottoman empire; and, having done this, he regards his analysis as superior and his economic history as global. We now have many comparative data sets, but ultimately how much of an advance

---

[23] Robert C. Allen, *The British Industrial Revolution in Global Perspective* (Cambridge, 2009), 106–31 and 135–55.

[24] Ibid., 138–40. See also Robert C. Allen, *Global Economic History: A Very Short Introduction* (Oxford, 2011), 31–5.

[25] On women's and children's wages, see Jane Humphries, *Childhood and Child Labour in the British Industrial Revolution* (Cambridge, 2010); Robert C. Allen, 'The High-Wage Economy and the Industrial Revolution: A Restatement', *Economic History Review* 68 (2015), 1–22.

[26] For a discussion of this historiography of technological change, see Joel Mokyr, *The Enlightened Economy: An Economic History of Britain 1700–1850* (New Haven, CT, 2009), 268.

[27] Jo Guldi and David Armitage, *The History Manifesto* (Cambridge, 2014).

is this on Simon Kuznet's Cold War projects of data collection on income and productivity in the 1950s?[28]

This type of recent global economic history is not where we find interest in and debate on the impact of trade and of the import of Asian goods on Europe in the early modern period. This debate is now taking place in the relatively new fields of material culture; and, connected with it, there is another new generation of work on consumer culture. This new research is less concerned with comparisons, across nations and regions, between resources and environmental factors, between wages and interest rates, between property rights and literacy, and more concerned with connections across regions and with the cultural impact of the exchange of objects and materials. New questions encircle objects and substances that once appeared only in trade statistics, probate inventories, and museum collections. Separate histories of objects in museums, once confined to a decontextualized material culture of elites, are now a part of our wider histories.

Working closely with museums, Giorgio Riello and Anne Gerritsen have led recent global commodities and luxury networks.[29] The Newberry Collection in the Ashmolean Museum, Oxford—a collection of 1,200 pieces of textiles dating back to the tenth century AD, made in Gujarat, and gathered in Egypt and South East Asia—now forms part of a large history of trade in the Indian Ocean that extends back to the ancient world.[30] Porcelain shards found in East Africa or the cargo of fine porcelain found in 1977 in the early seventeenth-century Dutch East India Company shipwreck of the vessel *Witte Leeuw* off St Helena are no longer curious finds and incidents added to the labels of museum collections and auction catalogues. They are part of a large global story of China's and India's manufacturing priority in the early modern world, their technological achievements, and the large scale of their trade with the rest of the world in exportable commodities like porcelain, silk, and cotton.[31]

Investigating the material culture of exchange raises more questions about these objects. There are issues of cross-cultural production and use, of the many objects produced in one place, traded to others, changed along the way, and acquiring new

---

[28] Simon Kuznets, *Modern Economic Growth: Rate, Structure and Spread* (New Haven, CT, 1966). This volume summarizes and advances arguments developed by Kuznets since 1949. Many of the early articles were published in the journal *Economic Development and Cultural Change* throughout the 1950s.

[29] Anne Gerritsen and Giorgio Riello, eds, *Writing Material Culture History* (London, 2015); Anne Gerritsen and Giorgio Riello, eds, *The Global Lives of Things: The Material Culture of Connections in the Early Modern World* (London, 2015). These two volumes were based on the Global Commodities Network (AHRC 2011–2012) and the Luxury Network (Leverhulme 2013–2015).

[30] Ruth Barnes, *Indian Block-Printed Textiles in Egypt: The Newberry Collection in the Ashmolean Museum, Oxford* (Oxford, 1969); Giorgio Riello, *Cotton: The Fabric that Made the Modern World* (Cambridge, 2013).

[31] Anne Gerritsen and Giorgio Riello, 'The Global Lives of Things: Material Culture, Commodities and History', in Gerritsen and Riello, *The Global Lives of Things*, 1–28, here 20; Anne Gerritsen, 'Global Jingdezhen: Local Manufactures and Early Modern Global Connections', paper presented at the workshop 'History of Commodities and Commodity Chains at the Center of Excellence "Cultural Foundations of Integration"', University of Konstanz, 27–8 February 2009; Anne Gerritsen, 'Fragments of a Global Past: Sites of Ceramic Manufacture in Song-Yuan-Ming Jingdezheni', *Journal of the Economic and Social History of the Orient* 52 (2009), 117–52.

uses and meanings. One classic example is the Chinese porcelain wine pot, which arrived in Italy through various stages of trade, then was fitted with gold and silver mountings and sent on to Northern Europe, where it was used as a teapot. Gerritsen and Riello emphasize the different meanings objects acquired as they were moved over wide parts of the world. Objects became goods, acquiring value as they came to be part of consumer cultures.

Consumer cultures were in turn reshaped by incorporating into the routines of everyday life substances and objects once viewed as exotic. Looking at objects in a museum is certainly not enough. Indeed, there are many different perceptions we project onto the objects of the past. Riello and Adamson recount interpretations of a Japanese suit of armour in the Tower of London that was dated to 1613 and sent as a diplomatic gift to James I by the Emperor Ieyasu. But, right through to the nineteenth century, other such suits of Japanese armour at various European courts were described as given by the emperor of the Mughal, or as the armour of Montezuma, or as the armour of the Moors of Grenada. We now see these sets of armour as diplomatic gifts, understood by both giver and receiver as a pact of trading privileges or as a token of 'commercial understanding'.[32]

Curatorial collections in museums give us access to examples of how objects became goods or gifts; but these collections need to be integrated with the kinds of sources that social historians are now investigating, such as the inventories of the Amsterdam Orphanage and the identifying marks (in the form of textile tokens) of the London Foundling Hospital. Other historians are making use of such English sources as the pauper letters and inventories of the English Poor Laws and of the records of theft kept in the archives of the Old Bailey.[33]

Riello's *Cotton: The Fabric that Made the Modern World* (2013) combined extensive research on museum collections of printed cotton textiles with archival research to argue for the existence of a wide globalized economy that was based on the wider world trade in printed cotton textiles from India throughout the early modern period. This trade stimulated industrialization in Europe, and especially in Britain, as Europeans sought to build an industry to match the fine material attributes of these cottons at low consumer prices.[34] Other researchers, for instance John Styles in his *Dress of the People*, challenged those who claimed easy and direct transfers of Indian textiles into European dress. First, the consumption of new goods had to be learned. Indian cottons did not displace linens worn next to the skin, and East India Company merchants learned this to their cost, through losses on huge shipments of ready-made shirts in the seventeenth century. Styles used unusual records, such as the mid- to late eighteenth-century Foundling Hospital records of

---

[32] Glenn Adamson and Giorgio Riello, 'Global Objects: Contention and Entanglement', in Maxine Berg, ed., *Writing the History of the Global: Challenges for the Twenty-First Century* (Oxford, 2013), 177–94, here 181–2.

[33] Anne McCants, 'Poor Consumers as Global Consumers: The Diffusion of Tea and Coffee Drinking in the Eighteenth Century', *Economic History Review* 61.S1 (2008), 172–200; John Styles, *The Dress of the People: Everyday Fashion in Eighteenth-Century England* (New Haven, CT, 2008); John Styles, *Threads of Feeling: The London Foundling Museum's Textile Tokens 1740–1770* (London, 2010).

[34] Riello, *Cotton*.

thousands of swatches of mothers' clothing that were attached to data about the infants they left in the orphanage. The large numbers of cotton, and especially fustian (a cotton–linen mixture), fabrics worn by predominantly poor urban women demonstrated not the huge penetration of Indian textiles, but the rapidly advancing imitations of Indian fabrics and prints made in small Lancashire mills.[35]

In her analysis of Dutch orphans' parental inventories, Anne McCants found wide evidence of Chinese and Japanese ceramics reaching right through to the middling classes, and even down to artisans of very modest income levels. In further research she has found a wide range of types of textiles owned by these groups, including some expensive Indian printed calicoes. Jane Humphries, Sara Horrell, and Ken Sneath used the records of stolen goods in the Old Bailey to show a much greater impact of aspirations related to fashion and the desire for variety and differentiation among common people than Horrell's and Humphries' earlier research on working-class budgets had conceded. Some of these goods had come from Asia, and many more were European imitations of such goods.[36]

THE ASIA–EUROPE TRADE: QUANTITIES AND IMPACT

Economic historians assessing the impact of trade on early modern European economies still do not accord it great significance. The trade they do recognize is a story of the Atlantic world—the exports of Europe's manufactured goods and the import of the colonial groceries of plantation agriculture: tobacco, sugar, and coffee.[37] The major commodities of wider world trade as a whole were sugar, tobacco, tea, coffee, cocoa, opium, pepper and other spices, silk, silver, wider cotton textiles, and porcelain. None of these was a basic necessity; many began and remained luxuries, and others spread into the consumption patterns of ordinary people in Europe. They were addictive goods or fashion goods—that is, among the goods that people could be induced to work longer and harder for after their basic needs were met, which led to what Jan de Vries called 'the industrious revolution'.[38]

Jan de Vries has recently surveyed the trade data we have and provided a sobering reminder of quantities and economies. The trade with Asia grew at 1.1 per cent per annum, a 25-fold increase over 300 years; the trade with the Americas was at

---

[35] John Styles, *The Dress of the People: Everyday Fashion in Eighteenth-Century England* (New Haven, CT, 2000).

[36] Anne McCants, 'Porcelain for the Poor: The Material Culture of Tea and Coffee Consumption in Eighteenth-Century Amsterdam', in Paula Findlen, ed., *Early Modern Things: Objects and their Histories, 1500–1800* (London, 2013), 316–41; Anne McCants, 'Becoming Consumers: Asiatic Goods in Migrant and Native-Born Middling Households in Eighteenth-Century Amsterdam', in Maxine Berg, Felicia Gottmann, Hanna Hodacs, and Chris Nierstrasz, eds, *Goods from the East: Trading Eurasia, 1600–1800* (Basingstoke, 2015), 197–215; Jane Humphries, Sara Horrell, and Ken Sneath, 'Consumption Conundrums Unravelled', *Economic History Review* 68 (2015), 830–57.

[37] Robert Findlay and Kevin O'Rourke, *Power and Plenty: Trade, War, and the World Economy in the Second Millennium* (Princeton, NJ, 2007), 304–10, 339–45.

[38] Jan de Vries, *The Industrious Revolution.*

least twice as much. At the end of the eighteenth century the volume sent annually from all of Asia to all of Europe was 50,000 tons; this sounds a great deal, but it could be fitted into one of today's container ships. It accounted for 11 per cent of the combined total imports of England, France, and the Dutch Republic and a good deal was re-exported. On average, these goods accounted for 2 per cent of annual earnings in Northern Europe; probably 3–4 per cent in Southern Europe; and 1 pound of goods per annum for each of Europe's 100 million (though, to be sure, these goods were very unequally distributed).[39] But, while the overall statistical estimates of the Asia–Europe trade do not appear to be large and are much lower than those for the Atlantic trade, the impact of this trade on European economies was significant when it comes to shifting material cultures and industrial priorities.

If we look at textiles and porcelain alone, we see prodigious amounts of these goods reaching Europe from the seventeenth century. Riello's recent estimates show that 1.3 million pieces of cotton textiles reached Europe by the late 1680s, and 24.3 million pieces over the period 1665–1799.[40] A typical order to Bengal in the 1730s was for about 590,000 pieces in thirty-eight different types and ninety-eight different varieties.[41] The indicators for porcelain are similar. The British alone imported between 1 and 2 million pieces of Chinese porcelain a year by the early eighteenth century. The Dutch imported 43 million pieces from the beginning of the seventeenth century to the end of the eighteenth century; the English, French, Danish, and Swedish companies imported another 30 million pieces. In just one year, namely 1777–8, European ships unloaded 700 tons of porcelain.[42]

A driving force behind the extensive trade in Chinese porcelain from the late seventeenth century was the new energy put into trading another fashionable, but also addictive substance: tea. Over the later seventeenth and early eighteenth centuries, tea imports into Europe increased steadily, being amplified over the period by smuggling. By the 1770s smuggling dominated the English tea trade; 7–8 million pounds were smuggled in, while legal tea in East India Company warehouses was 5.9 million pounds. The Tea Commutation Act of 1784 reduced the duty from 119 per cent to 12.5 per cent, and legal tea in the warehouses rose to 16.3 million pounds in 1785 and to 21 million pounds by 1800–1.[43]

Equally important to the history of this trade were the varieties and qualities of the goods traded. The trade contained many types of cotton textiles; East India companies standardized the range of porcelain imports they collected over the course of the eighteenth century, but private commissions to captains and supercargoes

[39] Jan de Vries, 'The Limits of Globalization in the Early Modern World', *Economic History Review* 63 (2010), 710–33.

[40] Riello, *Cotton*, 107, 116.

[41] Antony Farrington, *Trading Place: The East India Company and Asia* (London, 2002), 69.

[42] Maxine Berg, 'Britain's Asian Century: Porcelain and Global History in the Long Eighteenth Century', in Laura Cruz and Joel Mokyr, eds, *The Birth of Modern Europe Culture and Economy 1400–1800: Essays in Honour of Jan de Vries* (Leiden, 2010), 133–56; Robert Finlay, 'The Pilgrim Art: The Culture of Porcelain in World History', *Journal of World History* 9 (1998), 141–88, here 168; also Robert Finlay, *The Pilgrim Art: Cultures of Porcelain in World History* (Berkeley, CA, 2010).

[43] Hoh-Cheung Mui and Lorna Mui, *The Management of Monopoly: A Study of the English East India Company's Conduct of its Tea Trade, 1784–1833* (Vancouver, 1984), 91–3.

traded the hugely varied goods that filled Europe's porcelain cabinets over the period. British consumers acquired early on a taste for tea, which was fostered by European, and especially Swedish smugglers in the mid-eighteenth century. North British consumers preferred higher-quality Congua over lower-quality Bohea tea; merchants brought in several varieties of green and black teas to feed demands for different tea types at different times of the day.[44]

Levels of shipping and commitment of labour were high. Eleven thousand European ships set out for the Cape Route to India, Southeast Asia, and China. Eight thousand of them returned; many of those that stayed engaged in the private intra-Asian trade, which was equally vital in the chain of acquiring goods for Europe. The Dutch ships, like the Portuguese, grew in size from about 650 tons at the beginning to 1,000 tons in the 1770s. Although costs were high and risks even higher, the belief in the fabulous wealth to be gained in the trade in luxury goods brought from beyond the Cape prompted Europeans not just to invest in the companies but to devote enormous labour power to these ventures, long after monopoly company profits on these trade goods were declining. The manpower that conducted this trade was enormous. For the Dutch voyages alone, nearly 1 million took ship from Europe over the two centuries between 1602 and 1795; only a third of these returned to the Dutch Republic. The Vereenigde Oost-Indische Compagnie (VOC; United East India Company) relied on many foreigners, especially Germans and other North Europeans, to fill its large needs for sailors, merchants, clerks, and craftsmen for its overseas settlements—as well as for soldiers. It also made use of many Chinese and Indian seafarers.[45]

HOW WAS THE ASIA–EUROPE TRADE CONDUCTED, AND WHAT WERE ITS LIMITATIONS?

The voyages to acquire these goods from the East were long and costly, taking seven months to a year to Bombay and two to three hundred days to Canton in the first half of the eighteenth century. Many were also constrained in their sailing times by the monsoons. English East India Company ships sailed from the Thames in the spring. They were provisioned at St Helena, then had to arrive at the Cape of Good Hope by August to catch the north-easterly monsoons. They could then reach the Malabar or Coromondel coasts by November or December. After arriving and unloading at Surat, then later at Bombay or Madras, they often stopped at other ports along the coasts. Goods at the warehouses had to be selected and loaded, others sought out, orders, accounts, and correspondence exchanged, ships repaired and reprovisioned. Homeward journeys were timed for mid-December to mid-February,

[44] Andrew McKillop, 'A North Europe World of Tea: Scotland and the Tea Trade, *c.*1690–*c.*1790', in Maxine Berg, Felicia Gottmann, Hanna Hodacs, and Chris Nierstrasz, eds, *Goods from the East: Trading Eurasia, 1600–1800* (Basingstoke, 2015), 294–308.

[45] De Vries, 'The Limits of Globalization'; Jan de Vries and A. Van der Woude, *The First Modern Economy: Success, Failure and Perseverance of the Dutch Economy, 1500–1815* (Cambridge, 1997), 636–47.

in order for the ships to catch the south-westerly monsoon. Ships sought to leave Western India for their homeward journey by early December and Eastern India by early January. Journeys to India therefore took a year and a half to two years or more. Dutch ships sailed to Batavia in Indonesia (present-day Jakarta) but did so throughout the year, and so they were less constrained by the seasons than those of their rivals. The Dutch ran a Christmas fleet and an Easter fleet that left the Netherlands in the months of December and April. The return voyage had to reach the North Sea before the autumn gales and before the date of the auctions of Asian goods, that is, by the end of the summer; October was too late. Batavia was the centre of the company's intra-Asian trade and shipping. It was well provided with all the necessary warehouses, shipyards, and other workshops for the storage of all sorts of commodities and for the repair and maintenance of ships.[46]

The China voyages became very competitive during the eighteenth century. Smaller European companies—first the Ostend Company, then the Swedish and Danish companies—joined the race to acquire the best and cheapest tea to trade back to Europe. Speed was of the essence. The Ostend voyages averaged 198 days between 1724 and 1732. The Danes took 189 days between 1732 and 1772 and the Dutch averaged 225 days between 1734 and 1795.[47] The innovation required for achieving this kind of speed entailed new ship designs, with smaller ships and smaller crews—developments led by the smaller companies. States and navies played their part in reducing protection costs, piracy, and insurance rates.[48]

Much of this trade in eastern goods was organized and carried out by state monopoly companies, the East India Companies, but also by working in tandem with many private traders, including Indian merchants and shipowners, Armenian and Portuguese traders and intermediaries, and a wide range of European private traders who worked in the intra-Asian trade and also in the interstices of the companies.

As we know, the early modern trade to Asia was primarily conducted through national monopoly companies that competed vigorously with one another: the English East India Company (EIC) (1600), the VOC (1602), Companies des Indes Orientales (1684), the Ostend (1722), and Danish (1668 and 1732) and Swedish companies (1731). In addition to these there were numerous short-lived ventures or projects that failed before they got off the ground, all partially funded by European states, from Genoa to Trieste and Prussia.

Adam Smith blamed on the monopolies the fact that the growth of the East Indies trade was slower than that of the Atlantic trade: 'Europe, however, has hitherto derived much less advantage from its commerce with the East Indies, than from that with America.' He explained this by the exclusive privileges of the East India Companies. 'The English, French, Swedes and Danes have all followed their

---

[46] Femme Gaastra and J. Bruijn, 'The Dutch East India Company's Shipping, 1602–1795, in Comparative Perspective', in J. Bruijn and Femme Gaastra, eds, *Ships, Sailors and Spices: East India Companies and their Shipping in the 16th, 17th and 18th Centuries* (Amsterdam, 1993), 177–208, here 190, 199.

[47] Ibid., 195.

[48] Ken Pomeranz, 'Commerce', in Ulinka Rublack, ed., *A Concise Companion to History* (Oxford, 2012), 105–30.

[the Dutch] example, so that no great nation in Europe has ever yet had the benefit of a free commerce to the East Indies.'⁴⁹ Jan de Vries agreed with Smith that it was monopoly that limited the globalization of eastern trade. In addition, high shipping costs and high costs at the trading ports constrained innovation. The logistics of the Cape Route and high levels of manning on ships, which remained close to 20 men per 100 tons after 1620, added to the high costs of the protection and administration of trading ports, and the trade became less profitable over time.⁵⁰

Throughout the seventeenth and eighteenth centuries the companies maintained monopolies on the trade to Europe but had to compete and cooperate with one another and with private traders in the intra-Asian trade. They also had to compete back in Europe, selling their goods at auction to foreign and domestic merchants. The classic case was the tea trade, where the Ostend and the Swedish companies sold their tea at auction in order for it to be re-exported; then it was sold on the English market, competing with the EIC's tea, and frequently smuggled in to avoid the tea tax. The tea smuggled into Britain in this way equalled the tea sold on the legal market right up until the dramatic decline in the tea tax in 1784.⁵¹

The monopolies did not operate this trade on their own. Private merchant ventures and interlopers were there from the start and private trade became increasingly important, especially in the intra-Asian trade. After 1815 British private ships, now supported by the security of the Royal Navy, played a much greater part, and this coincided with the doubling of the growth rate in the volume of Asian exports to Europe after the 1790s. Private traders landed their goods in European ports for 20–23 per cent less than East India Company traders.⁵² What we also see, of course, in the nineteenth century is a shift in the composition of Asian imports into Europe: no longer the manufactured luxury goods of the East, they were increasingly raw materials.

KNOWLEDGE ECONOMIES AND INSTITUTIONS

Were there any advantages to this company organization of a trade in luxury goods that made a transition into export ware goods? Adam Smith, as we have seen, thought not. But this trade was not operated on an either–or basis. The companies interacted with private traders and allowed a large degree of privilege trade as an incentive to supercargoes, captains, and mariners.⁵³ It is important to look at the advantages that this interaction of monopoly and private trade brought to factors

⁴⁹ Adam Smith, *The Wealth of Nations* (Oxford, 1976 [1776]), vol. 1, 499 (Book IV).
⁵⁰ Jan de Vries, 'Understanding Eurasian Trade'.
⁵¹ William Ashworth, *Customs and Excise: Trade, Production, and Consumption in England, 1640–1845* (Oxford, 2003).
⁵² De Vries, 'Understanding Eurasian Trade', 33–4.
⁵³ Maxine Berg, Tim Davies, Felicia Gottmann, Hanna Hodacs, Chris Nieerstrasz, and Meike von Brescius, 'Private Trade and Monopoly Structures: The East India Companies and the Commodity Trade to Europe in the Eighteenth Century', in Emily Erikson, ed., *Chartering Capitalism: Organizing Markets, States and Publics*, special issue of *Political Power and Social Theory* 29 (2015), 123–45; Maxine Berg, 'Introduction', in Maxine Berg, Felicia Gottmann, Hanna Hodacs, and Chris Nierstrasz, eds, *Goods from the East: Trading Eurasia* (Basingstoke, 2015), 1–6.

recently considered, once again, in what economists refer to as 'the new trade theory' and 'new economic geography'. As Paul Krugman has outlined, economists have rediscovered the increasing returns of intra-industry specialization and localization outlined by Alfred Marshall a century ago. One key part of these externalities was 'knowledge spillovers'.[54] Economic and social historians who explored 'flexible specialization' in the 1980s had rediscovered the labour market pooling, the mysteries of the trade 'in the air', and regional concentrations of interconnected materials and parts suppliers.[55] These knowledge spillovers also applied to goods traded over very long distances, and in this case to the institutions of trade conducted through East India Companies and the trading factories they established around the Indian Ocean.

Knowledge economies and information flows connected with and benefited from those factors considered in the new institutional economic history, which incorporated relations of trust, informal credit and mercantile arrangements, legal and market frameworks, and modes of governance.[56] Factory production in the Indian Ocean world relied on knowledge economies, as discussed by Joel Mokyr, and on the nodes of mercantile networks, as discussed by Emily Erikson.[57] A vital connector was information flows. Historians of science discuss 'the brokered world' of intermediaries.[58] The factories and entrepôts were information nodes in Eurasian trade; they were information-rich in ways far beyond those of the bazaars and markets of independent merchants.[59] The factories and the company–private merchant connections also brought advantages in specialized trade and opportunities to gain from trade in different types and varieties of textiles, porcelain, and tea. As Krugman restated, 'consumers sought variety'. Even given that different national East India Companies supposedly fulfilled much the same function, there were new opportunities for trade to meet the demand for variety.

Despite limitations on profitability, over two centuries East India Companies brought key manufactured goods from Asia on a large scale—goods that were to have a profound impact on European material cultures and industrialization. Furthermore, quantities and varieties of goods arriving at a particular moment and in particular places could have an impact outweighing overall economic impact over the course of a century or more.

[54] Paul Krugman, 'Increasing Returns and Economic Geography', *Journal of Political Economy* 99.3 (1991), 483–99; Paul Krugman, 'The Increasing Returns Revolution in Trade and Geography', *American Economic Review* 99 (2009), 561–71.

[55] Charles Sabel and Jonathan Zeitlin, 'Historical Alternatives to Mass Production', *Past & Present* 108 (1985), 132–76.

[56] See Ann Carlos and Santhi Hejeebu, 'Specific Information and the English Chartered Companies, 1650–1750', in Leos Müller and Jari Ojala, *Information Flows: New Approaches to the Historical Study of Business Information* (Studia Historica 74) (Vammala, 2007), 139–68; Woodruff D. Smith, 'The Function of Commercial Centers in the Modernization of European Capitalism: Amsterdam as an Information Exchange in the Seventeenth Century', *Journal of Economic History* 44 (1984), 985–1004.

[57] Joel Mokyr, *The Enlightened Economy: An Economic History of Britain, 1700–1850* (New Haven, CT, 2010); Emily Erikson, *Between Monopoly and Free Trade: The English East India Company, 1600–1757* (Princeton, NJ, 2014).

[58] Simon Schaffer, Lissa Roberts, Kapil Raj, and James Delbourgo, eds, *The Brokered World: Go-Betweens and Global Intelligence, 1770–1820* (Purdue, IN, 2009).

[59] De Vries, 'Understanding Eurasian Trade', 14–17.

GLOBAL MICROHISTORY AND INDIAN MUSLINS

Rather than large data sets comparing factors of production and financial and property institutions over very long time series, micro and local studies of key conjunctural events can offer much by way of a historical explanation of the impact of the Asia trade on the European economic transition. Microhistories have frequently been contrasted with global histories as diametrically opposed approaches. Microhistory has been presented as an approach relying on close archival investigation and on the interrogation of a specific event and accessing different individual perceptions, frequently through the use of court or inquisition records.[60] Global history, by contrast, has recently been presented as the history of large areas of the world, written over the *longue durée* and relying on secondary sources.[61] But in reality its methods are ones of scale and point of view. Global history can bring two far parts of the world into focus; microhistorical investigation allows us to demonstrate their connections and the stimulus this provided to major historical transitions, such as industrialization and divergence. I, therefore, turn to one late eighteenth-century luxury and fashion manufacture, cotton muslins, to investigate how company merchants accessed these, the difficulties they faced, how a supply crisis developed by the later 1790s, and how a new British muslin manufacture emerged to meet these demands. Here I investigate two places, Dhaka in Bengal (today's Bangladesh) and Stockport in Lancashire; one decade, the 1790s, and specifically the final years of that decade; and a document, John Taylor's 'Account of the district of Dacca by the Commercial Resident Mr John Taylor' (1800).[62]

Consider a place of manufacture we should now all know of: Dhaka in Bangladesh, recently the site of the collapse, in April 2013, of the Rana Plaza factory, which produced cheap clothing for the West; we know it now as the place where at least 1,130 people were killed in a complex of badly constructed factories employing very low-wage workers to make cheap products for world markets. But Dhaka was another place in the eighteenth and even the nineteenth centuries. Robert Orme, the eighteenth-century orientalist, wrote in the early 1750s of Dhaka, where all the cloths for the use of the king and his seraglio were made in 'such wonderful fineness as to exceed ten times the price of any linens permitted to be made for Europeans, or anyone else in the kingdom'. In the 1760s the Dutch traveller Stavorinus wrote that 'Bengal muslins were made so fine that a piece of twenty yards in length or even longer could be put into a common pocket "tobacco box" (i.e. snuff box).'[63]

---

[60] Giovanni Levi, 'On Microhistory', in Peter Burke, ed., *New Perspectives on Historical Writing* (Cambridge, 2001), 97–119.

[61] Francesca Trivellato, 'Is There a Future for Italian Microhistory in the Age of Global History?' *California Italian Studies* 2.1 (2011), 1–26.

[62] Account of the district of Dacca by the Commercial Resident Mr John Taylor in a Letter to the Board of Trade at Calcutta dated 30th Nov. 1800. Home Miscellaneous 456E, India Office Records, Asia, Pacific, Africa Collections, the British Library.

[63] Cited in Sushil Chaudhury, *From Prosperity to Decline: Eighteenth Century Bengal* (New Delhi, 1995), 133. For further discussion of the Dacca muslin manufacture, see Maxine Berg, 'The Merest Shadows of a Commodity: Indian Muslins for European Markets 1750–1800', in Berg et al., *Goods from the East*, 119–34.

From the mid-eighteenth century the English East India Company's investment in South Asian textiles increased sharply; textiles accounted for 53.5 per cent of its total exports to Europe in 1758–60, but in 1777–9 the figure went up to 78 per cent.[64] European markets became increasingly dominated by textiles from Bengal; these provided 40 per cent of the cargoes exported to Europe. The internal market and private trade were even more important than company trade. The company controlled only 25 to 33 per cent of the weaving population, and private trade took over 60 per cent of the cotton-piece goods produced in Dhaka.[65] The key European framework for this muslin trade was an explosion, from the 1770s on, in the fashion demand for loose-fitting women's gowns made from this soft, fine, and even translucent fabric.[66] These were Jane Austen's muslins.

In the 1790s the quantities and qualities of Dhaka's cloth declined, and weavers were squeezed beyond their production capacity by pressures from local zamindars and company intermediaries. Some abandoned their manufacture, turning to agricultural employment; others absconded or died, their heirs inheriting their debts. Reports by the Dane Jacob Scavenius in 1790 and by John Taylor, the English chief resident in 1800, described the plight of the weavers: 'Through unwearying industry and with the help of a few paltry tools these poor people, nevertheless, are able to produce the prettiest and finest cloths without the use of machines.'[67]

In the later 1790s Taylor also wrote of the desperate state of the weavers. He connected it to the rise of a new cotton, and even muslin, manufacture in England.[68] Against the background of these difficult years of the 1790s in the production of Bengal muslins we can place the rising manufacture of new British muslins. Samuel Crompton's spinning mule, invented in 1779, was known as 'the muslin wheel'.

---

[64] Ghulam Nadri, *Eighteenth-Century Gujarat: The Dynamics of its Political Economy, 1750–1800* (Leiden, 2009), 136.

[65] Rajat Datta, 'The Commercial Economy of Eastern India under Early British Rule', in H. V. Bowen, Elizabeth Mancke, and John G. Reid, eds, *Britain's Oceanic Empire: Atlantic and Indian Ocean Worlds, 1550–1850* (Cambridge, 2012), 340–69, here 344 and 365; Rajat Datta, *Society, Economy and the Market: Commercialisation in Rural Bengal, c.1760–1800* (New Delhi, 2000). See also Om Prakash, 'From Negotiation to Coercion: Textile Manufacturing in India in the Eighteenth Century', *Modern Asian Studies* 41 (2007), 331–68, here 342 for discussion of India's internal market for cotton textiles as the exclusive preserve of indigenous merchants. Dhaka—more specifically Lakshmipur, a place of fine-quality textile manufacture 68 miles down the river from Dhaka—was the place where Linda Colley found the private trader James Crisp, Elizabeth Marsh's husband, seeking, like others in the 1770s, a lucrative private trade in the brilliantly coloured cloths of the area. He competed with the East India Company, other European private traders, and Asian merchants to attract indigenous weavers to his own trade. See Linda Colley, *The Ordeal of Elizabeth Marsh: A Woman in World History* (New York, 2007), 245–55. On the operation of private trade in the area, see Bishnupria Gupta, 'Competition and Control in the Market for Textiles: Indian Weavers and the English East India Company in the Eighteenth Century', in Giorgio Riello and Tirthankar Roy, eds, *How India Clothed the World: The World of South Asian Textiles, 1500–1850* (Leiden, 2009), 281–308.

[66] This point is made by John Styles in correspondence with the author, 26 May 2014. See also John Styles, *The Dress of the People: Everyday Fashion in Eighteenth-Century England* (New Haven, CT, 2007).

[67] Cited in Ole Feldbæk, 'Cloth Production and Trade in Late Eighteenth Century Bengal: A Report from the Danish Factory in Serampore', *Bengal Past & Present* 86.2 (1967), 124–41, here 126.

[68] John Taylor, *A Descriptive and Historical Account of the Cotton Manufacture of Dacca in Bengal, by a Former Resident in Dacca* (London, 1851). See a review and summary in *Athenaeum* no. 1253, 1 November 1851, pp. 130–40, 137–43, and 181–221; here 181.

One of the early Lancashire manufacturers to use it, Samuel Oldknow, competed directly with Indian products and faced a 'severe burst of competition' whenever East India Company vessels unloaded cargoes of textiles.[69] By 1784 Oldknow had over 1,000 weavers working for him, and his entire output supplied the London fashion markets for muslins and calicoes. His London merchants demanded frequent design change, month by month, and insisted on high quality. They conveyed a charged competitive atmosphere. By the spring of 1789 muslins made up nine-tenths of Oldknow's production; high proportions of these quality goods were figured and highly differentiated.[70] The London merchants at the time prepared a history of the rise and progress of British muslin and calico manufacture for the Lords of the Council for Trade, claiming that 'the object they [the inventors] grasped was great indeed—to establish a Manufacture in Britain that should rival in some measure the Fabrics of Bengall'.[71]

By the 1790s muslins were already high fashion, not just among the elites but among the middling classes too. Supply constraints in India's greatest textile region, as we have seen, were great. Competition there, in spite of the EIC, was as intense as among Lancashire's early cotton manufacturers, who were striving to meet, now with new machinery, the constantly changing fashion demands of London markets.

From the mid-eighteenth century on the consumption of British cotton calicoes (most of them made with cotton wefts and linen warps) boomed. The only Indian all-cotton fabric that retained a British market was that of plain muslins. They did not fall under the prohibitions on importing printed calicoes that prevailed at the time. They did face high tariffs, but this mattered little to wealthy high-fashion consumers. Lancashire manufacturers, John Styles has argued, were already providing British markets with lightweight printed cottons; Arkwright's water frame of 1769 allowed machine production of cotton warps, and thus a real British substitute for quality Asian cotton. This achievement was a response to technologies earlier developed for silk manufacture, and especially to the quality material represented by silk and by its nearest rival, high-quality Indian cottons. It was not quantity, but quality that drove this mechanization. It was not high wages in Britain, but the high prices of European silks and imported Indian cottons; it was the fashion markets in Britain and the American colonies that drove forward mechanization.[72] If this was the case for Arkwright's water frame, it was even more so for Samuel Crompton's spinning mule ten years later—a machine focused on producing quality muslins to compete with quality Indian muslins, which were becoming increasingly difficult to access.

[69] George Unwin, *Samuel Oldknow and the Arkwrights* (Manchester, 1924), 3.
[70] Ibid., 67 and 96 (Salte to Oldknow, 23 May 1786; 18 and 19 October 1787).
[71] Unwin, *Oldknow and the Arkwrights*, 63.
[72] John Styles, 'Fashion, Textiles and the Origins of the Industrial Revolution', *East Asian Journal of British History*, vol. 5, March 2016. Special Issue, Anglo-Japanese Conference of Historians 2015, pp. 161–91.

CULTURES OF CONSUMPTION
OF GOODS FROM THE EAST

What did the trade in goods from the East achieve? If we look at this question as economic historians, we see the Asia–Europe trade haunted by unpredictability, high risk, and eventually low and declining profit margins. But economic historians also accord other advantages to the Indies trade: the information that flowed through and from large trading organizations. The East India Companies could gather and analyse large quantities of commercial, political, and technical information. Along with this they gathered botanical, linguistic, and cultural information. Private traders both contributed to and benefited from it, as well as from the infrastructure and military security created by the companies. There were indeed many 'knowledge spillovers'. But there was another kind of information that was not just about enhancing the access and supply of Asia's goods to Europe. It was about understanding factors that stimulated changing consumer demand in Europe. This is where the economic historians need the cultural historians.

Economic historians Horrell and Humphries have very recently conceded the part played by fashion and tastes in the ownership of goods. Their data sets indicated that consumers moved towards more expensive cotton stockings and counterpanes and away from worsted and linen. This was not about emulation but about respectability, politeness, and differentiation. They sought greater variety and higher quality.[73] Jan de Vries argued that the information spread by trade with the East was also one of product differentiation; this information had a demonstration effect on European consumers.[74]

Lynn Hunt's recent *Writing History in the Global Era* (2014) links a cultural history of society and the self in later seventeenth- and eighteenth-century Europe to how exotic goods were experienced and chosen. Internal European factors interacted with wider global forces. Europeans developed a culture in which exotic goods made sense. Larger numbers, especially in specific places with higher discretionary incomes, wanted more choice. We have to ask what was in the minds of Europeans encountering strange goods, from chocolate and rhubarb to cottons and porcelain. This was about an interaction between self and society. A desiring, stimulus-seeking self developed in tandem with social awareness—different varieties and individual choices among these newly demarcated social groups. Tastes changed as experiences of the self changed.[75]

We can understand the varieties of goods carried in those East India Company cargoes and constantly sought in East India Company orders. This was no random collection of goods, but one constantly responding to large-scale buyers at the autumn and spring company auctions. These buyers were in turn closely affected by the choices of all the small retailers and peddlers they sold on to. French colourways

---

[73] Humphries, Horrell, and Sneath, 'Consumption Conundrums', 853–4.
[74] De Vries, 'Understanding Eurasian Trade', 17.
[75] Lynn Hunt, *Writing History in the Global Era* (New York, 2014), 114–41.

dictated Swedish silk imports from China; company orders went out with letters that criticized the colours of earlier cargoes and demanded dynamic, responsive, and intuitive designs and patterns.[76] Dutch and English East India Companies and private European and Indian merchants competed vigorously for the finest figured jamdani muslins.

The fashion demand that underlay the issues of agency and identity behind the sense of self also developed in a social framework. Cities were a part of this story. The close urban integration of towns and cities in the Low Countries and Britain provided a context for the sociability that fostered new experiences of consuming Asian goods. That sociability demanded goods that signalled gentility, politeness, and respectability—and, increasingly from the mid-eighteenth century, sensibility. This sensibility was sought in the appearance of modest dress, simple unstructured lines, and fine plain fabrics evoking country living.[77] Thus arose a new fashion for muslin dress fabrics and accessories differentiated by fineness, raised spotting, and embroidery.

Dhaka, and even the rest of Bengal, could not now provide for the wide social demand for this fabric. Newly mechanized cotton mills in Lancashire responded rapidly to the urgent letters of London merchants to 'raise the spots', produce more varieties of fineness, and make borders and cables.[78] The East–West trade was dynamic—knowledge about the goods, curiosity in their crafts and aesthetics, all those factors we now study under material culture—helped to change tastes. But it was also the self and society that changed those tastes.

The Asia–Europe trade changed consumer cultures; it also changed industries, but only in some places. Britain and Northern Europe were to make these gains, as were parts of southern France, Catalonia, and northern Italy. Imitative industries like Samuel Oldknow's muslin factory and Josiah Wedgwood's fine earthenware manufacture rose to the challenge of Europe's new taste for Asia. Why did goods from the East impact on the industries of some parts of Europe, which generated new industrial imitation and growth, but not of others? Many parts of Europe developed their own porcelain works; calico-printing works also proliferated. But the ones that reached deep into industrial structures, generating a new dynamic that lasted, developed in industrial regions already on their way and ready to receive them, such as Lancashire and Staffordshire. They also had the connections to the merchants who fed London's fashion markets. Those merchants had built their marketing expertise in the Indies trade, and this is why the major mercantile outlets for the new English-made products continued to centre on London. The economic advantages of these new British and European industrial regions paralleled the cultural and social advantages of the towns and cities of the Low Countries

---

[76] Hanna Hodacs, *Silk and Tea in the North: Scandinavian Trade and the Market for Asian Goods in Eighteenth-Century Europe* (Basingstoke, 2016).

[77] Styles, *The Dress of the People*, 181–94.

[78] Maxine Berg, 'Quality, Cotton and the Global Luxury Trade', in Giorgio Riello and Tirthankar Roy, eds, *How India Clothed the World: The World of South Asian Textiles, 1500–1850* (Leiden, 2009), 391–414, here 407.

and Britain; they, too, were already developing the sociability of experiencing the new goods of the wider world.

Global trading systems fed into the interconnectedness of economic development across Europe and Asia. A global history seeking the underlying connections between parts of the world can help us to understand a key stimulus to transformations within individual regions. This global history is not one that relies on large-scale comparisons over long time periods and builds large data sets. It relies instead on the new sources and methods historians have developed in recent decades, including microhistory, the study of material culture, and a cultural history connected to economic history. It seeks conjunctures and connections among specific places, times, and individuals.

Let us return now to Eric Hobsbawm. He attended the 'Writing the History of the Global' conference at the British Academy in 2009.[79] There he reconfirmed the key question of structure and chronology that has shaped his history writing: How did we get from the past to the present? Many will disagree with such a perspective on the past, but the present does shape the questions we take to our investigation of the past. He also challenged global history: Why had it thus far made so little reference to Africa and to the American world before Columbus? Eight years on from this we still need to ask: Just how global has our global history been, and how much of it is still separated off into area specialisms?

[79] Maxine Berg, ed., *Writing the History of the Global: Challenges for the Twenty-First Century* (Oxford, 2013).

9

Industrial History, Working Lives, Nation, and Empire, Viewed through Some Key Welsh Woollen Objects

Pat Hudson

This chapter illustrates the 'material turn' in history that has taken place in the past two decades or so: a shift involving the increasing use of objects and artefacts as historical evidence to be 'read' and interpreted in a similar way to documents.[1] Greater concern with objects in daily use and in social practice has stemmed from the wider flowering of cultural history that marked the 1980s and 1990s. With the latter's emphasis upon postmodern uncertainties and poststructural complexities, the cultural turn as a whole did not find favour with Eric Hobsbawm. However, greater emphasis upon material culture, as demonstrated here, can provide other-wise 'impersonal forces' of history with the sort of grounded human understanding that Hobsbawm often portrayed. The subject is approached in this chapter through study of the textile industry in Wales. I consider how analysis of specific items of woollen clothing can not only complement conventional archival research on the history of the industry and its region but also provide fresh insights into changes in manufacturing, trade, consumption, working lives, and national identity.[2]

This research feels particularly appropriate for the current volume because Eric Hobsbawm had a long and close connection with Wales, spending family holidays for more than two decades in a cottage on the Clough Williams-Ellis estate near Port Madoc. A large number of academics, intellectuals, and eccentrics could be found living in or visiting that vicinity between the 1960s and the 1980s, all attracted by a nucleus of Cambridge contacts of the Williams-Ellis family—and especially of 'Kitto' Williams-Ellis, who had been killed in Italy during the Second

[1] For more on this, see K. Harvey, ed., *History and Material Culture: A Student's Guide to Approaching Alternative Sources* (London, 2009); L. J. Jordanova, *The Look of the Past: Visual and Material Evidence in Historical Practice* (Cambridge, 2012); P. Findlen, ed., *Early Modern Things: Objects and Their Histories, 1500–1800* (Basingstoke, 2013); Anne Gerritsen and Giorgio Riello, eds, *Writing Material Culture History* (London, 2015).

[2] This chapter benefited from discussion at the international conference 'History after Hobsbawm', held at Senate House, London, 29 April–1 May 2014, and from the advice of the editors of this volume, particularly John Arnold. My thanks go also to Michael Freeman, former curator at Ceredigion Museum and an expert on Welsh national dress, who saved me from some important errors. Remaining faults are entirely my own.

World War. This visiting community included Bertrand Russell, Edward and Dorothy Thompson, the physicist and Nobel Prize winner Patrick Blackett, Joseph Needham and his mistresses, Munia and Cynthia Postan, John Maddox, the editor of *Nature*, and the antinuclear activist and painter Tom Kinsey, the 'only known anarchist Master' of the Snowdonia fox hounds.[3]

In his autobiographical volume *Interesting Times*, Hobsbawm asks what brought these outsiders to the Welsh mountains. He answers:

> Certainly not the search for comfort. In our Welsh cottages we voluntarily lived under the sort of conditions we condemned capitalism for imposing on its exploited toilers. None of us, *even given* the Spartan middle class styles of the 1950s, would have dreamed of accepting such standards in our everyday lives in London or Cambridge...It took two or three days after arrival to dry the house out enough to make it roughly habitable, and even then it was almost impossible to keep warm except in odd corners, in spite of paraffin heaters...and the fuel for our fireplaces which metropolitan intellectuals, dressed in the local style like tramps, could be seen chopping in the drizzle outside their back doors.[4]

In this essay I connect with Hobsbawm not only by looking closely at dress suitable for Welsh conditions, but also by seeking, through study of the material culture of the past, a political engagement with the present. I start by considering the material turn in general, its potential and its pitfalls. I then briefly outline the main features of the history of textile manufacturing and trade in Wales in recent centuries, deriving my story from business records, official reports and surveys, newspapers, and other conventional sources. Finally, some key products of the industry are introduced and examined. These suggest that an understanding of the human–object relationship can be central to blending together economic, social, and cultural history in a way that benefits all three.[5]

ECONOMIC AND SOCIAL HISTORY
AND MATERIAL CULTURE

Since their inception as professional disciplines in the early part of the twentieth century, economic and social history have drawn heavily upon the Cartesian approaches of social science: the positivistic analysis of cause and effect, achieved through a mix of qualitative and quantitative evidence and associated research methods. In economics in particular—but also in the broader field of social science—mechanical models, methods, and analogies have been dominant. In the humanities, by contrast, hermeneutic interpretive approaches have been given much greater scope, and these increasingly influenced the nature of history in the 1980s and 1990s, at the time of the ascendency of the cultural turn. The material turn took a lead from the latter: when applied to economic and social history, it takes us away from a primary emphasis on mechanical models of causation, production,

---

[3] Eric Hobsbawm, *Interesting Times: A Twentieth-Century Life* (London, 2002), 238–40, 241.
[4] Ibid., 240.   [5] Gerritsen and Riello, eds, *Writing Material Culture History*, 7.

and exchanges and orients us towards hermeneutic methods designed to tease out the *meanings* and the *feelings* of actions and things.

Early histories of material culture arose from the impulse to study how human beings in different cultures and contexts satisfied their fundamental needs for food, shelter, and clothing: how housing was constructed within the limits of locally available materials, how domestic warmth and lighting were created, how food was cooked, and how tools and technologies spurred changes and improvements in basic patterns and daily routines of existence, as well as in cultivation and in subsistence manufacturing.[6] Subsequently, the habitual character of the interaction between humans and material objects—an interaction that occurred through the pragmatic use to which objects and tools were put—has been regarded as a 'technoculture' of everyday life. Such a technoculture is seen to require ethnographic study in order to discover how 'things' shape daily lives and are constitutive of them.[7] The strong emphasis upon technologies and raw materials in material culture studies, particularly in the United States, was joined in the 1990s and afterwards by an equally important impulse to study the material cultures created by changing patterns of consumption and by the circulation of goods bought in the market.[8] This brought the material turn into closer alignment with parallel changes in economic and social history.[9]

Economic and social history, in Britain and elsewhere, had long privileged the study of production over that of consumption, of supply over demand. While the supply side remained the main focus, economic historians concentrated upon invention and innovation, production processes and productivity. The input from social history to economic history was largely confined to the areas of labour relations, the living standards of workers, and social conditions that affected the supply and quality of the workforce or of entrepreneurs. These were the main elements in the historiography of industry that preoccupied most British historians of the postwar decades. Eric Hobsbawm stood out at the time, because alongside these conventional topics he was engaged in analysing social conflict and was also interested in the symbols, rituals, and structures of the national imagination.[10] Nevertheless, his methods were and remained those of mid-twentieth-century social science. His use of microhistory was minimal and he was intolerant of the relativistic claims of postmodernism, implying that it could only be a diversion from the

---

[6] The key early work was Norman J. G. Pounds, *Hearth and Home: A History of Material Culture* (Bloomington, IN, 1989).

[7] See Phillip Vannini, ed., *Material Culture and Technology in Everyday Life: Ethnographic Approaches* (New York, 2009).

[8] The key authority is Daniel Miller, whose work has been at the forefront of material culture studies in Britain, inside and outside the home; an example is Daniel Miller, *Stuff* (Cambridge, 2010).

[9] Steven Lubar and W. David Kingery, eds, *History from Things: Essays in Material Culture* (Washington DC, 1993) includes contributions on technologies, raw materials, the formal attributes of artefacts, and utilitarian and social functions. For essays that bring historians and anthropologists together in their study of traded goods, including textiles, see Arun Appadurai, ed., *The Social Life of Things: Commodities in Cultural Perspective* (Cambridge, 1986).

[10] Eric Hobsbawm's classic collection of essays edited with Terence Ranger, *The Invention of Tradition* (Cambridge, 1983), though not without its later critics, remains a landmark in this field. My examination of Welsh textiles relates strongly to some of the themes explored therein.

political commitment that drove his sort of engagement with the past. There was little scope in Hobsbawm's history for the more speculative tools of hermeneutic enquiry or *Alltagsgeschichte*. Yet these are by no means antithetical to writing the sort of history that is relevant to the present and to the future, as I shall attempt to demonstrate here.

Once demand was in the ascendant in economic history, as it came to be from the 1980s or so, the way was open for new insights from archaeological excavation, cultural anthropology, fashion, design, museum studies, and art history. These joined with economic history in providing new perspectives on the processes of economic differentiation and betterment as driven by changes in work, technology, and consumption as well as in ideas and culture. Thus recent decades have seen major studies of artisanal skills, households and their contents; interpersonal relationships of material support and credit; solidarities and identities formed in common cultural values and symbols; textiles and dress; fashion and furnishings; reading and books; comestibles and the objects and rituals surrounding their consumption. But these phenomena cannot be studied in isolation from their impact upon changes in supply through shifts in manufacturing processes, techno-logical and organizational innovations, and the reorientation of national and global markets and exchanges. Thus there now exists a much livelier dialogue between economic history and cultural history than there was in Hobsbawm's heyday. It is a dialogue that breaks down the boundaries between the two and demands a wide range of non-documentary as well as documentary evidence to sustain it.

The material turn inevitably involves attention to the tools, possessions, cloth-ing, shelter, and adornments that frame everyday lives and to the personal, familial, and communal practices associated with them. It is not just about objects but about the meanings that 'things' hold for people in the processes of both producing and using them. It is thus deeply connected to forms of microhistory. Indeed the material turn lies at the point where the local or the micro and the wider—national or global—approaches to society and history coincide. Attention to the histories and mentalities embodied in material objects makes it impossible to study global history without also studying microhistory and, by the same token, makes micro-history into a source that can answer bigger, often global, questions.[11] The Welsh textiles studied here are treated not simply as objects but as sources and clues for understanding a wider array of issues related to the economic and social history of Wales as a national entity and as part of a wider imperial and global formation.

In western historiography, to date, the history of things has been dominated by counting possessions and by analysing them largely as communicators of personal and social identities expressed through display, manners, and the cult of the domes-tic or of male sociability and commerce. In this dispensation, as Trentmann has argued, 'things are interesting not in and of themselves or with respect to their material properties but solely because their appropriation promises to reveal

---

[11] There is an extensive historiography associated with microhistory in it various forms. For my own observations on the practice, see Pat Hudson, 'Closeness and Distance: A Response to Brewer', *Cultural and Social History* 7.3 (2010), 375–85.

processes of social stratification or identity formation...historical material culture studies have been more about culture than about material'.[12] Too often in the material turn objects have been instrumentalized, reduced to signifiers whose meanings and value lie not in their intrinsic qualities or in their being an embodiment of skills or quality, but in cultural convention and fashion. Thus 'recent research has...yielded teleological views, in which modern consumers and systems of meaning serve as the lens through which objects and materiality are observed'.[13] Studies covering the early modern period and onwards have focused, often somewhat anachronistically, upon consumer choice and shopping. The accent has been upon goods bought new in the marketplace by upper- and middle-class consumers, so that the material possessions of the working masses escape the net of things studied as material culture. What attitudes and sensitivities did ordinary workers and working consumers attach to objects and materiality? The question of how, and to what effect, substances and products, with their particular properties and 'personalities', are put to use in daily social practice is rarely considered, especially in anglophone historiography.[14] Often absent is a 'study of the way the specific character of people emerges from their interaction with the material world through practice'.[15]

Thus what I ask here is not whether people in a particular social hierarchy and regional context had more or fewer goods, whether they were voluntary or involuntary consumers, or whether they consciously and deliberately practised conspicuous consumption, using symbols to express a given social identity or to oil the wheels of social communication. I question the view that things are only instruments of meaning appropriated by a prior subject, suggesting instead that they are integral parts of relationships and subjectivities manifest in work and in leisure, in the private and in the public spheres. I consider how goods were habitually experienced in relation to weather, climate, cultivation and husbandry, labouring, crafting, and nurturing: how objects interacted in an organic way with their owners and, in the process, influenced work routines and social life.[16] Here materiality is seen as a process activated when the object (in this case, clothing) is put to use (in this case, worn). As Roger Pol-Droit has suggested, 'we

---

[12] Frank Trentmann, 'Materiality in the Future of History: Things, Practices, and Politics', *Journal of British Studies* 48.2 (2009), 283–307, here 288.

[13] Bert de Munk, 'Artisans, Products and Gifts: Rethinking the History of Material Culture in Early Modern Europe', *Past & Present* 224 (2014), 39–74, here 41.

[14] Here one might refer to Michel de Certeau's view of the often unconscious 'tactics' involved in using objects in everyday life. His co-author Luce Giard writes: 'This glass of pale, cool, dry wine marshals my entire life in the Champagne. People may think I am drinking: I am remembering' (Luce Giard, Michel de Certeau, and Pierre Mayol, *The Practice of Everyday Life: Living and Cooking*, Berkeley, CA, 1998, vol. 2, 188).

[15] Daniel Miller, 'Stone Age or Plastic Age?' *Archaeological Dialogues* 14.1 (2007), 23–7, here 26. See also Kim Siebenhüner, 'Things That Matter: Zur Geschichte der materiellen Kultur in der Frühneuzeitforschung', *Zeitschrift für Historische Forschung* 42.3 (2015), 373–409.

[16] The intellectual polarization of choice and habit in analysing market societies, despite the inherent compatibility of the two processes, is discussed in Pat Hudson, 'Choice and Habit in History', *Shakai-Keizaishigaku/Socio-Economic History* 72.3 (2006), 3–18 (initially a plenary lecture delivered at the Annual Japanese Economic History Society Conference Hitotsubashi University, Tokyo, April 2005).

live our clothes as though they were alive. Your trousers do the walking... they are integrated into the body's memory.'[17] The protective qualities, as well as the itch, of a flannel shirt on the skin, the heat generated by a milled woollen overcoat in the rain, the familiarity and protectiveness of miners' woollen drawers, the life-enhancing warmth of a specially designed knitted cap, the succour of large families enabled by the properties of a nursing shawl—all of these contribute to my story and to an interpretation of national and international history that I expose for consideration.

THE WELSH TEXTILE INDUSTRY: A BRIEF SURVEY

The textile history of Wales is largely the history of its woollen industry.[18] Although there were pockets of mechanized cotton manufacturing in the nineteenth century and of synthetic fibre production in the twentieth, especially in the north-east of Wales, the bulk of textile manufacturing, which used locally available wool and indigenous skills, lay in the production of woollen cloth and clothing. Localized woollen manufacture for subsistence was a vital element in the survival of a large proportion of the agrarian population of Wales from the thirteenth through to the twentieth century. The peripheral status of Wales reinforced the importance of cloth manufacture, alongside sheep farming, for poor farm tenants and cottagers on large estates, many of which were owned by unimproving English absentees.[19]

Knitting was also a vital and widespread by-employment. Knitting on a commercial scale, particularly hosiery, sustained an arc of the population of Mid and North Wales in the early modern period through an international market centred on Bala. Contemporary estimates suggest that, by the 1780s and 1790s, some 190,000 pairs of stockings valued at around £18,000 annually made their way from Bala to London and abroad.[20] Hand-knitting, from early modern times until well into the twentieth century, was a common by-employment for both women and men, undertaken indoors and outdoors, as they went about their other domestic and pastoral tasks, as illustrated in Plate 9.1.

---

[17] Roger Pol-Droit, *How Are Things? A Philosophical Experiment*, trans. Theo Cuffe (London, 2005), 52–3, 74. Attachment to a Welsh rural–industrial way of life might have been similarly conjured through the feel of wool flannel against the body.

[18] The history of the textile industries in Wales lacks a modern study. This section leans heavily upon the only substantial book on the subject: J. Geraint Jenkins, *The Welsh Woollen Industry* (Cardiff, 1969).

[19] Walter Davies, *General View of the Agriculture and Domestic Economy of North Wales* (London, 1810); Walter Davies, *General View of the Agriculture and Domestic Economy of South Wales* (London, 1815), vols 1–2; M. J. Jones, 'The Merioneth Woollen Industry, 1758–1820', *Y Cymmrodor* (1939), 181–208; Sir John E. Lloyd, ed., *A History of Carmarthenshire* (2 vols, Cardiff, 1935, 1939); C. A. J. Skeel, 'The Welsh Woollen Industry in the Sixteenth and Seventeenth Centuries', *Archaeologia Cambrensis* 47.2 (1922), 220–57.

[20] This is the equivalent of around £2M today. See Thomas Pennant, *Tours in Wales* (London, 1781), vol. 2, 211; Davies, *General View North Wales*, 404–6; Jenkins, *Welsh Woollen Industry*, 211; measuringworth.com (accessed 26 March 2016).

Pat Hudson

Historically one can get some idea of the ubiquity and spread of the wool textile industry from the location of place names that contain the word *pandy*, which is Welsh for 'fulling mill'. This criterion underestimates the numbers of fulling mills but is a useful indicator of their wide distribution. Many of the sites identified had a continuous history as centres of textile processing from medieval or early modern times to the early twentieth century (see Map 9.1).

When William Crankshaw was employed by the University of Wales to investigate the poor state of Welsh textile manufacturing in the mid-1920s, he found

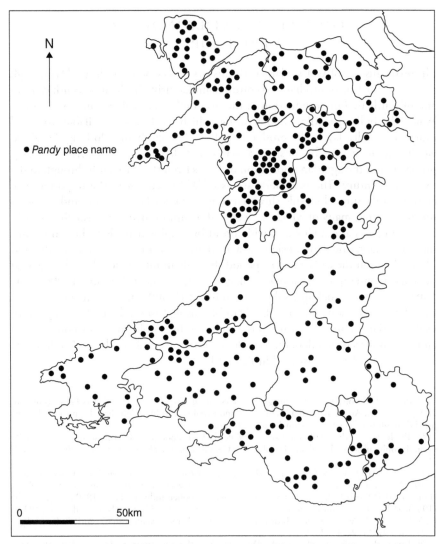

Map 9.1 Distribution of Pandy (fulling mill) place names in Wales. Based on J. Geraint Jenkins, *The Welsh Woollen Industry* (Cardiff, 1969), 103; redrawn by author.

small-scale establishments run by part-time farmers, elderly spinsters, fishermen, and poets with out-of-date water-powered technologies and handlooms, whose practices had changed little since medieval times. The majority employed only three or four part-time workers. Their main business was to take wool from local farmers and process it, to order, into cloth, shirts, coatings, blankets, and shawls, generally for the farmer's own use; money changed hands only at times of periodic reckonings.[21] A study undertaken a few months earlier than Crankshaw's had highlighted similar characteristics but that time with more than a tinge of nostalgia: it saw the textile industries of Wales as part of a distinctive communal culture and way of life.[22]

At the time of the Crankshaw survey in 1925, there were 192 textile factories in operation in Wales. Crankshaw visited 140 of them. Of these, sixty-seven had under four employees, a further forty had between four and twelve, and only twenty-six had more than twelve persons directly employed on the premises. Sixty per cent of the premises used *only* water power. Fifty-five mills had four looms or fewer, twenty-one had only handlooms, and twenty-six kept one or two handlooms alongside powered machines. Some mills were of course more commercialized, much bigger, and more technologically advanced; but even here the use of second-hand and second-rate technology from Yorkshire was common. Most mills, even those of the larger commercial variety, carried out all processes, from sorting wool to weaving and fulling.[23] Crankshaw was fascinated by the relaxed part-time communal and craft nature of the proliferation of small mills. One, run by two spinsters in Carmarthenshire, was immaculate, with roses on the outer walls and geraniums on the windowsills of the weaving room. But he found most mills to be dirty and disorganized. In one factory a butter churn turned by the spinning-machine shaft ran alongside the textile machinery, and cows were housed in the basement of the same building.[24]

The larger, more mechanized mills found by Crankshaw testified to the fact that, alongside localized part-time production, there had been and continued to be waves of serious commercial activity. The first had occurred in the thirteenth and fourteenth centuries, largely in the south and west, where Flemish weavers had settled and from where friezes were exported via designated ports such as Tenby and Carmarthen, to be then taken from Bristol via France into various parts of Europe. A significant trade in 'cottons' (not made of cotton but of wool) then grew from the late sixteenth century. These were produced largely in Mid Wales and traded via Shrewsbury to London or Bristol for export. 'Cottons' found a market particularly in France but also in Spain, Portugal (including the Canaries and the Azores), Russia, and New England.[25]

---

[21] William P. Crankshaw, *Report on a Survey of the Welsh Textile Industry Made on Behalf of the University of Wales* (Cardiff, 1927).

[22] Anna M. Jones, *Wales*, vol. 4 of *The Rural Industries of England and Wales* (4 vols, Oxford, 1927).

[23] Fine dyeing and finishing on the part of those few firms catering for the top end of the market was sometimes done in Yorkshire.

[24] Crankshaw, *Survey of the Welsh Textile Industry*, 7–9.

[25] Jenkins, *Welsh Woollen Industry*, 96–115; Skeel, 'Welsh Woollen Industry'.

The semi-colonial status of Wales dictated that all Welsh woollens for long-distance trade had to be sold through and finished by the monopoly of the Shrewsbury drapers between the late sixteenth and the early nineteenth centuries. This meant that the highest value-added process in the trade, and thus much of the profit of the industry, were not enjoyed in Wales.[26] For similar reasons the industry within Wales lacked native sources of capital, credit, and commercial enterprise. These factors undoubtedly held back industrial development but cannot fully explain the relative backwardness of the industry by comparison with its counterpart in England, because they themselves were partly a result of the much less commercialized nature of the industry west of the border.[27]

All-wool flannel, which was to become the dominant Welsh product in the modern period, started noticeably to figure in the trade from the mid-seventeenth century on.[28] Production was at first centred in Monmouthshire and Merioneth and was geared towards both domestic and transatlantic markets. Coarser webs or Welsh plains were also produced, especially in Merioneth and round Machynlleth. These were exported for slave blankets. As they needed little finishing, some of this trade was smuggled directly, via Barmouth, Derwen-Las, and the Dovey estuary, avoiding Shrewsbury.[29] The map in Plate 9.2 indicates the main locations of the commercial textile industry of Wales that are mentioned in this chapter.

By the early nineteenth century the industry was relatively buoyant, the Shrewsbury monopoly was finally broken, and manufacturing came to be centred in Newtown and Llanidloes, where cloth halls were established and where carding and spinning began to be mechanized in small workshops and factories. Nevertheless, crises in transatlantic markets in the 1830s, competition from Yorkshire, lack of capital, and poor market accessibility meant that the commercial industry of Mid Wales soon found itself in decline.[30] Labour unrest from exploited workers, who preferred agricultural work—generally better paid and more independent—and often combined it with textiles as a by-employment, aggravated matters; the area was, justifiably, a centre of bitter Chartist struggles.[31] Some firms survived into the later nineteenth century by finding a niche in high-quality flannels; they were aided by Pryce Jones, who pioneered mail order in Britain (from Newtown, Powys) and who initially promoted only Welsh flannels to his extensive client list.[32] A small number of other concerns in North and Mid Wales survived in the longer term, partly assisted by tourist demand and partly through

---

[26] T. C. Medenhall, *The Shrewsbury Drapers and the Welsh Wool Trade in the XVI and XVII Centuries* (Oxford, 1953). For more developed explanations, see Jenkins, *Welsh Woollen Industry*, 119–23, 183–6.

[27] The part-time employment and the craft nature of the bulk of the industry were major factors in the slow development of more commercialized manufacturing.

[28] A few forlorn early pieces have survived in the Foundling Museum (London) collection of tokens, dating from the mid-eighteenth century: see John Styles, *Threads of Feeling: The London Foundling Hospital's Collection of Textile Tokens, 1740–1770* (London, 2010).

[29] Jenkins, *Welsh Woollen Industry*, 126; Chris Evans, *Slave Wales: The Welsh and Atlantic Slavery 1660–1860* (Cardiff, 2010), 51–4.

[30] Skeel, 'Welsh Woollen Industry'.   [31] Jenkins, *Welsh Woollen Industry*, 148, 150, 167.

[32] Jenkins, *Welsh Woollen Industry*, 116–215; 165–7; for the Pryce Jones archive, see http://brecon-leisurecentre.powys.gov.uk/uploads/media/M_D_PJ_bi.pdf (accessed 3 November 2015).

the emulation of cheaper Yorkshire-style mixtures.[33] One or two continued well into the twentieth century, with success in exports, especially to the United States (see Plate 9.3). But the 1850s and 1860s brought bankruptcies and mill fires to many Mid Wales firms, accompanied by the immiseration and emigration of workers.[34]

The absence of coal and, more importantly, competition from Rochdale flannel in the Lancashire and Liverpool markets, opened up by the eighteenth-century Lancashire Canal and Leeds and Liverpool Canal and by improved road links, were factors in the decline of the commercial industry in Mid Wales. As many mill owners were part-time poets and clerics and some were dissolute characters, the poor quality of entrepreneurship may also have been important factors in the Mid Wales crisis. In 1806, for example, Reverend George Evors left his South Wales parish in charge of a curate in order to become *the* entrepreneur of the textile industry in Newtown. A magistrate, petty despot, and scourge of the Chartists, he accumulated a large fortune, little of which was ploughed back in the industry. He died in mysterious circumstances in 1844, after an overdose of laudanum, with £8,000 on his person.[35]

Revival and greater success for the Welsh woollen industry, from the 1860s, occurred 80 or 90 miles away, in South West Wales. By 1895 this regional shift had become very obvious: there were more than 300 mills in the Cardigan/Carmarthen/Pembrokeshire border area (see Plate 9.2), which had not previously been a major centre of the trade.[36] The speciality cloth of the region remained all-wool flannel, but the industry now concentrated almost entirely upon supplying occupationally and culturally specific cloth and clothing for the rapidly expanding population of the South Wales industrial region. The south-west took off in textile manufacturing with the coming of the railway to towns and villages of the area in the 1860s (see Plate 9.2). This linked the industry directly to its main markets. The efflorescence of the wool textile industry in South West Wales (c.1880–1945) and the nature of its products during this period are the main focus of this essay.

Demand was boosted by the rapid growth of proletarian consumers in the coal-field regions: at its peak in 1913, the coal mining industry alone employed over 230,000 men; perhaps a further 100,000 were employed in other mining, quarrying, the metalliferous trades, and heavy engineering.[37] Although bolts of cloth were sold directly to retailers, drapers, and outfitters, unlike in other parts of Britain, textile mills in Wales commonly had sewing rooms and employed resident and outworking knitters and sewers to make up speciality garments, particularly

---

[33] Crankshaw, *Survey of the Welsh Textile Industry*, 10.

[34] Jenkins, *Welsh Woollen Industry*, 156–70.

[35] In economic status, this was equivalent to over £12M in 2016. See Jenkins, *Welsh Woollen Industry*, 142–3, 146; and the issues of 21 March 1835, 10 November 1838, and 17 November 1838 of *Cambrian*—all at http://newspapers.library.wales (accessed 10 June 2013). For current values, see measuringworth.com (accessed 26 March 2016).

[36] Jenkins, *Welsh Woollen Industry*, 247–308.

[37] J. Williams, *Digest of Welsh Historical Statistics* (2 vols, Cardiff, 1985); Arthur H. John, *The Industrial Development of South Wales, 1750–1850: An Essay* (Cardiff, 1950); L. J. Williams and T. Boyns, 'Occupation in Wales, 1851–1971', *Bulletin of Economic Research* 29 (1977), 71–83.

workwear: primarily work shirts, drawers, skirts, aprons, shawls, and socks.[38] Suitings and coatings were also manufactured. These were repeatedly fulled, so they were very durable and almost impermeable to water.

With its main markets in the industrial valleys of South Wales, the fortunes of the Welsh woollen industry in the twentieth century became tied to the long-term fate of coal mining and the metalliferous trades and to the specialist requirements of Welsh male proletarian consumers in particular. Its prosperity was also linked, though to a lesser extent, to the popularity of linsey skirtings, woollen dress materials, and shawls that formed both everyday and ceremonial national dress for women.[39] Production of flannel mixes for uniforms during both wars temporarily boosted the industry. Wartime demand brought government grants for re-equipping but only increased the conservatism of the sector and its general unwillingness to develop new products and styles beyond flannels.[40] Cotton mixes (forming what was termed 'Angola flannel'), introduced during the wars for army cloths, under-mined the unique claim of the Welsh industry to be producing all-wool flannel and exacerbated the slack postwar demand. When the Rural Industries Bureau employed Marianne Straub in the 1930s to go around mills introducing their own-ers to new designs, in an attempt to rejuvenate the industry, she struggled against the conservatism of the sector.[41]

By the late 1960s and 1970s workers were starting to be issued with scientific-ally researched 'health and safety' workwear of enhanced durability. At the same time the domestic market for everyday and female workwear became increasingly flooded with fabrics and fashions made elsewhere that were cheaper and much more fashionable than Welsh woollens.[42] Both the nationalist impulse in consumer preference and the desire to fit in with a national cultural identity in dress were gradually diluted by large-scale immigration into the Welsh valleys from England and elsewhere in the late nineteenth and early twentieth centuries and by the spread of more cosmopolitan ideas via newspaper and magazine advertising, radio

[38] This is apparent in all of the surviving sales ledgers of textiles businesses in South West Wales from the later nineteenth century onwards. The business records at St Fagans National History Museum were researched in detail for this essay. Other records survive at the National Woollen Museum, Drefach Velindre.

[39] For histories of the Welsh working dress and its links to Welsh costume, see F. G. Payne, 'Welsh Peasant Costume', *Folk Life* 2 (1964), 42–57; Christine Stevens, 'Welsh Peasant Dress: Workwear or National Costume?' *Textile History* 33.1 (2002), 63–78; and Michael Freeman's website at https://welshhat.wordpress.com (accessed on 26 April 2017).

[40] Sometimes such grants encouraged the installation of machinery suitable only for Angola flannel and not for all-wool weaving, which made adjustment to postwar all-wool products difficult: see Crankshaw, *Survey of the Welsh Textile Industry*, 10. For more detail on post-1918 conditions, see Jenkins, *Welsh Woollen Industry*, 276ff.

[41] Ann Sutton, *The Textiles of Wales* (Ashford, 1987); Rural Industries Bureau Records D7, espe-cially D7/78 The National Archives (TNA). Straub is famous among other things for designing iconic patterns for the London Underground upholstery that are still in use.

[42] The history of flannelette (a brushed cotton made to look like flannel) is a particularly important part of this story, associated as it is with a rising number of deaths and injury from fires caused in circumstances where nightdresses and other items were getting too close to domestic coal fires in the early to mid-twentieth century: Vivienne Richmond, *Clothing the Poor in Nineteenth-Century England* (Cambridge, 2013), 69ff.

and the cinema. Some new products were introduced in the middle decades of the twentieth century and proved popular, especially with tourist and non-local markets: blankets (*carthenni*) with distinctive designs that dated from the late eighteenth century and double-weave bedspreads (most were necessarily woven on existing narrow looms and stitched up the middle), fabrics for furnishings, and some light tweeds, for example.[43] But the majority of producers remained wedded to traditional lines of flannel workwear, in the expectation that the heavy industries would eventually revive.[44] The bulk of mills disappeared between the 1940s and the 1970s. And the industry survives today only in a small number of high-end niche producers and in a few 'heritage sector' mills (some within museums), largely serving the tourist market (see Maps 9.2a–b).

THE APPROACH THROUGH OBJECTS

After this 'bare-bones' narrative of the industry based upon a range of conventional evidence, I turn now to the insights one can bring to the story of Welsh woollens by examining a selection of particular pieces of clothing that were some of the main-stays of the manufacture. Seemingly advantageous locational factors (including local wool supplies, indigenous skills, water power sites, and market potential), which are in many respects equal to those in Yorkshire, suggest that Wales might have been a major site of commercial, industrialized production in Britain in the nineteenth and early twentieth centuries. But the industry flourished commercially only within certain parameters, dictated by the political and cultural as well as by the economic environment and by the products that this environment demanded.

The Welsh Wig

I start my examination with a piece of early knitwear (see Plate 9.4). Although hand-knitted stockings were the foundation stone of commercial knitting in Wales for several centuries, the Welsh wig was an important piece of manufacture from the mid-eighteenth century, remaining popular until the late nineteenth century. Its particular properties and the circumstances that made it fashionable help us to understand how demand for hand-knitted items was sustained outside as well as inside Wales.

Welsh wigs were made in Hobsbawm's North Wales. Many were sold by itiner-ants and peddlers along the stagecoach route of what is now the A5 to Holyhead.[45]

---

[43] These fabrics are well described in Sutton, *Textiles of Wales*. The origins of the *carthenni* design are captured in the pattern book of William Jones, weaver of Holt, 1775–82. See the Denbighshire Record Office (a catalogue digitized by the National Archives, now at GB0209 BD-A.pdf).

[44] Jenkins, *Welsh Woollen Industry*, 276–87; Crankshaw, *Survey of the Welsh Textile Industry*, 15; Rural Industries Bureau: Welsh Textile Industry, Ministry of Agriculture and Fisheries, 1948–57, MAF 113/324 TNA.

[45] This was the major route for stagecoaches that carried passengers to Ireland via the ferry from Holyhead in Anglesey. Many such passengers were travelling long distances and, depending upon the class of their ticket, large numbers were partly or entirely exposed to the elements.

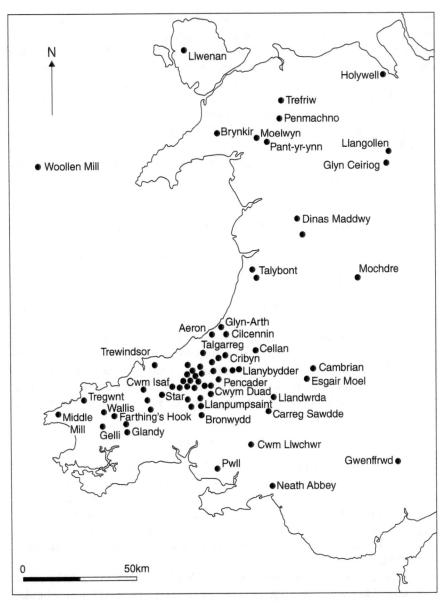

N

• Llwenan

Holywell●

● Trefriw
● Penmachno
●Brynkir ●Moelwyn
●Pant-yr-ynn
Llangollen
●
Glyn Ceiriog ●

● Woollen Mill

● Dinas Maddwy
●

Mochdre
● Talybont ●

●Glyn-Arth
Aeron ● ●Cilcennin
●
Talgarreg ●Cellan
Trewindsor ●Cribyn
Cambrian
● ●●Llanybydder ●
●Pencader Esgair Moel
Cwm Isaf ●Cwym Duad ●
●Star ●Llandwrda
Tregwnt ●Llanpumpsaint
Wallis ● Carreg Sawdde
Middle ●Farthing's Hook ●Bronwydd
Mill
Gelli ●Glandy
● Cwm Llwchwr
Pwll
Gwenffrwd ●
●Neath Abbey

0   50km

Map 9.2a–b Location of commercial wool textile mills in Wales 1947 and 1967. The white circles in 9.2b show weaving shops. Based on J. Geraint Jenkins, *The Welsh Woollen Industry* (Cardiff, 1969), 345–6; redrawn by author.

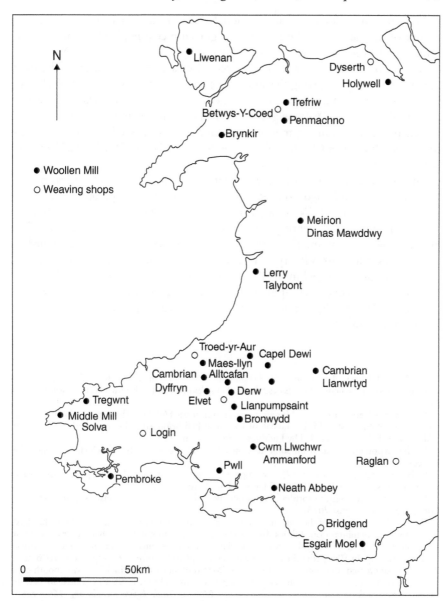

Map 9.2a–b Continued

Others entered national and international trade via the Bala market. After the decline of the hair wig at the end of the eighteenth century, balding men needed something to keep them warm, especially during road travel, and the Welsh wig could be worn under a normal hat, woollen loops at the back keeping the neck draught free as well as giving the appearance of a decent growth of hair. Such wigs were also worn by elderly men indoors and as nightcaps. Two Dickens characters are described wearing Welsh wigs that testified to their urban prominence far from Wales, particularly among men of a certain age: both Mr Fezziwig, Scrooge's former employer in *A Christmas Carol*, and Solomon Gill in *Dombey and Son* wore Welsh wigs.[46]

The example illustrated in Plate 9.4 dates from around 1854.[47] It was one in a sample sent from Bangor to Leeds with the intention of supplying soldiers who fought in the Crimea.[48] Welsh wigs are mentioned in relation to British imperial wars of the nineteenth century, and also in relation to exploration and the forging of new trade routes. They were on the list of pieces of clothing provided to men during the Ross Victory Expedition (1829–33), which pioneered steam power in ships and stayed in the Arctic for four years.[49] They were also included on the list of sledging equipment recommended by McClintock in 1851.[50] Indeed the Welsh wig was approved issue for polar expeditions as late as the Nares venture in 1875.[51]

---

[46] Charles Dickens, *A Christmas Carol* (London, 1858), 34; Charles Dickens, *Dombey and Son* (London, 1848), 42, where the wig is described as being 'as plain and stubborn a Welsh wig as was ever worn'.

[47] St Fagan's National History Museum; accession number F69.353. The wig was donated to the museum in 1969, by Miss M. L. Horsfall of Devon. It had belonged to her grandfather, the son of William Horsfall, who was killed by Luddites in Yorkshire in 1812.

[48] This hypothesis is based on some text on a label affixed to the tin in which it reached the museum.

[49] For this expedition, see http://www.rmg.co.uk/discover/explore/john-and-james-clarke-ross-north-west-passage-expedition-1829–33 (accessed on 26 April 2017).

[50] See http://erebusandterrorfiles.blogspot.co.uk/2011/12/black-men-welsh-wigs-and-knights.html (accessed 16 August 2013).

[51] The Welsh wig was not the only or the first piece of knitted headgear from Wales (or its borders) to add to Britain's military capabilities. Brown-wool knitted Monmouth caps had become the most common headgear in docks and at sea in the sixteenth and seventeenth centuries; see the article 'Monmouth Cap' in Wikipedia (https://en.wikipedia.org/wiki/Monmouth_cap, accessed 26 April 2017). Drake ordered 36 dozen such caps for his West Indies expedition in 1596. Monmouth caps were approved issue for the British Navy in 1663 (see Adm/2/1725, p. 95 PRO, cited in Beverly Lemire, *Dress Culture and Commerce: The English Clothing Trade before the Factory, 1660–1800*, Basingstoke, 1997, 14). Captain John Smith, a leader of the Jamestown Colony, wrote a pamphlet for English colonists with a Monmouth cap on the list of recommended kit: see Jennifer Carlson, 'A Short History of the Monmouth Cap', at http://www.personal.utulsa.edu/~marc-carlson/jennifer/Monmouth.htm (accessed 7 November 2015). Monmouth caps were ordered as part of the outfitting of 100 men heading for the New World in the 1620s by the Massachusetts Bay Colony. The caps were described as 'thick, warm, fulled by hand- and foot-beating and much favored by seamen' and some were red in colour (Anne L. Macdonald, *No Idle Hands: The Social History of American Knitting*, New York, 1988, 3). Monmouth caps were exported in large quantities from Bristol to the American colonies for settlers and for slaves; see Peter Kemp, ed., *The Oxford Companion to Ships and the Sea* (Oxford, 1979), 741–4; Diana de Marly, *Working Dress: A History of Occupational Clothing* (London, 1986). For more on the history and shape of the Monmouth cap, see Kirstie Buckland, 'The Monmouth Cap', *Costume* 13 (1979), 23–37.

Flannel Workwear

The crys fach

I now turn to a range of garments that were produced by the Welsh woollen industry from the mid-nineteenth century and that helped to sustain heavy industry and coal mining during the decades of British industrial prowess internationally. I start with the *crys fach* (small or short shirt), which appears to be a speciality garment unique to Wales (see Plate 9.5). Designed for maximum safety, comfort, and durability in the hot and dangerous foundry environments of the metalliferous trades, the shirt was worn alongside a piece of wet flannel, grasped between the teeth to prevent singeing to the mouth and face.[52] The *crys fach* was worn by furnace men in iron, steel, tinplate, and copper, by hot mill employees in tinplate, and probably also by roller men in copper and iron.

The *crys fach* is short at the front, to prevent any loose fabric from getting caught up in equipment or flames. It was worn loose and untucked over trousers, the open underarm gussets and absence of a collar contributing to the cooling circulation of air around the body. In arduous workplace conditions, before the invention and introduction of safety workwear and attendant legislation,[53] workers had to provide their own work clothes; and the safety properties of all-wool flannel in shirt designs were well known. The industry catered to this demand.

As shown in Table 9.1, wool has a much higher ignition point than any other fibre and a high limiting oxygen measure (LOI). Given that the ambient oxygen concentration in air is 21 per cent, the LOI of wool (25–6 per cent) makes it much more difficult than other common fibres to ignite. In addition, partly because of its high moisture content, it has a low heat of combustion and low heat release. While most textile fibres are polymers containing mainly carbon and hydrogen, which burn easily, wool contains nitrogen and sulphur, which make it harder to burn; and it does not melt or drip. Once ignited, the keratinized cells of wool fibre even create a self-extinguishing char.[54] Lady Bell considered a 'good-quality' flannel shirt 'absolutely necessary' for men in the Yorkshire iron works not simply to prevent chills but also because the gas and fumes destroyed cotton fibres. For the same reason she suggested that work trousers were often turned inside out when bought and resewn with woollen thread before use.[55] Welsh workwear destined for the metalliferous trades was generally sewn with wool or linen thread during manufacture. The decline of the *crys fach* was abrupt and can be dated to the 1950s and 1960s. This coincides with the beginnings of company-issue work clothing, but also with the transition from hand mills to strip mills in the tinplate industry.[56]

[52] For information on the kind of clothing worn in the metalliferous trades, and especially on the *crys fach*, I am indebted to Robert Protheroe Jones, Curator, Heavy Industries, Department of Industry, Museum of Wales.

[53] Mainly the Health and Safety at Work Act of 1974.

[54] Zirpro wool (an early flame retardant) was developed initially by the International Wool Secretariat; the idea was to make wool even more flame-retardant by using its reaction with zirconium or titanium salts. See L. Benisek, 'Zirpro wool textiles', *Fire and Materials* 8.4 (1984), 183–95.

[55] Lady Bell, *At the Works: A Study of a Manufacturing Town* (London, 1907), 71–2.

[56] Observation based on an array of visual sources: Robert Protheroe Jones, email communication, 3 March 2013. The *crys fach* was never the mainstay of the industry and may have been produced

Table 9.1 Flammability properties of selected fibres

Fibre	Ignition Temperature °C	Limiting Oxygen index (%)	Heat of combustion Kcal/g	Melting point °C
Wool	570–600	25.2	4.9	N/A
Polyester	485–560	20.6	5.7	252–292
Nylon	485–575	20.1	7.9	160–260
Rayon	420	19.7	3.9	N/A
Cotton	255	18.4	3.9	N/A

Miners' Drawers

Miners who worked underground were well aware of the hazards of explosion or spontaneous combustion and, partly for this reason, also favoured all-wool flannel. Miners' drawers (*draffers* or *drovers*) were made from underwear flannel (*gwalanen dronsus*) not just as a protection against fire but also for warmth, sweat absorption, and durability (see Plate 9.6, Plate 9.7, and Plate 9.8). Often striped and some-times yarn-dyed in darker weaves and checks, they were worn on their own in the depth of the mine, as shirts and trousers were stripped off in hot conditions. They remained common until the 1960s and 1970s, in firm preference to cotton under-pants. Before the 1974 Miners' Strike and the Health and Safety at Work Act of the same year, miners generally had to find their own workwear. Although the sector was very poorly paid before the mid-1970s and old, often second-hand clothes were common, the weight of demand, from around a quarter of a million men and boys, for low-flammability, durable, and sweat-absorbing drawers and shirts kept the textile industry of South Wales going.

Plate 9.9 shows three generations of miners in 1950. All three appear to be wearing their own, predominantly woollen clothing, and they were likely also to be wearing all-wool flannel drawers. This was to change after the nationalization of the coal mining industry in 1946, the slow development of health and safety legislation, and the advent of fire-retardant synthetics, which occurred over the following decades. However, the miners filmed digging desperately for the lost children of Aberfan as late as 1966 and coming straight off their shift were still wearing very similar clothing to that portrayed here (except for the addition of the hard hat).[57]

only by a small number of specialist mills that catered for the relevant occupations. The coal industry employed more than five times the number of men in the metalliferous industries, and within the latter only a minority of men were engaged in occupations that necessitated *crys fach*, the remainder wearing generic flannel work shirts. The *crys fach* was perhaps worn by only around 1 per cent of the entire population of male manual workers in Wales (Protheroe Jones, email communication, 4 March 2014), whereas the much longer—and also long-sleeved—flannel shirt was probably worn by 80 per cent or more of the same population.

[57] Type 'Google Images: Aberfan Disaster' (accessed 4 October 2016) and compare those pictures with Plate 9.9.

Flannel Work Shirts

All-wool flannel work shirts made from shirt flannel (*gwalanen crysau*) were by far the most important workwear produced by the industry (see Plate 9.10). They were worn by miners, agricultural workers, and workers in all other trades throughout Wales, especially those that involved outdoor operations: for example, by quarry men, lead miners, and workmen in building trades. Collarless but generally trimmed with linen at the neck, these were fairly loose garments, generally worn tucked in rather than over the top of trousers. This may have increased their suitability over smock garments (gathered and worn over trousers), whether of linen or of flannel, for indoor manufacturing that involved automated or belt-driven machinery: shirts were much less likely to get caught in the moving parts.[58] Flannel work shirts were cool and sweat-absorbing in summer, warm in winter. Their ubiquity in Wales from the eighteenth century to the interwar period (and, in rural areas, until later) crossed age boundaries: they were worn by all, from young boys to old men. These shirts were the equivalent, especially in rural and agricultural wear, to the linen smocks and shirts favoured in other parts of Great Britain. Although linen smocks were worn to some degree in Wales in the nineteenth century, especially near the Herefordshire border, it is clear that Welsh woollen shirts and jackets were preferred.[59]

Welsh flannel produced for workwear had yarn spun with a large amount of twist, to give strength and durability, and the cloth was shrunk to a maximum degree during finishing. The relative softness, durability, and non-shrinking quality that resulted appealed to working-class consumers.[60] Flannel shirts and underwear could be washed without damage at temperatures of up to 30°, a point stressed in newspaper adverts during the late nineteenth and early twentieth centuries, when cotton was beginning to make its way as a competitor in working-class underwear.[61] Flannel workwear may, however, have taken a little longer to dry than cotton or linen and appears to have been washed less frequently. New, or newly washed, flannel shirts and drawers were itchy garments when worn against the skin but grew less itchy with wear and age. Old and well-worn clothes were thus favoured and often regarded fondly. Rhys Davies describes the torture of a newly washed shirt on the Sabbath as 'a horror... because the fresh garment, by some vindictive alchemy of its washing day... carried extra crisp fire in its fangs', but 'by the middle of the week the sweat-impregnated garment would lose much of this

[58] A man was crushed in a punching machine in Aberdare in 1854, when his 'large smock-frock' became entangled in it: see the newspaper *Silurian, Cardiff, Merthyr, and Brecon Mercury, and South Wales General Advertiser*, 17 June 1854. I am grateful to Alison Toplis for this reference.

[59] Some embroidered smocks have survived in Welsh collections, but none is to be found in South West Wales and there is little mention of them in sources related to the industrial valleys of South Wales: see Tlid E. Anthony, *The Countrymen's Smocks in the Welsh Folk Museum* (Cardiff, 1974); Mair G. Rees and Christine Stevens, 'Smocks in the Welsh Folk Museum Collection', *Medal* 3 (1986), 32–8; Ann Buck, 'The Countryman's Smock', *Folk Life* 1 (1963), 16–34. Only one reference has so far been found to smocks worn in the heavy industries—namely the one mentioned in note 58.

[60] Crankshaw, *Survey of the Welsh Textile Industry*, 12.

[61] For example, *Aberdare Leader*, 24 September 1910.

punishment'.[62] After a week or so of hard work and sweating into the fibres of work shirts, the nap was calmed and fitted comfortably to the shape of the body: this appears to have been the main reason, along with the Welsh climate, for less frequent washing of workwear than in England. A cosy flannel shirt was also seen to have health-promoting qualities: it was a safeguard against bronchitis, whooping cough, and croup in youngsters and against chest ailments, coughs, and colds in adults.[63] Durable, old, rarely washed flannels were a daily accompaniment in the world of work and, although it is hard to find direct evidence of their meaning and value for their wearers, these garments were certainly regular and habitual 'friends' for months and even years.[64]

Woollen Jackets, Milled Overcoats, and Felt Hats

In the winter months, flannel work shirts were complemented by brimmed and felted woollen hats. For miners, these had a slightly curved brim on which a candle could ride while entering the darkness.[65] During the interwar years, wool cloth caps had become the most popular headgear, replacing the brimmed felt form. Rough woollen suiting (*brethyn cartref*), jackets, and rather shapeless heavy overcoats made of cloth milled many times in order to increase water-repellent qualities were also needed in winter. This was the tramp-like wear that Hobsbawm found ideal for chopping firewood. Woollens, especially of that density, generate heat when wet and are ideal for cold and wet conditions. Their use as winter workwear in the manual trades can be documented from contemporary paintings, sketches, and photographs from the late eighteenth to the mid-twentieth century. Plate 9.11 and Plate 9.12 depict felt hats and heavily milled suitings and coats from the late 1830s, which changed only little in fabric and shape during the following century.

Rational preference for the products of the Welsh woollen industry by Welsh workers was reinforced by nationalist campaigns aimed at supporting Welsh industry, especially (but not only) during the Depression years of the early twentieth century. Newspaper campaigns advocated the superiority and practical qualities of Welsh flannels, combined with the need to keep national industries going and

---

[62] Rhys Davies, *Print of the Hare's Foot* (Bridgend 1998), 16. I am grateful to Laura Ugolini for this reference.

[63] Ibid., 16. For nineteenth-century views on the health and healing properties of flannel, see Richmond, *Clothing the Poor*, 68–9. Soft Montgomeryshire flannels were noted by Walter Davies in 1810 as being suitable to wear next to the skin of the 'most delicate invalid': see Walter Davies, *General View North Wales*, 393.

[64] For Engels, the displacement of flannel by cotton in England in the nineteenth century represented an element in the degradation of the proletariat: he points out that the middle classes all wore flannel next to the skin. See Friedrich Engels, *The Condition of the Working Classes in England* (London, 1987 [1845]), 102–3. Compare this view with that of Gilbert White, who associated rarely washed woollens with a variety of 'cutaneous ails'. The persistent use of woollens in place of linens by the 'Welch' made them subject to 'foul erruptions': Gilbert White, *The Natural History and Antiquities of Selbourne* (London, 1789), 222.

[65] See https://welshhat.wordpress.com/elements-of-welsh-costumes/hats/miners-hats (accessed 10 October 2016).

Welsh workers off the dole.[66] The nationalist impulse was endorsed by flannel prizes at Eisteddfodau and by regular flannel fairs in the industrial valley towns.[67] To the same end most mills adopted labelling with nationalistic overtones, in drawers, shirts, and other items (see Plate 9.13 and Plate 9.14).[68]

Women's Wear

It is impossible to understand the popularity and longevity of items of woollen clothing made for women's wear without again referring to Welsh distinctiveness and Welsh nationalism. Two main types of gown were worn by women in Wales in the nineteenth and early twentieth centuries. The first, now generally referred to by Welsh dress historians as the *gŵn*, had a bodice with low-cut front, normally of striped flannel, finely cut and tailored (see Plate 9.15 and Plate 9.16). The other (the *betgŵn*—though not worn in bed) was a much simpler garment: a loose T shaped gown, like a kimono in shape (but shorter in length), made of light wool or of cotton by the later nineteenth century.[69] Such *betgŵns* were of mid-thigh length, worn over a skirt, wrapped across the front, and secured by a stringed apron. Several are depicted in Plate 9.17—*Market Scene in Wales*, by D. Fabronius— although this is a stylized image, probably made for the tourist industry, and hence it almost certainly exaggerates the ubiquity of the *betgŵn* and of the Welsh hat in everyday commerce.

The gŵn

The *gŵn* is a distinctive tailored flannel dress, as illustrated in Plate 9.15 and Plate 9.16. It was not initially unique to Wales but it continued to be worn in Wales long

---

[66] For example, in 1895 Blaiberg's Arcade in Cardiff was advertising South Wales Welsh flannel shirts at 4s. 11*d*. and flannel drawers at 1s. 10.5*d*., with the motto: 'By buying at Blaiberg's Arcade you support local work people' (see the issues of 5 March and 23 March 1895 and 31 March and 4 April 1896 of *Evening Express*). Carmarthen flannel was promoted with a plea to support local industry and local occupations with all-wool flannel guarantees (*Evening Express*, 12 October 1894). For real Welsh flannel and woollen goods, readers in Aberystwyth were encouraged to go to J. & E. Evans, General Drapers and Milliners, 40 Dark Gate St (*Aberystwyth Observer*, 12 April 1906, repeated in 1907 and 1908). Jothan & Sons sold 'real Welsh flannel shirts and shirtings', made from 'the best Welsh yarns', at 26 and 27, St Mary's Street, Cardiff (see *Cardiff Times*, 23 May 1885, and frequent repeats in *Weekly Mail* in the 1880s).

[67] The Mid Glamorgan Flannel Fair was held twice a year, for example, and gained detailed coverage in the local press: see the *Evening Express* issues of 2 February 1897 and 4 October 1898. The Eisteddfod flannel prizes sometimes drew controversy because of the difficulty of proving that the yarn was made in Wales (*Monmouthshire Merlin*, 18 November 1848).

[68] Superior flannels at the upper end of the market were also promoted for their 'Welshness', particularly those aimed at the tourist trade and those sold by Pryce Jones, pioneer of mail order in Newtown, who for two or three decades promoted only Welsh-made textiles through his Royal Welsh Warehouse, with the aid of pattern cards: see http://a-day-in-the-life.powys.org.uk/eng/home/eo_pryce.php (accessed 7 November 2015).

[69] The term *betgŵn* was rarely used in Wales until the 1920s, when it began to appear in academic articles. It is commonly used today and normally applied to the *gŵn*, but this is now considered inappropriate by dress historians: see https://welshhat.wordpress.com/introduction/terminology (accessed 26 April 2017).

after it died out in other parts of Britain and Europe, because it was incorporated into Welsh costume from the mid-nineteenth century and commonly worn on St David's Day, at Eisteddfodau, and on other ceremonial occasions, such as royal visits or civic displays.[70] It became the dress of Welsh women's choirs, harpists, folk dancers, and poets. The *gŵn*, worn over a skirt and with an apron cover, a small checked shawl and a tall 'beaver' hat, constituted an invention of tradition parallel to that of tartans and the kilt in Scotland.[71] It is no accident that the invention occurred around the same time as the kilt (1870–1914), a period singled out by Hobsbawm and Ranger as one in which Europe was undergoing the sorts of social and political change that made it fertile ground for nationalist imaginations, from outside as much as from inside these nations.[72] Welsh costume was much liked, photographed, and encouraged by tourists who wished to capture a quintessentially Welsh culture. Women were deliberately posed in Welsh dress, undertaking domestic and manufacturing tasks (especially spinning and knitting), which resulted in a proliferation of sketches, photographs, and postcards, as illustrated by the examples in Plate 9.18 and Plate 9.19.[73] These promoted a continued idealization of craft skills as well as of 'national costume', in tourist images that were reflected back to their subjects.

The incorporation of Welsh flannels, tweeds, and textiles into Welsh costume was sustained by support from key elite enthusiasts and by Welsh national revivals.[74] The *gŵn*—and Welsh national costume for women in its entirety, including the very tall and entirely impractical black hat—is partly an example of

---

[70] A least seventy survive in museum collections, all from Carmarthenshire and Ceredigion: see https://welshhat.wordpress.com/elements-of-welsh-costumes/gowns-and-bedgowns (accessed 30 November 2016). Four unprovenanced examples in Cyfarthfa Castle Museum, Merthyr Tydfil, may have come from persons who moved from those two counties in search of work (Michael Freeman, private communication, 24 November 2016).

[71] This may seem a bold statement, and it is of course debatable whether the word 'invented' should be used in connection with a combination of dress that existed long before the 1870s. Nevertheless 'Welsh national costume' began to appear in countless iconic images from this period onwards. For details of Welsh costume and the Welsh hat, see https://pilgrim.ceredigion.gov.uk/index. cfm?articleid=10006; https://welshhat.wordpress.com and http://www.welsh-costume.co.uk/welsh-high-hats.php (both accessed 20 November 2015).

[72] Hobsbawm and Ranger, *The Invention of Tradition*. Morgan's essay in their volume dates the lamented loss of a Welsh way of life, bardic culture and decline of the language to the late eighteenth century if not earlier, sparking a deliberate revivalism that came to a head after the mid-nineteenth century with the controversial criticism of Welsh culture and language that appeared in the Blue Books; see Prys Morgan, 'From a Death to a View: The Hunt for the Welsh Past in the Romantic Period', in Hobsbawm and Ranger, *The Invention of Tradition*, 43–100, esp. 92–4.

[73] See various illustrations collected on the website 'Gathering the Jewels' (http://www.gtj.org.uk, accessed 13 September 2015). Whether or not 'Welsh national costume' can rightly be described as 'national' when it was confined to photographic models and to women who could afford to have a costume made for them and the time to attend cultural events is highly debatable.

[74] For the role of Lady Llanover (and others), see Celyn Gurden-Williams, 'Lady Llanover and the Creation of a Welsh Cultural Utopia', unpublished PhD thesis, Cardiff University, 2008, available at http://orca.cf.ac.uk/54798/1/U585187.pdf; Michael Freeman, 'Lady Llanover and the Welsh Costume Prints', *National Library of Wales Journal* 34.2 (2007), 235–51. The Welsh Industries Association (1912–14), privately sponsored by a group of Welshmen living in London, organized sales and exhibitions to assist Welsh textile manufacturers, especially those specializing in dress flannels and suits; see Jenkins, *Welsh Woollen Industry*, 398.

Plate 9.1 Edward Lloyd, Ty Brics, the last stocking knitter in the town of Bala, *c.*1880.
© Gwynedd Library and Information Service.

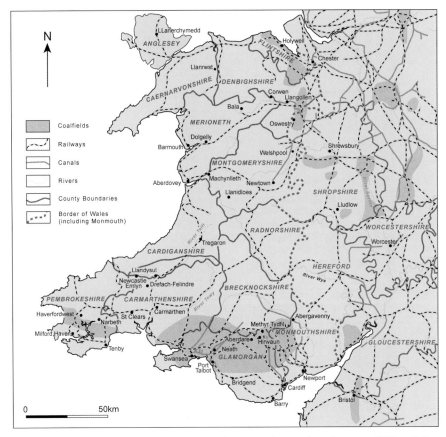

Plate 9.2 Important locations and routes relating to the textile industry in Wales. © Pat Hudson.

Plate 9.3 Women producing flannel for the United States at Holywell, inspecting the cloth, 1957: Rose Gallagher, Sara Price, Mary Evans, Brenda Wareham (Treffynnon). By permission of Llyfrgell Genedlaethol Cymru/The National Library of Wales.

Plate 9.4 Images of a Welsh wig dating from c.1854. © National Museum of Wales, reproduced by kind permission.

Plate 9.5 The *crys fach* (short shirt). All-wool flannel, collarless with open underarm gusset for air circulation, shorter at front for safety. © National Museum of Wales, reproduced by kind permission.

Plate 9.6 Miners' drawers (*draffers/drovers*). Blue/black check, all-wool underwear flannel (*gwalanen dronsus*), open fly, two buttons, drawstring waist and legs. © National Museum of Wales, reproduced by kind permission.

Plate 9.7 Miners' drawers (*draffers/drovers*). Self-coloured, all-wool flannel. Linen waistband, two buttons, open fly. © National Museum of Wales, reproduced with kind permission.

Plate 9.8 Miners' drawers (*draffers/drovers*), to illustrate the gathering on a buttoned cuff below the knee. © National Museum of Wales, reproduced by kind permission.

Plate 9.9 *Three Generations of Welsh Miners* (1950). Photo by William Eugene Smith. © Magnum Photos.

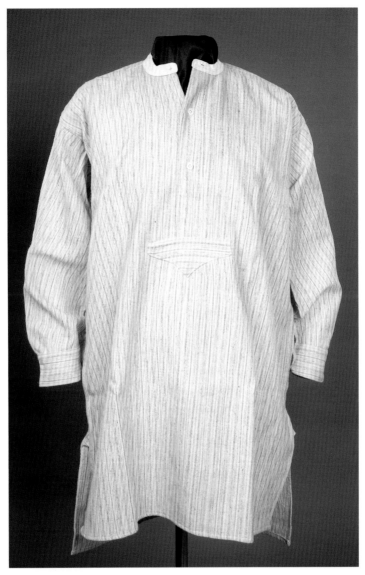

Plate 9.10 Flannel work shirt. All-wool, self-coloured flannel with stripe. Neck is taped/ reinforced with linen. Sleeves have buttoned cuffs. Side vents, back tail, buttoned front placket. © National Museum of Wales, reproduced by kind permission.

Plate 9.11 William Jones Chapman (attrib.), 1808–70, *David Davies, Cinder Filler, Hirwaun*. Plates 9.11 and 9.12 reproduce two of 17 extant paintings of workers at Treforest Tinplate Works and at Hirwaun Ironworks, commissioned in 1835–40 by Francis Crawshay, their employer. © National Museum of Wales, reproduced by kind permission.

Plate 9.12 William Jones Chapman (attrib.), 1808–70, *Thomas Francis, Quarryman, Forest*. © National Museum of Wales, reproduced with kind permission.

Plate 9.13 and 9.14 Labelling on miners' drawers (Plate 9.7) and flannel shirt (Plate 9.10), designed to appeal to nationalist sentiment. © National Museum of Wales, reproduced by kind permission.

Plate 9.15 The *gŵn*: front view. All-wool flannel, red/black stripes. Low neck, 24–6-inch tailored waist, front chest flaps traditionally held in place with a thorn. Watered silk cuffs. Worn (as here) over a skirt with linen waistband. An apron would generally be worn on the top that would hide the waistband. Amgueddfa Ceredigion Museum. I am grateful to Michael Freeman for permission

Plate 9.16 The *gŵn*: back view, opened out to show inserted fabric at tail and two cloth-covered buttons at waist. Amgueddfa Ceredigion Museum. I am grateful to Michael Freeman for permission to use his image.

Plate 9.17 *Market Scene in Wales*. Drawn by D. Fabronius; printed by Day & Son, 1850s. By permission of Llyfrgell Genedlaethol Cymru/ The National Library of Wales.

Plate 9.18 Two women in traditional dress, knitting. Photo (*c.* 1875). John Thomas Collection. By permission of Llyfrgell Genedlaethol Cymru/The National Library of Wales.

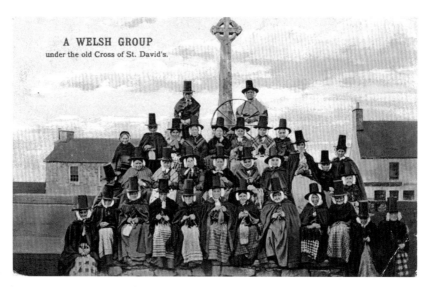

Plate 9.19 Women around the cross at St David's, Pembrokeshire, said to be a group who welcomed the duke and duchess of Edinburgh to St David's in 1882. Many copies were made depicting an idealization of Welsh national dress, hand-knitting, and spinning (see https://welshhat.wordpress.com/chronological-survey/1880s-3/1882-2). Amgueddfa Ceredigion Museum, reproduced by kind permission.

Plate 9.20 Tourist postcard of three women in Welsh national costume. © National Museum of Wales, reproduced by kind permission.

Plate 9.21 *An Unidentified Girl Carrying a Baby in a Shawl 'Welsh Fashion'.* Photograph by Tom Mathias. Courtesy of Pembrokeshire Museum Service. The Tom Mathias Collection of glass plate negatives forms part of the Pembrokeshire Museum Service photographic collection held at Scolton Manor.

Plate 9.22 Woman and baby in a smaller checked-flannel nursing shawl, possibly a converted whittle. © National Museum of Wales, reproduced by kind permission.

Welsh Pit Disaster. A little mother waiting for news.

Plate 9.23 Postcard depicting the aftermath of the Senghenydd Colliery Disaster, which occurred at the Universal Colliery near Caerphilly on 14 October 1913. The explosion and the subsequent release of poisonous gas killed 439 miners. The nursing shawl depicted here is typically of large size and loose (handloom) weave. © National Museum of Wales, reproduced by kind permission.

Plate 11.1

(a) Top left: Arminius Kaffee, 1903. Reproduced with kind permission of Staatsbibliothek zu Berlin—Preußischer Kulturbesitz, Signatur Oo 1519/5.
(b) Top right: Jeanne d'Arc chocolate, c.1910. Reproduced with kind permission of Musée Gourmand du Chocolat, Paris.
(c) Bottom left: Cadbury's 'The Good Old English Cocoa', 1901. *The Penny Illustrated Paper* and *Illustrated Times*.
(d) Bottom right: The Paula Girl, 1926. Reproduced with kind permission of The Paulig Company, Helsinki.

Plate 11.2 The loyal helpers of the housewife: 'We, too, will all come back—Electricity: Don't waste it—use it properly!' Posters from Berlin, 1948–9. Reproduced with kind permission of BEWAG Archiv, Vattenfall, Berlin.

dominant groups (from inside and outside Wales) misunderstanding (in this case exaggerating) the culture (in this case the costume) of subordinate groups and having 'the power to make their misunderstandings stick'.[75] The postcard in Plate 9.20 typically illustrates Welsh costume in total, including checked shawl, apron, *gŵn*, and hat. Such idealization of Welsh costume and Welsh identity was encouraged by the elite participants in the tourist industry of the nineteenth and early twentieth century and by manufacturers and merchants, such as Pryce Jones, who saw in this imagery the extension of a market for their products.

Flannels for women's clothing tended to be dark-dyed, often black with a red stripe or a red-and-black or white-and-black check. The woollen skirt worn under the *gŵn* (and generally of the same fabric) had pleats towards the hem that could be let out as a child or a teenager grew taller. *Gŵns* and skirts were durable, made to last, and likely to have been passed down within families.[76] Crankshaw saw the declining demand, in the interwar period, for linsey skirtings and woollen dress materials for women—including those that were intrinsic to national costume— as a major problem of the industry, aggravated by the disappearance of village tailors and by the advent of the merchant tailor, who was unwilling to make up a customer's own cloth.[77]

The Nursing Shawl

My final object of analysis is the nursing shawl (*siôl magu* or *siôl nyrsio*). This was one out of four or five shapes and styles of shawl in Wales. Generally around six feet square with a six-inch fringe, it was commonly used in the South Wales indus-trial valleys, from the late eighteenth century (if not before) to the 1960s or 1970s. Another—generally smaller—type of shawl was the 'whittle', sometimes fringed and often checked. Varying in colour over different regions of Wales, it was worn across the shoulders secured by a thorn or pin (as in Plate 9.20). The nursing shawl may have evolved from the whittle but was predominantly confined to South Wales (within Britain).[78] The nursing shawl enables babies up to the age of eighteen

---

[75] Peter Burke, 'Review of Hobsbawm and Ranger, eds, *Invention of Tradition*', *English Historical Review* 101.398 (1986), 316–17. The distinctive Welsh hat characterized Welsh costume in the nine-teenth century across South Wales, and in the north-west of the country in particular. It appears to have been taller and more conical in South Wales than in the north, where brims were smaller and shapes generally more cylindrical. Such hats are likely to have developed out of existing hat shapes in the early nineteenth century. They were made outside Wales by Carver and Co. in Bristol or by Christys or Dale and Co. in London and Stockport. They were probably going out of production by the 1880s. Those worn later either were handed down within families or were copies made from infer-ior materials. I am grateful to Michael Freeman for this point. See also Huw Roberts, *Traditional Welsh Costume in Nineteenth-Century Anglesey* (Anglesey, 2006).

[76] It is sometimes in the form of heirlooms that they have reached museums; see, for example, St Fagan's collection in the National Museum.

[77] Crankshaw, *Survey of the Welsh Textile Industry*, 4; Jenkins, *Welsh Woollen Industry*, 280.

[78] They were worn more widely within Wales, especially in the northern quarrying, mining, and industrial areas (Michael Freeman, private communication, 24 November 2016), but appear to have been thickest on the ground in the region of the South Wales coalfield. For more on Welsh shawls, see https://welshhat.wordpress.com/elements-of-welsh-costumes/shawl-siol (accessed 10 October 2016).

months or so to be securely strapped to their mother or carer's body and carried that way. At night it could be used as a cot cover.[79] As it left women's hands free for other tasks, it was particularly useful in large working families. Miners' families remained well above average in size in Britain until after the interwar period: the demographic transition occurred late in mining communities, which meant that miners' families continued commonly to comprise ten children or more.[80] In such families nursing shawls were invaluable.

The shawls varied in size, were often as big as two metres square, and were generally fringed. Often plain and mostly 'natural' in colour but sometimes checked or striped with black or grey, nursing shawls were loosely woven on a handloom and were flexible in all directions for tying and fitting to the baby's growing shape. Many mills kept a handloom largely for this purpose, which accounts to a great extent for the large number of handlooms found by Crankshaw in 1925. To *cwtch* comes from the verb for carrying in the shawl and means something like (but more than) 'to cuddle'. Nursing shawls of various types and from different periods are illustrated in Plate 9.21, Plate 9.22, and Plate 9.23.

CONCLUSION

The purpose of this essay has been to demonstrate that products of the Welsh wool textile industry can be used as a starting point to read history backwards, from ownership and use back to production and to the context of manufacturing. Close attention to objects and their intrinsic qualities not only enables an improved understanding of quotidian experience, the nature and feel of working lives, but also enriches our appreciation of the links between industry and attachment or belonging to landscape and climate, an attachment that fed into working practices and into nationalistic expression. Much of the current literature on materiality suggests that, with modernization, the intrinsic quality and the agency of objects became subordinated to the meaning that Cartesian subjects attached to them as markers of social status or class.[81] But this is hard to accept in the case of the work clothes and ceremonial dress that was valued and used by the working masses of South Wales. The strong attachment to nation and to a Welsh rural–industrial way of life embodied in such clothing makes is hard to impose an analysis of the industry that derives solely from the linear trajectories of modern social science.

The Welsh wig assisted in promoting British power and influence through more comfortable and sartorial national and international road and sea travel and in

---

[79] From the illustrations, prints, and photographs that have survived it appears that babies were held up high in the shawl, between the waist and the shoulder, generally on the left, which left the right hand entirely free—the left hand also being used to provide additional support when needed for walking. Some illustrations show the baby anchored to the right; this may have occurred if the mother or the carer was left-handed.

[80] Simon Szreter, *Fertility, Class and Gender in Britain, 1860–1940* (Cambridge, 1996), 58–9.

[81] Bert de Munk, 'Artisans, Products and Gifts', 61, refers to Bruno Latour's idea that a 'purification' process took place in the early modern period, in which objects became mere signifiers.

Polar exploration. Occupationally specific and practical workwear such as the flannel shirt, the *crys fach*, and miners' drawers supported Britain's industrial prowess and global trade for a century before safety workwear had been researched or routinely supplied. The long-term popularity of *gŵns* resulted in demand for flannels in darker colours and, like workwear, was promoted by a strong sense of Welsh national revivalism, expressed in popular support for Welsh products and ceremonial dress. Finally, the nursing shawl gave greater manual freedom to the mothers of large families, enabling them better to raise, support, feed, and clothe the predominantly male workforce of the 'old staple' export-oriented industries of South Wales. Endorsed by their practical qualities and appropriate designs, by the nationalist impulse, and by the picturesque imaginings of gentry and tourists, particular sorts of Welsh woollen garments remained in currency long after similar fabrics and styles had ceased to be fashionable elsewhere in Britain. It is only by a close consideration of the materiality of these garments, in their context and in relation to their meaning for, and centrality to, the lives of their wearers, that the story of the industry can be fully appreciated. It is also in this manner that the links between the local and the global, the experiential and the social, the personal and the political can begin to be explored.

10

Social and Environmental History in the Anthropocene

Paul Warde

Environmental history emerged not so much from new methods, but as a *political demand*: a renewed solidarity among historians interested in human life as lived in nature and from the sense that environmental problems, though largely identified by scientists, required political solutions and that this was a domain on which historians could comment.[1] Environmental historians could act as a bridge across what Bruno Latour called 'that division of labour between human politics and the science of things'.[2] The emergence of the field since the 1970s was not because of a previous absence of historical work on what we now called 'environmental' issues. There was already a rich tradition of work produced by historians and historical geographers on the histories of pollution, landscapes, conservation, energy, animals, and many other themes, although the volume of output in these and other areas has certainly accelerated in recent times. What was new was the desire to associate.

For the most part, 'environmental history' has introduced into historical scholarship areas of concern that were in fact bread-and-butter issues for other disciplines, particularly anthropology and human geography: humans had serious impacts on their environment, and environments might shape the way in which humans behaved, and hence their well-being and their experience of justice. Many of the histories produced in this vein have been, in themselves, quite conventional (which is not to belittle their value in any way). Environmental historians write social, political, and cultural histories of environmental scientists, of managers of resource extraction or national parks, of foresters and conservationists, of explorers and dam builders. This is virtuous work; but it represents an extension of the actors that historians consider interesting, rather than constituting a new kind of history.

---

[1] John Robert McNeill, 'Observations on the Nature and Culture of Environmental History', *History and Theory* 42 (2003), 5–43; Alfred W. Crosby, 'The Past and Present of Environmental History', *American Historical Review* 100 (1995), 1177–89; Sverker Sörlin and Paul Warde, 'The Problem of the Problem of Environmental History: A Re-Reading of the Field and its Purpose', *Environmental History* 12.1 (2007), 107–30; Donald Hughes, *What Is Environmental History?* (Cambridge, 2006) (also at http://aseh.net/about-aseh/history-of-aseh, accessed 13 July 2015).

[2] Bruno Latour, *Politics of Nature: How to Bring the Sciences into Democracy* (Cambridge, MA, 2004), 5; Kristin Asdal, 'The Problematic Nature of Nature: The Post-Constructivist Challenge to Environmental History', *History and Theory* 42 (2003), 60–1.

This is not, however, the only possibility on offer. Some historians expanded the world of historical 'actors' into hitherto unexplored or unelaborated areas, including those of microbes, parasites, animals, or hurricanes.³ Of course, none of these was entirely novel, especially not disease; but such non-human actors were rarely placed at the centre of the story (even in the case of plague). Other historians have argued for the advantages of taking on the conceptual apparatus of the natural sciences, a move that was, itself, the latest manifestation of a quite venerable two-way traffic.⁴ Still others sought to take more account of data produced by natural scientists in understanding the human impact on the environment and how it was refracted in social and economic change, although this had also long been in the purview of landscape historians and archaeologists; and a few, particularly in the field of historical climatology, sought to demonstrate how historical records could be turned into serial 'proxy data' of use to natural scientists.⁵

These are in themselves significant developments. It has become harder, rightly, to think of writing a history of the 'age of capital' or of the 'age of extremes' without commenting on the concomitant 'great acceleration' of resource depletion and biodiversity loss, or without addressing how empire and colonial settlement were shaped by disease, environments, resources, and the 'naturalizing' ideologies of race and management.⁶ These themes, now decades in the making, would seem peculiar absences from any ambitious historical narrative of the kind that Hobsbawm produced so adeptly as an account of how we got here and where we are going—although, in his framing, 'ecological problems' took up only a small part of the *Age of Extremes*, largely in the prospective final section, and were given about the same amount of space as the marginal references to feminism.⁷ In this chapter, however, I want to make a claim that environmental history can go beyond introducing a new set of relevant facts and some actors traditionally overlooked by social (and other) history. The greater claim is that environmental history can help to designate a new field of concern, which draws attention to the inadequacy of previous categories in history more widely. Yet in this, we find as so often in historical writing, a certain continuity of historians discovering how their comprehension of their own era opens up new modes of interrogating the past.

³ For example, Alfred W. Crosby, *Ecological Imperialism: The Biological Expansion of Europe, 900–1900* (Cambridge, 1986); Sherry Johnson, *Climate and Catastrophe in Cuba and the Atlantic World in the Age of Revolution* (Chapel Hill, NC, 2011); John Robert McNeill, *Mosquito Empires: Ecology and War in the Greater Caribbean, 1620–1914* (Cambridge, 2010).
⁴ Edmund Russell, *Evolutionary History: Uniting History and Biology to Understand Life on Earth* (Cambridge, 2011).
⁵ The literature in historical climatology is now very large. For one example of synthesizing 'big history' in surveying all of these approaches, see John L. Brooke, *Climate Change and the Course of Global History: A Rough Journey* (Cambridge, 2014).
⁶ For a series of survey essays, see William Beinart and Lotte Hughes, *Environment and Empire* (Oxford, 2007); on the 'great acceleration', see Will Steffen, Paul J. Crutzen, and John R. McNeill, 'The Anthropocene: Are Humans Now Overwhelming the Great Forces of Nature?' *AMBIO: A Journal of the Human Environment* 36 (2007), 614–21.
⁷ Eric Hobsbawm, *Age of Extremes: The Short Twentieth Century, 1914–1991* (London, 1994); see in particular the index entries on page 618 and the sections referenced there.

This move seems all the more pertinent with the rapid growth of interest in the concept of 'the anthropocene', the 'age of humans', a term first coined in 2000 by Paul Crutzen, an atmospheric chemist and oceanographer, denoting a new geological epoch, in which humans have become the most significant force shaping the planetary system—a force of nature, so to speak.[8] At the time of writing this proposition is under discussion by the International Commission on Stratigraphy (a body of geologists) as to whether it will be formally accepted into the consensus periodization of the earth sciences, an imprimatur that appears significant and authoritative in the wider media[9]—although this attention in itself raises questions as to why the conventions of geology, designed to indicate agreed signifiers of change in deep time, should carry such weight in the articulation of what is significant about our present predicaments. The International Commission's Anthropocene Working Group, which includes the historians Naomi Oreskes and John McNeill, is already serving to highlight the under-researched material impacts of humans on the planet, not just through climate change but equally through the role of fertilizers, metals, and new alloys, chemicals, cement, erosion, and biodiversity decline—mostly subjects that have received little sustained attention even from economic historians, and often only in the context of business history.[10] However, whether it achieves the accolade of formal acceptance or not, the idea already has a prominent and disputed position in environmental debate, spawning academic journals, exhibitions, and numerous articles.[11] Perhaps paradoxically from a historical point of view, this represents what Earth systems scientist Will Steffen has called 'a "no analogue" situation'.[12] From the point of view of the scientific study of the planetary environment, the possibility that a capricious humanity is strongly affecting trajectories in the Earth system is an unsettling challenge for prediction and implies enormous risks for us all. From the point of view of historians, the primacy of humanity has been a disciplinary conceit all along and, arguably before the emergence of the modern earth sciences, geological phenomena were largely interpreted as consequences of human action, albeit mediated by divine intent. The idea that people have only very recently made the history of the Earth a story about themselves could indeed be seen as another example of what Hobsbawm called '[t]he destruction of the past, or rather of

[8] Paul J. Crutzen and Eugene F. Stoermer, 'The Anthropocene', *IGBP Newsletter* 41 (2000), 17; Paul J. Crutzen, 'Geology of Mankind', *Nature* 3, January 2002, 23.

[9] See http://www.bbc.co.uk/news/science-environment-31836233 (accessed 14 July 2015).

[10] For membership and themes of the group's work, see http://quaternary.stratigraphy.org/workinggroups/anthropocene (accessed 14 May 2017).

[11] See useful summaries of this very rapidly expanding cross-disciplinary literature in Helmuth Trischler, 'The Anthropocene: A Challenge for the History of Science, Technology, and the Environment', *NTM: Zeitschrift für Geschichte der Wissenschaften, Technik und Medizin* 24 (2016), 309–35; Jamie Lorimer, 'The Anthropo-Scene: A Guide for the Perplexed', *Social Studies of Science* 47.1 (2016), 1–26, doi: 10.1177/0306312716671039; and discussions in Clive Hamilton, Christophe Bonneuil, and François Gemenne, *The Anthropocene and the Global Environmental Crisis: Rethinking Modernity in a New Epoch* (London, 2015).

[12] Noel Castree, 'Geographers and the Discourse of an Earth Transformed: Influencing the Intellectual Weather or Changing the Intellectual Climate?' *Geographical Research* 53.3 (2015), 244–54, here 244.

the social mechanisms that link one's contemporary existence to that of earlier generations'—and 'one of the most characteristic and eerie phenomena of the late twentieth century'.[13] There are plenty of analogues from the perspective of human *beliefs*, but none of them could be validated by modern science.

The idea of the Anthropocene implicitly makes all human action, in some sense, environmental. Just as all weather—even the kind that seems unremarkable to us—is already the consequence of global warming in that it is the outcome of a hotter world, so now all human action is entangled with environmental consequences, unless we think that some actions demonstrably have no influence on any others. Equally, if social choices have unavoidable environmental consequences, then arguably the life of everything on the planet has become embroiled in social history, and there is no obvious demarcation of these fields of action. Hobsbawm provided 'a bird's eye view' of the short twentieth history. In the Anthropocene, all of human history literally comes to be beheld by the bird, as it makes its way in the world; equally, the bird is an actor in our history too.[14] This view was summarized in an influential set of theses by Dipesh Chakrabarty in 2009, his first thesis proclaiming 'the collapse of the age-old humanist distinction between natural history and human history'.[15] Aristotle's demarcation of 'nature', as the world of things that possess their own inner principles of movement and rest and that are, so to speak, their own cause, dissolves—or at the very least the expected dividing line between nature and the action of conscious human agents has to be redrawn.[16] Both approaches, the environmental and the social, extend so as to be found 'everywhere and nowhere', to borrow a phrase from the historian Mark Elvin. We should still note, however, that such arguments of integration are not entirely new and have their own long history, despite the particular form in which we now encounter them.

HISTORICIZING 'THE ENVIRONMENT'

Oddly enough, historians have not done much historicizing of 'the environment'. They have tended to treat it as a self-evident object, composed of various interrelated parts (animate and inanimate, of various topographies, watery and non-watery, atmospheric and climatic, and so on) that scientists, we hope, convey accurate information about. Its essential unity is unquestioned; why things are now considered linked as 'environmental' when they were previously not studied together at all, much less regulated by the same ministry, is rarely asked. Knowledge of the environment, now and historically, is thus often treated as a problem of 'discovery' rather than of construction and conceptualization, even though the history of

---

[13] Hobsbawm, *Age of Extremes*, 3.   [14] Ibid., 1–16.
[15] Dipesh Chakrabarty, 'The Climate of History: Four Theses', *Critical Studies* 35 (2009), 197–222, here 201.
[16] This is not necessarily the same as nature–culture boundaries becoming redundant—boundaries that anthropology has long demonstrated are in any case contingent.

the life sciences, for example, has become quite thoroughly historicized.[17] Yet, like any concept, much work went into its creation, and even such a universal category has its exclusions as well as its connections.

Thinking a little more about the history of this term can, arguably, help us to think about the specific character of our environmental age.[18] The word 'environment' was popularized in English in the second half of the nineteenth century by Herbert Spencer, who adopted it to describe those external conditions that exerted evolutionary pressure on the subjects of his narrative (which were various, but included human societies). He did not imagine that this environment had any fundamental unity or interconnectedness; rather, he made it into an aggregate of causal agents in stories of adaptation and selection. This was how the term was widely adopted in the social sciences, and notably in ecology, by the late nineteenth century—at first as an explanatory framework for variations in plant physiology, but later in a wide range of fields, including economics and sociology.[19] The concept of environment as a disparate set of characteristics that *acted upon* rather than *was acted upon* was prevalent in what we now look back on as environmental determinism, often accompanied by unsavoury racial overtones, something that persisted into the interwar period. This idea of environment is obviously not that which has informed modern environmental history. The latter has rather taken its cue from a meaning that emerged clearly only in the postwar period: the environment as a system under threat, in a narrative where humans had become the destructive agents rather than the ones acted upon; and the precise scope of the damage was increasingly measured, modelled, and managed by groups of scientists who came to be understood as 'environmental' experts.

In 1963, a year after the appearance of Rachel Carson's famous *Silent Spring*, Lynton Caldwell, an American planner with substantial experience of urban development in South East Asia, published an influential call for 'environmental policy'.[20] Caldwell argued that development was altering the world in which humans lived in ubiquitous and unanticipated ways and that this quite general phenomenon demanded an integrated policy response. For him, the term 'environment' could perform the work required to bring a repressed and degraded nature into social life, but also that acknowledged the interconnections between different fields of social activity. It denoted, in other words, a perception of changes

---

[17] For example, Lynn K. Nyhart, *Modern Nature: The Rise of the Biological Perspective in Germany* (Chicago, IL, 2009); Eugene Cittadino, *Nature as the Laboratory: Darwinian Plant Ecology in the German Empire, 1880–1900* (Cambridge, 1990); Gregg Mitman, *The State of Nature: Ecology, Community, and American Social Thought, 1900–1950* (Chicago, IL, 1992); Sharon E. Kingsland, *The Evolution of American Ecology, 1890–2000* (Baltimore, MD, 2005).

[18] See also the discussion in Sara B. Pritchard, 'Joining Environmental History with Science and Technology Studies: Promises, Challenges, and Contributions', in Dolly Jørgensen, Finn Arne Jørgensen, and Sara B. Pritchard, eds, *New Natures: Joining Environmental History with Science and Technology Studies* (Pittsburgh, PA, 2013), 1–20.

[19] Paul Warde, 'The Environment', in Peter Coates, David Moon, and Paul Warde, eds, *Local Places, Global Processes* (Oxford, 2016), 32–46.

[20] Rachel Carson, *Silent Spring* (New York, 1962); Lynton K. Caldwell, 'Environment: A New Focus for Public Policy?' *Public Administration Review* 23 (1963), 132–9.

in the natural world as being a social problem, uniting a range of new categories of measurement and policy by which scientific expertise attempted to police and regulate the impacts of social behaviour.[21] 'Environmental history' arose in the aftermath of this postwar agglomeration of environmental expertise, bringing together ecologists, economists, planners, demographers, and conservationists in conferences such as the 1965 'Future Environments of North America'; and by 1970 it was manifest in new governmental institutions.[22] A significant, but by no means the only, strand in this thinking was a continuation of Malthusian fears formulated in relation to global food supply in the 1920s, and sometimes with links to eugenics.[23] The concept was explicitly political, in that the degrading trajectory of the environment was connected to a range of other problems and demanded political action for redress. Environmental history, especially in its North American incarnation, at first took up the task of explaining how ingrained cultural attitudes or economic imperatives caused environmental damage, often with some reference to an older tradition that valued outdoors and wilderness experiences, especially in the style of nineteenth-century transcendentalist thinkers.[24]

This short survey draws attention to the fact that 'the environment' is the product of work, namely of a wide range of scientific and discursive practice. It denotes an area of social anxiety. In pieces published in 2007 and 2009, Sverker Sörlin and I argued that, in light of this history, environmental history had hitherto missed the opportunity to put the term to use *conceptually* rather than simply *descriptively*. Environmental history could engage in some ontogenetical thinking in order to analyse how human societies, and perhaps also the 'humanities', worked to constitute themselves, allocate expertise, and manage the awkwardly permeable boundary between what lay inside and what lay outside the 'social' realm.[25] There are other analogues to this story of emergent and differentiated expertise and systems of governance, to be found, for example, in the way in which certain areas of government action—such as the utility industries, infrastructural development, or public health—were portrayed in the nineteenth and twentieth centuries as 'technical' rather than 'political' questions, although without, in the end, preventing the

---

[21] Of course, there were much more limited examples of this in the past, especially with regard to public health, disease prevention, and pollution control. See, for example, Thomas Le Roux, *Le Laboratoire des pollutions industrielles: Paris, 1770–1830* (Paris, 2011).

[22] Paul Warde and Sverker Sörlin, 'Expertise for the Future: The Emergence of Environmental Prediction, *c.*1920–1970', in Jenny Andersson and Eglė Rindzevičiūtė, eds, *The Struggle for the Long-Term in Transnational Science and Politics: Forging the Future* (New York, 2015), 38–62; Frank Fraser Darling and John P. Milton, eds, *Future Environments of North America* (Garden City, NY, 1966).

[23] Alison Bashford, *Global Population: History, Geopolitics, and Life on Earth* (New York, 2014); Thomas Robertson, *The Malthusian Moment: Global Population Growth and the Birth of American Environmentalism* (New Brunswick, 2012); Fabien Locher, 'Cold War Pastures: Garrett Hardin and the "Tragedy of the Commons"', *Revue d'Histoire Moderne et Contemporaine* 60 (2013), 7–36.

[24] For example, Roderick Frazier Nash, *Wilderness and the American Mind*, 4th edn (New Haven, CT, 2001[1967]); Donald Worster, *Nature's Economy: A History of Ecological Ideas*, 2nd edn (Cambridge, 1994 [1977]).

[25] Sörlin and Warde, 'The Problem of the Problem'; Sverker Sörlin and Paul Warde, 'Making the Environment Historical: An Introduction', in Sverker Sörlin and Paul Warde, eds, *Nature's End: History and the Environment* (Basingstoke, 2009), 1–19.

emergence of new kinds of politics.[26] Reflection on the debates, practices, and problems of the postwar period for which the environment was presented as conceptual tool for thinking-through, could help us now in thinking about how such processes have continually emerged historically. These processes, which we called 'environing', seemed richly exemplified in a work that lies far from modern environmental concerns: *Nature and Policy*, Kirsten Hastrup's 1990 study of medieval and early modern Iceland.[27] The book demonstrated how Icelanders, in an increasingly hostile and isolated place, responded to difficulties by acting according to categories derived from their Scandinavian origins, as to what were or were not appropriate areas for social action, and which equally apportioned the land and sea between regions of social regulation, supernatural agency, and different modes of economic activity.[28] This was a particular variety of what we called 'environing' and it was constitutive of both expectations and actions about the natural and the social worlds. In this understanding, environmental history is not just a history of how humans relate to, or influence, what is out there; it is a work of grasping how people have constantly sought to define what should be the proper territory of human reflection, interaction, and conversation (let us call it 'society') as against everything else that just happens (let us call it 'nature'). In Hastrup's account, in the early modern period deteriorating conditions for Icelandic societies and a decaying farming infrastructure meant that 'the natural world...expanded into and took over parts of the social. The "movements" of nature accumulated to such an extent that counter-movements became more or less impossible',[29] inducing a paralysing fatalism. The situation seems almost reversed today, when the complexity of social life paralyses our capacity to implement solutions to environmental dilemmas with which science allegedly stands waiting.

This boundary between society and environment (or, as is well known, culture and nature) is not as easy to find as we might expect.[30] Today, for example, at what point does a scientist who measures and reports on mercury levels according to disciplinary expectations and government regulation depart from the social and become the purveyor of information solely about the environment?[31] These distinctions require work, as does the recognition that she is really a scientist, that her equipment works properly, that certain measured levels actually have implications for all the things that live in the lake, and that these might be relevant for the society she reports to (which society is that?). Or, to state the case more accurately, distinction requires *works*, which according to one's taste might undermine the very notion of a 'Nature with a capital N', or at least make one wonder how it is

[26] Frank Trentmann, 'Materiality in the Future of History: Things, Practices, and Politics', *Journal of British Studies* 48 (2009), 283–307, here 300–3.
[27] Kirsten Hastrup, *Nature and Policy in Iceland, 1400–1800: An Anthropological Analysis of History and Mentality* (Oxford, 1990).
[28] Ibid., 247–76.   [29] Ibid., 275–6.
[30] Raymond Williams, *The City and the Country* (Oxford, 1973).
[31] Michael Egan, 'Communicating Knowledge: The Swedish Mercury Group and Vernacular Science, 1965–1972', in Dolly Jørgensen, Finn Arne Jørgensen, and Sara B. Pritchard, eds, *New Natures: Joining Environmental History with Science and Technology Studies* (Pittsburgh, PA, 2013), 103–17.

that all these different works that seek to identify the environment can be connected into a singular identity, and to what purpose.[32]

THE ANTHROPOCENE AND SOCIETY

If the environmental is, at best, a hybrid category, in a certain sense social, what does this make the social itself? If we are to understand the environmental as the co-product of works both human and non-human, then this must apply to the social realm too. Social history emerged as a way of both analysing aggregates and allowing collectives to 'act'. By and large, social history, to generalize somewhat, has followed a line that may be traced back to Vico, as a history fundamentally concerned with human agency and above all, with political and institutional life (institutions later conceived in the broadest sense, to include the family, voluntary associations, campaigning movements, churches, and so forth).[33] Social history extended the terrain of this agency into the subaltern but did not fundamentally alter the conception: history was made by conscious agents, even if not in circumstances of their own choosing, and many of its narratives have been preoccupied with the possibilities of articulation and realization in public life that are attendant upon urbanization, industrialization, and mass literacy. In its determination to restore dignity and agency to the mass of the population, including women, social history has resisted investing too much power in objects or in natural forces. Society, after all—even the most rigidly structured—was about choice, negotiation, subterfuge, and performance. An exemplar of this approach—and there could be legion—would be a minor aside from David Sabean in his magisterial demographic study of the German village of Neckarhausen. In this study he noted that 'property is not a relationship between people and things but one between people about things'. A fence does not constitute a boundary as such; it is only the social convention about what a fence is, a matter of the mind, that grants it this effect.[34] And yet, while the meaning of the fence is clearly important, so is the materiality of the boundary itself. Historians of agrarian societies know well that the lack of a physical demarcation of agreed property rights has its own set of implications for how livestock are managed, who does the managing, who pays for it, what levels of penalty there are for transgressions, and what forms of engagement with the landscape are possible. The matter of the fence really matters. Indeed, a turn towards 'materiality' and 'things' (whether this constitutes a return is another matter) has been visible for some time within strands of sociology, anthropology and history, notably with 'material culture', although the emphasis is more frequently on 'culture' than on its qualifier.[35]

[32] Asdal, 'Problematic Nature', 72.   [33] Chakrabarty, 'Climate of History'.
[34] David Warren Sabean, *Property, Production and Family in Neckarhausen, 1700–1870* (Cambridge, 1990), 18.
[35] For a useful and thoughtful survey, see Trentmann, 'Materiality in the Future of History'.

Earlier schools of historical thought have consciously engaged with geography, notably the *Annales* school pioneered by Lucien Febvre. Indeed, Febvre spoke of 'the problem of environment' alongside 'the problem of race' as the two great questions confronting any historian, but did so to lambast ideas of determinism in each case.[36] Nevertheless, despite Febvre's insistence that 'men... utilize their geographical circumstances, more or less, according to what they are, and take advantage more or less completely of their geographical possibilities',[37] and despite his discussion of environmental transformations, for the most part the *Annalistes* persisted in employing a 'base–superstructure' model of society, according to which the environment defined the conditions of possibility of a society while being itself shaped by the forms of production undertaken by that society.[38] This is perhaps because of the *Annalistes*' tendency to examine the *longue durée* of a peasant world, 'a history of constant repetition' that itself was 'almost timeless'.[39] The kind of distinctions that Braudel made, between timescales that were geographical (often proxied as environmental), social, and of events, is not one that we feel at ease with any more. Of course, Braudel and his successors wished to draw attention precisely to the inseparable fates of the human and the non-human; and yet making such distinctions allowed for the persistence of a gap between three domains of study. It is not enough to say, as Braudel did, that 'Everything is history: soil, climate, geological movements'; or indeed claim, as Le Roy Ladurie did in 1974, that the *Annales* had 'long since' addressed 'ecological history'.[40] Great though the achievements of these scholars have been, such statements indicate that they had not fully absorbed the potential of 'the environment' as a category. A similar effect is mandated by a now traditional tripartite division of environmental history into the study of human impacts on nature, socioeconomic organization, and ideas about the natural world.[41] This division says very little about how thought and practice actually negotiated such boundaries and made sense of their activity and possibilities for action. This underscores the reality of much historical writing that remained in the same bunkers as before.

More recent social history has been shaped by a strong desire to reassert in new forms the notion that 'man makes himself'[42]—a determination to make people 'actors' instead of seeing them as part of statistical aggregates or classes. Such determination was common in more social structural approaches to history and, at times, in the *Annales* tradition. This turn against a more sociological history was perhaps no more than a political wish to accord all people the same kind of individual dignity that we would like ourselves to be awarded in the age of universal

---

[36] Lucien Febvre, *A Geographical Introduction to History* (London, 1925), 1.   [37] Ibid., 315.

[38] Most strikingly in Fernand Braudel, *The Identity of France*, 3 vols (London, 1990).

[39] Fernand Braudel, *The Mediterranean and the Mediterranean World in the Age of Philip II*, 2nd edn (London, 1972), vol. 1, 20; see also Emmanuel Le Roy Ladurie, 'History that Stands Still', in idem, *The Mind and Method of the Historian* (Brighton, 1981), 1–27.

[40] Cited in José Augusto Pádua, 'The Theoretical Foundations of Environmental History', *Estudos Avançados* 68 (2010), 81–101, here 81–2.

[41] Donald Worster, ed., *The Ends of the Earth: Perspectives on Modern Environmental History* (Cambridge, 1988).

[42] V. Gordon Childe, *Man Makes Himself* (London, 1936).

human rights and reflects a view adopted by many within social history—where, somewhat in the vein of Collingwood, the historian's job is argued to be to 'discern the thought of [an action's] agent', as a reaction against quantifying and aggregating approaches. Of course, history has never lived up to Collingwood's ideal in practice, nor have many practitioners wanted it to.[43] Foucauldian approaches have objected to the very possibility of such discernment.[44] Nevertheless, one can see the workings of this self-same sensibility in some debates about incorporating non-humans into historical and sociological thought. The question becomes one of whether animals, or even hailstorms or soil types, should be understood as 'actors', and thus achieve some kind of planetary citizenship in a way that does not have to relinquish the autonomy of the liberal (and liberated) subject. This probably says more about our politics than about the non-human world.

Yet greater attention to diversity, agency, and movement in social history has also drawn attention back to the inescapably material conditions of existence, in that the development of industries or the self-fashioning of identity is seen as inextricably linked to increasingly global flows of commodities. It is but a short step to see these ramifying connections, or 'circulatory histories', as being related to environmental circumstances with sometimes astonishing effects, such as those elaborated in John Soluri's study of the multifaceted impact of the banana trade in the Americas or in John Tully's work on gutta-percha (a kind of rubber) and the enormous environmental impact of demand for that product, which permitted the development of effective cabling for telegraph and electrical systems (and also revolutionized the game of golf as the heart of the ball).[45] The shape of social life can hardly be imagined in these works as independent of the availability and potentialities of other forms of life. All of the three great transformations of the twentieth century identified by Hobsbawm are brought into play in these histories: declining Eurocentrism; the globe's becoming more of 'a single operational unit'; and the severing of traditional social relationships.[46] 'Globalization' has been a common shorthand for all these, but the globalized environment also represents a way in which the concerns of earlier, structural and material histories are given new life and significance, while the notion of the globe as a 'single operational unit' was also itself a construction of the emerging environmental and climatic sciences, which led towards the emergence of earth systems science and the Anthropocene.[47] In his recent book *The Crisis of Global Modernity*, Prasenjit Duara declared that 'tension

---

[43] Collingwood, cited in Chakrabarty, 'Climate of History', 203.

[44] Hence Foucault's careful distinction between 'proposition' and 'statement'. An excellent exposition of this view is given in Gilles Deleuze, *Foucault* (London, 1999); or, in the words of de Certeau on Foucault, 'the ground of our certainty is shaken when it is revealed that we can no longer think a thought from the past': Michel de Certeau, *Heterologies: Discourse on the Other* (Manchester, 1986).

[45] John Soluri, *Banana Cultures: Agriculture, Consumption and Environmental Change in Honduras and the United States* (Austin, TX, 2005); John Tully, 'A Victorian Ecological Disaster: Imperialism, the Telegraph, and Gutta-Percha', *Journal of World History* 20 (2009), 559–79.

[46] Hobsbawm, *Age of Extremes*, 14–15.

[47] See, for example, Paul N. Edwards, *A Vast Machine: Computer Models: Climate Data, and the Politics of Global Warming* (Cambridge, MA, 2010).

between circulation and misrecognition is the political logic of the modernity of nation-states'.[48] By this, he meant to contrast the reality of regionally and globally circulating ideas, not least the very concepts through which the nation-state was imagined, and the 'misrecognition' of every nation-state as something authentic, autonomous, and endogenous. Indeed, an appeal to place (or environment), sometimes spliced with race, was a method by which nationalist 'misrecognition' proceeded and that brought down the ire of Lucien Febvre. We might turn this observation so as to argue that societies have equally been dependent on circulations or flows from nature, but with the misrecognition that social life is self-constitutive and essentially autonomous, which generates a tension frequently articulated along a continuum from 'determinism' to 'agency'. In the case of nation-states that traced their vigour back to a particular place or climate, the line of progress was often found in their capacity to transcend that essential origin and expand into new locations.[49] On the broader scale of humanity, such a narrative can still be found embedded in accounts, most often related to climate and found in perfectly respectable historical works, that human history, when viewed in the long run, is a kind of emancipation from environmental constraints. From an evolutionary perspective, so the argument goes, environments exerted pressures that tested the adaptive mettle of particular societies and rewarded those who responded well and thus liberated themselves.[50]

The Anthropocene would be an ironic counterblast to such dreams of emancipation: if humanity was previously chained to Gaia but now holds the reins, well, humanity is still inextricably hitched to Gaia. The point of departure for this section was not, however, to put the whole of humanity in its place, but simply to enquire what it is that we might understand as the 'social', or whether a new understanding of the hybridity of the 'environmental' required us to reconsider the social too.[51] If it requires so much work to hold a social realm aloof from the determinisms of technology or environment or to insist that exerting power over nature is just a way of exerting power over people (or indeed of naturalizing power over people) without also finding the reverse to be equally true, we might suggest that this is a rich vein for historical enquiry rather than a place where one needs to take sides. In the final section I will provide further examples of what such histories look like; but first I examine how historians might usefully engage with historical periodizations that emerge from outside the discipline.

[48] Prasenjit Duara, *The Crisis of Global Modernity: Asian Traditions and a Sustainable Future* (Cambridge, 2015), 103.

[49] David Arnold, *The Problem of Nature, Environment, Culture and European Expansion* (Oxford, 1996).

[50] See, for example, Brooke, *Climate Change*; Geoffrey Parker, *Global Crisis: War, Climate Change and Catastrophe in the Seventeenth Century* (New Haven, CT, 2013).

[51] This question has of course been posed in an analogous fashion within the history of science, in especially trenchant form in Bruno Latour, *Reassembling the Social: An Introduction to Actor-Network Theory* (Oxford, 2005).

THE MATERIALITY OF THE SOCIAL

Evoking the Anthropocene is not simply yet another repetition in a long history of appeals for interdisciplinarity and the dissolution of old boundaries (although it belongs there too). It can be viewed as a new point of departure and as a reason to reflect on the process of drawing boundaries rather than on their abolition. But to where do we depart, in the age of humans, where humanity *appears* to be more invested in the state of nature? The use of the term 'Anthropocene' in the earth and social sciences has swiftly generated anxious debates about its meaning and the questions it poses. Does 'the age of humans' imply responsibilities, or the identification of the whole species as a *causal agent*? If so, what kind of entity would that species be? And is such an identification a hazardous form of essentializing, beyond any explanation based on 'class' or similar social categories? Objections have been raised that the damage to the environment produced by climate change relates to the activity of a relatively small share of the Earth's human population (the developed nations) and is arguably driven by an even smaller group, those who steer the capitalist economy. The very notion of the 'Anthropocene' represents, in this view, a form of mystification or an absolution of social inequality and capitalism.[52] Jean-Baptiste Fressoz has pointed out, perhaps somewhat tongue-in-cheek, that at least until 1950 the Anthropocene might better be named the 'Anglocene', as English speakers were responsible for the majority of carbon emissions.[53] A riposte to such concerns might be that using the word 'Anthropocene' posits a useful set of questions that touch precisely upon these issues, as it is by no means clear a priori that capitalism (however defined) by necessity causes climate crises, nor what characteristics define humanity as a species.[54] That use of the 'Anthropocene' might automatically 'introduce a powerful degree of essentialism in our understanding of humans' seems no more warranted than the idea that studying 'anthropology' by necessity seeks a reductive account of human behaviour.[55] Nor, one might add, is the idea itself of a 'species' as essentialist as is sometimes implied. Certainly, as we write the history of *other* species, we find our own conceptions of what is 'essential' about them shifting, as demonstrated brilliantly in D. Graham Burnett's history of cetacean studies, *The Sounding of the Whale*.[56] In a different vein Daniel Lord Smail has reached towards primatology to provide perspectives on human behaviour and

---

[52] Andreas Malm and Alf Hornborg, 'The Geology of Mankind? A Critique of the Anthropocene Narrative', *Anthropocene Review* 20 (2015), 62–9; Alf Hornborg, 'The Political Economy of the Technocene: Uncovering Ecologically Unequal Exchange in the World-System', in Hamilton et al., *The Anthropocene*, 57–69; Castree, 'Geographers'.

[53] Jean-Baptiste Fressoz, 'Losing the Earth Knowingly: Six Environmental Grammars around 1800', in Hamilton et al., *The Anthropocene*, 71.

[54] See Dipesh Chakrabarty, 'Climate and Capital: On Conjoined Histories', *Critical Inquiry* 41 (2014), 1–23.

[55] Chakrabarty, 'Climate of History', 214.

[56] D. Graham Burnett, *The Sounding of the Whale: Science and Cetaceans in the Twentieth Century* (Chicago, IL, 2012).

to refute notions of evolutionary fixity from a hunter-gatherer past.[57] How would humans shape up, one wonders, in a comparative history of species? A species understood as a locus of diversification, reproduction, and selection that has been ongoing for hundreds of thousands of years and is part of a still longer genealogy of life.[58]

Perhaps more alarming for historians—although probably also an unrealistic proposition—are calls for methodological monism and for an integration of sciences and humanities (often in fact meaning natural and social sciences), not least when one can argue that methodological diversity is itself a source of resilience.[59] Yet, if natural scientists are already pondering how to integrate 'society' and historical processes into systems analyses, would it be perverse if those whose bread and butter it is to study societies were not involved, even if critically, in the enterprise? There is certainly a risk if historians are not able themselves to choose what is significant about their discipline in any such 'integration'. As a starting point, history can provide rich insight into and demonstration of how 'entangled' thought about environments (or biology) and society has long been. There is absolutely no novelty in decrying or attempting to overcome a boundary between the 'natural' and 'cultural'. Still less has it been a condition of modernity or of the Enlightenment to assume and then reify such a boundary; as I have argued above, this has always been the product of *work*, in this and any other age. The study of boundary conditions has been a particular preoccupation in the history of science but has also received wider scrutiny in works such as Alison Bashford's *Global Population*, which traces the myriad connections, in mid-twentieth-century thought, between demography, eugenics, ecology, and human (particularly women's) rights.[60]

Historians have been notably absent from debates about the dating of the Anthropocene,[61] although the protagonists have had significant recourse to arguments about historical process in making the case for particular 'markers' (given the predilection of geology for using physical boundary markers to demarcate time). We find various start dates offered as prehistorical agricultural and pastoral clearances (Ruddiman);[62] 1784 as the (wrongly attributed) date for Watt's invention of the steam engine: that was in fact the year when he took out a patent for his engine in combination with new gearing, to produce rotary motion (Crutzen); 1945 for the explosion of the first atomic weapons and the beginning of the postwar 'Great Acceleration' (Steffen, McNeill, Hamilton); 1610 as a change in atmospheric carbon levels resulting from the demographic collapse of the post-conquest Americas (Lewis and Maslin) or possibly 1964 (also Lewis and Maslin).[63] Arguably such 'golden spikes' are fundamentally sterile, in that they confuse event with

[57] Andrew Shryock and Daniel Lord Smail, eds, *Deep History: The Architecture of Past and Present* (Berkeley, CA, 2011).

[58] Chakrabarty, 'Climate of History', 213.

[59] Castree, 'Geographers', 6–7.   [60] Bashford, *Global Population*.

[61] With the exception of John McNeill. See also Libby Robin, 'Histories for Changing Times: Entering the Anthropocene?' *Australian Historical Studies* 44 (2013), 329–240.

[62] William F. Ruddiman, 'The Anthropogenic Greenhouse Era Began Thousands of Years Ago', *Climatic Change* 61 (2003), 261–93.

[63] S. L. Lewis and M. A. Maslin, 'Defining the Anthropocene', *Nature* 519 (2015), 171–80; Jan Zalasiewicz et al., 'Colonization of the Americas, "Little Ice Age" Climate, and Bombproduced Carbon: Their Role in Defining the Anthropocene', *Anthropocene Review* 2 (2015), 117–27.

process in a manner very familiar to historians in dealing with periodization; it is well understood that periodization is already contingent on the narratives that frame conventions in a particular field of interest.[64] Yet the challenge also runs in the other direction. If, in the longer term, we discover that the human impact on the environment has become so extensive as to require the energies of a significant amount of society's activities and resources to mitigate or manage it, then the periodization of environmental change must be at the forefront of how social change is narrated. This is, in fact, not an observation solely about our present dilemmas or future hazards. It is not trivial that the introduction, even on a small scale, of monocultural field agriculture means that somebody (probably women or children) must subsequently spend a lot of time weeding or carting manure, or that most of the world's coastal communities ebb and flow with the availability of and market for seafood. Thus the story of the Anthropocene, however narrated and given empirical foundations, in fact highlights the role of ecological processes in social processes that have always been there (and indeed that many works of history have recognized). This is not to deny that the Anthropocene, as a shift in the 'earth system', represents an altogether new scale of impact from human behaviour. But, scale aside, it is not clear that this represents any epistemological break with how humans understand their predicaments, even if it gives us cause to reflect anew on our social and ecological life.

While some disciplines prefer to wield Occam's razor, history's inclination to complication can also make clear that there is no easy allocation of 'responsibility' or 'virtue' to particular groups, populations, or indeed species. The cross-generational passage of benefits from extraction, carbon emissions, empire, and suchlike (measured against a putative counterfactual of 'what if they had not done this' or 'follow the money'), or indeed the identification of a consistent population across time that might reap rewards or be sustainable, is no simple matter, as any economic or demographic historian will attest. Nevertheless, the simple metrics (albeit with complex dynamics) of a global systems model can equally present the historical discipline with some blunt questions, often too easily ignored amid historians' habitual embrace of the singular and irreversible. What would a world without fossil fuels really look like? This does not require a very clear answer, nor could it have one; but it serves the purpose of focusing attention on what properties of our world *are* related to fossil fuel consumption and on the fact that society's capacity to alter the world is clearly related to particular technologies.

These matters do not have to be considered on the grand scale to make great history. The historian of technology Finn Arne Jørgensen, for example, offers a microhistory of why the automatic bottle-recycling machine was invented and adopted in Norway, a history of income, retailing practices and community scale, social expectation, government legislation, bottle-making technology, and commercial and manufacturing practices—as well as, somewhere down the line, environmental thinking. The recycling device was successful because it could be aligned with the expectations of consumers and recyclers, who operated through

---

[64] See also Clive Hamilton, 'Getting the Anthropocene So Wrong', *Anthropocene Review* 2 (2015), 102–7.

small-scale grocery stores, while its designers were able to respond rapidly to the entrepreneurial challenges in developing technology that matched changing bottle design, material, and drinking habits, as well as expectations about returning vessels for reuse (a habit inculcated in an earlier, more austere, and poorer age). Nearly all of this story would have been missed in an account that simply focused on 'green thinking', 'environmentalism', and the willpower of Norwegian citizens, or indeed some characteristic of 'Norwegian society'. As it happens, it is precisely the kind of story that policymakers should take cognizance of today.[65] Such a history—a history of consequences—does not necessarily change the practice of history itself; nevertheless, the *kinds* of questions opened up in Anthropocene debates draw lines—lines of effects—that transcend the traditional boundaries of historical inquiry. The history of liquid refreshment looks different when we know that a plastic bottle drunk from for a couple of minutes and cast away may well end up in a vast array of similar waste in the middle of the Pacific Ocean, which takes centuries before it is dissolved by sunlight into tinier particles that attract pollutants and are readily absorbed into marine lifeforms, to continue through the food chain.[66]

These considerations may also return us to some old matters of concern that many historians have neglected or avoided for fear of getting tarnished through association with determinism—or worse. One such matter is the soil. It is of course not really news to anyone working in landscape or agricultural history that the soil shapes practice and possibilities (at the very least, the cost of inputs required to enable certain outputs); and it is now equally well understood that soil itself is not a static category but varies within historical time as a result of processes of weathering, hydrology, and management. However, how people interact with the soils on which they live is also itself shaped by whether they consider it as something fundamentally fixed and constraining or as a matter of 'choice' and malleability, which has itself been shaped by shifting notions of what the soil consists of and how it relates to living things (which may be codified in systems of chemistry or soil science) as well as by learning processes from farming or gathering.[67] Again, to look 'out' and down to the soil may shift attention to how *social* and *intellectual* boundedness operate, as well as to ecological processes. Indeed, it is worth being reminded at this point that looking at 'the soil' or at 'the forest' as central subjects of environmental history is to replicate a certain kind of environmental paradigm of fairly recent vintage, where nature is above all a matter of exterior phenomena. We might wonder how this boundary is drawn and maintained, while matters of health and the body, for example, are generally related to interior and social qualities. This division of labour—the existence of 'environmental health' notwithstanding—was not yet completed in the late nineteenth century, as the history of medicine has demonstrated.

[65] Finn Arne Jørgensen, *Making a Green Machine: The Infrastructure of Beverage Container Recycling* (New Brunswick, 2011).

[66] Tony Juniper, *What Has Nature Ever Done for Us?* (London, 2013).

[67] Paul Warde, 'The Invention of Sustainability', *Modern Intellectual History* 8 (2011), 153–70; Benjamin R. Cohen, *Notes from the Ground: Science, Soil and Society in the American Countryside* (New Haven, CT, 2009).

Such approaches have the potential to cast new light on the materiality of social interactions that go beyond traditional demarcations and on (still worthy) topics where 'environment' and 'society' were assumed to be separate but set in relation to each other, such as nature protection or conservation, the environment as base and raw material for a social superstructure, or the problem of pollution. I am not proposing that necessity is imposed either on society by the environment or vice versa. Rather *both* certainly confront people, individually and collectively, with a round of what we might paradoxically call 'involuntary choices', which are handed down by circumstance and may differ significantly across the social scale.[68] How we might imagine such hybridity evolving over time can be glimpsed in histories such as Pekka Hämäläinen's *Comanche Empire*, which tells a revisionist history of the American West and of how the culturally and ethnically fluid society of the Comanches was able to carve out an aggressive power (*imperium*) in the interstices of American and Spanish colonial power, shifting social organization in the face of climatic variability, economic opportunities, and especially changing ecology of bison and horses on the Great Plains and in the regions in which Comanches raided and traded.[69]

Just as environmental historians have deconstructed the naivety and elisions that lurk within the idea of 'wilderness'[70] as a space clear of people, so all historians must guard against histories that float miraculously free of material and place. We are, in the end, a worldly profession, and creatures of incarnation more than creatures of assumption. None of this necessitates some deep break in the wider practices of the historical discipline, which has always been in a process of adaptation and contestation of one sort or another. A history that was more conscious of the role played by the non-human in the constitution of society and of the *work* required to maintain human distinctiveness might be adequate to the Anthropocene precisely because it does not proclaim the new geological period as one of domination of nature, thus deifying its subject, *anthropos*, but helps in *normalizing* human behaviour as of this Earth.

ACKNOWLEDGEMENTS

I would like to thank Libby Robin and Sverker Sörlin for comments on drafts of this text. References are intended to be indicative rather than comprehensive in regard to the many issues addressed.

---

[68] I have borrowed this notion from the social historian John Styles's idea of 'involuntary consumption', the second-hand acquisition of consumer goods in a variety of contexts; see John Styles, *The Dress of the People: Everyday Fashion in Eighteenth-Century England* (New Haven, CT, 2007).

[69] Pekka Hämäläinen, *The Comanche Empire* (New Haven, CT, 2008).

[70] See the essays in William Cronon, ed., *Uncommon Ground: Rethinking the Human Place in Nature* (New York, 1995); see also the forum arranged by the journal *Environmental History* for the fiftieth anniversary of the Wilderness Act in 2014 (http://environmentalhistory.net/wilderness-act-forum, accessed 14 July 2015).

11

Material Histories of the World
Scales and Dynamics

Frank Trentmann

In 1823 John Potter Hamilton was on his way to Bogotá as one of Britain's first commissioners to the new state of Colombia. It proved a strenuous journey. In the Valle del Cauca, on the Pacific side of the country, Hamilton's trek faced mountains, jungle, and, above all, mud. One day he and his mule got stuck in such 'deep slough' that he had to get off the animal to try and pull them both out—only to sink in deeper and deeper in the process, much to the 'merriment and amusement of my secretary, servants [and] muleteers'. This was 'rather an annoyance', he recorded in the book of his travels, because he was due to make his 'debut' at Mr and Mrs Arboleda's, a wealthy local family. Mr Arboleda duly apologized for the bad state of the roads, pointing to the surrounding red hills, where 800 of his slaves were washing the soil for gold dust. 'After making ourselves clean and comfortable, we sat down to an elegant dinner served on massy [massive] silver dishes and French china, and soon forgot all our past grievances.' Before the Civil War, Mr Arboleda had counted 10,000 head of cattle his own. Now they were barely a tenth. Still, his estate was hardly a poorhouse. In one room, which 'he called his study', he had managed to bring together an extensive library of French, English, Italian, and of course Spanish books. When Hamilton entered his guest room, he was struck by the 'luxuries provided for the toilet which are only found among rich families in Europe'. His bed was 'completely in the French style', the curtains 'ornamented with artificial flowers'. On the table lay 'eau de Cologne, Windsor soap, *huile de Macassar* [a hair conditioner], *crème d'amandes amêres* [*sic*] [an almond lotion], brushes, &c.'. In the morning a servant announced that 'a cold bath' was ready.[1]

Hamilton found himself in a secluded valley in deepest Colombia, a universe far, far away from the metropolitan bustle of London and Paris; and yet he was greeted by a collection of domestic comforts and luxuries familiar from home. Travel accounts like his give us a snapshot of the material world *in situ*: individuals find and handle objects in a local setting and often describe them in fine detail. The historian who studies such a source is not so different from a visitor who

---

[1] John Potter Hamilton, *Travels through the Interior Provinces of Colombia* (London, 1827), vol. 2, 114–21.

presses his nose against a showcase in one of today's museums of decorative arts and design.

But this is only one perspective on the material world. A radically different vantage point is obtained by looking through the other end of the lens and seeing the material mass of the world as a whole. One way of doing this is by measuring material flows across time and space, a method developed by social ecologists and environmental economists. Each household, community, and country has material inputs and outputs—things and resources that are being sucked in while others are being spat out. National accounts measure these flows within the territories of a state. Put them together and you will find the social metabolism of the world.

This method is not perfect—no method is. For one, it does not discriminate between different types of materials; it lumps them together instead. A ton of coal carries the same weight as a ton of wool, but the former is much more harmful to the planet than the latter. Water tends to be excluded altogether in most accounts because it is heavy and its extraction, distribution, and use are so ubiquitous that adding it would render numbers meaningless; think of all the things in which water is 'embedded', such as cotton. Some households and communities have a faster metabolism than their neighbours, but this disappears in aggregates. Still, notwithstanding these and other problems, material flow analysis has the merit of giving us at least an overall sense of the total amount of stuff and material in use in the world. The twentieth century, for which we have good figures, saw a dramatic growth in material appetite.[2] In 2009 the world went through more than ten times as much matter as in 1900. Even when adjusted for population and taking into consideration that societies were much more efficient in 2000 in their use of goods than they were in 1900, a person today goes through twice as much material as his or her great-grandparent did.

As sources for historical study, Hamilton's *Travels* and global material use may seem worlds apart, one giving us French curtains and a bar of soap, the other giga-tons of resources. But it would be wrong to try and fit them neatly into micro or macro accounts familiar to historians since the 1970s and to treat them as mutu-ally exclusive alternatives.[3] Rather, we should see them as prompts to think about the linkages between the local and the global and between humans and things. The phenomenal rise in consumption and material use is a dynamic process and, to understand it, we need to reconstruct the linkages that have propelled it forward. This also requires us to take a longer and broader view of consumption. Goods have a life before and after the point of purchase; and this includes the materials that go into their making, as well as their disposal and mutation into waste. In

---

[2] Fridolin Krausmann, Simone Gingrich, Nina Eisenmenger, Karl-Heinz Erb, Helmut Haberl, and Marina Fischer-Kowalski, 'Growth in Global Materials Use, GDP and Population during the 20th Century', *Ecological Economics* 68.10 (2009), 2696–705. See also Marina Fischer-Kowalski et al., *Gesellschaftlicher Stoffwechsel und Kolonisierung von Natur* (Amsterdam, 1997).

[3] For different points of entry into these methodological genres, see, e.g., Charles Tilly, *Big Structures, Large Processes, Huge Comparisons* (New York, 1984); John Brewer, 'Microhistory and the Histories of Everyday Life', *Cultural & Social History* 7.1 (2010), 87–110; and Filippo de Vivo, 'Prospect or Refuge? Microhistory, History on the Large Scale', *Cultural & Social History* 7.3 (2010), 387–97.

addition to the goods in our shopping bag, we carry on our back an invisible 'ecological rucksack', to use the image of the climate expert Friedrich Schmidt-Bleek. This backpack contains all the materials needed to produce, deliver, and dispose of our goods, including the fuel for shipping, cooling, and heating and the tapioca and soy that feed our livestock. Looking at that backpack widens our view of material processes considerably: in addition to the contents of this or their shopping bags, the average person in advanced societies today uses between 45,000 kg and 85,000 kg of materials and resources (coal, oil, metals, minerals, grain etc.) in the course of one year.[4] That is a lot of stuff.

In his work as in his life, Eric Hobsbawm had an ambivalent relationship with consumption. He was deeply in tune with jazz music, but jeans and other aspects of popular youth culture from the 1960s left him cold.[5] Consumption was never absent from his writing—after all, he made the pessimist's case in the debate about the standard of living in the late 1950s, emphasizing that there is more to quality of life than wages. The shift from luxury trades to mass consumption in textiles, too, received its mention in subsequent work. Nonetheless, industry and finance remained, for him, the drivers of capitalism, and consuming tended to appear more as an effect of these forces than as a historical phenomenon in its own right. A partial exception is his treatment of the 1960s as a cultural revolution. As he put it in a characteristically controversial passage in *Interesting Times* (2002), the 'year 1968 may prove to be less of a turning-point in twentieth-century history than 1965, which has no political significance whatever, but was the year in which the French clothing industry for the first time produced more women's trousers than skirts'.[6] It was in the 1970s and 1980s that a new generation of anthropologists and historians reclaimed consumption as a major source of social identity for class and gender. But giving attention to goods and their use need not mean shelving Hobsbawm's main project and his interest in the history of capitalism. Quite the contrary: consuming not only creates identities; it also generates demand, which in turn propels capitalism, production, and social and material change. The pages to come should therefore be read as an extension of Hobsbawm's intellectual architecture—a plea for making us think about ways to historicize demand and to understand how the lifestyles that generate it stimulate capitalism. Consumption, in other words, is an input of capitalism as well as an output.

Consuming is private and intimate, but also public and global. Getting a grip on it therefore raises interesting challenges about the scale of historical inquiry. Recent environmental historians have stretched the scale of this research to 'deep

---

[4] Albert Adriaanse et al., *Resource Flows: The Material Basis of Industrial Economies* (Washington DC, 1997).

[5] In *The Age of Extremes* (London, 1994), Eric Hobsbawm noted how consumer culture unsettled generational identities: 'Blue jeans, the deliberately demotic wear pioneered on American college campuses by students who did *not* wish to look like their elders, came to appear, on weekdays and holidays, or even, in "creative" or other hip occupations at work, below many a grey head' (326). Eric was not one of those grey heads.

[6] Eric Hobsbawm, *Interesting Times: A Twentieth-Century Life* (London, 2002), 261.

history', making it run across centuries and millennia.[7] This chapter argues that we should also travel further between spatial scales (macro and micro, global and local) if we are to understand better the dynamic expansion of our material world. The following sections explore some of the chains in these spatial connections, starting with trade and empire, then turning inwards to the material self, before tracing connections between modern networks, energy use, and people's habits. I will conclude by reflecting on the methodological challenges that face historians of the material world.

TRADE AND EMPIRE

One way to connect the local and the global is by tracing the life of a commodity. At their best, commodity biographies can illuminate the links between sites of production and consumption on opposite sides of the world. Sidney Mintz's pioneering account of sugar, *Sweetness and Power* (1985), is a towering example.[8] Yet many such works have limitations not dissimilar to those of conventional biographies. There is a danger of methodological solipsism, as if everything in the world turned around the chosen commodity as the main protagonist in history. But, of course, the world is full of commodities and objects. Very few objects are, so to speak, their own masters. Tea, coffee, and cocoa in the Atlantic world, for example, and also maté in Latin America, were all part of larger cultures of sociability and comfort that involved many other objects and services, from drinking utensils and furniture to ideas about appropriate dress and behaviour. While commodities leave their mark on the organization of labour and leisure—the plantation and the tea party—they are also the products of larger historical forces. Commodity biographies tend to exaggerate the former and to downplay the latter. To try and pin the rise of Protestant Northern Europe in the seventeenth and eighteenth centuries and the decline of the Catholic south onto their respective taste for coffee versus chocolate is not very illuminating.[9] Commodities circulated through the veins of empires and trading networks in a larger body politic with its own ideas, interests, and institutions. And these larger structures underwent fundamental changes between 1500 and 1900 that, in turn, helped to transform the world of goods.

---

[7] From the growing literature, see Julia Adeney Thomas, 'History and Biology in the Anthropocene: Problems of Scale, Problems of Value', *American Historial Review* 119.5 (2014), 1587–607; Andrew Shryock and Daniel Lord Smail, eds, *Deep History: The Architecture of Past and Present* (Berkeley, CA, 2011). See also the chapter by Paul Warde in this volume.

[8] Sidney Mintz, *Sweetness and Power: The Place of Sugar in Modern History* (New York, 1985). For different approaches, see Robert J. Foster, 'Tracking Globalization: Commodities and Value in Motion', in Christopher Tilley, Webb Keane, Susanne Kühler, Mike Rowlands, and Patricia Spyer, eds, *Handbook of Material Culture* (London, 2006), 285–302. See also the chapter by Pat Hudson in this volume.

[9] Britons are renowned tea drinkers, but it tends to be forgotten that in 1900 they also drank as much chocolate as the Spanish. Nor should the sober atmosphere of the coffee house in earlier centuries be overdone; see Brian Cowan, *The Social Life of Coffee: The Emergence of the British Coffeehouse* (New Haven, CT, 2005).

Goods had travelled between continents since ancient times. By AD 100 textiles, indigo, and spices reached the Roman empire from Asia via the Silk Road, coins, fine glass, and coral moving in return. By 1000 the Indian Ocean had become such a lively trading zone that it was common to see cottons dyed and printed in Gujarat in the markets of Cairo and Zanzibar.[10] Inventories, diaries, and other gazettes reveal a growing number of chests, shirts, cutlery, oriental carpets, and musical instruments from Asia in Renaissance Italy in the fifteenth century, including in the homes of artisans.[11] Late Ming China enjoyed its own commercial heyday as more sugar, books, and porcelain circulated in the empire.[12] Still, goods also confronted many obstacles in these settings. Italian cities like Florence were essentially small, high-end artisanal markets for the European elite. Their fortune rose and fell with that of a fairly small, exclusive clientele. It was a highly vulnerable position. The discovery of the Americas in 1492 was part of a long-term shift in trade from the Mediterranean to the Atlantic and from Venice and Florence to Amsterdam and London. Then the Thirty Years War (1618–48) cut the Italian cities off from markets in Northern Europe. Late Ming China, meanwhile, had commerce but few cities, and thus also few urban consumers. And, with the exception of the voyages to India in the early fifteenth century, the late Ming emperors were oriented inwards, not outwards. This territorial orientation had a cultural counterpart: what was primarily valued was domestic antiques, not novelties or exotic goods from afar. Like Renaissance Italy, late Ming China prized land over commerce. Consumption remained suspect, denounced for eroding social and gender hierarchies, for corrupting the soul, and for draining the coffers of cities and states.

By contrast, the European empires, first and foremost the Dutch and the British, carved out a new, more dynamic world of goods. Bits of the New World were carried across the world in the shape of mined silver and gold, being used as payment for porcelain and cotton from China and India. Imperial commanders and soldiers of fortune returned with loot from India and Egypt.[13] The Caribbean became a major site of transplantation. Enslaved people and plants from one part of the world were uprooted and grafted onto another.[14] Sugar and coffee plantations opened up new zones of cultivation. It is debatable whether this ecological annexation (together with coal fields at home) was decisive and gave Britain a head start in industrialization and led to the 'great divergence' between Northern

[10] Peter Frankopan, *The Silk Roads: A New History of the World* (London, 2015); Ruth Barnes, *Indian Block-Printed Textiles in Egypt: The Newberry Collection in the Ashmolean Museum* (Oxford, 1997).

[11] Isabella Palumbo-Fossati, 'L'interno della casa dell'artigiano e dell'artista nella Venezia del cinquecento', *Studi Veneziani* 8 (1984), 109–53; Marta Ajmar-Wollheim and Flora Dennis, eds, *At Home in Renaissance Italy* (London, 2006).

[12] Timothy Brook, *The Confusions of Pleasure: Commerce and Culture in Ming China* (Berkeley, CA, 1998).

[13] Maya Jasanoff, *Edge of Empire: Lives, Culture, and Conquest in the East, 1750–1850* (New York, 2005).

[14] Alfred W. Crosby, *Ecological Imperialism: The Biological Expansion of Europe, 900–1900* (Cambridge, 1986).

Europe and China.[15] What is indisputable is that imperial expansion played an important role in widening the range of goods and foods available to Europeans and their cousins overseas and, with that, people's norms and expectations. In North America, it was the experience of a rising standard of living in the early and mid-eighteenth century that turned colonial consumers into revolutionary patriots in the 1760s and 1770s, when Westminster reverted to taxing the colonies.[16] Mercantile tariffs and shipping restrictions certainly meant that prices were steeper and access more limited than in a free market, but it is difficult to see how these new zones of cotton, coffee, and sugar could have been brought into existence in the first place without the force of empire, the navy, and the slave trade.[17]

If the eighteenth century was marked by imperial rivalry and protectionism, the nineteenth brought British hegemony and free trade. In 1846 Britain repealed its protectionist corn laws, and shortly thereafter its restrictive navigation acts. The new open-door policy triggered a series of some fifty European trade treaties in the 1860s; in this it was a forerunner of the European single market in the 1970s. While Britain's European trading partners reverted to protectionism in the 1880s, Britain kept its door wide open. For the world of goods, this liberal opening was hugely consequential. Not only did consumers in Liverpool and London get more stuff at cheaper prices, but people in Vienna and Stockholm, too, began to enjoy the fruits of foreign colonies more easily. In fact, by 1914, Scandinavians were drinking more coffee per person than anyone else in the world, something inconceivable without the more liberal architecture of world trade.

Free trade, steamships, and cooling technology fostered a more integrated world economy than ever before. Price, not origin, was now decisive, and this changed the quantity and quality of things in circulation. By 1900, for example, Britons consumed 90 lb. of sugar per person, but most of this now came from beet in Germany and continental Europe, not from sugar cane on Jamaican plantations. As the material world bulged, then, there were also big shifts in material flows between regions. The crisis and decline of the British Caribbean after slavery and in the era of free trade was one part of this story.

The more 'liberal' circulation of goods changed the look of things as well and, with it, the creation of value. In the seventeenth century, coffee and cocoa had been prized for their distant, exotic qualities. Their value was authenticated by travellers, scientists, and *virtuosi* connoisseurs who communicated their tastefulness

---

[15] Kenneth Pomeranz, *The Great Divergence: China, Europe, and the Making of the Modern World Economy* (Princeton, NJ, 2000); Prasannan Parthasarathi, *Why Europe Grew Rich and Asia Did Not: Global Economic Divergence, 1600–1850* (Cambridge, 2011); Stephen Broadberry and Bishnupriya Gupta, 'The Early Modern Great Divergence: Wages, Prices and Economic Development in Europe and Asia, 1500–1800', *Economic History Review* 59.1 (2006), 2–31.

[16] See T. H. Breen, *The Marketplace of Revolution: How Consumer Politics Shaped American Independence* (New York, 2004), and now Steve Pincus, *The Heart of the Declaration: The Founders' Case for an Activist Government* (New Haven, CT, 2016).

[17] Here as elsewhere, I am simplifying a very complex and long-standing debate. A good starting point is Patrick K. O'Brien, 'Fiscal and Financial Preconditions for the Rise of British Naval Hegemony, 1485–815', *EH Working Paper*, 91/05, 2005 (http://www.lse.ac.uk/economicHistory/pdf/WP9105. pdf, accessed 19 May 2017).

and appropriate consumption. By the late nineteenth century, by contrast, they had become mass consumer goods and were increasingly repackaged as industrial foods. Their value now derived not from their exotic origin but from European technology, standards, and marketing. The technique of extracting butter from the cocoa bean opened the door to chocolate bars and cocoa powder. When Europeans brewed their coffee in 1900, they now mostly drank a blend of beans from Brazil, Kenya, and Mysore.

Some writers have presented this period as launching a form of 'commodity racism'.[18] This is too simple. The reality was more surprising and more troubling. Instead of vilifying colonial 'others' openly, Europeans erased them altogether from the brands and advertisements of coffee, cocoa, and chocolate. Cadbury advertised its 'authentic English cocoa', manufactured to scientific standards in the healthy air of its Bournville factory. Coffee brands in imperial Germany included 'Industrie', which showed a proud German worker in front of smokestacks, not an indentured labourer on an exotic plantation, and 'Arminius', named after the German national hero who defeated the Romans in the Teutoburg Forest in AD 8.[19] At the 1893 world fair in Chicago, Stollwerck created a 38-foot-tall chocolate temple of Germania. The French had 'Jeanne d'Arc' chocolate bars, the Swiss had 'Toblerone' with a bear on the Matterhorn. In Finland, after the First World War, the Paulig company sent the so-called Paula Girls in folkloristic Sääksmäki costumes up and down the country to teach housewives how to brew proper 'Finnish' coffee. Exotic origins never entirely disappeared—rum is one example. Still, the domestication of previously exoticized products is striking. The era of mass consumption, then, must be thought of together with free trade, the new imperialism, and the creation of national publics. In addition to ransacking Africa, Asia, and Latin America for resources for European industry, Europeans also nationalized the image of many colonial things (see Plate 11.1a–d).

Materialization, then, is not straightforward, either culturally or economically. Nor is the physical flow of materials between different regions of the world. The total volume of stuff circulating in the world increased eight times between 1962 and 2005—from 2,400 to 19,000 million tonnes; roughly half of that comes in the shape of fossil fuels; the rest is biomass, metals, and minerals. But the relative position of regions shifted in this period. In the 1960s, Europe, the United States, and Japan were the principal net importers of resources. By 2000 they had been joined by China, India, South Korea, and Malaysia, which now exceeded the demands of many European countries. The largest net exporter of resources is Australia; it is followed by Canada and Brazil, which exports growing amounts of biomass. So far these figures refer to actual physical exchanges between countries, for instance in the form of shipping oil from Venezuela to China. The picture becomes more complex and gloomier if we recall the 'ecological rucksack' full of all

[18] Anne McClintock, *Imperial Leather: Race, Gender and Sexuality in the Colonial Contest* (London, 1995).
[19] Julia Laura Rischbieter, *Mikro-Ökonomie der Globalisierung: Kaffee, Kaufleute und Konsumenten im Kaiserreich 1870–1914* (Cologne, 2011).

the things and materials needed to produce the goods that countries purchase. Since the 1970s, Britain, for example, has seen a sharp decline in direct use of material, thanks to deindustrialization: fewer factories and plants translate into less demand for coal, iron and steel. But, on their own, national material accounts produce an optical illusion. They need to be placed in their true global, environmental context if we are to recognize the hidden resources that lie embedded in imported things produced elsewhere. A British person buying a car made in Brazil, for example, is responsible not only for the 2 tons of steel, glass, and plastic that end up rolling down a suburban street in Peckham. Manufacturing this vehicle required a lot of fossil fuel, iron, and various other resources in Brazil, Spain, and Poland. At least some of these materials should be laid at Britain's door. Calculations of such indirect flows for the period 1962–2005 show that South America, Australia, and Central Asia have been increasingly bearing the environmental burden for the rest of the world. Put differently, Western Europe and Japan—and, increasingly, also the United States and China—have been enjoying plenty of materials while offshoring most of the environmental damage involved in their production.[20]

The legacies from such regional imbalances in material flows are not just a matter for ethical and ecological debate today. They also invite us to widen our perspective on past developments. The Victorian and Edwardian story of free trade, for example, to this day is overwhelmingly told as a liberal success story of market integration, of putting 'a girdle around the earth' as Victorian liberals liked to say, with cheaper food and benefits for all, and the occasional acknowledgement that it also involved imperial wars, famines, and force.[21] But the quickening metabolism in the era of free trade also involved the unprecedented extraction and use of resources. And this had profound consequences for landscapes and environments, both within Britain itself and for the rest of the world. By 1900, some 80 per cent of the world's coal trade was in British hands. At the end of the First World War, it was estimated that Britain pumped 10 million tons of smoke and soot into the air.[22] The long-distance trade in bulk foodstuffs had already been a feature of the early modern world. In the eighteenth century, the Dutch shipped herring from the North Sea to Northern Europe and to the German states; in exchange, grain from Prussia, Poland, and Bohemia moved west. By the early 1830s, wheat and flour had travelled over 2,000 miles before they reached

[20] Monika Dittrich and Stefan Bringezu, 'The Physical Dimension of International Trade, Part 1: Direct Global Flows between 1962 and 2005', *Ecological Economics* 69.9 (2010), 1838–47; Monika Dittrich, Stefan Bringezu, and Helmut Schutz, 'The Physical Dimension of International Trade, Part 2: Indirect Global Resource Flows between 1962 and 2005', *Ecological Economics* 79 (2012), 32–43.

[21] The Whiggish narrative persists in spite of recent and older critical accounts: John Gallagher and Ronald Robinson, 'The Imperialism of Free Trade', *Economic History Review* 6.1 (1953), 1–15; Anthony Howe, *Free Trade and Liberal England 1846–1946* (Oxford, 1997); Mike Davis, *Late Victorian Holocausts: El Niño Famines and the Making of the Third World* (London, 2001); Frank Trentmann, *Free Trade Nation: Commerce, Consumption, and Civil Society in Modern Britain* (Oxford, 2008).

[22] Chris Otter, 'Liberty and Ecology: Resources, Markets, and the British Contribution to the Global Environmental Crisis', in Simon Gunn and James Vernon, eds, *The Peculiarities of Liberal Modernity in Imperial Britain* (Berkeley, CA, 2011), 182–98.

breakfast tables in London. Free trade (after 1846), steamboats, and refrigeration stretched food even further, and now also more perishable items. In the eighteenth century a Londoner's butter, cheese, and eggs used to come from a few hundred miles away. By the 1870s, they had travelled over 1,300 miles.[23] Before 1846 fruit and vegetables and live animals had been sourced locally or regionally. By the 1890s, these, too, had travelled over 1,000 and 3,000 miles respectively. Under free trade, Britons not only developed a bigger appetite: their appetite also left its legacy on ever more distant parts of the world.

Free trade and laissez-faire did not win out everywhere—in colonial India, for example, concerns over the conservation of native forests made colonial administrators look to government and regulation.[24] But the revolution in transport, mobility, and communication in these decades unquestionably reinforced the pull on overseas resources. The transatlantic cable that connected Valentia Island in the west of Ireland with Heart's Content in eastern Newfoundland in 1866 required copper for 340,000 miles of wire, which were coated with gutta-percha, a natural rubber from Borneo. The cable did not only speed up communication, it also involved the annual destruction of 26 million trees in Borneo. By the 1880s, western experts warned of how the 'gradual scarcity, and threatened extinction of the guttifers, has for some years been the cause of much anxiety' and threatened the future of the electrical industries.[25]

Historical studies of consumption and research on resources tend to be separate fields. The former chart the rise of affluence, leaving scarcity to the latter. The dominant narrative of 'consumer society' is thus a story of more and more, in which shortages and environmental consequences appear, if at all, as an effect or afterword, most notably since the oil crises of the 1970s. Bringing consumption and the flow of materials into the same analytical frame creates the opportunity to tell a radically different story. It enables us to view affluence and scarcity in a dialectical relationship, in constant interplay. Rising demand and diminishing resources are the see-saw of modern capitalism.

Scarcity long predates the environmental concerns and 'postmaterialist' values of the 1970s. More coal burning in domestic fires and industrial furnaces led Victorians to worry about a 'coal famine'.[26] In 1908 US President Roosevelt set up a National Conservation Commission, because it was feared that the United States was burning through its own resources so fast that the country was at risk of decline and exhaustion. In 1951 Truman followed with the President's Materials Policy Commission, in order to show that America still had the ability to grow. The warning

[23] J. Richard Peet, 'The Spatial Expansion of Commercial Agriculture in the Nineteenth Century', *Economic Geography* 45 (1969), 283–301.
[24] See Emma G. Reisz, '"Provident" Political Economy in Indian Forests', in Martin Daunton and Frank Trentmann, eds, *Worlds of Political Economy: Knowledge and Power in the Nineteenth and Twentieth Centuries* (Basingstoke and New York, 2004), 115–35.
[25] Charles Bright, *Submarine Telegraphs: Their History, Construction, and Working* (London, 1898; repr. Cambridge, 2014). The quotation comes from page 258, which also gives calculations about the destruction of trees.
[26] There is a forthcoming study on coal by Fredrik Albritton Jonsson, *Cornucopia and the Stationary Future: The End of Growth in the Age of Industry*.

that the world was reaching the 'limit of growth', often associated with the Club of Rome's report published in 1972, was already made by the American conservationist Samuel Ordway in 1955, in the very midst of the postwar boom.[27]

What changed in the modern period was the remedies offered for the problem. And these reflect the governing ideologies of their day. During the progressive era, in the early twentieth century, responsible stewardship was in the moral purview of all citizens. By the 1950s, in the era of the Cold War, thinking about future resources had become inseparable from a defence of freedom, choice, and the market. Truman's commissioners noted with concern the 'lavish use of materials'—richly ornamented cars with single passengers who enjoyed the roar and acceleration of heavy engines—but to interfere with rising consumption and private lifestyle was now off the political table. Private enterprise, individual choice, and growth would guide the use of energy and resources, with a minimum of government guidance.

Shortages, moreover, were not only about the absence of things at that particular moment. Efforts to persuade people to conserve resources now often came with promises of a brighter future, in which goods and comforts would return as a reward for temporary sacrifice. Thus, in the late 1940s, amid an energy crisis, Germans were urged to conserve electricity, switch off their heaters and appliances, and monitor their meters daily, while posters announced the impending return of electrical helpers. In this way shortages also created expectations of plenty (see Plate 11.2).

THE MATERIAL SELF

Trade flows of fossil fuels, biomass, and minerals, measured in billions of tons, give a valuable sense of the changing scale of the material world and of the problems arising from it. But they can also appear abstract and lifeless and do not explain *why* people and societies came to pursue and devour so much more stuff over time. This is not the place to discuss all the various factors behind the growth of consumption—factors that, in addition to empire, would need to include purchasing power, urbanization, innovation, and the rise of a middle-class culture.[28] Instead I would like to turn now to one critical dimension: people's changing view of things and, by extension, of themselves. The expansion of the material world involved a fundamental sea change. Everyone, from Plato to the Christian Fathers, had preached that humans and things were fundamental opposites, the mind or

[27] Samuel Ordway, 'Possible Limits of Raw Material Consumption', in William. L. Thomas, ed., *Man's Role in Changing the Face of the Earth* (Chicago, 1956), 987–1009; Donella Meadows, Dennis L. Meadows, Jorgen Randers, and William W. Behrens III, *The Limits to Growth: A Report for the Club of Rome's Project on the Predicament of Mankind* (New York, 1972). See also Libby Robin, Sverker Sörlin, and Paul Warde, *The Future of Nature: Documents of Global Change* (New Haven, CT, 2013), esp. Part 2.

[28] Frank Trentmann, ed., *The Oxford Handbook of the History of Consumption* (Oxford, 2012); Frank Trentmann, *Empire of Things: How We Became a World of Consumers, from the Fifteenth Century to the Twenty-First* (London, 2016).

soul being in need of protection from the corrupting lure of objects. Between the seventeenth and the nineteenth centuries a new mindset was gaining ground that appreciated things as essential elements of what it meant to be human. Without an appreciation of this rapprochement between humans and things, it is impossible to understand the dynamic growth of the world of things. For more and more stuff to enter people's lives, things had to enter their hearts and minds.

Our understanding of this transformation has suffered from two distorted perspectives which have portrayed modernity as a socioeconomic system that separated humans from things. The first is Marxism. Here the rise of capitalism in the West is linked to the triumph of money and markets. Wage labour alienated workers from the products of their own hands. Whereas older cultures fetishized goods for their supernatural or animalistic powers, products in capitalist societies were given a price tag, which turned them into an abstract unit that could be exchanged for money. The capitalist market economy conjured up an unnatural equivalence between all sorts of different products: 20 yards of linen = 1 coat = 10 lb of tea = 1 quarter of corn = ½ ton of iron, to use Marx's own example in the first volume of *Capital*.[29] The materialist conception of history carried its name for a reason. Marx's followers were convinced that only socialism truly appreciated matter as the foundation of nature and society.[30] Capitalism might throw up shiny products, but deep down it did not care about stuff and naturally led to a squandering of resources. In reality, of course, socialist countries turned out to be even more wasteful and polluting than their capitalist neighbours.

The second perspective comes from a more recent socio-technological view of the modern world, which was championed by the French sociologist and thinker Bruno Latour and attracted an influential international following in the social sciences in the 1990s and in the first decade of the twenty-first century. Latour reacted against the indifference to things then dominant in the social sciences, where states, social movements, and human actors did all the running. At a time of growing concern about climate change and the escalation of material use, this disregard for things was profoundly problematic, politically as well as scientifically. In his early work in the 1970s and 1980s, Latour had shown how in real life science did not advance through rational principles but was a social construct, shaped by interactions in a laboratory between scientists, their ideas, and, critically, their instruments.[31] More generally, he argued, a lot of what people did and of how society functioned was only made possible by material 'actants', from keys and doors that opened and shut spaces to tools and machinery that enabled people to express themselves and put virtual ideas into physical reality. Pistols, bullets, fridges, and plastics do matter. This rallying call for the 'missing masses' retains a lot of its original force.[32] In subsequent work, however, Latour went a big step

---

[29] See Karl Marx, *Das Kapital* (Frankfurt, 1987 [1867]), 43 (Book I, ch. 1).

[30] See John Bellamy Foster, *Marx's Ecology: Materialism and Nature* (New York, 1999).

[31] Bruno Latour and Steve Woolgar, *Laboratory Life: The Construction of Scientific Facts* (London, 1979); Bruno Latour, *The Pasteurization of France* (Cambridge, MA, 1988).

[32] Bruno Latour, 'Where Are the Missing Masses? The Sociology of a Few Mundane Artifacts', in Wiebe E. Bijker and John Law, eds, *Shaping Technology/Building Society* (Cambridge, MA, 1992),

further and imposed his critique of the contemporary silencing of things onto modernity as a whole. In this view, as in Marx's, modernity was founded on a widening gulf between humans and things. But here, unlike in Marxism, it was reason (not markets and capital) that advanced the illusory idea of a civilization and progress propelled by the human mind alone. A direct line ran from Hobbes, Rousseau, and Kant in the seventeenth and eighteenth century to Rawls and Habermas in the twentieth. A clean break with this reason-based modernity was necessary in order to give things back their agency and get them heard: Latour aptly called for *Dingpolitik*.[33]

Alongside an emphasis on critical reason, however, modernity in fact gave rise to a new appreciation of things. Critics who warned against luxury and the power of things to corrupt the mind did not disappear, but they were confronted and outflanked by a growing number of voices who defended and embraced objects and possessions as sources of human identity, social advancement, and economic progress. These ideas came in several forms. One was a religious argument. God had furnished people with multiple and insatiable desires, wrote Robert Boyle, the great seventeenth-century Anglo-Irish scientist who is remembered today for his experiments with the air pump. He wanted people to be inquisitive and industrious. In seeking to satisfy their own desires, people were therefore not straying from a divinely ordained path, let alone selling their soul to the devil. Quite the contrary, Boyle wrote: it led them to a 'more exquisite admiration of the omniscient Author'.[34] Things could be friends of the spirit, not just their enemies.

A related argument connected the desire for novelty to the pursuit of trade and exploration. In the 1630s, Caspar Barlaeus, the Dutch polymath, praised trade for making people appreciate new things.[35] The world was full of undiscovered goods and objects, Thomas Sprat, one of the founders of the Royal Society in England, wrote three decades later. Why else would God have put them in the world, if He did not want humans to find them and use them? New fibres and new objects such as optical glass were vehicles of progress that opened up the universe in all its divine splendour.[36] In the mid-eighteenth century, the Scottish Enlightenment thinker David Hume refined these ideas into a general secular defence of moderate luxuries as a source of national wealth and cultural progress. New fashions and comforts made people more creative, productive, and civilized, which in turn made countries stronger as well as richer.

225–58; Bruno Latour, *Reassembling the Social: An Introduction to Actor-Network Theory* (Oxford, 2005).

[33] Bruno Latour, 'From Realpolitik to Dingpolitik', in Bruno Latour and Peter Weibel, eds, *Making Things Public: Atmospheres of Democracy* (Cambridge MA, 2005). The split between mind and body is often associated with Descartes, but recent philosophers have pointed out that Descartes, too, had a much richer view of the self; see Karen Detlefsen, ed., *Descartes' Meditations: A Critical Guide* (Cambridge, 2013).

[34] Robert Boyle, *Some Considerations Touching the Usefulness of Experimental Natural Philosophy* [1663], in idem, *Works of the Honourable Robert Boyle* (London, 1772), vol. 2, 5–63, here 31.

[35] Harold J. Cook, *Matters of Exchange: Commerce, Medicine, and Science in the Dutch Golden Age* (New Haven, CT, 2007).

[36] Thomas Sprat, *History of the Royal Society of London, for the Improving of Natural Knowledge* (London, 1667); Sprat became the bishop of Rochester.

Here was the mental furniture not only for traders and improvers but also for people at large. It was this new orientation towards the material world that made many flock in the seventeenth century to cabinets of curiosities and *Wunderkammern*, to admire everything from automatic clocks and exotic plants to the tusk of a narwhal. The idea that God had wanted people to discover and enjoy beautiful things also left its mark on a central stage of consumption: the home. Domestic possessions and the domestic interior came to demonstrate the spiritual development of their owners. Puritan austerity was out; a celebration of divine beauty was in. In Britain, one Baptist minister preached in the 1860s: 'We have left the old Puritan error. We no longer despise the beautiful and artistic, but claim them as divine things, and enlist them in divine service … all man's life and work can be dedicated to heaven.'[37]

In the context of Victorian Britain, these new attitudes have been traced to the rising doctrine of incarnationism and the decline of a more tortured evangelicalism, which had been fixated on sin and atonement. But the greater friendliness towards things gained a larger international momentum and advanced across a surprising number of Protestant doctrines and denominations, from the Reformed Church in Switzerland to the Mormon tabernacle in Salt Lake City. Among Mormons, letters and diaries in the 1860s–1880s give testimony to the growing importance attached to cultivating one's personal taste through beautiful objects.[38] Possessions refined the person through a higher symbiosis of aesthetics and spirituality.

In the years around 1900, the material turn was discernible across western thought and culture, from psychology and literature to early anthropology and the display of indigenous and 'traditional' lifestyles at exhibitions and museums. In the *Principles of Psychology* (1890), William James noted the significance of objects for emotions and identity. People had not only a 'social self' and a 'spiritual self'; they also had a 'material self'. 'The body', he wrote, 'is the innermost part of the material Self in each of us.' 'The clothes come next' and were a central source of personal identity. Then—and only then, in James's account—came our immediate family, 'bone of our bone and flesh of our flesh. When they die, a part of our very selves is gone.' People identified with their home: 'its aspects awaken the tenderest feelings of affection'. Homes were projects for improvement and sites for collecting more objects. Losing possessions, James wrote, did not only depress people because of a 'feeling that we must now go without certain goods that we expected the possessions to bring in their train'. It also involved 'a sense of the shrinkage of our personality, a partial conversion of ourselves to nothingness'.[39]

Contemporary writers and novelists, including William James's own younger brother Henry, explored how objects created meaning and helped build and destroy relationships between people.[40] During the First World War the artist Marcel Duchamp retrieved a bicycle wheel and a urinal and exhibited them as

[37] E. Luscombe Hull, quoted in Deborah Cohen, *Household Gods: The British and their Possessions* (New Haven, CT, 2006), 26.

[38] Greg ('Fritz') Umbach, 'Learning to Shop in Zion: The Consumer Revolution in Great Basin Mormon Culture, 1847–1910', *Journal of Social History* 38 (2004), 29–61.

[39] William James, *Principles of Psychology* (New York, 1918 [1890]), vol. 1, 292–3.

[40] Bill Brown, *A Sense of Things: The Object Matter of American Literature* (Chicago, IL, 2003).

pieces of art. Such 'ready-mades' may have attracted few admirers at the time, but fascination with objects was widespread, especially as old objects were falling into disuse. In London, Paris, and New York this was a golden age for second-hand and antique shops and those producing historical lookalike furniture.[41] As it churned out a lot of cheap new stuff, mass manufacturing also triggered a demand for old or authentic-looking vintage goods. Collecting expanded into a popular pastime. At a time of rapid social and technological change, everyday objects appeared to hold out a spiritual as much as a physical lifeline to the past. 'Ordinary' things acquired extraordinary value.

What role did this growing cultural sense of things play in the larger material history of the world? A recognition of the flux between humans and the material world was hardly unique to Europeans and Americans at the time. In Asian religions, things can have a soul. In Buddhism, they can strive towards liberation. Asian cultures were (and arguably remain) far less suspicious of objects and wealth than European ones, but that did not give them a head start in the consumer revolution or in the Industrial Revolution; nor, I should add, have fetishistic elements prevented them from exploiting markets and rapid development in recent decades. In other words, we must guard against monocausal explanations in which culture is treated as a simple economic asset. At the same time, the parallel expansion of things in trade and mentality deserves emphasis. The growing sensibility and receptiveness towards things gave objects greater room for physical circulation than they previously had. Restraints on demand never entirely disappeared; but they certainly loosened.[42] The appreciation that people had a 'material self' gave possessions a new legitimacy, as tools of self-cultivation and social advancement. This insight did not automatically favour liberal solutions. Totalitarian regimes, too, tried to exploit it for their ends. The campaign for *kulturnost* (a cultured lifestyle) in Stalin's Russia looked to the mirror, soap, and clean shirts to turn peasants into socialists. Political regimes differed in their methods, but across the board there was a growing tendency to see objects as a critical marker of personal and national identity. It is difficult to understand the material expansion of the modern world without these widening cultural horizons.

DEMANDING INFRASTRUCTURES, DEMANDING LIFESTYLES

So far, I have stressed the physical and cultural materialization of the modern world. These two processes worked in tandem. Networked infrastructures—such as those of gas, water, and electricity—brought material flows, social norms, and practices into immediate and intensive interplay. In the course of the nineteenth

---

[41] Manuel Charpy, 'Le Théâtre des objets: Espaces privés, culture matérielle et identité bourgeoise, Paris 1830–1914', unpublished PhD thesis, Université François-Rabelais de Tours, 2010.

[42] For a discussion of how sumptuary laws repressed demand and especially punished women, see Sheilagh C. Ogilvie, *A Bitter Living: Women, Markets, and Social Capital in Early Modern Germany* (Oxford, 2003).

and twentieth centuries these centralized networks and grids advanced into models of development. It is only in the last few decades that they have, once again, been challenged by calls for greater local self-reliance, off-grid, renewable solutions, or smart minigrids in which consumers are also producers of energy, so-called 'prosumers'.

Networks fundamentally altered the relationship between what people do, the appliances or machines they employ to accomplish their tasks, and their contact with the resources they need. Consider a typical household in a European city in 1900, which was dependent on a coal fire for heating, cooking, and washing. The household had to have the coal delivered, but, once that was accomplished, it could go about its domestic duties whenever it chose, regardless of what the neighbours did or when. The coal fire was physically prepared in the late evening for the following morning, mostly by older children—that is, as long as there was enough coal in the house. Most working-class tenements lacked a storage place and scraped by with small (and overpriced) deliveries, week after week. At a time of crisis, like the First World War, this meant irregular deliveries and little heat, or sometimes none at all. As a British government inquiry at the time showed, the coal crisis in London and southern England was one of distribution rather than supply: the railroads were congested by trains with troops and ammunitions.[43]

Electricity grids introduced very different relationships from the 1920s onwards. Alternating current electricity cannot be stored at home. It required a flick of the switch and no advance preparation or particular care to keep it going. Networks were much more efficient in balancing supply with demand by pooling power and distributing it where and when it was needed. On the other hand, by connecting many different users, the network also created new temporal vulnerabilities: peak demand. If every household switched on its electric heater or kettle at the same hour, it would create such a surge that it could bring down the entire system. Unlike the personalized, free-standing power plant of the individual fire, the electrical grid needs to be able to have enough extra capacity (peaking stations, backup generators, and pumped storage reservoirs) for multiple users to switch on appliances at the same moment. On the demand side just as on the supply side, coal and electricity therefore involve fundamentally different material relationships.

The era of networks came with phenomenal changes in consumption. In Europe, the total energy consumption per person doubled between 1930 and 2000. Electricity alone increased twenty times per capita.[44] In the United Kingdom, in 1974, households were responsible for 43 per cent of the total electricity demand— the bulk was for heating space and water. Thirty years earlier, that amount had been just 7 per cent. How and why did demand grow so quickly? We know a fair bit about the individual pieces of this puzzle. In industrial societies, the postwar

[43] *Report of the Committee Appointed by the Board of Trade to Inquire into the Causes of the Present Rise in the Retail Price of Coal Sold for Domestic Use*, Parliamentary Papers 1914–1916, Cd. 7923. See also Armin Triebel, 'Coal and the Metroplis', in Jay Winter and Jean-Louis Robert, eds, *Capital Cities at War: Paris, London, Berlin 1914–1919* (Cambridge, 1997), 342–73.

[44] See Astrid Kander, Paolo Malanima, and Paul Warde, *Power to the People: Energy in Europe over the Last Five Centuries* (Princeton NJ, 2013), 5 (figure 1.1), and 267 (table 8.3).

years saw unprecedented growth, an extension of the grid, and more power plants.[45] These are the same years when more washing machines, fridges, and TV sets were sold.[46] What we do not currently understand very well is how these pieces fit together. Put differently, what drives demand? Again, it is helpful to put consumption and material resources in the same frame of analysis. In this case, we need to think about the relationship between people's practices, such as cooking, washing, and heating, the appliances enabling these practices, and the networks providing the necessary power. How do infrastructures and daily practices relate to each other?

From the perspective of the engineer and economist, the answer is fairly straight-forward. Networks make power readily available. Once power reaches households through cables, people use it to switch on the lights, bake bread, or heat the house. This is helpful, but only up to a point. Infrastructures and power plants are enormous and expensive projects—Hinkley Point C, the new nuclear power station planned for Britain, is scheduled to cost £18 billion, the equivalent of 50 per cent of what the government spends on housing and the environment in a whole year. To be viable, such long-term projects must not merely meet but antici-pate and generate future demand. But this supply-oriented perspective only gets us so far. In the final analysis, networks depend just as much on the needs of various users; and, for households, this means the daily practices that are energy-hungry.[47] Ultimately it is heating, cooking, and taking a hot shower or bath that creates the demand for electricity or gas that infrastructures try to meet. And these practices have a life of their own, which is at least as much a product of social norms and cultural changes as of supply and technology. Take the transformation of personal hygiene, which has made heating hot water for baths and showers a major source of energy demand. The late nineteenth century saw the growing popularity of a weekly bath in well-off middle-class families in English and American cities. From the 1960s to the 1980s the daily shower became the norm in the western world. Since 2000, the younger generation has started to move on to two or three daily showers, to the concern of public health officials who warn of the risk of allergies and skin diseases from 'overbathing'.[48] This development has more to do with changing notions of cleanliness, fitness, and beauty and associated exercise and grooming regimes than with infrastructures as such. A similar example is the growing frequency with which individual items of clothing are put in the washing

---

[45] See the seminal account by Thomas P. Hughes, *Networks of Power: Electrification in Western Society, 1880–1930* (Baltimore, MD, 1983).

[46] Avner Offer and Sue Bowden, 'Household Appliances and the Use of Time: The United States and Britain since the 1920s', *Economic History Review* 47.4 (1994), 725–48.

[47] For this interplay, see Elizabeth Shove, Frank Trentmann, and Matt Watson, eds, *Infrastructures in Practice: The Evolution of Demand in Networked Societies* (forthcoming).

[48] See the article 'Do You Shower Every Day? Science Says…', in the 8 June 2016 issue of the *Health Science Journal* (http://www.thehealthsciencejournal.com/shower-every-day-science-says, accessed 29 August 2016). See also Elizabeth Shove, *Comfort, Cleanliness and Convenience: The Social Organization of Normality* (Oxford, 2003). Among historians, there has been less sustained attention to 'ordinary' consumption. A rare exception is Daniel Roche, *A History of Everyday Things: The Birth of Consumption in France, 1600–1800* (Cambridge, 2000 [1997]).

machine. Consuming needs hardware—the shower, the pipes, the cables, and the washing machine. In the end, though, it is shaped by how (and how frequently) people use that hardware. To understand these processes, we need social history and sociological attention to the evolution of practices.

Infrastructures and practices rarely fitted together smoothly in modern societies. Today's talk of 'energy transition' conjures up a shift from one resource era (fossil fuels) to another (renewables). But, as with the original 'Industrial Revolution', energy changes are not sudden. Societies were caught in processes of transformation throughout the modern era. They mixed different fuels and appliances. As late as 1949, 42 per cent of British households used coal to heat the water for their laundry in the summer (43 per cent used gas, 15 per cent electricity); in the winter the proportion climbed to 53 per cent, as many households relied on the coal fire as their primary source of heat.[49] Coexistence and combination of fuel types remain widespread in rich societies, as evidenced by the staying power of kerosene in Japan. In West Germany in the early 1980s, 46 per cent of households switched on an electric heater in spring and autumn, regardless of whether their primary heating was with petroleum, gas, or coal.[50]

Such coexistence also points to the slow speed and selective adoption of new networks and technologies and to the resistance they faced. In Europe, electricity in homes was almost exclusively used for lighting in the interwar years, in spite of massive spectacles, showrooms, and promotions by utility companies that celebrated electricity as clean, easy, and modern. Outside a few corners of America, the 'all-electric home' remained an ideal, not a reality. Other fuels faced similar obstacles. Supply did not automatically create demand. In the 1930s, for example, the private Gas Light and Coke Company was pressing the London County Council (LCC)—the largest provider of municipal housing in Britain—to expand gas appliances and to roll out smokeless gas-lit coke fires across its estates. But the LCC was cautious about how much unsatisfied demand for gas and coke its working-class tenants had. Almost all were used to a coal fire. An experimental trial in a couple of blocks produced a wide spectrum of reactions. Some felt that the smokeless fires were 'very comfortable'; others did 'not like it' at all. Many did not use the gas to light the fire, as intended, but resorted to wood or paper instead. Some placed coal on the fire instead of coke. Yet others were used to seeing with their own eyes when the fuel was alight and kept the gas to ignite the coke burning for so long that it made the whole fire prohibitively expensive.[51]

This does not mean that societies were static. Town gas, electricity, kerosene, and, from the 1960s, natural gas did advance. But their use was uneven and related to changing lifestyles, sense of comfort, and use of space at home. In England in

---

[49] Leslie T. Wilkins, *Social Survey: Domestic Utilization of Heating Appliances and Expenditures on Fuels in 1948/49* (London, 1951).

[50] Vattenfall, Berlin, BEWAG Archiv: BEWAG 'Haushaltskundenbefragung 1981' durch die BEWAG Anwendungstechnik-Energieberatung, pp. 20–31.

[51] London Metropolitan Archive, LMA, GLC/HG/HHM/10/L055 Part 1, Survey Responses and Analysis by Officers, Spring 1936; Report by Surveyor, 14 May 1936, and tenant responses, 3 February 1938.

the 1940s, for example, household coal was limited and several million homes bought portable electrical or gas heaters. In war-torn Germany, where many families were quartered in other people's flats, a small electrical hotplate offered a little piece of privacy, reducing conflict over access to the shared kitchen. Portable heaters provided 'part-time space heating', a critical step in the diffusion of thermal comfort into bedrooms and other spaces in the home that had previously led a cold existence. Bedrooms became spaces to study or to hang out with friends, not just to sleep in at night. Instead of most family life taking place around the hearth, social practices branched out into other parts of the home. It was this spatial diffusion of heat and practices that paved the way for central heating, not the other way around.

Infrastructural changes to the built environment, in short, changed the capacities for consumption, but their actual use depended on lifestyles, habits, and the socio-economic conditions of their inhabitants. By retrieving the diverse experiences of people who lived through such transitions, historians can illuminate the processes of change. Take, for example, changes in heating in England in the 1960s. In the early 1960s, the LCC introduced new centrally provided underfloor heating in several blocks of flats. By 1963, the buildings were showing unexpected physical problems that baffled the engineers and town planners, who had put their faith in the technical superiority of the new heating system. The resultant survey gave a snapshot of how tenants actually lived. Usage varied hugely. In fact several tenants were not using their underfloor heating at all. Some had given up after a few trials because they felt they were only heating the neighbour's flat below, which did not use it either. Of those tenants who did use it, many complained that it was not warm enough, or not the right kind of heat. There were many reasons for the wide range of responses. Some had to do with money—people on hire-purchase agreement were more like to switch on their underfloor heating than those paying directly. But age and custom were just as important. Many of the older tenants had been used to heating with solid fuel (coal or coke) before moving into a modern flat. To them, a proper fire was what was 'normal'. It had flames, colour, smoke, and smell, as well as thermal heat measured in Fahrenheit. Many contemporaries commented on the 'cheerfulness' and 'psychological tonic' of the open fire, which made it popular in spite of its inefficiency—a place that would be filled by the TV set in the course of the 1960s.[52]

What is considered 'normal' use, of course, is not entirely up to the individual. It is the result of social conventions, norms, and standards. Buildings, pipes, wires, and lighting materialize those standards. A home or an office comes with a certain material endowment, an existing number of sockets, light bulbs, and boilers. How these standards evolve is poorly understood at present and deserves much greater research. Their development was certainly not a foregone conclusion. It involved an ongoing struggle between urban planners, the utility providers, architects, the

---

[52] Rupert Francis and Brooks Grundy, 'The Economics of a District Heating System for 500 Houses at Harrow', *Journal of the Institution of Municipal Engineers* 71.12 (1945), 393–412, here 393 and 411.

building sector, government, and tenants. Electrical wiring in new homes in California was often so dodgy in the 1930s that Southern California Edison ran a public campaign against 'bad' wiring.

In general, raising standards took a lot of effort and had to overcome a lot of resistance. The road to our own materially intensive lifestyle has been littered with obstacles and failures. A single-minded concern with eventual outcomes tends to forget that. At the end of the Second World War, it was far from clear whether higher standards for all were either feasible or desirable. In Britain there was a fundamental debate about raising heating standards in the new homes 'fit for heroes' that were being planned. Was it the right social democratic thing to provide everyone, poor and rich, with cosy warm air, all day and all year round? Or, as the critics held, was this a dangerous kind of paternalism that would force working-class families to spend much more money on fuel than they otherwise would and that ignored the fact that most workers were accustomed to quite different temperatures? In the 1950s–1960s it was common for the poor to spend around 12 per cent of their total expenditure on fuel and light.[53] Perhaps it was wiser to prioritize exporting coal to other nations and earn much needed hard currency?[54] Official standards for space, flushing toilets, and heating systems that would warm living and dining spaces to at least 18°C when the outside temperature dropped below freezing were only introduced in the United Kingdom in 1961, after the Parker Morris report, and revised in 1967; their mandatory nature was, significantly, abolished in 1980 by the Conservative Thatcher government keen on cutting costs. In West Germany in the early 1960s, in the middle of the boom, housewives despaired about the so-called 'socket bottleneck'. Forty-one per cent of kitchens only had one socket, and almost as many were smaller than 8 m². Housewives wanted more sockets and space; manufacturers wanted to sell more fridges, toasters, and electric mixers. It did not matter. When the space standard came up for renewal in 1965/6—new kitchens only needed to be 5.8 m²—they were sidelined by the building industry and urban planners, who put quantity of new homes above quality.[55]

We have become so accustomed to higher standards and find it so difficult to imagine lifestyle change today that it is critical for historians to retrieve such earlier moments and to remind us just how recent even the idea of universal standards is, even in the most advanced societies, where 'energy poverty' and uneven provision across classes and regions remain a reality.

Following the interplay between material infrastructures and people's daily lives brings us back to a consideration of habits. We have seen that a lot of the use of

---

[53] Ministry of Labour, *Family Expenditure Survey: Report for 1957–59* (London, 1961); Ministry of Labour, *Family Expenditure Survey: Report for 1963* (London, 1963).
[54] (Egerton) Heating and Ventilation Committee, Building Research Board, 1945; C. A. Masterman to A. C. G. Egerton, 1 March 1945, in Churchill Archives Centre (Cambridge), Harold Hartley Papers, Box 116.
[55] Sophie Gerber, *Küche, Kühlschrank, Kilowatt: Zur Geschichte des privaten Energiekonsums in Deutschland, 1945–1990* (Bielefeld, 2015), 174–83. See also Frank Trentmann, *Materielle Kultur und Energiekonsum: Verbraucher und ihre Rolle für eine nachhaltige Entwicklung* (Munich, 2016).

materials and objects cannot be understood in terms of individual choice. Cooking, heating, bathing, watching television, and indeed shopping involve repetitive sequences of actions. But how exactly do habits emerge, evolve, and (sometimes) die? One approach to habits comes from microeconomics. In the 1960s the Nobel prizewinner Gary Becker studied how and why households shifted time and money from home production (cooking, cleaning, making clothes) to consumption (buying ready meals and clothes, hiring a cleaner, etc.), or vice versa. Consumer demand here emerged as a physical outcome, not as an expression of psychological desire. It was mediated by household technology. Behaviour was the result of fairly stable desires hitting a set of constraints.[56] But what if some habits also acquire a life of their own, promoting a set of social practices that then create expectations and produce constraints? The sociologist Elizabeth Shove argues that habits acquire people, not the other way around, as the familiar saying has it. From this perspective, habits are social practices that compete with one another and in the process 'recruit' individual 'practitioners' who develop the competence necessary to perform them.[57] Routinized actions, such as daily showering or going to the gym, are not, then, simply outputs of desires and constraints. Quite the opposite: they help to shape them. And they have knock-on effects on time, mobility, and resource use. They can change physical constraints—one bathroom for each bedroom provides a different setting for daily life from that of an arrangement with no bathroom and a portable tin tub; the habit of using digital devices 24/7 is creating new demands and expectations for utility and digital communication providers, batteries, and storage devices and their accessibility on trains, planes, and in many other places. The study of habits presents a fertile field with plenty of opportunities for future historians interested in engaging with the recent rediscovery of habits in the social sciences.

THINGS MATTER . . . BUT SOME MATTER MORE THAN OTHERS

When historical studies of consumption took off in the 1980s and 1990s, they focused on shopping and possessions and their role in providing meaning and identity. These are and remain important topics. But, as we have seen in the previous pages, consuming reaches well beyond representations and the point of purchase. It is linked to political power as well as to markets. And it involves social habits, norms, and conventions, not just individual choice and preferences. Climate change has made it urgent for historians to inquire into the full story of humans' relationship with things, from desire and acquisition through to disposal. Such broader material histories can no longer stop with a physical object—be it decorated curtains or a fashionable coat—but need to extend to the many materials

---

[56] Gary S. Becker, 'A Theory of the Allocation of Time', *Economic Journal* 75.299 (1965), 493–517. See also Kevin M. Murphy, 'Gary Becker as Teacher', *American Economic Review* 105.5 (2015), 71–3.

[57] See Elizabeth Shove, 'Habits and their Creatures', in Alan Warde and Dale Southerton, eds, *The Habits of Consumption* (Helsinki, 2012), 100–12; Elizabeth Shove, Mika Pantzar, and Matthew Watson, *The Dynamics of Social Practice: Everyday Life and How it Changes* (London, 2012).

and resources that service and maintain our increasingly intensive lifestyle. Attention to the work done by things as well as to their meanings thus widens the cast of characters for material history considerably.[58] It extends it from luxury goods and 'conspicuous' consumption to basic goods and utilities like water, gas, and electricity. It is a history of both needs and wants.

To recognize the longer material tail of consumption, however, also creates fresh challenges: just how far back in the chain of material processes should we go? In the beginning, when the study of consumption was fighting to establish itself as a field, there was sometimes an understandable urge to carve out its own terrain as distinct from that of work and production, which had been dominant for so long. This is no longer true and the interplay between these spheres is today more widely recognized, in research on product innovation and design, the work carried out by consumers on a daily basis (recycling, repairing, booking their own flights, etc.), and the role of the workplace in providing goods and services and in shaping desires, norms, and habits.[59]

The question that now arises is *how* we connect the use of materials in consumption with what is happening in production. Of course, in the final analysis, 'consumption is the sole end and purpose of all production', as Adam Smith pointed out in *The Wealth of Nations* (1776).[60] Ultimately, a car factory exists to make cars for consumers. But this does not offer the historian much direction. The path we choose depends on the question that is guiding our interest in the material world. What are we seeking to explain? If the question is to get a sense of the total flow of material in a region or in the world as a whole, then yes, it is imperative to study mining, the scars left by cement, and the amount of fossil fuels used, regardless of whether they are burnt in an industrial furnace or in a fireplace at home. From the perspective of the planet, it does not matter whether the cement went into a factory building or into basement extensions accommodating kitchens and games rooms. But this is not the only question, and material histories should not be limited to explaining climate change. If we want to understand the evolution of modern lifestyles and what people do with things, the material chains of interest will be different ones. Modern living uses up coal, oil, and aluminium; but, while an analysis of lifestyle can reveal all sort of material insights, it does not and cannot produce an account of the total demand for material. This would require an investigation of the efficiency of boilers and engines, industrial processes, farming methods, and economic development, among other things. Power plants also consume coal and gas but these are different social processes from a family cooking a meal. That the thermal efficiency of a coal-fuelled electricity power plant rose

---

[58] See also Frank Trentmann, 'Materiality in the Future of History: Things, Practices, and Politics', *Journal of British Studies* 48.2 (2009), 283–307.

[59] Maxine Berg, 'In Pursuit of Luxury: Global History and British Consumer Goods in the Eighteenth Century', *Past & Present* 182.1 (2004), 85–142; Kathryn Wheeler and Miriam Glucksmann, *Household Recycling and Consumption Work: Social and Moral Economies* (London, 2015); Trentmann, *Empire of Things*, 522–61.

[60] Adam Smith, *An Inquiry into the Nature and Causes of the Wealth of Nations* (Chicago, IL, 1976 [1776]), 179 (= bk IV, ch. 8).

from 5 per cent to 46 per cent in the last century is a fact and a precondition for cheaper electricity, but as such does not do much to help us understand why and how people live the material lives they do. If the latter is the overarching question, then it would probably not be a good idea for a historian to spend a lot of time researching coal bunkers or the changing design of turbines.

To be interesting and meaningful, therefore, material historians should reflect on what things are used for. These meanings and functions are social processes. The great challenge today is that these processes do not fit into the analytical containers we have inherited, but this challenge is also an opportunity for historians to develop their own approaches to those aspects of the material world that interest them. 'Consumption' does not have an inherent, self-explanatory meaning that is ready-made for historical use. In one extreme version that gained ground in twentieth-century economics and beyond, it came to stand for an end user's individual preferences. Arguably, this led to an overly discrete treatment of private consumption. At the same time, it would be a mistake to rush to the very opposite end and lump together all forms of material use, private and industrial, and include under consumption all the coal and matter used up in a factory, a view still held in the early nineteenth century. Private demand does have a life of its own: it is not just a function of supply. Between these two extremes lies a rich field for future historians to explore.

ACKNOWLEDGEMENTS

This chapter draws on reflections arising from work on my last book *Empire of Things: How We Became a World of Consumers, Fifteenth Century to the Twenty-First* (London and New York, 2016) and from research on two current projects: 'Material Cultures of Energy', funded by the Arts and Humanities Research Council, grant no. AH/K006088/1, and the research centre 'DEMAND: Dynamics of Energy, Mobility and Demand', funded by the Engineering and Physical Sciences Research Council and the Economic and Social Research Council, no. EP/K011723/1. Thanks to colleagues and the research councils for their generous support.

III

PEOPLE AND POLITICS

12

Five Swans over Littleport

Fenland Folklore and Popular Memory, c.1810–1978

Andy Wood

This chapter engages with two marginalized fields of historical inquiry: folklore and local history. Its empirical basis comprises a blend of folkloric studies and texts on memory. In particular I draw on interviews conducted with old fenmen and women in the postwar period by the great folklorist Enid Porter.[1] Often in their eighties at the time at which they spoke with Porter, they discussed tales told by their grandparents, so carrying us back by up to a century and a half.

I ought to say straightaway that my aim is not to use use these memories in an attempt emprically to reconstruct 'how things really were' (although I believe that some can be used to that purpose) so much as to engage with what popular memory tells us about the condition and subversion of the category of the subaltern. As historians, we may want to dismiss 'myths' and stories about the past that seem to us to have no connection to the 'real' past. But this is to miss their significance; the verifiable truth or otherwise is less important in this context than the authority that these beliefs about the past are accorded.[2] Moreover, folklore is far from a stable category: as Dell Hymes has suggested, 'intact tradition is not so much a matter of preservation, as it is a matter of re-creation, by successive persons and generations, and in individual performances'.[3] In its protean richness, then, folklore can be seen as paradigmatic, offering us privileged access into the culture that generated and sustained it.

The pasts constructed in the folkloric imagination were not the top-down impositions on which Eric Hobsbawm and Terence Ranger focused; they were instead generated from within the culture of the subaltern classes.[4] The Hobsbawm and Ranger volume has been hugely influential, and for its time represented an important intervention in understanding the ways in which histories are constructed.

---

[1] For her magnum opus, see E. Porter, *Cambridgeshire Customs and Folklore* (London, 1969).

[2] Moses Finley's early discussion of the subject remains highly perceptive. See M. I. Finley, 'Myth, Memory and History', *History and Theory* 4.3 (1964–5), 297–302.

[3] D. Hymes, 'Folklore's Nature and the Sun's Myth', *Journal of American Folklore* 88.350 (1975), 345–69, here 354–5. See also J. E. Limon, 'Western Marxism and Folklore: A Critical Introduction', *Journal of American Folklore* 96.379 (1983), 34–52, here 39.

[4] E. J. Hobsbawm and T. Ranger, eds, *The Invention of Tradition* (Cambridge, 1992).

But, arguably, the pieces in the collection gave too much significance to state- or elite-sponsored constructions of history and paid little attention either to the reception by subalterns of those histories or to the capacity of subordinates to articulate their own histories. This chapter tries to set that story straight.

The chapter's claim to originality therefore lies not so much in its empirical base as in the integration of that material into an argument that engages with subalternity.[5] In particular, the chapter challenges modernizing accounts of social and cultural change that present oral tradition as being in decline during the nineteenth and twentieth centuries.[6] It is an exercise in what Malcolm Gaskill has called 'history from within'—that is, it tries to get at the history of mentalities, world views, and senses of place.[7] In particular, the chapter seeks to establish the nature of social subordination in the fens by looking at the ways in which that subordination was negotiated and confronted over the period 1810–1978 and at the extent to which folklore and popular memory proved to be enabling forces in the culture of the working people of the region.

The area of fenland with which I am concerned lies on the western edge of Norfolk and Suffolk and in the eastern half of Cambridgeshire.[8] It is easily ignored, remaining as marginal as the sources on which this essay depends. The fens are passed through on the traveller's way to somewhere else—a cruciform of major arteries take the driver from Cambridge to Norwich, or from London to the North. It is a scruffy region, neither entirely solid land nor fluid water. As the oral historian Mary Chamberlain has observed, 'Poverty and isolation are synonymous with the fens.'[9] The history of the fens has been in part that of the struggle against the sea and the tides. Yet it has its own still beauty. In some ways, despite its contemporary integration into capitalist agribusiness and the presence of a great university on its doorstep, it remains the epitome of the local.

The people with whom this essay is concerned are 'ordinary'—but the stories they tell are extraordinary.[10] For a long time they have been known as 'Fen Tigers'. Enid Porter believed that they acquired the name way back in the 1640s and 1650s, during the anti-enclosure struggles against fen drainage led by the Dutch

---

[5] On western Marxism and the subaltern, see M. Green, 'Gramsci Cannot Speak: Presentations and Interpretations of Gramsci's Concept of the Subaltern', *Rethinking Marxism* 14.3 (2002), 1–24. On subaltern resistance and local culture, see R. Maddox, *El Castillo: The Politics of Tradition in an Andalusian Town* (Urbana, IL, 1993), 9, 11; K. Crehan, *Gramsci, Culture and Anthropology* (London, 2002), 104.

[6] For such accounts, see D. Vincent, 'The Decline of the Oral Tradition in Popular Culture', in R. D. Storch, ed., *Popular Culture and Custom in Nineteenth-Century England* (London, 1982), 20–47. Patrick Joyce has observed the continuing vitality of oral culture in Victorian industrial Lancashire; see P. Joyce, *Industrial England and the Question of Class, c.1848–1914* (Cambridge, 1993).

[7] M. Gaskill, *Crime and Mentalities in Early Modern England* (Cambridge, 2000).

[8] For a useful introduction to its landscape history, see J. Ravensdale and R. Muir, *East Anglian Landscapes: Past and Present* (London, 1984), 177–203.

[9] M. Chamberlain, *Fenwomen: A Portrait of Women in an English Village* (London, 1975), 19.

[10] For ordinariness and working-class culture, see M. Savage, G. Bagnall, and B. Longhurst, 'Ordinary, Ambivalent and Defensive: Class Identities in the Northwest of England', *Sociology* 34.4 (2001), 875–92.

engineer Cornelius Vermuyden.[11] In 1966, the 65-year-old Arthur Randall recalled for Enid Porter:

> In the old days the people who lived on the other side of the Ouse river were called High Norfolk folk; those on the other side where my parents were born were called Fen Tigers. The ways and customs and speech of the Fen Tigers, even the work they did on the land, were quite different from those of the High Norfolk people who were always referred to as 'Foreigners' by the Tigers.

William Edwards, speaking to his daughter in the early twentieth century, observed:

> I don't claim to 'av no ancestors, but I did 'ave some forebears, on'y they were really tigers—fen tigers. I don't know why old fenmen were allus called tigers, unless it were because they used to act so wild and shy, not being used to seeing many folks, or whether the strangers thought they looked a bit fierce.[12]

In particular, I am concerned with the ways in which popular memory was inflected by a sense of the local and with how that sense connected to the condition of sub-alternity.[13] Writing about the fenmen and women represents a methodological challenge. As Keith Snell puts it, 'We are dealing with one of the most illiterate, subdued, silent, maligned and shadowy classes in nineteenth-century society.'[14] Yet the challenge is there: and its fruits take us far from the world of educated elites, states, and governors. They take us instead into a rich, complex culture that has thus far attracted little attention from professional historians.[15]

Our story begins in the Cambridgeshire village of Littleport on 28 June 1816, when five swans were seen in flight overhead. They landed in the nearby Great Ouse river, where they nested for some years. At the same time as the swans landed in the village, five men from Littleport were hanged in the nearby county town of Ely. The story was confirmed by the fenman Jack Barrett in his conversations with his aged neighbour Chafer Legge, who spoke to Jack about his grandfather's stories. In Chafer's memories:

> When grandfather got back [from witnessing the executions at Ely], he was told that, just about the time those men were hung, five swans flew over Littleport and came

[11] See A. R. Randall, *Sixty Years a Fenman* (London, 1966), 2. For those struggles, see K. Lindley, *Fenland Riots and the English Revolution* (London, 1982). Of Cornelius Vermuyden's fate, Ernie James recalls: 'It is said that such was his enthusiasm for the project that he invested much of his own money in the [drainage] scheme and as a result died almost penniless'. See A. James, *Memoirs of a Fen Tiger: The Story of Ernie James of Welney as Told to Audrey James* (Newton Abbot, 1986), 11.

[12] S. Marshall, *Fenland Chronicle* (Cambridge, 1967), 8.

[13] Social memory is therefore seen as a potential resource for subaltern agency. For a Norfolk example of the consequences of communal forgetting, see L. Rider Haggard, ed., *I Walked by Night: Being the Life and History of the King of the Norfolk Poachers, Written by Himself* (Ipswich, 1935), 110–11. For an excellent survey, see J. Fentress and C. Wickham, *Social Memory* (Oxford, 1992).

[14] K. D. M. Snell, 'Deferential Bitterness: The Social Outlook of the Rural Proletariat in Eighteenth- and Nineteenth-Century England and Wales', in M. L. Bush, ed., *Social Orders and Social Classes in Europe since 1500: Studies in Social Stratification* (Harlow, 1992), 158–84, here 162.

[15] Geoff Eley and Keith Nield have put this well, arguing that 'the life of a subaltern class encompasse[s] something fuller, richer, and more complex than simply the reflexes of its subordination'. See G. Eley and K. Nield, *The Future of Class in History: What's Left of the Social?* (Ann Arbor, MI, 2007), 144.

down on the river and, what's more, when he crossed the bridge on his way home he saw them still there, and he said they stayed on the river for years.[16]

The unstated inference was clear: these were the souls of the five men, returned to their home.

The five Littleport men who were hanged on 28 June 1816 were named William Beamiss, George Crow, John Dennis, Isaac Harley, and Thomas South. Along with many others from across the fenlands, the Breckland, and the city of Norwich, they had taken part in large-scale rioting that was intended to lower food prices. The slogan of the rioters had been 'Bread or Blood'.[17] At that time, in the aftermath of the Napoleonic Wars, England was gripped by a fatal combination of economic depression, unemployment, and high food prices. Dragoons and Hanoverian infantry were dispatched to the Fens and Brecks to quell the protest, which led to severe repression and the execution of the five men at a Special Assizes presided over in full pomp by the bishop of Ely. The repression was scorched into local memory. Many years later, a fenland vicar reported how 'Local tradition' had it that a body of Hanoverian troops (probably from the King's German Legion) mistook a thatcher's cries to his assistant as an insult to them and so shot him dead. His body fell from the roof of the barn on which he was working to its great folding door and 'there it hung, dripping with blood for over three days, the officer swearing that anyone who dared to remove it should share the same fate, as an example to all to behave with due respect to their oppressors'.[18]

Chafer Legge went on to: 'I want to tell you bor [that is, Jack Barrett], don't you believe it when people tell you that those men stood on the scaffold snivelling and praying, because Grandfather said they didn't, they died like Fenmen are expected to.'[19] Prior to their execution, the condemned men signed a confession in which they 'acknowledge[d] and confess[ed] our sins in general, and we most sincerely beg of God to pardon our sins: fervently hoping and trusting that God Almighty will, for the sake of the all-atoning merits of the Redeemer, receive our precious and immortal souls into his favour'. A different tone was struck by William Beamiss at his execution, who started to forgive one Mr Tansley for bearing false evidence against him; the drop cut off the rest of Beamiss's words.[20] After the event, the bodies were laid out for public exhibition. Chafer Legge mentioned one particular moment:

> Five other old chaps from the fen went in with Grandfather and Robert Norman, who was over ninety, made them swear over the coffins that they'd tell their children,

---

[16] W. H. Barrett, *Tales from the Fens*, ed. by E. Porter (London, 1963), 98. Familial memory is also important: an old man aged 85 in 1901 noted that he had been born in 1816, 'two days after my father was hung at Ely for the part he took in the Littleport riots'. See W. H. Barrett and R. P. Garrod, *East Anglian Folklore and Other Tales* (London, 1976), 3. Chafer felt a close bond between the fens and his kin: he 'used to boast that his ancestors were living on the isle of Southery when Norman soldiers were afraid to venture there'. Jack Barrett describes him as 'the last of the real old Fen tigers' (ibid., x).

[17] A. J. Peacock, *Bread or Blood: A Study of the Agrarian Riots in East Anglia in 1816* (London, 1965), 80, 88, 103, 116.

[18] Ibid., 109.   [19] Barrett and Porter, *Tales*, 97.

[20] Peacock, *Bread or Blood*, 128–9.

generation after generation, about what the Bishop and the gentry had done to those Fenmen... Then old Norman cut a bit of rope off one of the bodies and cut it into pieces and gave one to each of them, and if you're round my back door any time, go in and ask my old woman to show you Grandfather's bit of rope stuck behind the glass of that picture over the hearth.[21]

In the end, despite the strikes, incendiarism, and campaign of terror against the farmers and gentry, the Fen Tigers had to accept defeat: 'they had to tell themselves that, for the first time since the Fens were made, those living in them were beaten'.[22] Yet remembrance imposed duties:

Now, bor, I want you to remember this story just as I've told it to you and, what's more, perhaps, when you're older, you'll write it down so that, when I've thrown my last clay hole out [i.e. to finish his labours], there'll still be people to remember the terrible thing that was done to those innocent men all that time ago.[23]

Chafer Legge followed his account of the events of 1816 with a grim description of the long hunger that followed. As Chafer told his story, the experience of defeat changed things among the Fen Tigers.[24] In the 1840s a pair of outside radicals arrived in the area. The fenland folk, feeling that 'they weren't having people like them coming into the fen and telling them to do things that would make them a sight worse', responded by tarring and feathering the interlopers. Shortly after, the magistracy arrived in the village. At first, the justices behaved as though they intended to punish those responsible for the tarring and feathering. Yet the fenmen stuck together, saying that they were *all* responsible. On hearing this answer, the gentry explained that they had been hunting the radicals across the area, and that it was therefore their duty to treat *all* of those present to a series of rounds of beer in the village pub. An old man named Turfy Rowell then stood forth. Turfy expressed his dislike at the idea of rick-burning and class war, adding: 'the only thing he and his pals ever did that the squires might not see eye to eye with was a bit of poaching, and there were a few chaps in the room who'd spent a week or two in Norwich [gaol] because of it. That made the gents laugh.' The old man then told the squires about the hunger in the fens 'and how he knew some old people who'd starved to death. He was scared, he said, that some of the things those two men [that is, the outside agitators] had talked about [might happen], and then there'd be more hangings like there had been forty years ago.'[25]

---

[21] Ibid., 98. There is a memory of martyrdom at work in the story about the Littleport executions. The tradition might be related to that noted by the Hammonds in 1911, according to which snow never settled on the grave of a young ploughboy called Henry Cook, executed in 1831 for his participation in the Swing Riots. See J. L. and B. Hammond, *The Village Labourer, 1760–1832* (London, 1911), 284–6. See also the stories, communicated both in print and by speech to Dave Douglass in the 1970s, concerning the public exhibition of the tarred body of an executed coal miner in the 1830s. See D. Douglass, '"Worms of the Earth": The Miners' Own Story', in R. Samuel, ed., *People's History and Socialist Theory* (London, 1981), 61–7, here 64.
[22] Barrett and Porter, *Tales*, 96. [23] Ibid., 98.
[24] Peacock, *Bread or Blood*, 133, notes the quietude of the areas affected by the 1816 riots during the agrarian troubles of the 1820s–1840s.
[25] Barrett, *Tales from the Fens*, 109–10.

Chafer Legge's narrative, in which local people humiliate outside agitators, might be read as an acceptance of an organic social order, contemptuous of literate, modern radicalism and hostile to any larger vision of the world.[26] At least in this fenland village, it seems that localism triumphed over class. But there is more at work in his story. Chafer's story also addressed local solidarity (the whole village refused to disclose the identity of those responsible for the tarring and feathering) and plebeian articulacy (Turfy Rowell's effective account of village suffering). Most importantly, a deep memory of 1816 ran through Chafer's stories. Chafer had been told by his grandfather that he needed to hold hard to a memory of the executions of that year. In mid-Victorian Littleport, this memory had been turned into a story that confirmed the futility of popular agency: what Chafer feared above everything else was that 'there'd be more hangings like there had been forty years ago'. Richard Hoggart's words apply here:

> When people feel that they cannot do much about the main elements in their situation, feel it not necessarily with despair or disappointment or resentment but simply as a fact of life, they adopt attitudes towards that situation which allow them to have a liveable life under its shadow, a life without a constant and pressing sense of the larger situation.[27]

Fenpeople were painfully conscious of their lack of education and apparent lack of intellectual capacity. In conversation with his daughter in the early twentieth century, William Edwards worried that 'our lives were so simple and we were so ignorant that we talked and listened to each other so much, but I'm often wondered if other folks used to go away laughing at me an' at what I'd said'. He put this down to a long history of isolation. Looking back on the nineteenth century, Edwards suggested: 'A lot on [the fenmen and women] cou'n't read and di'n't want to, and a few on 'em were so isolated where they lived that they were frit [i.e. frightened] to be in company.'[28] Fenpeople were aware that their body language and seeming taciturnity confirmed in outsiders' minds the cultural inferiority of the Fen Tigers. In 1978 the local journalist Eric Fowler had this to say: 'The weather has a bit to do with it all—it's responsible for the way we mutter, talk with our mouths shut because we don't want to let this east wind in. Another thing is frugality, a product of 19th century poverty.'[29] This taciturnity in the presence of outsiders was picked up on by other fenpeople. In his semi-autobiographical novel *Bicker's Broad* Alan Bloom points to the taciturnity of fenpeople when around outsiders: 'The habit of using as few words as possible and keeping most of his thoughts to himself was

---

[26] For more, see K. D. M. Snell, 'The Culture of Local Xenophobia', *Social History* 28.1 (2003), 1–20. See also the comments in E. P. Thompson, 'Folklore, Anthropology and Social History', *Indian Historical Review* 3 (1978), 247–66, here 265.

[27] R. Hoggart, *The Uses of Literacy: Aspects of Working-Class Life with Special Reference to Publications and Entertainments* (London, 1957), 92.

[28] Marshall, *Fenland Chronicle*, 137. For the wider context, see Snell, 'Deferential Bitterness', 163–5; B. Reay, *Rural Englands: Labouring Lives in the Nineteenth Century* (Basingstoke, 2004), 145.

[29] M. Watkins, *This Other Breed: East Anglians* (Ipswich, 1978), 55.

already part of his own make-up.'[30] Anne Barrett, writing in the mid-twentieth century, observed:

> the cream of the fens was the farm worker. He knew all there was to know about his job. To strangers he appeared sullen. It was not so. It was reserve, and once this was broken and you received an invitation to enter his home and try a glass of his home-made mead, you were treated as a brother.[31]

We might call this body language and taciturnity—this way of holding one-self—*composure*. It excluded the outsider and enabled the maintenance of a defensive local working-class culture. It was, then, about *survival*. Generated from the memory of generations of malnutrition, poor housing, lack of education, unemployment, and low pay, composure allowed the fenman and fenwoman to hold onto his or her identity and values by shutting them off from the ears and eyes of the outsider. As the historian Alun Howkins observes, 'The rural poor seemed to many to be completely alienated from their "betters", a separate, secret people, impervious to change and influence.'[32]

Yet the fenpeople's composure had its active, creative side. Storytelling underwrote composure. Jack Barrett remembers old men in the pub spinning their yarns: 'The faces of these men, as they sat in the glow of the fire, looked as if they were carved from bronze. Slow in speech they were often thought, by strangers, to be dull-witted, but this was far from true.'[33] As the historian Penny Summerfield suggests, 'The starting point of the cultural approach to oral history is to accept that people do not simply remember what happened to them, but make sense of the subject matter they recall by interpreting it.'[34] Storytelling allowed fenpeople to contextualize their lives, generating a sense of the past that was rooted in the land, in a memory of suffering and survival, and in a rich tradition that was endlessly intelligent. In all of these respects, storytelling contested the view of fenfolk as taciturn and slow: rather, in storytelling, we find a liveliness and a protean creativity.

Storytelling constituted a way of understanding and reconciling oneself to what outsiders saw as the bleak environment of the fens. Ernie James recalled:

> Most Saturdays I visited Will Kent, my father's old friend; he fascinated me and I listened for hours to the stories he had to tell about the old Fen characters he knew when he was a lad. It was Will who first encouraged me to appreciate the beauty and solitude of the Fens.[35]

For Jack Barrett, who spoke of his youth in the late nineteenth century, storytelling was a way of overcoming the deadening loneliness of the fens. Barrett was aged

---

[30] A. Bloom, *Bicker's Broad* (Thetford, 1974), 17.
[31] Barrett and Garrod, *East Anglian Folklore*, 127.
[32] A. J. Howkins, *Reshaping Rural England: A Social History, 1850–1925* (London, 1991), 65.
[33] Barrett and Porter, *Tales*, xii.
[34] P. Summerfield, 'Culture and Composure: Creating Narratives of the Gendered Self in Oral History: Interviews', *Cultural and Social History* 1 (2004), 65–93, here 67.
[35] James, *Memoirs of a Fen Tiger*, 22.

11 when he left school; in the early years of his working life he found himself out in the fenland emptiness, employed at crow scaring and tending to sheep. 'I eased the loneliness by memorizing the tales I had heard the old men tell of Fenland's past.' The old men

> were past masters in the art of story-telling. Untutored and unread, they had been reared in an age long before the Education Act of 1870 was passed. Each one was a storehouse of folk-lore stories, many of which had been handed down from generation to generation, told and re-told in the days when listeners sat enthralled by what was, more or less, their only means of recreation.

'Old Pegleg', for example, told the young Jack Barrett many a tale. He spoke of the impact of parliamentary enclosure, the Game Laws, and his father's poaching adventures on the squire's estates and subsequent transportation to Australia, along with Old Pegleg's experiences in the Crimean War, in the course of which he had lost a leg. Jack Barrett says of Old Pegleg: 'He was getting an old man when I first met him, and for a period he was my tutor of early eighteenth century social history and its folklore.'

One centre of storytelling was the male world of the pub. Jack Barrett said: 'The cream of the stories which I heard were told on Saturday nights at the Ship Inn near my home in Brandon Creek. Here one adept in the art of entertaining his fellow men would be sure of free beer, with an ounce of shag thrown in.'[36] Ernie James remembered how:

> When Georgie Butcher and I were old enough, we often met in the pub after a day's work. It was a social centre of the village as far as the men were concerned, and we used to sit in a corner listening to the old men telling yarns and reminiscing about their younger days. Georgie's father, Joey, was a master story-teller, and once he started he could entertain the other customers in the tap room all night. He had a fund of wonderful tales because he had a vivid imagination and was into everything.[37]

One unnamed old fenman with whom Jack Barrett spoke in 1902 reflected on earlier riots. The man was employed on parish relief, spending his time breaking stones. Citing the local proverb 'It's the poor that helps the poor' (folk wisdom similar to Evans Pritchard's observation that 'It is scarcity not sufficiency that makes people generous'), Jack Barrett explained that he had brought the old man a jug of hot tea.[38] They fell to talking: the old man was born in 1820 and had begun his working life at the age of seven. Sipping the tea, he reflected on the poverty of his upbringing and of days when his meals consisted of boiled turnips or cabbage soup. In particular he remembered machine-breaking riots. One year, when the harvest season began, the workers were ready to elect their harvest lord (an honoured labourer who oversaw the harvest) but found that they had been

---

[36] Barrett and Garrod, *East Anglian Folklore*, ix, xii, 51.
[37] James, *Memoirs of a Fen Tiger*, 45.
[38] M. Fafchamps, 'Solidarity Networks in Preindustrial Societies: Rational Peasants with a Moral Economy', *Economic Development and Cultural Change* 41.1 (1992), 147–74, here 149.

replaced by reaping and threshing machines. Migrant Irish workers began an agitation that ended with

> Gangs [roaming] the countryside during the nights...harvest operations came to an abrupt halt; came the period when the night sky was all aglow with burning fields of ripe corn. Dragoons were sent from Norwich to knock a bit of sense into Silly Suffolks' heads.

With their fancy uniforms, the Dragoons were doubly resented for their success with the local girls. The old man went on: 'The winter that followed was one of the bitterest in memory.' When steam engines came to power the new farming technology, '[t]he men, who always found work in the winter threshing corn with a flail, said that the engine was nothing less than the handiwork of the devil'. Winter unemployment deepened social conflicts: 'in those perilous times, no well-to-do farmer lived at his farm; he went into the towns, leaving a foreman in charge'. On the night of the threshing machine's arrival, the whole farmhouse and cornfields went up in flames. 'There was hell to pay when the horse soldiers arrived. I was dragged out of bed, kicked and clouted; then with several others was driven like sheep to Thetford.' They were taken before a magistrate, who sent the men to gaol in Norwich Castle. The old man was given three years' hard labour: 'Here I had time to think. Why did I move out of Silly Suffolk into cruel Norfolk, where it seemed to me that just a few folks held reign, who believed God is on my side, and, bugger the lower classes.' Jack Barrett went on: 'After expressing his thanks for hot tea, he added: "God is up above, so all is well with the world." My answer to that was: "How do you make that out, existing as you do, on near starvation poor law parish relief?"' Barrett did not record the old Fen Tiger's answer.[39]

Other than in the pub, memories were communicated in the less gendered environment of the home. Arthur Randall remembered how, in the years before the First World War, the children would sit around the fire of an evening

> as our parents talked of a variety of things but nearly always of events or people they could remember or had heard of long ago. You couldn't say that they were all complete or connected stories that we heard, more often it was a casual reference to an almost-forgotten bit of village history which had been called to mind, perhaps because of some more recent happening.[40]

Clearly, then, both mother and father had their role in forming the social memory of the home and of the village. The only woman whom Jack Barrett mentions as a spinner of local tales was 'Granny Hall, who, when she was over ninety, could make one's flesh creep with tales of ghouls, witches and ghosts'.[41] But it was assumed that the first training in the history and folklore of the fens would come

---

[39] Barrett and Garrod, *East Anglian Folklore*, 74–7.   [40] Randall, *Sixty Years*, 72.
[41] For a remarkable account of the endurance of magical beliefs, see K. Bell, *The Magical Imagination: Magic and Modernity in Urban England, 1780–1914* (Cambridge, 2012).

from the mother: like his informant Chafer Legge, Barrett assumed that the male storytellers 'had learned the history of the Fens at their mothers' knees'.[42]

Mary Chamberlain concluded from her conversations in the early 1970s with the women of Gislea that they

> have little confidence in their skill at story-telling. They see this as a man's prerogative and are silent when their men are around, leaving the talking to the 'professionals'. Few people hear a woman's tale, remembering instead the old rustic character who entertained them so well around a pint, for pub going is not a women's tradition.

Chamberlain went on, however, to observe that 'gangs of women working on the land and mothers' stories to their children provide as great a creative field for story-telling as the old boy in the pub'.[43] The 86-year-old Mary Coe, for instance, told Chamberlain:

> Gleaning we used to go, at harvest, after they got the corn in...we was on holiday then from school. That was our summer holiday...we'd be sitting with the older women till the Church bell went [signifying the start of gleaning for the day], and I was sometimes sorry to start gleaning, because the best part was before, listening to the older women's stories.[44]

Chamberlain tells us that 'One very old lady remembers her grandmother telling her that "when the women went on the land" "the men used to stand over them with whips"'.[45] My rough guess, assuming that the story was collected around 1974, is that the 'very old lady' was then aged around 80 and that her grand-mother was also aged 80; so this story takes us back to the 1820s—about a century and a half. There are, then, long-term women's memories that remained alive in the postwar period and told of a patriarchal order that could be violently oppressive. But, just among their menfolk, fenwomen's memories could provide an assertive sense of rights and entitlement. In the 1930s one old fenwomen remem-bered her childhood days back in the 1850s: 'when the corn was cut the whole families [of the labourers] would go gleaning the corn left in the fields, *this being, of course the gleaners own property*. A great many families gleaned sufficient to keep them in bread for the whole of the winter.'[46]

It is significant that the wealthy farmers tended to live in the larger villages or in market towns. Especially in the aftermath of 1816, the suffocating darkness of the night-time fenland could make the fens a dangerous place to be. Chafer Legge had many a story to tell to that effect. In one, a farmer handed a man over to the magistracy for stealing a sheep; the man was hanged, his wife went insane and killed herself and their three children, and the farmer was found tied to the water-wheel of the village mill, his drowned body cycling round and round. A variation on such stories presented the enemies of the Fen Tigers as vanishing, their bodies sometime later to be found in fen drains.[47] One story commands our attention.

---

[42] For the quotations, see Barrett and Porter, *Tales*, xi, xii, 85.
[43] Chamberlain, *Fenwomen*, 12.   [44] Ibid., 29.   [45] Ibid., 91.
[46] M. Llewwlyn Davies, ed., *Life as We Have Known It: By Co-Operative Working Women* (London, 1931), 112.
[47] Barrett and Porter, *Tales*, 86, 87; see also 96.

During the 1816 riots, Bob Dewey and a friend had been repairing the banks of Wellmere Fen, which had sprung a leak in the previous winter. Dewey invited his mate home, where they discovered a shocking scene. Dewey's newly married bride was naked and unconscious on the floor, while her rapists, two soldiers, were sleeping off the effects of the hard drink they had consumed. Dewey took his wife up to their bedroom; she recovered and told him

> what those soldiers had done to her and she said all she wanted to do was die. Dewey said she wasn't going to do that; if there was any dying to be done it wouldn't be her that did it...What happened after that is anyone's guess. Forty years afterwards, that bank [of Wellmere Fen] was leaking again and when they opened the trench again and got almost to the bottom, they found two skeletons, right where the leak was, as the clay hadn't been puddled over them. Nobody could do anything about it as Dewey and his wife and his mate were all dead by then, and the officers had thought that those two soldiers had deserted.[48]

Yet other memories spoke of social relations as being less antagonistic. Every year there was a moment when the labourers had the capacity to assert themselves over the farmers when, before the harvest came in, a process of collective bargaining began between worker and employer. All of a sudden, for a period of weeks, their labour had a special value. Arthur Randall had a clear recollection of being involved in the forging of a harvest contract:

> It was quite a business when the harvest men met the farmer each year to fix the price per acre for tying, shocking and carting...Often they would argue for as much as half a day but in the end they always came to some agreement and then the farmer would send for some beer to seal the bargain and a start could be made on the work.[49]

Randall gives an account of the feasts laid on for harvest workers after the harvest had been brought in:

> rows of trestle tables...plenty of beer...huge joints of beef and pork...when the meal was over 'our' farmer and the others who were giving the feast with him, each made a little speech thanking everyone for all the work that had been done...there would be loud shouts of 'For he's a jolly good fellow, and so say all of us'.

Randall adds the threatening note that 'probably only the day before some of the workers had been calling [the farmer] anything but a good fellow'.[50]

For some, looking back on stories they had been told about the small change of everyday social relations, the gentry seemed not to be so bad. Eric Fowler was presented with positive stories about the squirearchy, which he summarized in 1978:

> There was paternalism among employers, a willingness to look after their people, to take an interest in their families, but it didn't include paying them any money that still

---

[48] Ibid., 91–2.

[49] Randall, *Sixty Years*, 23. For more, see D. H. Morgan, 'The Place of Harvesters in Nineteenth-Century Village Life', in R. Samuel, ed., *Village Life and Labour* (London, 1975), 27–72.

[50] Arthur Randall, *Fenland Memories* (London, 1969), 17. On harvest celebrations, see also W. B. Gerish, 'An East Anglian Harvest Custom, Known Locally as "Hallering Largees" ', *Folklore* 5.2 (1894), 167–9; J. Glyde, *A Dyshe of Norfolke Dumplings* (London, 1898), 102–3; J. Hooper, 'Horkeys, or Harvest Frolics', in W. Andrews, ed., *Bygone Norfolk* (London, 1898), 196–209.

exists... [then in the next breath] ... Feudalism? If you like, but those old squires were a darned sight more liberal and fair-minded in their administration than the new generation of bureaucrats dominated by people I would call commuters—they're more harshly Tory than the old squire was.[51]

This rose-tinted view elides the massively unequal power relations between the Fen Tigers and those whom they called the 'mighty men'.[52] Farmers, the gentry, and the Anglican clergy all expected ritual displays of deference—the women had to curtsey and the men to touch their caps.[53]

The expectation of deference from the Anglian clergy may have been especially galling to a people whose own confessional identity was Baptist or Primitive Methodist (these were locally known as 'Ranters'). In a penetrating piece of analysis, Alun Howkins shows the ways in which, in rural England after 1850, there was a conscious ideological offensive waged by the Anglian clergy to win back flocks who, during the vicious conflicts of the first half of the nineteenth century, had been lost to the established church. This offensive was stitched into a wider set of claims of the gentry to represent a paternalist, benevolent social force. Closer analysis of the effects of this offensive in the fens in the mid- and later Victorian period would be very valuable. For now, we might fall back on the memories of Chafer Legge, who, in discussing the riots of 1816, added:

> The parsons were as bad [as the farmers], if they weren't worse. They wanted to keep people in with the gentry so they used to tell the people to put up with their miseries and not grumble, then, when they got up top [to heaven] they'd be ever so happy listening to the sound of harps; but those who grumbled and tried to alter things would just be stoking up fires in Hell.[54]

In this respect Primitive Methodism represented a counter-hegemonic force, mentally freeing workers from an ideological compact known in Norfolk as 'parsonocracy'. Jack Barrett, for example, recalled a sermon given by the Methodist lay preacher Rhiny Fletcher at the Steam Engine Primitive Methodist Chapel around 1900:

> Who was Job? Well, I'll tell you. He was a fenman. You want to know how I know that? It's in the book he wrote, thousands of years ago, where he says 'Behemoth lieth in covert of reed and fen.' I don't know who [the Biblical monster] Behemoth was, he might have been a gamekeeper or something like that, but what I do know is, that there's reed and there's fen, and if Job hadn't lived in the Fens, how would he have known about reeds and fen?[55]

The preacher's sermon naturalized a radical reading of the Old Testament within the fenland landscape in which Behemoth became the hated gamekeeper and the Prophet Job was transformed into a Fen Tiger.

---

[51] Watkins, *This Other Breed*, 55.   [52] Marshall, *Fenland Chronicle*, 103.
[53] Ibid., 93. For the apparently passive acceptance of deference, see Norfolk Federation of Women's Institutes, *Within Living Memory: A Collection of Norfolk Reminiscences* (King's Lynn, 1972), 77. For a counterexample, see Snell, 'Deferential Bitterness', 164–5.
[54] Barrett and Porter, *Tales*, 88.   [55] Ibid., 53.

But in many fenland villages outward disrespect could be a dangerous luxury. Lily Levitt was 83 when she was interviewed by Mary Chamberlain, around 1974. She remembered being in service at the Coatsworths' household—a big farming family in Meachem—in her teens. She recalled:

> Everyone in that village was subservient to them. They got to be. They were old-fashioned farmers. They were the owners of the village, really, they owned all the land. I suppose they thought they were good in their way. People used to sometimes go to them if they was [*sic*] in trouble, and they gave them perhaps a shilling, if they went to Church, and thought they were doing wonderful things.[56]

Shivers of fear reverberated into the present. Margaret Gott, the wife of the Baptist minister in Gislea, was in her thirties when Mary Chamberlain interviewed her. She suggested that women in the village

> have a tremendous inferiority complex. They very quickly feel inferior when we have speakers from Cambridge, you know, ladies with huge hats who all talk down, I curl up because I can feel the barrier coming up then. I suppose it's from the days when there was [*sic*] land workers and the gentry and you got the separation of the classes.[57]

All of this represented the political background to the post-1870 trade unionism and radicalism manifested among East Anglian rural workers. But there is an important caveat to what might seem like a triumphalist (and ultimately tragic) story of poor labouring men struggling for rights, resources, and freedom. Mary Chamberlain reminds us that, 'while the men were agitating for a living wage, the women were continuing their unsung battle to keep a home together and starvation at bay: as well as, in most cases, working on the land'.[58] Rather as with the Peruvian peasants studied by the anthropologist Gavin Smith, what was really important in the fenwomen's retelling of their survival was not so much their tales of celebrated moments of outright rebellion, but rather

> another element, *a far more important element*...that of sheer endurance: from week to week, year to year, decade to decade, through years of oppression to the capturing of the advantage of a correctly judged conjuncture, when the centre did not hold.[59]

The defence of the working-class home as an autonomous space, just as much as the forging of a new tradition of rural radicalism, represented a major achievement: one mostly won by women.[60]

---

[56] Chamberlain, *Fenwomen*, 99. For a brilliant discussion of household service in the early twentieth century, see S. Todd, 'Domestic Service and Class Relations in Britain, 1900–1950', *Past & Present* 203.1 (2009), 181–204.

[57] Chamberlain, *Fenwomen*, 124.   [58] Ibid., 16.

[59] G. Smith, 'Pandora's History: Central Peruvian Peasants and the Re-Covering of the Past', in G. Sider and G. Smith, eds, *Between History and Histories: The Making of Silences and Commemorations* (Toronto, 1997), 80–97, here 86.

[60] For a much more pessimistic assessment, see W. Johnson, 'On Agency', *Journal of Social History* 37.1 (2003), 113–24.

Landscape archaeologists, anthropologists, and social historians have recently emphasized the ways in which the material environment conditions mentalities and how rural people might read the world around them as much more than a repository of material resources.[61] This phenomenological, sensory understanding of the landscape comes through strongly in the fenland material. Young Fen Tigers were taught to respect what could be a dangerous landscape: many of the memoirs and oral interviews used in this piece mentioned the dangers of the fens, of children falling into sinkholes or being dragged into deep streams. Ernie James remembered: 'Fortunately it was very rare that a child drowned in Welney, because we were all taught by our parents from a very early age to respect the rivers and be aware of their potential dangers.'[62] When he went out to catch birds, fish, or eels, James always listened to what was told him by older men: 'They had a rich and fascinating store of knowledge about the Fens and the creatures who inhabit them, handed down by their forefathers.'[63] This sense of landscape and memory extended to discussions of the fossilized remains of long-dead forests and to prehistoric trackways.[64] Fenmen and fenwomen had a close attachment to the land, which they saw as the bearer of their historical culture and the basis of their living. A petition to the governors of Bedford Level signed in 1810 by 174 men and women with an interest in the fens in Littleport and Downham Market emphasized these factors: they explained that, '[f]rom time immemorial', their lands had drained into Grunty Fen; the drainage of that fen would have the effect of excluding them from 'their just and to them most valuable Right'.[65]

Stories were grafted into the land. Jack Barrett remembers how 'Old John Dewey, of Dutch extraction, could...spin a fine yarn; his stories told how Fen folks reacted during floods and disasters.'[66] In 1974 Mary Chamberlain noted that, although the people of Gislea were not given over to superstition, the older villagers told with pride the story of one particular landscape feature: 'Lying a few miles out of the village, and supposed to be that of a young boy who was hung for stealing a sheep, the "Grave" has been mysteriously and defiantly maintained ever since.'[67] Stories were bearers of truths—in this case, the harshness of property laws of the past and the cruelty of farmers and magistrates.

One story passed around fenmen and fenwomen, first recorded in the 1898, was that of John Leaford, who lived in Oxlode in later Stuart times. Like all fenmen and fenwomen, he worked hard on his flood defences. But over five years of good weather there were no floods; Leaford neglected the flood defences and grew rich,

---

[61] N. Whyte, *Inhabiting the Landscape: Place, Custom and Memory, 1500–1800* (Oxford, 2009); A. Wood, *The Memory of the People: Custom and Popular Senses of the Past in Early Modern England* (Cambridge, 2013); D. Massey, *Space, Place and Gender* (Cambridge, 1994); R. Bradley, *The Past in Prehistoric Societies* (London, 2002); J. Thomas, 'Archaeologies of Place and Landscape', in I. Hodder, ed., *Archaeological Theory Today* (Cambridge, 2001), 165–86; C. Tilley, *A Phenomenology of Landscape: Places, Paths and Monuments* (Oxford, 1994).
[62] James, *Memoirs of a Fen Tiger*, 24.   [63] Ibid.,13.
[64] See, for instance, Marshall, *Fenland Chronicle*, 108–15; Bloom, *Bicker's Broad*, 35.
[65] Cambridgeshire Archives, S/B/SP889.
[66] Barrett and Porter, *Tales*, xi.   [67] Chamberlain, *Fenwomen*, 17.

expanded his landholdings, and built a fine mansion. He came to be hated by everyone and was widely known by the name 'the Rich Fool'. The next time there was a flood, all of Leaford's achievements were washed away. The landscape attested to the story:

> you can still see at Oxlode, the great Hundred-Foot Bank standing as a memorial to the patience of the fen-men, who began all over again and rebuilt that rampart so that it rests upon a secure foundation, nor will there ever be another flood so disastrous, provided the necessary repairs are not neglected.[68]

The story is a commentary on those who give themselves airs and graces. All stories do things. In this case, the story of the rich fool did two things: it acted as a warning to the socially aspirant not to forget where they had come from; and it emphasized the importance of collectively guarding against the waters by maintaining flood defences. The waters also affected the reading interests of the Fen Tigers. In her sketch of the fenman, Anne Barrett observes:

> Not having had much schooling, books were not of great interest. He possessed two: a bible, his knowledge of which was obvious to all he came into contact with, and *Old Moore's Almanack* which gave him the phases of the noon and timetable of high water at King's Lynn, vital information to one living in constant fear of burst banks and flooded fen. A staunch liberal, in his view Cromwell was the greatest man in history and Gladstone was his prophet.[69]

The struggle of the Fen Tiger has been in part the struggle against water. This makes her or his attachment to the land especially poignant. The Fen Tigers' struggle against the waters reached far back in the distant past and defined their local culture.[70] When further fen drainage and enclosure came in the late eighteenth and early nineteenth centuries, much more than an ancient landscape was disrupted: so was a way of *being*. In 1904 the Cottenham man Jacob Sanderson wrote a powerful comment on the cultural impact of enclosure:

> Now a great change came over Cottenham, the Enclosure. Old times were to pass away and all things to become new. No more stocking of the Commons on Old May Day, not Dye Feast, or Officers chosen, nor Auditermakers Days. Nearly all the old landmarks were removed and a fresh order of things substituted in their place. Three old watermills taken down, Undertaker, Chare Fen and Setchell, and two steam engines in their place, Smithe Fen and Chare Fen. New drains were dug or made, and fresh roads made through the Fens and Fields, everyone knowing his own allotment. There is not one now in all the Town but what has changed hands since then, both in the Town Fields and on the Fen. In my time one generation passeth away and another cometh.[71]

---

[68] C. Marlowe, *Legends of the Fenland People* (London, 1926), 133–7, here 137.
[69] Barrett and Garrod, *East Anglian Folklore*, 127.
[70] Cambridge University Library, EDR.A/8/1.
[71] J. R. Ravensdale, *Liable to Floods: Village Landscape on the Edge of the Fens, AD 450–1850* (Cambridge, 1974), 34.

What is described here is the generation of a kind of *anomie*—a sense that has been seen as characteristic of the experience of urban modernity.[72] All of this was so different from the world before large-scale enclosure and drainage.

Yet there remained parts of the fens that were never drained. Throughout the texts on which this essay has depended runs a profound sense of attachment to the land, a way of reading the landscape as much more than a set of resources: rather the fenland landscape was read, felt, *experienced*. Labour upon the land generated what archaeologists have called a taskscape, a sense of place that was built around the experience of work and movement, a way of being in the land.[73] Alan Bickers's semi-autobiographical novel gives some sense of this attachment:

> The soft black earth, the livestock and the horses, the routine of cultivation, sowing and harvesting, these were things to be in love with. They held a challenge and in accepting it [the fenman] became so absorbed that he could not help but give all that he had. But this was not all. He could feel part of this landscape, on which his fore-bears—especially old Amos Bickers, had left their mark. He had been a pioneer in these fens, and Uncle Albert had told him much more of the family history, how the Bickers had originated from the Fenland village with that name. At least that was the family legend and Cyril was the only one left in the Fens to carry on the name.[74]

So, to what wider issues do the stories told in this piece speak? What great issues of historiography or grand theory are illuminated by the women of Gislea, or by Chafer Legge, or by Jack Barrett? Where do the grandiose priorities of 'Big History' fit in these emphatically local, working-class stories?[75] First of all, let us acknowledge that marginality runs through this whole piece. The fens are marginal: on the edge of East Anglia, they are a farming region worked for generations by wage labourers bonded to the land, and now by migrants from the poverty-stricken edges of Eastern Europe. They are also culturally marginal. Graham Swift's bleak novel *Waterland* attests to this marginality, to the ghosts of the past that hover over the fens, and to the constant struggle against flood and hunger. Finally, the sources on which this essay has depended have been selected, at least in part, because of their historiographical marginality: these are not the state papers of the great, not the estate records of the gentleman, not the careful accounts of the prosperous farmer. There is no 'Big History' here. They are sources that academic historians are trained to disdain, turning up their noses at the nostalgia, the gossip, the local worlds to which my sources have spoken.[76] It is significant, I think, that much of the material I have deployed was printed in local publishing houses.

[72] For placelessness and memory, see T. Judt, 'The Past Is Another Country: Myth and Memory in Postwar Europe', *Daedalus* 21.4 (1992), 83–118.

[73] T. Ingold, 'The Temporality of the Landscape', *World Archaeology* 25.2 (1993), 152–74. For the application of the concept in historical analysis, see K. Navickas, 'Luddism, Incendiarism and the Defence of Rural "Task-Scapes" in 1812', *Northern History* 48.1 (2011), 59–73; S. Sandall, 'Industry and Community in the Forest of Dean', *Family and Community* 16.2 (2013), 87–99.

[74] Bloom, *Bicker's Broad*, 25.

[75] J. Guldi and D. Armitage, *The History Manifesto* (Cambridge, 2014); at http://historymanifesto. cambridge.org (accessed 15 July 2015).

[76] For nostalgia as agency, see B. Jones, 'The Uses of Nostalgia: Autobiography, Community Publishing and Working-Class Neighbourhoods in Post-War England', *Cultural and Social History* 7.4 (2010), 355–74.

If there is a larger meaning to be taken from the memories and stories recorded here, it is that of the importance of the historian keeping her or his ear open to voices from the margins, of attending to small places—places about which large questions might be asked, but that might remain marginal. Much of the time, this is where subaltern history happens. In their study of the Captain Swing protests of the 1830s, Eric Hobsbawm and George Rude wrote of rural labourers' world views as merely 'the common luggage of the pre-political poor'.[77] For all that Hobsbawm and Rude shared membership of the Communist Party Historians' Group with Edward Thompson, it is hard not to contrast this assessment with Thompson's desire for a history of the worlds that workers made.[78] The tension here is partly one between different versions of Marxism; but it is more than that. It is a contrast between different ways of understanding the past.

In the end, we are left with the five swans over Littleport. On that summer's day in 1816, the birds carried with them the burden of loss. Nesting in the river, they fostered a fierce urge to survive which subsequently defined the cultural and material worlds of generations of Fen Tigers. This is a story that has its own validity and that deserves to be read in its own terms.

ACKNOWLEDGEMENTS

I am grateful to John Arnold for reading this chapter at very short notice, and to the thoughtful comments of the anonymous reader for Oxford University Press.

---

[77] E. Hobsbawm and G. Rude, *Captain Swing* (Harmondsworth, 1973), 43.
[78] For a passionate restatement of this tradition, see S. Todd, *The People: The Rise and Fall of the Working Class* (London, 2014).

13

Rethinking Gender and Labour History

Sonya O. Rose and Sean Brady

Gender and labour history matter. A gendered account of labour history is significant to our understanding of past lives as well as to the lives we live now. Its significance, along with that of race and ethnicity, is related to one of the most important issues in today's world as well as in times past: social and economic inequality. It has bearing on a range of related historical and contemporary concerns as well. This chapter discusses the ways in which questions of gender and of global history have revitalized and expanded labour history as a historical subdiscipline.

Labour history once focused almost exclusively on the development of trade unions and on the industrial labour force. The field became reinvigorated and expansive in the 1950s and 1960s, as the interests of historians widened to include the everyday lives and political activism of members of the working class. The struggle of feminist historians to incorporate women's labour as a crucial site of analysis in labour history and the economy of the working-class household was born out of critical disagreements within labour historiography. Although Eric Hobsbawm recognized in the late 1970s that the history of women and of their labour was neglected, he and other labour historians were roundly criticized for perceived antipathy to women's history and to gendered identity politics in general. As Sally Alexander, Anna Davin, and Eve Hostettler stated in 1979, Hobsbawm and other male historians of labour seemed unable to 'include as class consciousness...women homeworkers, housewives, or the many who earned during marriage by a wide range of strategems'.[1] Nonetheless, with the rise of women's history from the 1970s and early 1980s, historians began to focus on the lives of women workers in industrializing Europe and North America. There was recognition that working-class women laboured to support family livelihoods and did so at a disadvantage. From the mid-1970s, and especially in the 1980s, questions of gender that included not only women as workers but working men as men broadened the field of labour history even more. Historians' attention to men as men began to flourish, especially as scholars became interested in the family wage, the respectable artisan, and the relationship between men's employment and household status, their right to vote, and then, later, embodied labour. Feminist historians emphasized

---

[1] Sally Alexander, Anna Davin, and Eve Hostettler, 'Labouring Women: A Reply to Eric Hobsbawm', *History Workshop* 8 (1979), 174–82, here 175.

the significance of reproductive labour—the work of women in their households, which enabled those formally considered 'workers' to labour. Attention was also paid to women's struggles for inclusion in unions and for better working conditions and higher wages. Scholars attended to women's participation in and instigation of collective action and protest. There was an outpouring of work on the gender segregation of jobs that helped to explain why women's earnings were lower than men's and showed that job segregation by sex was woven into the very fabric of industrial capitalism. In other words, industrial capitalism as it developed in the nineteenth and early twentieth centuries was gendered.

Scholarship on gender and labour flourished through the 1990s and into the twenty-first century. Some brief examples illustrate how a focus on gender adds to our understanding of labour history and its influence on men as men—on masculinities. In 2004 the *Labour History Review* devoted a special issue to a theme that produced the volume title *Working-Class Masculinities in Britain, 1850 to the Present*. An article by Ronnie Johnston and Arthur McIvor used oral testimony to examine how working in hazardous Clydeside heavy industries in the period 1930–70 cultivated and buttressed masculine identities such as the 'hard man' and at the same time the culture of work and its dangers threatened 'provider masculinity'.[2] Karen Hunt dealt with socialist masculinities before the First World War, and Pat Ayers wrote about the cultural and racial context of the remaking of masculinities in the face of the dramatic economic restructuring of Liverpool in the period after the Second World War.[3]

Feminist-inspired labour and working-class historical scholarship continues to probe the lives of women in the workplace and family situations—especially in the interconnection between the so-called 'public' and 'private'. One example, published in 2013 by Ileen DeVault in the US journal *Labor History*, documents the contribution of American wives and mothers to the economic survival of families through a variety of forms of work that brought cash into their households during the period from 1880 to 1930, supplementing the earnings of 'male breadwinners'.[4] Selina Todd's 2005 study of young women, work, and family in England between 1918 and 1950 demonstrated the interrelatedness of women's employment opportunities and workplace experiences with their familial relationships and leisure activities.[5] In recent years there has been a surge of scholarship on 'caring' as gendered and racialized labour, as well as on domestic servants.[6]

[2] Ronnie Johnston and Arthur McIvor, 'Dangerous Work, Hard Men and Broken Bodies: Masculinity in the Clydeside Heavy Industries, c.1930–1970s', *Labour History Review* 69.2 (2004), 135–52.
[3] Karen Hunt, '"Strong Minds, Great Hearts, True Faith and Ready Hands"? Exploring Socialist Masculinities before the First World War', *Labour History Review* 69.2 (2004), 201–19; Pat Ayers, 'Work, Culture and Gender: The Making of Masculinities in Post-War Liverpool', *Labour History Review* 69.2 (2004), 153–69.
[4] Ileen DeVault, 'Family Wages: The Roles of Wives and Mothers in US Working-Class Survival Strategies, 1880–1930', *Labor History* 54.1 (2013), 1–20.
[5] Selina Todd, *Young Women, Work, and Family in England, 1918–1950* (Oxford, 2005).
[6] On caring, see Eileen Boris and Jennifer Klein, *Caring for America: Home Health Workers in the Shadow of the Welfare State* (New York, 2012) and Evelyn Nakano Glenn, *Forced to Care: Coercion and Caregiving in America* (Cambridge, 2010). For research on the issue of contemporary care workers, see

Of course, feminist scholarship on servants has a distinguished history. Leonore Davidoff, for example, published her essay 'Mastered for Life', on household servants and working-class wives in Victorian and Edwardian England, in 1974.[7] But there seemingly has been a flurry of recent scholarship on the subject of domestic service. Carolyn Steedman's study on eighteenth-century domestic service is notable here. In 2007 she published *Master and Servant*, which detailed the relationship between a male employer and his young domestic servant, as told through the employer's diaries.[8] In 2009 Steedman followed this book with a collection of essays titled *Labours Lost: Domestic Service and the Making of Modern England*, in which she demonstrates the centrality of domestic service to the social and cultural history of the period between 1760 and 1830. The essays show domestic labour to be an integral part of the working class and part of a modern labour force, as indicated by the nature of labour relations in which domestic labourers were involved, wage payment systems, and employment contracts.[9] Lucy Delap's work expands our understanding of domestic service and its complexities in twentieth-century Britain by focusing on its varied forms and their emotional resonances.[10] Selina Todd has underscored the significance of domestic service and its transformations, both for working-class women and for their middle-class employers in the first half of the twentieth century.[11] In a recent essay, Laura Schwartz has exposed the ambivalence of Edwardian feminists towards the efforts of some domestic workers to form the Domestic Workers' Union, created in 1910, and then to engage in it.[12] Bringing race into the mix of gender and class, an essay by Caroline Bressey discusses the involvement of black women in England in domestic service, as well as in caring work such as nursing, from 1880 to 1920.[13] Importantly, there has been a recent spate of scholarship on domestic work, migration, and globalization that will be discussed later in this chapter.

Although scholarship on gender and labour has continued in important ways, labour history itself has been seen by scholars to be in decline. In 1993, for example, a special supplement to the *International Review of Social History* was published with the title *The End of Labour History?*. In 2010 *Labour History Review*, the

for example Fiona Williams and Deborah Brennan, eds, *Care, Markets and Migration in a Globalising World*, special issue of *Journal of European Social Policy* 22.4 (2012).

[7] Leonore Davidoff, 'Mastered for Life: Servant and Wife in Victorian and Edwardian England', *Journal of Social History* 7.4 (1974), 406–28, here 406–8.

[8] Carolyn Steedman, *Master and Servant: Love and Labour in the English Industrial Age* (Cambridge, 2007).

[9] Carolyn Steedman, *Labours Lost: Domestic Service and the Making of Modern England* (Cambridge, 2009).

[10] Lucy Delap, *Knowing their Place: Domestic Service in Twentieth-Century Britain* (Oxford, 2011).

[11] Selina Todd, 'Domestic Service and Class Relations in Britain, 1900–1950', *Past & Present* 203 (2009), 181–204; recently Selina Todd, *The People: The Rise and Fall of the Working Class* (London, 2015), 13–99.

[12] Laura Schwartz, 'A Job like Any Other? Feminist Responses and Challenges to Domestic Worker Organizing in Edwardian Britain', *International Labor and Working-Class History* 88 (2015), 30–48.

[13] Caroline Bressey, 'Black Women and Work in England, 1880–1920', in Mary Davis, ed., *Class and Gender in British Labour History: Renewing the Debate (or Starting It?)* (Powys, 2011), 117–32.

journal of the British Society for the Study of Labour History, published a special issue on the preceding fifty years of labour history. The volume contained Neville Kirk's essay 'Challenge, Crisis and Renewal?'. In a multicontributor volume edited by Joan Allen, Alan Campbell, and John McIllroy and published in the same year under the title *Histories of Labour: National and International Perspectives*, the essays seemed to portray the field of labour history as a discipline under threat. If labour history was seen by many observers as becoming eroded, the blame for it was variously placed on the rising emphasis on cultural approaches to history, on the increasing interest in historical scholarship on gender and racial identities, which ignored or seemed to downplay social class, and on the fact that the political climate in both the United Kingdom and the United States had taken the lifeblood from working-class activism, especially as trade union membership plummeted in both countries.

Trade union membership in the manufacturing sector of the British economy (the traditional focus of labour history) has continued to fall. UK trade union statistics for the year 2014, published in May 2015, reveal that, while in 1995 only one third of trade union members were employed in manufacturing, this percentage dropped to 18 per cent in 2014.[14] Another interesting finding in the report for 2013 is that employees in professional occupations were more likely to be trade union members than those in other occupations and thus accounted for 37 per cent of all trade union members, although only 21 per cent of all UK employees worked in these occupations.[15] Professional occupations included teachers, speech and occupational therapists, and nurses. In an analysis of trade union density by industry, the education sector was found to have the highest proportion of trade union members, 52 per cent of employees being members of unions.[16] Not surprisingly given the gender dimension of these occupations, women outnumbered men as trade union members overall. These statistics raise important questions about the changing relationship between gender and labour. Questions such as how gender relations change and how the meanings of masculinity and femininity change as the occupational structure and modes of production are transformed seem especially relevant. Questions like these would be relevant not only to the present but also to the past, as the ways of producing goods and services and the social characteristics of producers themselves have been changing over a very long historical period.

There are many examples of occupations that have undergone gendered transformations. An interesting one is clerical work—what would now be part of the service sector of the contemporary economy, where people serve as 'administrative assistants'. Labour and working-class history, given its traditional focus on industrialized workplaces and organized labour, would not have incorporated studies of the changing nature of clerical work—which once had been the preserve of young

[14] Department for Business Innovation and Skills, *Trade Union Membership 2014: Statistical Bulletin,* National Statistics, June 2015 (also available at https://www.gov.uk/government/uploads/system/uploads/attachment_data/file/431564/Trade_Union_Membership_Statistics_2014.pdf, accessed 20 May 2017), 10.
[15] Ibid., 9. [16] Ibid., p11.

men who were clerks and were probably considered to belong to the lower middle class. The relevance of labour and working-class history to histories of gender and labour is demonstrated in a recent study by the US historian Carole Srole, who examines the changing meanings of clerical work and the creation of professional labour in nineteenth-century courts and offices in the United States.[17] Her work underscores the simplicity of our current vocabulary of gender and class in the context of what might be considered a 'middle-class workplace'. Srole examines office work as a route to gendered middle-class identity and explores how both men and women attempted to assume the respectability of middle-class status. She argues, however, that, when women first entered office work, they were cast as degraded workers on account of their working-class status. If men did work that women also did, they tried to distinguish their employment, seeing themselves as clerks and women as copyists. Srole's investigation of the middle-class workplace underscores the need to question categories of analysis, not of gender, but of those other concepts that labour history took for granted—labour, class, and the working class.

If labour history as a field of study is concerned primarily with the development of the labour movement and the working class, how would a study of masculinity and femininity in office work fit into this definition? It would not—not given the taken-for-granted meaning of 'working class', at least as this class was viewed in its relationship to industrial capitalism. Class was itself understood in terms of the relations of production, most particularly as it concerned the making of the proletariat. More than that, the working class was assumed to consist of men who did manual work—labour involving muscle and strength as well as skill. But what if one is concerned with the relationship between labour and gender, gender being defined as the set of ideals and practices that give meaning to and socially differentiate the male and the female? How are gender relations and the construction of gender differences shaped by class distinctions or work of various kinds, or indeed by economic transformations? Or what if one questions how, in turn, gender relations or the constructions of masculinities and femininities affect workplace organization and practices or the making and unmaking of class identities, collective action, or—importantly, as will be discussed later—the globalization of labour and capital?

So how do we understand the concept of 'class' and the meaning of 'the working class'? Much has been written of late about class having dropped out or being muted in analyses of gender and labour. But there are also some 'green shoots'— suggestions about how to think of class in a commodious way in order to make it both a useful category of historical analysis and one that might have some political resonances in today's world. The US historian Eileen Boris has suggested that, with a focus from scholars on the global political economy, class has re-emerged as an expansive category of analysis.[18] She does not succinctly define class in her essay

[17] Carole Srole, *Transcribing Class and Gender: Masculinity and Femininity in Nineteenth-Century Courts and Offices* (Ann Arbor, MI, 2010).
[18] Eileen Boris, 'Class Returns', *Journal of Women's History* 25.4 (2013), 74–87.

published in 2013 but suggests that skill, education, occupation, and the nature of one's relationship to the means of production define class. She further suggests that class may be configured differently by sex and influenced by kinship status and by the division of labour, all of which lead to differences in wealth and income, property and ownership, and access to the means that distinguish social groups in a hierarchical manner. In other words, she seems to see class both as entangled in the means of production and social reproduction or household labour and as the means by which people or groups are distinguished from one another in terms of access to economic and social privilege.

In her recent book *The People: The Rise and Fall of the Working Class*, Selina Todd defines class as a 'relationship of unequal power'.[19] Given the growing disparities in wealth in today's world—especially considering the United States, where the top 10 per cent own 76 per cent of the country's net worth, and the ways in which wealth is increasingly becoming central to politics and is reshaping democratic institutions—Todd's definition holds a great deal of purchase.[20] We might tie a definition of class more directly to the question of how people earn a living, building on Eileen Boris's conceptualization by defining classes as patterned differences in life chances that are given meaning and recognition through socially and economically structured relations, both at work and beyond the workplace and through cultural mechanisms that create 'distinctions' (in Bourdieu's meaning of the term).[21] In the end, however, the political meaning of 'class', as Todd's definition suggests, concerns inequality—unequal life chances—as the phrase 'life chances' refers to (or designates) the economic circumstances that influence the manner in which people live their lives.

But who, then, comprise the working class, whose gendered histories gender and labour historians are interested in understanding? To address this question, it is necessary to ask: what *is* work? There probably is no definition of 'work' that would be meaningful for all societies and cultures across historical time. Marcel Van der Linden has defined work as 'the purposive production of useful objects and services'.[22] Jurgen Kocka has defined it as the 'purposeful application of physical and mental forces to fulfil needs'.[23] Van der Linden's and Kocka's similar definitions are capacious enough to include slave, indentured, and conscripted labour, sharecropping and subsistence agricultural labour, unwaged household labour, and, of course, all manner of wage labour. They would include office or clerical work and the varieties of service work that have replaced industrial production in many societies that were formerly devoted to manufacturing.

---

[19] Selina Todd, *The People*, 369.

[20] Statistics are from OECD, *In It Together: Why Less Inequality Benefits All* (Paris, 2015; also available at http://www.keepeek.com/Digital-Asset-Management/oecd/employment/in-it-together-why-less-inequality-benefits-all_9789264235120-en#.WSQpajPMyuU#page3, accessed 20 May 2017), 1.

[21] Pierre Bourdieu, *Distinction: A Social Critique of the Judgement of Taste* (Cambridge, MA, 1987).

[22] Marcel Van der Linden, 'Studying Attitudes to Work Worldwide, 1500–1650', *International Review of Social History* 56.19 (2011): 25–43, here 27.

[23] Jurgen Kocka, 'Work as a Problem in European History', in Jurgen Kocka, ed., *Work in a Modern Society: German Historical Experience in Comparative Perspective* (Oxford, 2010), 2.

The US historian Alice Kessler-Harris has emphasized that the turn to global history forces scholars of gender and labour to question the 'particularity of Western cultural standpoints, encouraging us to investigate how racialized-gendered power relations infuse the distribution of work and shape the meaning of the family' and expose 'the multiple ways that gender participates in structuring changing systems of work organization'.[24] She suggests that relationships to work—both paid and unpaid—have provided the 'informal claims to dignity' that at the same time have both produced and reflected distinctions based on race and gender.

An expansive definition of work is important in thinking about histories within national or regional boundaries as well as globally. The distinction between 'formal' and 'informal' labour in the recent past was used by scholars to contrast modern industrial economies in which waged, primarily 'blue-collar' work predominated and underdeveloped, 'traditional' economies mired in earlier modes of production such as subsistence agriculture or reliant on bartering and trading.[25] Social science scholars are increasingly arguing that such a binary view is off the mark; they speak of the 'blurring of the formal/informal economy divide' and are seeking new ways to conceptualize the diverse labour practices that intersect and are conjoined.[26] This reconceptualization abandons the idea of a unilinear shift from informal to formal labour as societies become industrialized and transformed. As Jennifer Klein has noted, 'Although there's been greater industrialization and enmeshment in the global economy... it has been accompanied by the dramatic increase in casualized or precarious employment and even unemployment all over.'[27] Such forms of work are proliferating not just in 'less developed' regions of the globe, but also in the West.[28] A reconceptualized, inclusive understanding of work, then, would include such forms as paid and unpaid domestic labour and caring, sex work, and varieties of coerced, trafficked labour as well as small-scale self-employment or market activities and agricultural production, all of which have a long history that continues to the present day.[29]

Given a capacious definition of 'work' and a turn to global labour history, how might the concept of 'the working class' be understood? Marcel van der Linden, who has been at the forefront of arguing for a 'global labour history', sees the working class as including 'all carriers of labor-power whose labor-power is sold or hired out to employers under conditions of both economic or non-economic compulsion regardless of whether these carriers of labor-power are themselves selling or

[24] Alice Kessler-Harris, 'Reframing the History of Women's Wage Labour: Challenges of a Global Perspective', *Journal of Women's History* 15.4 (2004), 186–206, here 189.

[25] Sara Nadin and Colin C. Williams, 'Blurring the Formal/Informal Economy Divide: Beyond a Dual Economies Approach', *Journal of Economy and its Applications* 2.1 (2012), 85–103 here 86.

[26] Ibid., 86; see also Miriam Glucksmann's conceptualization of a 'total social organization of labour approach' in Miriam Glucksmann, 'Shifting Boundaries and Interconnections: Extending the 'Total Social Organisation of Labour', *Sociological Review* 53.1 (2005), 19–36.

[27] Jennifer Klein, 'New Directions in Labor History around the Globe: Introduction', *International Labor and Working-Class History* 82 (2012), 114–16, here 115.

[28] Nadin and Williams, 'Blurring the Formal/Informal', for example, examine the variety of labour practices in English localities.

[29] See, for example, Benjamin N. Lawrance and Richard L. Roberts, eds, *Trafficking in Slavery's Wake: Law and the Experience of Women and Children in Africa* (Athens, OH, 2012).

hiring out their labor-power; and also regardless of whether these carriers themselves own the means of production'. In other words, the global working class would include waged workers, forced, bonded, or slave labourers, as well as self-employed contractors and street market traders. He argues that what such workers have in common is the commodification of their labour power.[30] In sum, it is the more or less 'coerced' contribution of its labour power to capital that defines the working class.

Van der Linden's reference to the 'coerced' contribution of labour power to capital is suggestive, as it opens up the possibility of exploring forms of work or labour that are neither 'free' nor 'enslaved' and of considering the mechanisms through which different forms of labour or work are coerced as well as the extent of coercion involved. In a provocative essay, the Canadian historian Peter Way proposes that military labour might be investigated by labour historians. He suggests that the military played an increasingly important role in the early modern transition to capitalism and in the process of primitive accumulation. He argues that the paid labour of soldiers, seen as a collectivity, as an army, 'contributed directly to the political economic project of the imperial state'.[31] Thinking about war, empire building, and colonization moves the discussion of labour history, making it encompass a much broader time span than the period of industrial and proto-industrial production. Way suggests that production or labour need not be restricted to the 'generation of a commodity for market consumption' and may be understood as 'proletarian labor'. 'Wherever European nations fought for territory and access to trade across the globe, the labor of soldiers and sailors comprised crucial components to empire building.'[32] Considering how soldiers and sailors were recruited—including through impressment, lifelong contracts, volunteering for the military for economic motives, and conscription—the amount of discipline they were subjected to once they were on the job, and the dire consequences of their attempting to quit collapses even further the distinction between free and unfree labour and opens a new and potentially fruitful path for historians of labour as well as for military historians. The fact that until fairly recent times soldiers and sailors were predominantly male does not make a history of gendered labour irrelevant. It opens a door to exploring the way in which the different kinds of work of soldiers and sailors affected how they were regarded as men and how gender relations were affected when, in the twentieth century, women were given the 'privilege' to fight.[33]

---

[30] Marcel van der Linden, 'The Promise and Challenges of Global Labor History', *International Labor and Working-Class History* 82 (2012), 57–76, here 66–7.

[31] Peter Way, '"Black Service...White Money": The Peculiar Institution of Military Labor in the British Army during the Seven Years' War', in Eric Leon Fink, ed., *Workers across the Americas: The Transnational Turn in Labor History* (New York, 2011), 57–80, here 62.

[32] Ibid., 63.

[33] For examples of research that addresses that issue regarding the Soviet Union in the Second World War, see Anna Krylova, *Soviet Women in Combat. A History of Violence on the Eastern Front* (Cambridge, 2010); Steven G. Jog, 'Red Army Romance: Preserving Masculine Hegemony in Mixed Gender Combat Units, 1943–1944', *Journal of War & Culture Studies* 5.3 (2012), 321–34.

Van der Linden's reference to the term 'commodity' implies a connection between the history of work and capitalism in its various forms, historically and in the present. Although a discussion concerning the debates over definitions of capitalism and its histories is beyond the scope of this chapter, it is important to note that, at least among US historians, those debates are flourishing.[34] Louis Hyman, a participant in that debate, has suggested that 'the problem with capitalism is not defining it, but figuring out why it resists easy definitions'.[35] More than its being impossible to give a simple definition of capitalism as an economic system, it would seem to be more to the point to speak of *capitalisms* that are diverse and constantly changing economic and political forms or processes.[36] Labour history, then, is concerned with work over capitalism's *longue durée*, beginning with the production of sugar in the sixteenth century and, later, of cotton on plantations in colonized areas of the Americas with the help of slave labour from Africa that contributed to and was connected with the rise of industrial capitalism.[37]

The turn to global labour history reinvigorates some aspects of earlier scholarship concerned with household strategies for economic survival, as it moves away from the history of proletarianization and labour unions bound to the era of industrialization and focuses on households as well as on individual workers in different interrelated regions of the globe, thus opening the field to a longer time period. The Indian labour historian Prasannan Parthasarathi has noted, for example, that the study of 'Indian labor has shifted decisively from the male (unionized) factory operative and has come to recognize the diverse forms of employment, status, work and organization that characterize the past as well as the present'.[38] He proposes that a focus on 'survival strategies' broadens the study of labour, making it include 'family, household and gender'.[39] Van der Linden also suggests that households are a better unit of analysis for working-class or labour history than individuals and quotes Jean Quataert's point that this unit 'permits keeping in focus at all times the lives of both men and women, young and old, and the variety of paid and unpaid work necessary to maintain the unit'.[40]

---

[34] See the section 'Interchange: The History of Capitalism', in *Journal of American History* 101.2 (2014): 503–36.

[35] Ibid., 513.

[36] For a thoughtful discussion and historiographic overview, see Sven Beckert, 'History of American Capitalism', in Eric Foner and Lisa McGirr, *American History Now* (Philadelphia, PA, 2011), 314–35.

[37] Famously, it was Eric Williams who first advanced this idea, in a much debated thesis in his *Capitalism and Slavery* (Chapel Hill, NC, 1944). The argument that plantation slavery was crucial to industrializing Britain has continued to be advanced. See, e.g., Emmanuel Akyeampong, 'Slavery, Indentured Labor, and the Making of a Transnational World', in Ato Quayson and Girish Daswani, eds, *A Companion to Diaspora and Transnationalism* (Oxford, 2013), 163–71. See also the acclaimed book by Sven Beckert, *Empire of Cotton: A Global History* (New York, 2014).

[38] Prasannan Parthasarathi, 'Indian Labor History', *International Labor and Working-Class History* 82 (2012), 127–35, here 129.

[39] Ibid., 130.

[40] Marcel van der Linden, 'Global Labor History: Promising Challenges', *International Labor and Working-Class History* 84 (2013), 218–25, here 222; Jean H. Quataert, 'Combining Agrarian and Industrial Livelihood: Rural Households in the Saxon Oberlausitz in the Nineteenth Century', *Journal of Family History* 10.2 (1985), 145–62, here 158.

Interestingly, numerous studies of manufacturing in pre-industrial or 'proto-industrial' and early industrializing Europe attended to household labour and economic strategies. Prior to the location of manufacturing goods in factories, and even in the early years of textile manufacturing, production took place not only in workshops, but also in households where family members participated in operating such machinery as spinning wheels and weaving looms, or finished items by hand.[41] Historical scholarship on this topic, however, was generally published as research on family history. What is being suggested here with regard to household survival strategies is to bring together the fields of labour and family history where they intersect and to see household economic strategies as playing a long and important role in gendered regimes of labour.

Research on industrializing Bengal underscores the importance of household or family strategies to histories of work, illustrating how a turn to global labour history expands the field to make it incorporate the ways in which families sustain themselves through different forms of labour. In the early years of industrialization—in the late nineteenth and early twentieth centuries—many rural people became increasingly impoverished, due to declining incomes from labour, land, and crafts. As a consequence, men moved to the city or overseas to earn an income, while wives and children remained to work intensively for subsistence in the rural economy: 'The typical working-class family was spatially fragmented and was as crucially dependent on the unpaid (or poorly paid) labour of women and children in the rural economy as on men's industrial wages.'[42] As Willem van Schendel has argued, 'The power of kinship and family ideologies in deploying the labour of household members, parcelling out entitlements and shaping household strategies needs to be taken more seriously. This requires us to focus on the agency of workers and the transformative role of their living strategies, cumulating over generations.'[43]

Sociologist Mike Savage has suggested that structural insecurity is the distinctive feature of working-class life and that workers adopt a variety of coping strategies in response that involve households, neighbourhoods, and communities.[44] The notion of 'structural insecurity' brings to mind publicity in 2014 and 2015 about the number of people employed on 'zero-hours contracts' in Britain. The Office of National Statistics in the winter of 2015 estimated that nearly 700,000 people were on such contracts, as their main employment and that around 1.8 million contracts that do not guarantee a minimum number of hours were given out in mid-August 2014.[45] The International Labour Organization (ILO) reported in May 2015 that

---

[41] For a fairly recent contribution to that literature by a sociologist, see Jane Gray, *Spinning the Threads of Uneven Development: Gender and Industrialization in Ireland during the Long Eighteenth Century* (Lanham, MD, 2005).

[42] Samita Sen, 'Gendered Exclusion: Domesticity and Dependence in Bengal', *International Review of Social History* 42 (1997), 65–86, here 73.

[43] Willem van Schendel, 'Stretching Labour Historiography: Pointers from South Asia', *International Review of Social History* 51 (2006), 229–61, here 244.

[44] Mike Savage, 'Class and Labour History', in Lex Heerma Van Voss and Marcel Van der Linden, eds, *Class and Other Identities: Gender, Religion, and Ethnicity in the Writing of European Labour History* (Oxford, 2002), 61.

[45] Office for National Statistics, 'Analysis of Employee Contracts that Do Not Guarantee a Minimum Number of Hours', 25 February 2015, http://webarchive.nationalarchives.gov.uk/

three-quarters of the world's workers were employed on temporary or short-term contracts and worked often without contracts, were self-employed, or worked in unpaid family jobs.[46] While such reports offer a good illustration of 'structural insecurity' in today's world, it is important to note that structural insecurity in different forms has been an issue for working people worldwide historically. This line of thinking leads us back once again to a consideration of household survival strategies and, in the context of global history, to the complex livelihoods of households in which the distinctions between formal and informal labour continue to be blurred. With regard to Indian labour history, Parthasarathi suggests that 'issues of survival strategies shaped the politics of workers from the eighteenth century to the present'.[47] He maintains that a focus on survival strategies sheds light on the diversity of types of work and labour relations in Indian history. While employers sought to secure profitability in a competitive world, workers sought survival and security. He underscores the point that 'a focus on survival strategies... broadens the study of Indian labor, most importantly to include the family, household and gender'.[48] Additionally, Parthasarathi argues that state policies regulating and affecting labour as well as gender and household survival strategies are important to consider in a broadened field of labour history.[49]

While attending to a world or global history approach to labour or working-class history suggests investigating large historical transformations comparatively, as a consequence of regional interdependencies, or transnationally, it need not necessarily do so, although such investigations are significant in shedding light on local, national, and regional cases. Thinking globally raises numerous questions that might be addressed for different time periods, regions, and local settings. For example, studies of coerced and voluntary migration or of the movement of people across space and its consequences for gender and work offer a fruitful line of historical inquiry—one that deals with slavery across time—as well as a host of issues concerning indentured workers, refugees, economic migrants, and the importation of foreign labour to meet temporary economic demands such as 'guest worker' programmes and seasonal workers. Importantly, the turn to global labour history brings together two areas of historical scholarship—histories of migration and histories of labour—that until fairly recently had been separate domains of scholarship. Some of this recent scholarship focuses on transnational history: histories that cross national or, to be more inclusive, political borders; these would also include studies of regional migrations during the period of European imperial domination of Asia, Africa, and Latin America and would predate the formation

20160105160709/http://www.ons.gov.uk/ons/rel/lmac/contracts-with-no-guaranteed-hours/zero-hours-contracts/art-zero-hours.html, accessed 20 May 2017.

[46] International Labour Organization, 'World Employment Social Outlook 2015: The Changing Nature of Jobs', ILO, 2015, at http://www.ilo.org/wcmsp5/groups/public/---dgreports/---dcomm/---publ/documents/publication/wcms_368626.pdf, accessed 20 May 2017. See especially Chapters 1 and 5.

[47] Parthasarathi, 'Indian Labor History', 130.

[48] Ibid.   [49] Ibid., 131–3.

of what we call 'nation-states'.[50] Dirk Hoerder has thoughtfully argued that, to grasp the movements of working men and women, especially when considering their movement to and from different labour markets, it is helpful to think of 'transcultural' spaces. By 'culture' he means to include all aspects of people's lives as they change locales.[51] Hoerder makes the important point that, while the term 'globalization' is usually thought to describe a very modern phenomenon, the processes involved in fact stretch back in time at least to the early modern period. He uses the seventeenth-century fur trade as an example that extended 'from Alaska via Labrador and Scandinavia to Siberia, and [was] capitalized from London, Paris, Amsterdam, and Moscow'. The trade depended upon the migration of traders and producers and involved the gendered work processes of women and men.[52] Hoerder attends specifically to the gendered labour patterns of the global textile trade. While steel and heavy industry 'privilege[s] the northern Atlantic world and men's over women's work', textile production was another matter altogether. As suggested earlier, it involved family economies and the production of fibre of various sorts, 'local, macroregional, and global'. Nineteenth-century merchants and producers in Lanarkshire in Scotland 'depended on fleece from specific regions in Australia, light alpaca from the Peruvian Andes, or mohair from specific regions of Turkey'.[53] Labour historians might examine the various work processes involved in this global trade: not only the production of cloth, but the rearing and shearing of the animals from which the fibres were harvested. Although gender is not the site of Sven Beckert's analysis, his work on the 'empire of cotton' emphasizes the transnational interconnectedness and global struggle between planters, slaves, merchants, and factory owners through the nexus of cotton fibre and cloth production.[54] Focusing upon the historical production of a specific, industrialized commodity such as cotton cloth would further reveal the gendered division of labour not only in the production of the cloth, but in many other products such as steel, iron, rubber, and palm oil, which originated in various regions and went into the production process. Additionally, the production process depended upon the labours of women and men who migrated across borders using family strategies and relying upon networks of former migrants to establish new communities.

Historians of chattel slavery in various regions of the globe have paid continuing attention to the consequences of and for gender and labour post-emancipation, as well as to the contribution of slavery and the slave trade to the growth of capital and to industrialization.[55] While such historical studies have been cordoned off from labour or working-class history, this need not continue to be the case. This is especially so given the current attention being paid internationally to the trafficking

---

[50] For a set of essays that discuss the concept of 'transnational', see Part I, 'Overview: The Challenge of Transnational Labor History', in Fink, ed., *Workers across the Americas*, 3–48.

[51] Dirk Hoerder, 'Overlapping Spaces: Transregional and Transcultural', in Fink, ed., *Workers across the Americas*, 33–8, here 33.

[52] Ibid., 35.   [53] Ibid.   [54] Beckert, *Empire of Cotton*.

[55] See, for example, Catherine Hall, Nicholas Draper, Keith McClelland, Katie Donington, and Rachel Lang, *Legacies of British Slave-Ownership: Colonial Slavery and the Formation of Victorian Britain* (Cambridge, 2014).

in persons at global, regional, and national levels—even leaving aside the concern, in the middle of the second decade of the twenty-first century, about the illegal transport of migrants from war-torn countries in Africa and the Middle East and about ethnic and religious minorities in South and South East Asia. A report issued by the United Nations Office on Drugs and Crime in 2014 indicated that victims of trafficking who were citizens of 152 countries were found in 124 countries worldwide during the period between 2010 and 2012. Most were females, trafficked for sexual exploitation but also for forced labour. Significant numbers of men and boys were also trafficked, as were, more generally, children in increasing numbers. The numbers reported were based only on those detected by national authorities and thus under-represent the volume of trafficking.[56] It is interesting to note, given the definition of 'work' discussed above, that the report stated that the 'vast majority of trafficking is aimed at obtaining economic benefit from the labour and services extorted from the victims'.[57] A recent volume, focused primarily on Africa, has argued that an 'historical analysis of trafficking in dependent laborers—women and children—into economic conditions not of their choosing must be situated within the wider literature on slavery, the transformations in and decline of slavery...and the deeper economic transformations wrought by expanding colonialism and globalization'.[58] The authors go on to assert that, in Africa, 'economic transformations during the twentieth century, including the growth of industrial production, actually increased the demand for coerced labor'.[59] This analysis is also reflected in the volume *Global Sex Workers* (1998), where coercion, trafficking, and transnational sex work are examined by the authors as gendered forms of work in the context of the expanding contemporary global economy.[60] Illustrating the argument that connects forced labour with colonialism and postcolonialism in Africa is scholarship on the continuation and growth of unfree female domestic labour in Ghana (formerly the Gold Coast), which involves primarily children. During the colonial period, by the Second World War, abolition ended 'domestic slavery...debt-bondage, and forced labor' for males, but involuntary labour for young females continued.[61] The practice of deploying prepubescent females in forced domestic labour was known traditionally by the Akan word *abaawa* and has expanded due to regional disparities in economic development. In recent years '[p]repubescent females are brought to the southern regions, especially major urban centers, not only to work as traditional *abaawa*, but also to provide involuntary

[56] United Nations Office on Drugs and Crime, *Global Report on Trafficking in Persons* (New York, 2014), also available at https://www.unodc.org/documents/data-and-analysis/glotip/GLOTIP_2014_full_report.pdf, accessed 20 May 2017.

[57] Ibid., 50.

[58] Benjamin N. Lawrance and Richard L. Roberts, 'Introduction: Contextualizing Trafficking in Women and Children in Africa', in Lawrance and Roberts, *Trafficking in Slavery's Wake*, 3.

[59] Ibid.

[60] Kamala Kempadoo and Jo Doezema, *Global Sex Workers: Rights, Resistance, and Redefinition* (London, 1998).

[61] Kwabena O. Akurang-Parry, 'Transformations in the Feminization of Unfree Domestic Labor: A Study of *Abaawa* or Prepubescent Female Servitude in Modern Ghana', *International Labor and Working-Class History* 78.1 (2010), 28–47, here 33.

labor service for traders, chop-bar operators, and owners of cottage industries'.[62] The *abaawa* institution is a long-standing one that has undergone changes in the nature of the forced labour involved, but what has not changed is that it is 'fraught with abuse, exploitation, harshness', and entails 'structures of gender inequality and the feminization of poverty and marginality'.[63] Currently it stems from 'the social inequalities between upwardly mobile and urban-educated and the rural backwater poor'.[64]

Bringing together colonial domination, forced labour, and gender, historian of Africa Marie Rodet has recently suggested that resistance to forced labour from the period 1919–46 was interwoven with differing conceptions of masculinity.[65] While colonial authorities attempted to base their conception of West African masculinity on wage labour, which in practice was forced labour that required men to leave their communities, the consequence was to keep young men from marrying and becoming involved in family life in those communities, which was traditionally crucial to what it meant to be a man in their cultural understanding:

> Resistance against forced labor in this context has therefore to be understood as a response not only to employment-centered frustrations but also to clashing definitions of masculinity, with the colonial state trying to promote an idea of *productive* masculinity, to which African workers opposed a *family-oriented* masculinity with its specific social claims and needs.[66]

Returning more directly to the issue of migration, substantial scholarly work has highlighted the globalization of domestic labour. In an historical overview of migrant domestic service in Europe, Raffaella Sarti has argued that 'The "new" domestic service is…less new than one might think.'[67] She discusses the migration of servants or domestics from the early modern period to the present, suggesting that until the mid-nineteenth century it was more common for international and intercontinental servants to go from richer to poorer countries, but after that the pattern was reversed and servants migrated from poorer to richer countries. While in the early modern period male domestics were common, domestic service became a predominantly female occupation from the nineteenth century on. The demand for domestic workers and carers has been growing in recent years, including for live-in servants; and, interestingly, large numbers of international domestics are married with families left behind, whereas earlier most were young and single or remained single.[68] The large numbers of migrant domestic workers has thus led in recent years to the 'feminization of outmigration'.[69]

---

[62] Ibid., 36.   [63] Ibid., 41.   [64] Ibid.

[65] Marie Rodet, 'Forced Labor, Resistance, and Masculinities, in Kayes, French Sudan, 1919–1946', *International Labor and Working-Class History* 86 (2014), 107–23.

[66] Ibid.. 119.

[67] Raffaella Sarti, 'The Globalisation of Domestic Service: An Historical Perspective', in Helma Lutz, ed., *Migration and Domestic Work: A European Perspective on a Global Theme* (Aldershot, 2008), 77–98, here 77.

[68] Ibid., 91.

[69] Annelies Moors, 'Migrant Domestic Workers: Debating Transnationalism, Identity Politics, and Family Relations: A Review Essay', *Comparative Studies in Society and History* 45.2 (2003), 386–94,

Studies of migration history in the past focused attention on the movement of men across boundaries; but, as Christiane Harzig has put it, 'Looking into domestic service migration, it can be seen that the unattached, single male *homo migrans* does not adequately reflect the universal experience of migration. Migration is a profoundly gendered process and experience, and should be analysed as such.'[70] As Harzig and others have argued, the numbers of women who crossed borders to work as domestics, carers, 'nannies', and so on were profoundly undercounted and even ignored, such work being invisible labour.[71] But whether or not women migrated to places like North and South America to work in domestic service varied depending upon where they came from. For example, during the mass emigrations of Italians in the late nineteenth and early twentieth centuries, '[w]aged work in garment, textile, and cigar factories was the single most important occupation "niche" for Italian immigrant women'.[72]

A focus on cross-border contract labour migrations has opened up a fertile arena for labour history that also crosses historical time periods and raises interesting questions about the distinction between free and unfree labour discussed earlier in this chapter. Indenture, or labour contracts that bound workers to their employers for a specified period of time, was a prominent feature of labour migration, primarily of men across the Atlantic to the British colonies of North America, from the 1600s to the War of American Independence. Indentured labour from India and China replaced slave labour in the British Caribbean from the 1830s and, as other European imperial states emancipated slaves in the Americas, indentured foreign workers replaced them. A new kind of state-authorized temporary contract for foreign workers came into being in Prussia in the 1890s as a consequence of 'native' hostility toward immigrant workers who had been crossing borders on their own initiative or as a result of recruitment by estate owners who depended upon seasonal agricultural workers from Poland. According to Ulrich Herbert, only single men were allowed in, and they were required to leave every winter.[73] The First World War also led the United States to encourage the importation of migrant farm

here 386. See also Rhacel Salazar Parrenas, *Servants of Globalization: Women, Migration, and Domestic Work* (Stanford, CA, 2001).

[70] Christiane Harzig, 'Domestics of the World (Unite?): Labor Migration Systems and Personal Trajectories of Household Workers in Historical and Global Perspective', *Journal of American Ethnic History* 25.2/3 (2006), 48–73, here 69.

[71] Ibid.; see also Dirk Hoerder, 'Transcultural Approaches to Gendered Labour Migration: From the Nineteenth-Century Proletarian to Twenty-First Century Caregiver Mass Migrations', in Dirk Hoerder and Amarjit Kaur, eds, *Studies in Global Migration History*, vol. 1: *Proletarian and Gendered Mass Migrations: A Global Perspective on Continuities and Discontinuities from the 19th to the 21st Centuries* (Leiden, 2013), 19–64, here 21–33.

[72] Donna R. Gabaccia and Franca Iacovetta, 'Introduction', in Donna R. Gabaccia and Franca Iacovetta, eds, *Women, Gender, and Transnational Lives: Italian Workers of the World* (Toronto, 2002), 3–42, here 16.

[73] Ulrich Herbert, *A History of Foreign Labor in Germany, 1880–1980: Seasonal Workers/Forced Laborers/Guest Workers* (Ann Arbor, MI, 1990), 20. For an informative overview of the history of guest workers, see Cindy Hahamovitch, 'Creating Perfect Immigrants: Guestworkers of the World in Historical Perspective', *Labor History* 44.1 (2003): 69–94.

workers from Mexico, Canada, Puerto Rico, and the West Indies.[74] These workers
were to be hired 'for the duration', although many stayed on after the war was over.
It was the Second World War and the postwar period that witnessed the growth of
what became known as 'guestworker' programmes in many European countries
and of similar schemes in the United States, where they were known as 'H2 workers' and 'Braceros'. Such programmes blossomed until the early 1970s, as a way to
provide employers with temporary workers who could labour without the same
rights as citizens. Scholarship on these programmes that raises the issue of gender
is suggestive of the value of a gendered labour history approach to cross-border or
transnational programmes and to their impact upon workers' lives. Deborah
Cohen's study of Mexican men who were employed as temporary contract workers
in the United States in the Bracero Program, which existed from 1942 to 1964, is
illustrative. The programme was established by an agreement between Mexico and
the United States. The United States originally wanted Mexico to send families, so
that wives and children could be put to work at lower wages than the men in the
family; and it would prevent the men from becoming involved with local women
or from making use of prostitutes in the United States. But Mexico wanted only
men to go across the border, in order to make sure that they would return. Mexico
hoped that the men's experience in US agriculture would turn them into yeoman
farmers in Mexico. Because the men worked without families present, employers
kept the wages low. Their all-male living quarters challenged their sense as 'properly gendered beings' because they had to do 'women's work'—their own domestic
labour—and the 'migrants sought to recuperate their patriarchal claims through
social rituals of drinking and socialising, often with women other than their wives
or girlfriends'.[75] The men who refused to join in such activities did so for the moral
and gender-affirming reason that they needed to send money home to families.[76]
But, interestingly, Cohen argues that the way men recuperated their sense of man-
liness was through their 'subjectivity as workers...created in the fields vis-à-vis
white and Mexican American bosses and foremen, and other Mexican migrants'.[77]
She concludes: 'Braceros mobilized their position as (proto)patriarchs and thus, as
honorable heterosexual men with (future) families to advocate for themselves as
workers.'[78] Whether the programmes recruited only men or men and their families
differed according to the agreements between the receiving and the sending countries. The consequences of these programmes for masculine and feminine subjectivities and gender relations, both in the countries where people worked and in
their communities of origin, therefore undoubtedly varied culturally and socially.

[74] Ibid., 80. For a more extended discussion, see Cindy Hahamovitch, *The Fruits of Their Labor: Atlantic Coast Farmworkers and the Making of Migrant Poverty, 1870–1945* (Chapel Hill, NC, 1997), 79–97.
[75] Deborah Cohen, 'From Peasant to Worker: Migration, Masculinity and the Making of Mexican Workers in the US', *International Labor and Working-Class History* 69 (2006), 81–103, here 89. For an extended analysis of Braceros as 'transnational subjects', see Deborah Cohen, *Braceros: Migrant Citizens and Transnational Subjects in the Postwar United States and Mexico* (Chapel Hill, NC, 2011).
[76] Ibid., 90.　　　[77] Ibid., 95.　　　[78] Ibid., 99.

Research into gender and cross-border labour migration, broadly considered, would add considerably to our knowledge in various fields of historical inquiry.

Labour history, with its emphasis upon traditional industrial labour movements and concepts of the working classes that focus on relations of production and the making of a delineated urban proletariat, may indeed have been eroded in recent decades, alongside the disappearance of the manufacturing sector and decline in trade union membership in industrial economies such as Britain's. But an over-reliance on national and subnational issues in labour history in Britain and the disconnectedness of the subdiscipline from intellectual developments in other strands of social and cultural historiography in Britain, from Britain's history, and from the approaches adopted by historians of labour in other national contexts have arguably led to this decline of a once vibrant field. Reconceptualizing what is meant by work and who or what constitutes 'the working classes' expands enormously the scope of inquiry into historical forms of labour. Furthermore, the examination of gender and of the gendering of various forms of work and occupations stimulates inquiry into the ways in which gender and gender relations are shaped and influenced by class distinctions, workplace organization, and work of various kinds. A more expansive and gendered definition of work allows historians to encompass casual and precarious forms of work, and therefore to get to the heart of questions of social and economic equalities, which of course had been a central ambition in the development of labour history since the 1950s. Examination of gender and labour in a global historical context expands and invigorates the field even further. Global labour history fosters analysis of historical transformations comparatively, through examination of regional and global interdependencies, and also of transnational movements of workers. Expansion of the sites of analysis of labour and reconceptualization of what is meant by labour foster historical discussion that addresses and illuminates some of the world's most pressing concerns about inequalities—historically and contemporaneously—with nuance and rigour, in fascinating and critically incisive ways.

14

Postcolonial History as War History in the Twentieth Century

Yasmin Khan

Clive Branson (1907–44) was a poet, a painter, and a war hero. Born in London to a privileged family, he was killed in action in Burma in 1944. He was fighting with the Allies, trying to recapture South East Asia from the Japanese. A committed communist, he had already volunteered for the International Brigades during the Spanish Civil War and had been captured and held as a prisoner of war in a Francoist Camp.

Branson arrived in India in 1942 as a soldier in the British army. He wrote a series of evocative letters home, to his wife and parents, which were published posthumously by the Communist Party of Great Britain in a small pamphlet entitled *British Soldier in India*. In these letters he records his experiences of being a soldier and expresses views both on the war and on his daily life stationed in India. He displays there an acute awareness of the ways in which warfare and the preparation for fighting had consequences for lives far beyond the theatres of war. He writes with perception and horror about food shortages and the terrible famine in Bengal of 1943, notices racial discriminations and slights against local people, reflects on the ways in which agricultural farmland was ruined by battles and the effect that this had on peasant farmers, and writes disparagingly of the visits paid by military men to local brothels. He also dissects the effects of imperialism in India both in its economic and in its racial aspects, and reflects on how soldiers interact among themselves and with the South Asian society around them. He demonstrates both sympathy for Indian nationalism and a serious commitment to defeating the fascists.[1]

Clive Branson's experiences remind us of the profound connections between Britain and India in the 1940s and of the fact that the Second World War was an imperial war. Branson interests me in particular because of the ways in which he appreciated the global inequalities and hierarchies that accompanied the fighting of the Second World War in the British empire while remaining committed to the anti-Japanese cause. In the 1940s this tension between anti-imperialism and anti-fascism remained a fault line for many people across the world. Yet the imperial

---

[1] Clive Branson, *British Soldier in India: The Letters of Clive Branson* (London, 1944).

dimensions of Europe's great wars—and the wars of decolonization that ensued after 1945—have been ghostly presences in much history writing and hover uneasily at the edges of much twentieth-century European history.

Although a soldier himself, Branson reflects with great humanism on the changes wrought by war on individuals and on their lives caught in the crux of fighting a battle. He also reveals his own inner ambivalence and contradictions towards war and violence, his own understandings of militarism and of how it structures social and cultural interactions along certain lines. Branson's letters bring me to consider how historians can contribute to a radical approach to writing war histories, enhancing perhaps even a less militarized future. In particular, in the twentieth century historians could show how one is to reckon with the entwined nature of Britain and its colonies and how this imperial context shaped war, both before and after 1945. Marxism is not incompatible with this project, but I will argue that postcolonialism can help us to think through a truly global and democratic approach to war histories.

At the heart of Branson's thinking was an internationalism developed from his Marxist training and commitment. It placed an equal value on human life. This was also a hallmark of the thought of Eric Hobsbawm, who was born ten years after Branson. (Hobsbawm may not have met Clive, but he knew Noreen Branson, Clive's widow, who published in a series edited by Hobsbawm in the 1970s.) And, like many in this generation of British Marxists, Hobsbawm was also a friend of India: he was widely admired and influential there and always knowledgeable about the latest political developments on the subcontinent. Many of the thinkers at the heart of 'British' leftist writing—from George Orwell to E. P. Thompson— were closely connected to India through family networks and had deep links with the colonial world. The Communist Party Historians' Group was forged in the late 1940s and the 1950s, not only against the backdrop of the Cold War but also in a Britain that was reeling from the reconfigurations of its vast overseas empire.

Eric Hobsbawm was a historian of Britain, Europe, and the world and was too gifted and knowledgeable to think in terms of simple blocs or essentialist categories. He could make deft connections vertically between places and events, linking the dots between local and global events. He insisted on the interconnectedness of Europe, Britain, and the world 'long before the global turn', writing in 1996, for instance, 'it is impossible to sever European history from world history'.[2] He was (and is) widely admired in India in return. He paved the way, particularly through his engagement with Gramsci, for the Subaltern Studies Collective—the emergence of an influential group of historians of India who, like Hobsbawm, were concerned with capturing the sheer energy and agency of the marginalized, the oppressed, and the forgotten in world history. Hobsbawm's own emphasis on the peripheral and the excluded in European history, for instance in *Bandits*, was an approach that translated well in India when historians sought new ways of telling the story of Asian colonialism and nationalism from the left.

[2] Jan Rüger, 'Britain, Empire, Europe: Re-Reading Eric Hobsbawm', *Journal of Modern European History* 11 (2013), 417–23, here 419.

Hobsbawm's Marxist approach did have historicist limits and the explanatory force of his models often seemed to place emphasis on European heartlands as the engine room of history—as when he said, 'That the forces which transformed the world since the fifteenth century were geographically European is patent,' for instance.[3] This pushed the subalterns into creative tension with Hobsbawm, especially in their attempt to convey the distinctive political rationality of peasants or poor workers in Asia. Ranajit Guha used Hobsbawm's description of the pre-political as a springboard for working out his own ideas in the foundational text of subaltern studies, by suggesting more plural tracks towards modernity and by looking beyond the western Marxist categories of analysis for the political consciousness of peasants.[4] And, as the Subalterns themselves became more fragmented, more removed from hard economics, and consciously distanced from their Marxist roots, they critiqued the traditions of historical thought itself, dismantling many of the ideas that underpinned narrative history writing and, again, drawing on Hobsbawm for inspiration and counterpoint.[5]

Putting these historiographical debates aside for a moment, where does all this leave the writing of war histories and the histories of empire in the twentieth century? In what ways did Hobsbawm's global perspective open up the possibilities of writing new kinds of global histories of war and decolonization? Hobsbawm obviously understood the global repercussions of war on empire and of empire on war, but these were less urgent for him than other questions. For Hobsbawm, the Second World War was profoundly personal and essentially European. 'Every historian has his or her lifetime, a private perch from which to survey the world,' he said in his Creighton Lecture in 1993.[6] His political commitment was chalked out in his early life in Vienna and as a youth attending school in Weimar Berlin as Hitler ascended to power. This was the 'perch' from which he viewed history, the basis of his politics. And yet his personal experience of the war was dispiriting; he was confined to Britain with a Sapper regiment and, later, with the Army Education Corps, was regarded with suspicion by the War Office for his Austrian background and political affiliations.[7] The shift in scale from the personal to the global and his own subjectivities were writ large in his own memories and histories of the war. The individual and personal commitment to defeating fascism, seen from a central European perspective, made other sacrifices pale by comparison; 'In the Second World War, 50 million died. Was the sacrifice worthwhile? I frankly cannot

---

[3] Eric Hobsbawm, 'All Peoples Have a History', in idem, *On History* (London, 1997), 171–8, here 172.

[4] Ranajit Guha, *Elementary Aspects of Peasant Insurgency in Colonial India* (Delhi, 1983); 'Contra Mundam' *London Review of Books*, 9 March 1995, pp. 22. Similarly, Edward Said expressed some unease about the vague but persistent idea, in Hobsbawm's *The Age of Extremes*, that the non-West tagged behind where the capitalist West led; and he argued, among other things, that this left a blind spot around the question of religious radicalism and fundamentalism.

[5] Dipesh Chakrabarty, *Provincializing Europe: Postcolonial Thought and Historical Difference* (Princeton, NJ, 2000).

[6] Eric J. Hobsbawm, *The Present as History: Writing the History of One's Own Times*. The Creighton lecture, 8 November 1993 (London, 1993).

[7] Eric Hobsbawm, *Interesting Times: A Twentieth-Century Life* (London, 2002).

face the idea that it was not,' he told the *Guardian* in 2002. 'I can't say it would have been better if the world was run by Adolph Hitler.'[8]

Few would disagree with the moral case for the Second World War and with the case for 'a just war' at the heart of modern European history, a war waged to defeat fascism. The Holocaust makes this position incontrovertible. But the reasoning behind the war did look different for contemporaries in other parts of the world. The moral ambiguities and grey zones were far sharper in places outside Europe, where people faced a war that brought havoc but lacked the power to control it. Indians charted a course between support for antifascism and resistance to a wartime imperial state that had become ever more authoritarian and exploitative in the 1940s. Thousands were killed during wartime protests in India. Bengal, incidentally one of the intellectual incubators of subaltern studies, was the home of Subhas Chandra Bose, leader of the Indian National Army who sided with the Japanese in the 1940s, and the location of the catastrophic famine of 1943, which was a direct result of wartime food distribution. The Indian communists—who attempted to square anti-imperialism and antifascism, just like Clive Branson, and who actively backed the war—actually ended up neglected or even tainted rather than lionized in postwar national memory. The moral and national categories of memorialization after the war had been inverted in India, a reflection of the strength of nationalism, but also of the intense adversities of this historical period in South Asia.

And after 1945 a difference in sensibility and perspective remained. On the subject of war, Hobsbawm was clear that the postwar world had entered a new phase of violence and disarray in the twentieth century that he called 'barbarity'. 'We have learned to tolerate the intolerable. Total War and Cold War have brainwashed us into accepting barbarity. Even worse: they have made barbarity seem unimportant, compared to more important matters like making money.'[9] People had become accustomed, even acclimatized, to extreme violence. Civilians had become the chief sufferers of war after 1939, as refugees and as casualties. During the First World War only 5 per cent who died were civilians; in the Second World War this percentage increased to over a half, and by the end of the century some 90 per cent of those killed in war were civilians. Civil wars had become more prevalent than wars between states in the later twentieth century; new kinds of quasi-official henchmen and 'killer squads' now stalked war zones. States that should have known better returned to the use of torture, a practice outlawed in many places in the late eighteenth century. Hobsbawm also stressed the damage wrought by the totalizing propaganda needed in order to win over modern nations to war, and how the need to create identifiable enemies meant a complete demonization of the opponent, in ways unknown to earlier generations.[10]

---

[8] Interview with Maya Jaggi in *Guardian*, 14 September 2002 (https://www.theguardian.com/books/2002/sep/14/biography.history).

[9] Eric Hobsbawm, 'Barbarism: A User's Guide', in idem, *On History*, 253–65, here 265. See also Eric Hobsbawm, 'War and Peace in the 20th Century,' *London Review of Books*, 24.4 (2002), 16–18.

[10] Ibid.

The question that lingers is why this descent into barbarism happened. Here the place of empire and of the European wars of decolonization after 1945 become, for postcolonial historians at least, essential to the story. Why did this new way of doing war become the norm in the twentieth century? Hobsbawm suggested that this was 'curious'—it was a failure in many ways to root the lessons of the Enlightenment, a breakdown of empires not quite replaced by fully functioning nation-states, and the general descent into anomie and alienation that was at fault, unleashing civil factions, quasi-nationalist groups, and terrorism. Yet, as Hobsbawm also showed, depictions of fully functioning European nation-states in the nineteenth century could only ever be partial, and empires emanating from Europe exported and enhanced violence around the globe in ways that were unthinkable to their earlier inhabitants. Many would go further and suggest that the crisis of the late twentieth century was one made by the West and that global forms of violence were rehearsed through empire. The so-called 'boomerang' argument of Hannah Arendt—that systemic imperial violence in the nineteenth century rebounded in Europe in the form of totalitarianism in the twentieth (notwithstanding debates about the nuances of Arendt's meanings)—was seized on with alacrity by historians in the 1990s.[11] The juxtaposition of these two strands of supposedly separate history—the European imperial past and the totalitarian 1940s—fuelled new and imaginative readings of imperial effects. It generated new debates about the plurality of genocides. It also helped to further the understanding of Europe's own experience as one of continental imperialism, and of fascist ambitions to colonize the continent. Europe's empire and continued imperial commitment after 1945 are, then, in this light, absolutely essential for understanding the course of world history.

Hobsbawm saw the world wars as taking place between territorial states or alliances of states, and only secondarily as wars of empires. He identified Europe as the heartland of those wars, while also acknowledging the 3 million killed by famine in Bengal, or the histories of Hiroshima. There was an international breakdown in the 1940s, and the global death toll and sheer loss of human life in warfare was staggering. In the short twentieth century alone, Hobsbawm stated that 187 million people had died, or had been allowed to die, 'by human decision'—a powerfully telling phrase. For Hobsbawm, it was a failure of the post-1945 era to stabilize peace; for postcolonialists and the so-called 'new imperial historians', that failure was inherent in the imperial states that were at war in the first place, not least because of their determination to reassert those empires in the aftermath of 1945—by British action in Malaya and South East Asia, by American basing strategies, or in the French relationship with Algeria and Vietnam.

War in the twentieth century, seen from the perspective of the European empires, adds a new edge to our vision. Looking at war from 'the other end of the telescope' helps to rethink colony and centre, and also helps to rethink British and European history in two key ways. The chronologies of the twentieth century's global histories that Hobsbawm did so much to establish are enhanced by this viewpoint: first, the

[11] Dan Stone, 'Defending the Plural: Hannah Arendt and Genocide Studies', *New Formations* 71 (2011), 46–57.

complex entanglement of colonial armies and colonized land in both the First and the Second World War; and, second, after 1945, the persistence of wars of decolonization in the short twentieth century. European and colonial histories were inextricably entangled through warfare. This is sometimes, in British history at least, the elephant in the room. After the Second World War, decolonization was only just beginning to register, but the Colonial Office was growing and many in Britain felt duty-bound to reassert and revitalize the British empire in the East. In South East Asia, indeed, Chris Bayly and Tim Harper described this move as 'a second colonial conquest'. The extent of military force, internment, extrajudicial torture and killings, authoritarianism and concealment of archives has only recently started to truly resonate in British histories of the later twentieth century and, still often, with a sense of deference to an idea of 'fair-minded' interpretations of empire's balance sheet.[12]

* * *

How far do our histories published today respond to this urgent need to democratize the victims of war, to call out barbarism when we see it? How far are we self-reflexive, as historians, about our own role in normalizing militarism?

Are there dangers of losing this sensibility, while the descent into barbarism continues? There is certainly a martial corner of British history writing that continues to be very successful. War histories sell copies, and well-written military histories are popular and profitable. Military history saturates bookshops, libraries, television, and popular culture. Inside professional history departments, military history is viewed with more circumspection for certain traits: proximity to defence academies and officer training schools, an emphasis on operational and campaign history, obscure and specialized terminology, and, at its most extreme, a sort of macho enjoyment of the spectacle of war and a risk of overidentification between historian and commanding officer. Strategic histories are often embedded in familiar conceptual landscapes and continue to reflect official policy discourse. They underpin contemporary military adventurism and work to enhance the prestige of military institutions and of the military establishment.[13]

But other historical studies have broadened the historical interpretations of war and moved very far from operational and conventional military histories of strategy to encompass the social terrain, including the experiences of civilians—men, women, and children—and there has been extensive study of the aftermath of war, the plight of refugees and expelled peoples, the memories and memorialization of war, and the ways in which war continues to reverberate socially and culturally for long into peacetime.

Feminist scholarship has pioneered alternative approaches, illuminating a far more complex and contested history in which masculinity itself, the actions of

---

[12] Caroline Elkins, 'The Re-Assertion of the British Empire in Southeast Asia', *Journal of Interdisciplinary History* 39.3 (2009), 361–85; Yasmin Khan, 'Upending the Telescope', *History Workshop Journal* 75.1 (2013), 259–64. 'To upend the telescope' is Antoinette Burton's metaphor for writing imperial history.

[13] Michael J. Shapiro, *Violent Cartographies: Mapping Cultures of War* (Minneapolis, MN, 1997). An early exception was in the work of Joanna Bourke, *An Intimate History of Killing: Face-to-Face Killing in Twentieth-Century Warfare* (London, 1999).

armies and the ways in which soldiers interact with local societies all come under the microscope. Sexual violence seems to have been an endemic part of modern warfare; for example, it has reframed the history of the American liberation of France after 1944 by considering the interactions between American men and local French women, to argue for a hidden history of rape and sexual abuse.[14] Or it has revisited debates about the so-called 'comfort women' in Japanese and Chinese histories. The presence of foreign soldiers often created domestic issues caused by consensual interracial relationships as well as by sexual predation.[15]

Prostitution has generated a disproportionate amount of historical attention, partly because it is so visible in the historical record. Militaries were greatly concerned with regulating, policing, and controlling sex workers, and this creates a well-documented trail for seeing where the intimacies of war and the greater 'war machine' collided. Histories of women in war have extended across many other subjects, including children born of wartime relationships, interracial relationships, and women's work, from nursing to the factory floor. The wives and mothers of soldiers are also important for tracing influences on recruitment, alongside the power of women's patriotism and grief. In the post-1945 era, Cynthia Enloe's work, among that of others, draws explicit lines between gender and militarism on a global scale, looking at the gendered cultures of US army bases in Asia, for instance, or at the ways in which American communities support military action overseas.[16]

Gendered histories of global warfare in the twentieth century are, then, about far more than restoring women's voices and agency to an otherwise static picture—the real challenge for historians is to reframe war, to reveal the layers of coercion and the hierarchies of gender and race that intersected with war efforts. Such histories point to the collusion between military officials and men across the borderlines of military and intimate lives, to the ways in which warfare encouraged misogyny and was often at the expense of the welfare of women. They cut across national boundaries and often intersect with imperial histories. Gendered histories of war, then, help to redefine the concepts and chronologies through which we think about war more generally.

But perhaps the historian's most radical departure—which has often been aligned with gendered histories—has been to globalize and decentre narratives of war from the margins. This can be done many ways, from rethinking the major dates and episodes of world history at the macro level to recapturing the peasant consciousness of *tirailleurs* in the French army or the oral history of Gurkha families from Nepal. There has been considerable movement in this direction in

---

[14] Mary Louise Roberts, *What Soldiers Do: Sex and the American GI in World War II France* (Chicago, IL, 2013), 11.

[15] For example, Dagmar Herzog, ed., *Brutality and Desire* (London, 2009); Maki Kimura, *Unfolding the Comfort Women Debates* (London, 2016). On relationships in the United Kingdom, see Sonya Rose, *Which People's War? National Identity and Citizenship in Wartime Britain, 1939–45* (Oxford, 2003).

[16] Cynthia Enloe, *Bananas, Beaches and Bases: Making Feminist Sense of International Politics* (Berkeley, CA, 2014); Cynthia Enloe, *Nimo's War, Emma's War: Making Feminist Sense of the Iraq War* (Berkeley, CA, 2010).

histories of Africa, Algeria, India, and South East Asia, reinforced by new engagement with the history of the First World War, which was itself stimulated by the anniversary of the start of that war.

The original 'subaltern' was a junior soldier—or a mercenary in the service of empire. The global networks of mercenaries through which Britain and other European empires controlled and annexed more territory suggest the foundational imbrications of warfare and empire. In the eighteenth century the European powers routinely recruited slaves as soldiers, and this was commonplace in the British West Indies and during the fighting of the revolutionary wars. Later on Indian soldiers were the motor of expansion and in the vanguard of imperial defence from the nineteenth century on in Java, Malacca, Penang, Singapore, and China. Indian troops fought against the Mahdi uprisings in Sudan, in the Boxer Rebellion in China, in the Afghan Wars and in Tibet. They both triggered and helped to suppress the Indian uprising of 1857. In the First World War, 1.3 million Indian soldiers left the subcontinent to fight in France and Belgium, in Gallipoli, Salonika, and Palestine, in Egypt and Sudan, in Mesopotamia, at Aden and in the Red Sea, in East Africa, and in Persia; and the recent anniversary of the First World War has been a spur to a flurry of global interpretations of First World War experiences. Different, decentred readings of the two world wars show how far global war has connected the West and the non-West in the twentieth century.[17] Every European power used forced or conscripted labour in the First World War, from Egypt, South Africa, Fiji, China, and India. In the East African theatre, the British drew on manpower from up to a million Africans in the Carrier Corps. Historians of the colonized world have begun to place histories of subalterns in different historical genealogies, to forge different narratives of war, which put European experiences in a global context. The subjectivities of families experiencing famine in India and China can now sit alongside accounts of how famines were structurally connected to war.[18]

Binaries between loyalists and rebels unravel under closer scrutiny. Loyalist soldiers (the classic mercenaries for British rulers, in the eyes of some postcolonial leaders) were themselves caught between competing demands, which ranged from poverty and tradition to familial pressures, and 'loyalist' soldiers themselves were able to subvert and resist their colonial overlords, while negotiating the tricky space between paid state employment and the pull of political emancipation.[19] Militaries have operated historically through entrenched hierarchies, in which ethnic, class, and racial groups have often been relegated to lesser positions by comparison to the heroic white male. Black American soldiers often did manual labour far from the

---

[17] Heike Liebau, Katrin Bromber, Katharina Lange, Dyala Hamzah, and Ravi Ahuja, eds, *The World in World Wars: Experiences, Perceptions and Perspectives from Africa and Asia* (Leiden, 2010); Santanu Das, ed., *Race, Empire and First World War Writing* (Cambridge, 2011).

[18] Richard Smith 'Soldiery', in Philippa Levine and John Marriott, eds, *The Ashgate Research Companion to Modern Imperial Histories* (London, 2014), 359–77, here 365. An excellent recent account of the 1943 famine in Bengal and of its links to warfare is Janam Mukherjee, *Hungry Bengal: War, Famine and the End of Empire* (London, 2015).

[19] Gajendra Singh, *Testimonies of Indian Soldiers* (London, 2014); Gregory Mann, *Native Sons: West African Veterans and France in the Twentieth Century* (Durham, NC, 2006).

front line. Chinese workers dug graves and trenches across Europe from 1914 to 1918. Refugees could also be soldiers: 6,000 Ethiopian refugees who had found safety in Kenya or Sudan in the 1940s were recruited into Allied battalions that fought in North Africa. Conversely, military histories have also tended to favour those on the front line who were doing the work of killing; they paid far less attention to nursing, non-combatant, and auxiliary roles. Yet it was often the labour of these men and women that propped up the war-making capabilities of the modern state, and consequently these histories are a part of labour history as much as they are a part of military history.[20]

In empirical ways, the contemporary British warfare state rests on imperial and global lineages. Historians have begun the important work of revealing how the warfare and the developmental state emerged together and how imperial control was extended through hybrid military and civilian technologies; Priya Satia has offered an important analysis of the British engagement with the Middle East which suggests how aerial surveillance and military airpower in the First World War and afterwards were tied to governance and shows how air policing and aerial bombardment became a regularized element of colonial control—an element based on environmental imaginings of the desert. She stresses the way in which aerial photography, signalling and surveillance, and certain types of aerial bombardment were pioneered during the Mesopotamian and Palestine campaign in the First World War and how myths of successful imperial control were managed in the face of very real limitations. Minimizing casualties on one side and inspiring fear and awe on the other were both embedded in the development of the technology. It is not too far-fetched, she argues, to see the present-day emergence of drones as a logical outgrowth of imperial technologies of control and domination.[21]

In the Second World War the domestic changes affecting the empire restructured societies and left scars on the landscape. The inflated wages of the wartime economy in Allied zones pulled villagers across North Africa, the Middle East, and South Asia into rapidly expanding cities, in order for them to work in industrial production. The rapid building of aerodromes, ports, and roads and the new opportunities for work in mines sucked in new wage labourers from around the British empire. Slums developed in scale around the edges of many imperial cities. In South Africa restrictions were placed on urban migration to no avail. Seasonal or casual migrations often became permanent or left people living in new and precarious ways, as food shortages and wartime inflation began to escalate. Mexican *braceros* moved to the United States, leaving families behind in Mexico. Soldiers recruited into forces such as the Indian army often never returned home, beginning

---

[20] On African experiences of war, the authority to consult is David Killingray. There is an extensive literature on black American experiences, for example Kimberley L. Phillips, *War! What Is It Good for? Black Freedom Struggles and the US Military from World War II to Iraq* (Chapel Hill, NC, 2012). For an analysis of *lascars* (Indian merchant seamen) as a form of Marxist labour history, see Ravi Ahuja, 'Mobility and Containment: The Voyages of South Asian Seamen', *International Review of Social History*, 51 (2006), 111–41.

[21] Priya Satia, *Spies in Arabia: The Great War and the Cultural Foundations of Britain's Covert Empire in the Middle East* (Oxford, 2008); see also Priya Satia, 'The Defense of Inhumanity: Air Control and the British Idea of Arabia', *American Historical Review* 111.1 (2006), 16–51.

a long chain migration, sometimes back to the postwar industrial cities of Britain. As Pamela Ballinger has argued, more expansive interpretations of what constituted a displaced person are relevant. Refugees came in many different guises, and some of them were never labelled as such. Thinking about these population movements in their most diverse forms allows space for those who fall outside state categories and legal classifications into 'refugee' or 'displaced persons' to be subjected to historical scrutiny.[22] Decolonization and the aftermath of war were also entangled, of course. The end of the Italian empire also meant the repatriation of Italian settlers from Eritrea, Ethopia, Somalia, and Libya. Former European settlers displaced by the Japanese from the Dutch and British empires in South East Asia never returned, often finding new homes in Australia, South Africa, and other parts of the white settler world.

The recalibration of chronology and the realization of the continued commitment of European states to empire after 1945 form another important part of recasting these binaries of war and peace in the short twentieth century. Over the past twenty-five years David Edgerton has redefined analysis of British liberal militarism by stressing the false perception and erroneous chronologies that are used as commonplace understandings of wartime in Britain. For instance, by stressing the high levels of civilian and military technological interdependence and the high levels of defence spending and arms production in the United Kindom after 1945, he revisits the assumption that the post-1945 period was a time of welfare spending and peace. As he writes, 'we are apt to forget the deep structural impact of the Cold War on post-war Britain'.[23]

Such alternative binaries of times of peace and times of war put British twentieth-century histories in a new light. Wars in Malaya (1948–58), Kenya (1952–6) and Cyprus (1954–9), as well as operations in Suez and Ireland, resist being uncritically cast as counterinsurgency or neglected in cultural and historical memory making. As Paul Gilroy has particularly noted, the selectivity of British historical memory and the centrality of the Second World War to British cultural life may be explained as manifestations of postcolonial melancholia, a form of nostalgic militarism prompted by the loss of imperial greatness but remedied or redeemed by the national role in the Second World War.[24] The military campaigns of Britain overseas after 1945 have a key part to play in the important work of connecting imperial and domestic histories and, to use Bill Schwarz's term, in understanding 'the re-racialization' of Englishness in the 1950s and 1960s. As Britain ambivalently 'decolonized' its empire and disconnected itself from white settlers overseas, postwar military experiences became a cornerstone of understanding this disentanglement.

---

[22] Pamela Ballinger, 'Entangled or "Extruded" Histories? Displacement, National Refugees, and Repatriation after the Second World War', *Journal of Refugee Studies* 25.3 (2012), 366–86. See also Elizabeth Buettner, *Europe after Empire: Decolonization, Society, and Culture* (Cambridge, 2016).

[23] David Edgerton, 'War, Reconstruction, and the Nationalization of Britain, 1939–1951', *Past & Present* 210 (2011), 29–46.

[24] Paul Gilroy, *Postcolonial Melancholia* (New York, 2010). On the intersection between colonial wars, decolonization, and Britishness, see Bill Schwarz, *The White Man's World* (Oxford, 2011); Wendy Webster, '"There'll Always Be an England": Representations of Colonial Wars and Immigration, 1948–1968', *Journal of British Studies* 40.4 (2001), 557–84.

Caroline Elkins' advocacy for victims of torture during the Mau Mau rebellion has proven the urgency of methodological innovation and the validity of oral histories as a parallel source to archives. The revelation that the British Foreign and Commonwealth Office secretly stashed thousands of imperial-era documents at Hanslope Park is a wake-up call for any historian who works with modern British archives.

How else might progressive or subaltern war histories develop in the future? One answer lies in the turn away from the 'front line' towards an analysis of the long trail of non-combatants and global supply networks that were necessary to sustain war. Twentieth-century and twenty-first-century wars relied (and still rely) on supply chains. These rest on a bedrock of casual labourers and poorly paid workers, often from the poor world, drawn to war zones by relatively higher wages. Around bases there have always been food sellers and caterers, transport workers, sex workers, purveyors of alcohol and black market goods, and entertainers. These differential forms of wartime employment and experience have attracted more attention in recent years. In the more recent past, countries such as India have had many thousands of citizens working near the American bases in Afghanistan and Iraq, and some who were part of a Kuwaiti company that sent military supplies to the US forces were kidnapped in a high-profile case in 2004.[25] Within armies themselves, there have always been many more men who do not see the front line than men who experience combat, and the former are crucial to the war's prosecution; they include those who cook and run stores and offices. Such differential employment, too, has often been stratified and racially defined in the past. Emergent histories of military bases, basing strategies, and interactions between soldiers and the local societies they encountered present another potential counternarrative to state-centred histories of war.

Similarly, medical and technological histories can shift the limelight away from battles and campaigns. Some recent environmental histories that focus on the extraction of resources in the 1940s also reframe war histories by making them part of a longer story of developmentalism, of the application of expertise, of state planning, and of scientific attempts to control and direct resources. By inserting themselves into the geopolitics of environmental contestation, these histories of resource extraction globalize our understandings of the Second World War and the rise of US power in the mid-century. Judith Bennett's history of the South Pacific during the Second World War reflects on how an influx of Allied soldiers radically altered the landscape and the environment on the islands in attempts to control disease and food production and how, by introducing patterns of trade and exchange, these soldiers opened the door to further environmental degradation. Seth Garfield describes, in his history of the Amazon in the 1940s, the bilateral race to control rubber supply from the Amazon once the Japanese entered the war, after the Americans lost access to Asian markets. This race resulted in mass Brazilian migration, scientific experimentation, and ultimately in the restructuring of local societies and economies. A major plank of his work is the migration of tens of

---

[25] Some 20,000 Indians were working in Iraq during the war in 2004.

thousands from north-eastern Brazil to the Amazon in the 1940s. Garfield reflects on the agency of the tappers and of the migrants themselves and on the interplay of private business and state involvement.[26]

The production of arms and the origins of the global arms industry delimit another area that is under-researched but that raises major questions of power relations between states, the chains involved in the hard material production of guns and bombs, and the military–civilian networks that undergird our modern world. Recent studies have started to open up this area of research. Jonathan A. Grant argues for the internationalization of the arms market with the advent of the First World War and speaks of the ways in which nation-states made purchases from arms dealers and from other states, according to quality and price rather than along lines of national allegiance. In his analysis, banking and industrial interests could run counter to (and indeed undermine) diplomatic powers. Hence Russian purchases saved the German arms industry on several occasions, and one quarter of the Russian naval fleet was made up of foreign-built ships in the 1890s.[27] Here, then, are many of the ironies and interdependencies of the global arms trade that foreshadow our present day. Using a different approach, Priya Satia's forthcoming book on a Quaker family, the Galtons, investigates the moral dilemma of pacifists who were the largest gun manufacturers in eighteenth-century Britain and also promises to reveal the linkages between industrial production and imperial warfare and expansionism. It will also situate the production of arms in the age of the Enlightenment.

*   *   *

What are the ethical implications of people publicly grieving terrorist attacks in Paris or Brussels but remaining indifferent to lives lost in Pakistan or Syria? How do we find empathy with victims of violence who are different from us or far away from us? Everyday we are confronted by an ethical dilemma when we read the media. The global relativism of grief is writ large on a daily basis. The equality of human life in the historical record is of urgent importance. A universal and democratic approach to human life ultimately rests on a simple but important humanist principle of giving equal value to all human life (and death).[28]

Hobsbawm paved the way for thinking about global and transnational connections between Britain, Europe, and their empires. The ways in which past wars have been waged, sustained, and justified are essential to thinking about the future of global interactions; and postcolonial historians, perhaps as an overcorrection, have tended to create their own vanishing points, letting Europe's experiences of the twentieth century recede in importance. This is not to fall back on crass relativism or dogmatic pacifism, or to displace the centrality of the defeat of fascism

[26] Judith Bennett, *Natives and Exotics: World War II and the Environment in the Southern Pacific* (Honolulu, 2009); Seth Garfield, *In Search of the Amazon: Brazil, the United States, and the Nature of a Region* (Durham, NC, 2014).
[27] Jonathan A. Grant, *Rulers, Guns, and Money: The Global Arms Trade in the Age of Imperialism* (Cambridge, MA, 2007).
[28] Judith Butler, *Frames of War: When Is Life Grievable?* (London, 1999).

from our collective past. For Hobsbawm and others of his generation, defeating fascism was both history and lived experience. As historians living through the twenty-first century and reading Hobsbawm, we are prompted to question the conditions under which war occurs and the conditions under which future fascisms may grow. As Clive Branson's writings suggest, attentiveness to the ways in which warfare restructures and impacts society can be an integral part of being opposed to authoritarianism in all its guises. And Hobsbawm reminded us with prescience that the Hague Conventions of 1899 and 1907 no longer worked in a world where the lines between war and peace had become blurry and where the line between combatants and civilians was vanishing. The structural entanglements of 'the West and the rest' during wartimes speak to a world in which Europe has always been more deeply integrated and dependent on non-Europeans than many of its inhabitants imagine.

15

The People's History and the Politics of Everyday Life since 1945

Jon Lawrence

Eric Hobsbawm set a high bar for the study of 'history from below'. For him, the recovery of 'lost' subjectivities represented the beginning of the historian's task, not the end point. Hobsbawm insisted that history from below must seek to *explain* the lives and actions of people who had left few written records, not simply rescue them from the 'condescension of posterity'.[1] For him, this was about building models capable of re-establishing the connections between micro and macro; between Geertzian 'thick description' and the large structures of the economy and the polity. But by 1988, when Hobsbawm penned his reflections on history from below, a new linguistic turn in history was already seeking to reassert the (relative) autonomy of politics from social and economic determination.[2] Most advocates of a more discursive approach to politics remained deeply interested in what Hobsbawm called 'grassroots history' and paid close attention not just to the representation of voters in political language, but also to the interactions between grassroots activists and elite politicians.[3] However, studies written in this tradition still tended to start with formal politics and to work outwards: in that sense they were not history from below even if they gave popular politics pride of place.

But it *is* possible to start from below—with the non-activist majority—and still place questions of politics centre stage. Particularly for the post-1945 period, we are fortunate to have access to rich qualitative sources collected in the field by social scientists who were also interested in the everyday (though often for different reasons from those of the historian). Revisiting the transcripts of postwar social science encounters can tell us much about vernacular understandings of the social world, including what one might call the informal politics of everyday life.[4] Too

---

[1] Eric J. Hobsbawm, 'History from Below: Some Reflections', in Frederick Krantz, ed., *History from Below: Studies in Popular Protest and Popular Ideology* (Oxford, 1988), 13–27.

[2] Gareth Stedman Jones, *Languages of Class: Essays in English Working-Class History, 1832–1982* (Cambridge, 1983).

[3] For an overview, see Jon Lawrence, 'Political History', in Stefan Berger, Heiko Feldner, and Kevin Passmore, eds, *Writing History: Theory and Practice*, 2nd edn (London, 2010), 213–31.

[4] For discussion of the issues raised by reanalysing social science interviews, see Martyn Hammersley, 'Qualitative Data Archiving: Some Reflections on its Prospects and Problems', *Sociology* 31 (1997), 131–42, and Mike Savage, 'Revisiting Classic Qualitative Studies', *Forum: Qualitative Social Research* 6.1 (2005), Art. 31. Important studies deploying 'secondary analysis' include Mike Savage, 'Working-Class

often we forget that it is a natural part of the human condition to search for meaning and pattern in life, and especially to tell stories about where we have come from in order to make sense of where we might be heading. It is not just writers and academics who seek to impose meaning on the chaos of everyday life. This reflexive, meaning-generating activity takes many forms, but perhaps most relevant for understanding the politics of everyday life are vernacular understandings of recent history, what we might call 'shallow' as opposed to 'deep' history.[5] These are the master narratives people weave to make sense of change in their own lives and in the lives of those around them. Certainly, people often turn to the wider culture for the raw material of such narratives, but this is what makes analysing contemporary vernacular voices rewarding. We gain an insight into the strands of mainstream cultural debate and political argument that became woven into everyday speech (and thought) and those that did not. Emily Robinson and Joe Twyman have recently shown that politicians' use of the term 'progressive' bears little relationship to the term's meaning to ordinary voters.[6] Reanalysing the transcripts of major postwar social science studies allows us to explore the relationship between 'official' and vernacular languages of politics historically.

It is only recently that politicians have begun to talk explicitly about the importance of 'narrative' for capturing the political agenda, but the battle to shape the first draft of history has always been central to party politics.[7] Arguably, historians have paid too little attention to the ways in which this struggle to define the past has shaped not just popular perceptions of present and future, but also what it is possible to imagine as achievable through politics. In his influential work on the development of historical sensibilities as a defining feature of modernity, Reinhart Koselleck focuses primarily on higher forms of political and social discourse; but everyday speech also displays distinctive modes of temporality. Reconstructing this temporality can help us to understand important changes in the dominant ways in which individuals have connected past, present, and future across the postwar period, and hence their basic orientation to politics.[8]

Identities in the 1960s: Revisiting the Affluent Worker Study', *Sociology* 39 (2005), 929–46 and Selina Todd, 'Affluence, Class and Crown Street: Reinvestigating Post-War Working Class', *Contemporary British History* 22 (2008), 501–18. For a discussion of the reuse of working-class oral history narratives, see Andy Wood's chapter in this volume.

[5] Andrew Shyrock and Daniel L. Smail, *Deep History: The Architecture of Past and Present* (Berkeley, CA, 2011).

[6] Emily Robinson and Joe Twyman, 'Speaking at Cross Purposes? The Rhetorical Problems of "Progressive Politics"', *Political Studies Review* 12.1 (2014), 51–67; Emily Robinson, 'The Meanings of Progressive Politics: Interpretivism and its Limits', in Nick Turnbull, ed., *Interpreting Governance, High Politics and Public Policy* (New York and Abingdon, 2016), 115–30.

[7] Sanford F. Schram and Philip T. Neisser, eds, *Tales of the State: Narrative in Contemporary US Politics and Public Policy* (Lanham, MD, 1997); Frederick W. Mayer, *Narrative Politics: Stories and Collective Action* (New York, 2014); David Reynolds, *In Command of History: Churchill Fighting and Writing the Second World War* (London, 2004).

[8] Reinhart Koselleck, *Futures Past: On the Semantics of Historical Time*, trans. Keith Tribe (New York, 2004); for a discussion of popular mentalities registering these discursive shifts, see Reinhart Koselleck, '"Progress" and "Decline": An Appendix to the History of Two Concepts', in idem, *The Practice of Conceptual History: Timing History, Spacing Concepts*, trans. Todd Presner et al. (Stanford, CA, 2002), 218–35.

Koselleck reminds us of the interconnection between how people assign meaning to past experiences and how they conceptualize the future: what he terms their 'horizons of expectation'.[9] However, social theorists such as Hartmut Rosa argue that since the 1970s the acceleration of social change has disrupted this capacity, leaving people struggling to project their lives into a coherent, imaginable future.[10] But is such grand theorizing borne out by the fine-grain qualitative material deposited in contemporary field notes? If we turn our attention to the archived testimony of ordinary people, it becomes possible to explore shifting conceptions of historical time from below.[11] In doing so we certainly find examples of vernacular speech mirroring the language of formal party politics, but it can often be difficult to establish who may have been imitating whom. Politicians constantly search for vernacular idioms to make their ideas appear more grounded and vivid. At the same time their arguments are so widely disseminated through the mass media and party propaganda that they naturally form part of the cultural scrabble bag through which people rustle when trying to make sense of their own lives. But, while questions of causality may prove elusive, there is still much to be learned from exploring the conceptions of past, present, and future that people use when trying to articulate a 'common-sense' understanding of everyday life.

In order to provide some sense of context (both personal and social), the discussion that follows focuses solely on speech recorded in the field notes of studies focused on a specific time and place (beginning in Bermondsey in the late 1940s and ending on Tyneside in 2007–8). The story that emerges is a broadly familiar one, but constructing it from below—from the snatches of vernacular speech recorded in social science field notes—nonetheless raises major questions about the connection between political discourse and everyday life. The patriotic celebration of 'the People' during the Second World War does appear to have been internalized as the defining myth of the postwar social democratic settlement.[12] Labour played its part here, constantly reworking memories of mass unemployment and poverty in the 1930s to feed a popular narrative about social progress as a society-wide journey towards a fairer and better life. But Labour did not own this narrative, and from the beginning it can also be found being mobilized against its perceived failings in power.

The elderly, in particular, sometimes questioned the benefits of postwar 'progress', notably by complaining about a growing materialism and individualism. However, both materialism and individualism had deep roots in English popular culture, and one could argue that what was most distinctive about postwar popular

---

[9] Reinhart Koselleck, '"Space of Experience" and "Horizon of Expectation": Two Historical Categories', in idem, *Futures Past*, 255–75.

[10] Hartmut Rosa, *Social Acceleration: A New Theory of Modernity*, trans. Jonathan Trejo-Mathys (New York, 2013); also Guy Standing, *The Precariat: The New Dangerous Class* (London, 2011), esp. ch. 5.

[11] For a fruitful discussion of the issues raised by seeking to reclaim 'voices from below', see the various contributions in Mark Hailwood, Laura Sangha, Brodie Waddell, and Jonathan Willis, eds, *The Voices of the People: An Online Symposium*, 2015, https://manyheadedmonster.wordpress.com/voices-of-the-people, accessed 24 May 2017. On politicians' varied, multispeed conceptions of historical time and 'progress' in mid-twentieth century Britain, see Jeremy Nuttall, 'Pluralism, the People and Time in Labour Party History, 1931–1964', *Historical Journal* 56 (2013), 729–56.

[12] On the exclusions at the heart of this mythology, see Sonya O. Rose, *Which People's War? National Identity and Citizenship in Wartime Britain, 1939–1945* (Oxford, 2003).

conceptions of progress was in fact the newly found ability to reconcile ideas of personal advancement with collective, society-wide social improvement. We see this most clearly in a testimonial from the postwar new town of Stevenage, itself a giant experiment in collective improvement; but deep into the 1960s we hear of similar sentiments from places as diverse as Luton and Tyneside.

However, historical sensibilities were beginning to change by the late 1960s. Stories about the hungry 1930s were beginning to lose their power to mobilize. Instead, recurrent economic crises and revelations about the persistence of poverty and social deprivation began to destabilize postwar understandings of progress, especially the notion that it represented a *shared* experience. At the same time new social movements, and to a lesser extent large-scale immigration, began to challenge postwar conceptions of 'the People' and their supposedly common past, present, and future. Thatcherite politics worked with the grain of these changes, but did not cause them. Thatcherites certainly wove powerful self-legitimizing narratives about recent history (stories of crisis focused on national 'decline', economic failure, and, of course, industrial chaos, as exemplified by Labour's 'winter of discontent'), but they were not the reason why postwar social democratic concep-tions of history broke down. This owed more to the left's inability to develop powerful counternarratives about the recent past.

Ironically, the democratization of history may have played its part here. Popular representations of the past increasingly focused on the lives of ordinary people, but in doing so they arguably encouraged a fractured sense of history, organized around the gulf between past and present rather than around the connections.[13] At the same time, as Rosa suggests, rapid social change may have been disrupting estab-lished ways of imagining the connection between present and future. It probably did not help that many analyses of Thatcher's new brand of populist, radical con-servatism presupposed the collapse of social democracy; but, viewed from below, it is not clear that any discursive strategy could have restored popular belief in a progressive social democratic future.[14] The autonomy of politics is not absolute.

THE PEOPLE'S HISTORY

When Raymond Firth and an impressive team of anthropologists from the London School of Economics went to Bermondsey to study working-class kinship in 1947, they found local people echoing many facets of Labour's powerful case for social progress as reward for the past sacrifices of 'the People'. In its 1945 manifesto, *Let Us Face the Future*, the Labour Party used the phrase 'the people' fifteen times,

[13] Tristram Hunt, 'Reality, Identity and Empathy: The Changing Face of Social History Television' *Journal of Social History*, 39.3 (2006), 843–58; Emily Robinson, ' "Different and Better Times"? History, Progress and Inequality', in Pedro Ramos Pinto and Bertrand Taithe, eds, *The Impact of History? Histories at the Beginning of the 21st Century* (Abingdon, 2015), 110–22.

[14] Stuart Hall and Martin Jacques, eds, *The Politics of Thatcherism* (London, 1983); Stuart Hall, *The Hard Road to Renewal: Thatcherism and the Crisis of the Left* (London, 1988); Bob Jessop, Kevin Bonnett, Simon Bromley, and Tom Ling, eds, *Thatcherism: A Tale of Two Nations* (Cambridge, 1988).

and variations such as 'our people' and 'the British people' on a further thirteen occasions. Its central message was that only through a radical reform of the social and economic system based on 'fair shares for all' would 'our people reap the full benefits of this age of discovery'.[15] This language of 'fair shares' was central to Labour discourse in the 1940s, playing a central role in its defence of the continuation of rationing long after the end of hostilities.[16] Both 'fair shares' and 'the people' were distinctively Labour concepts in 1945; by contrast, the Liberal and Conservative manifestos used the phrase 'the people' only three times each in 1945.[17] It is therefore striking that we frequently hear this partisan language echoed on the streets of Bermondsey during Firth's 1947–8 anthropological study of the borough. Perhaps more importantly, we also hear local people echoing Labour's distinctive take on the meaning of recent history; namely that the hardships of the past justified radical policies in the present so that a better future could be secured for all. This social democratic narrative put down deep roots in Labour heartlands like Bermondsey. Firth's field notes offer little support for the thesis that there was a radical disconnection between Labour and 'its people' in the 1940s.[18]

When Firth and his colleagues went to study the Snowsfields Guinness Trust Buildings in Bermondsey, local people frequently emphasized the dramatic improvements that had been secured since the war. They often did so by telling graphic stories about the hardships of the 1930s, including that at least one local woman had 'died of starvation' rather than submit to the Means Test.[19] Grim stories about conditions in the 1930s were deployed both as a measure of recent progress and as an explicit justification of the government's postwar rationing policies, which were said to be 'very fair'.[20] Memories of the 1930s also underpinned a strong local culture of anti-Conservatism, even among those who professed to be uninterested in politics.[21] Again, the parallels with Labour Party propaganda were strong. The risk of a return to mass unemployment formed a central plank of the party's case against the Conservatives in 1945, 1950, and 1951. In Bermondsey, Labour propaganda recalled how local people had starved or been forced into the workhouse while the wealthy continued to dine lavishly in the West End.[22]

But it would be wrong to imagine that the people of Bermondsey simply parroted Labour arguments about history and progress. On the contrary, Firth's field

---

[15] Labour Party, *Let Us Face the Future: A Declaration of Labour Policy for the Consideration of the Nation* (London, 1945), http://www.politicsresources.net/area/uk/man/lab45.htm, accessed 26 May 2017.

[16] Mark Roodhouse, *The Black Market in Britain, 1939–1945* (Oxford, 2013).

[17] Liberal Party, *20 Point Manifesto of the Liberal Party* (London, 1945); Conservative Party, *Mr Churchill's Declaration of Policy to the electors* (London, 1945).

[18] Steven Fielding, Peter Thompson, and Nick Tiratsoo, *England Arise! The Labour Party and Popular Politics in 1940s Britain* (Manchester, 1995).

[19] London School of Economics Library, London, Sir Raymond Firth Papers (hereafter Firth Papers), 3/1/8 'Miscellaneous Notes and Reports', untitled paper [4 pp., 1947], p. 3.

[20] Firth Papers, 3/1/11 'Reports', 'Darts Report' [Geddes, 28 October 1947].

[21] Firth Papers, 3/1/8, untitled paper, p. 3; also 3/1/4 'Notes on Informants' Attitudes', 'Politics' report.

[22] Southwark Public Libraries, Bermondsey Labour Party Collection, 1980/54 F/5, 'Mellish: Of the People, for the People' [Bermondsey Election Special, 1950], p. 2.

notes suggest that they took their own measure of both past and future, rooting their thinking squarely in personal experience. A conversation about social security brought this out especially vividly. Two brothers who had grown up in the Guinness Buildings quizzed Firth about welfare provision in his native New Zealand. Frank, the older brother, insisted that social security in Britain remained inadequate despite Labour's reforms. He complained that, after a man had worked 'for his country' for more than fifty years, 'pensions of 26/- [shillings] per week [were] not enough to live on decently'. The government, he insisted, 'ought to see that he gets more'. When his brother suggested that 'by that time he should have put something by', Frank retorted that things had been harder before the war—wages had been lower, and men like their father had had to spend every penny on feeding and clothing their families.[23] In the popular narrative of progress, the rising living standards and improved security of the postwar era, which were widely commented on in Bermondsey, were understood to be a rightful reward for the sacrifices of two world wars. State welfare was understood in contractual terms, but in the popular mind this was a contract paid in blood and sweat over the preceding decades rather than through individual monetary contributions to the 'national insurance' fund.

In fact almost every aspect of daily life was interpreted through an historical frame that supposed not just change, but social improvement. For instance, Sid Morris insisted that Bermondsey's reputation for toughness was no longer deserved: 'It used to be tough in [my dad's] day, when policemen had to walk in pairs, but not now. [There are] a few gangs but they are under control.' According to the researcher, Morris insisted that 'The emphasis now is on sociability and friendliness, particularly in pubs.'[24] Older residents were not always convinced that change was for the better, but they still recognized the language of 'progress'. Mrs Harvey noted pithily: 'In those days [her youth] we had large families and small wages; nowadays they have small families and big wages'—but she doubted whether people were happier as a result.[25]

In his work on the nearby East End borough of Bethnal Green a few years later, Michael Young also found people mobilizing nostalgia in order to add rhetorical weight to present discontents.[26] This did not mean that they necessarily felt that life had been better before the war, but they did feel that progress had come at a price—most commonly people were said to be less friendly now that they needed one another less. Mrs Instone told Young: 'People in the East End seem to keep more apart than they used to; young married couples keep to themselves.'[27] Some older residents even questioned whether people were better off materially, perhaps projecting personal experience rooted in the economics of the life cycle onto the

[23] Firth Papers, 3/1/1 *Field Notebook 1*, pp. 21–2.
[24] Firth Papers, 3/1/11 'Reports', 'Darts Report' [Geddes, 28 October 1947]. All names in this chapter are either original or invented pseudonyms.
[25] Firth Papers, 3/1/1 *Field Notebook 1*, p. 9.
[26] Ben Jones, 'The Uses of Nostalgia: Autobiography, Community Publishing and Working-Class Neighbourhoods in Post-War England', *Cultural & Social History* 7 (2010), 355–74.
[27] Churchill Archive Centre, Cambridge, Young Papers, Acc. 1577 (hereafter Young Papers), Case BG31, Instone family, p. 3.

wider society. Mrs Parfitt told Young that in the old days 'we were all huddled together and were we worse off? Money bought something then and mothers looked after their children: now they don't bother to look after them and they can't cook.'[28] But, if Young registered dissentient voices, he insisted that overall the people of Bethnal Green were 'well aware of the change which has come upon them in the course of a few decades'; their 'mentality', he argued, was shaped by 'the comparisons they make between the old and the new'.[29] In short, their politics came from making sense of their own experience, rather than from external party discourses.

THE PEOPLE'S JOURNEY

Down to the 1960s the popular narrative of progress tended to blend personal and public improvement; there was no hard line between individual and collective progress. People might place special emphasis on improvements in their own lives and in the lives of their immediate family, but they did so through a frame that presented these as part of the shared experience of 'people like us' (a phrase that vies for ubiquity with the idea of 'bettering' oneself in postwar social science transcripts, nicely capturing the dynamic tension between collective and individual idioms). Class was present, but not through an explicit language of class—in fact the dominant message was that 'the people' were escaping from the harsh conditions that had once allowed others to define them as 'working class'. We find such sentiments especially strongly in the postwar new towns—planned communities designed to alleviate overcrowding in the major conurbations. In such places people regularly portrayed themselves as both pioneers in a great new social project and as individuals on a personal, familial journey towards social improvement and prosperity.

In 1959, when the young Raph Samuel interrogated newcomers to Stevenage New Town about their attitudes to class and politics, he elicited many interesting answers. People repeatedly spoke of how they *and their neighbours* had embarked on a journey away from the impoverished, overcrowded conditions that had once been their lot. Jean Proctor, an instrument maker's wife from Ruislip, explained: 'I come from working-class people—my father was just a tradesman [skilled worker]. With the standard of living in this town *most of us people* would be lower-middle-class.'[30] Many of the newcomers to Stevenage seemed to have internalized the social democratic vision of the politicians and planners who had brought it to fruition in the years immediately after the war. Asked whether there were still people in poverty, Jack Bannister, a young tool designer from Glasgow, replied: 'I don't

---

[28] Young Papers, Case BG26, Harvey family, p. 9.

[29] Michael Young and Peter Willmott, *Family and Kinship in East London* (London, 1957), 5. On the centrality of change to Young and Willmott's study, see Mike Savage, *Identities and Social Change in Britain since 1940: The Politics of Method* (Oxford, 2010), 157–9.

[30] Bishopsgate Institute, London, Ruskin Papers (hereafter Ruskin Papers), RS1/302, Interview 22, p. 1 (emphasis added).

know too much about other places. There's no poor here, but you see them in Glasgow and London. They can better themselves if they want to: that's what the new towns are for.'[31] Brian Smith, a young draughtsman from Cambridge, also stressed the centrality of the new towns programme to social progress, arguing: 'The lower class is coming into the middle class in *this* area but not in all—that depends on housing.'[32]

Such comments certainly had a judgemental, individualist flavour, but there was a strong assumption that the people who made a new life together in Stevenage shared broadly the same outlook and values—imagined out-groups, be they rich or poor, lived beyond the new town's boundaries. Time and again, they used variations on the theme that they were 'bettering' themselves by moving to Stevenage. People rarely feel comfortable talking about their own social class in England—the concept is freighted with too many social taboos and anxieties about 'status'. Certainly, Samuel's attempts to quiz people directly about class frequently extracted tortured answers. Many were keen to stress that they saw moving to the new town as part of a conscious strategy to 'better' themselves; but they were also keen to disown any suggestion that they might be 'putting on airs'. George Metcalfe, an instrument maker from Kentish Town, acknowledged that he would 'like a better home and so on' but immediately insisted that he 'wouldn't like to be known as middle class. I've no illusions about myself.'[33] Similarly, Patricia Thompson, a factory inspector's wife with two young children who had grown up in Walthamstow, insisted that 'everyone's very much the same [in Stevenage], we're all working people here, of course there's some earning more than the others, but that's all'.[34]

Crucially, many of the incomers appear to have embraced Stevenage as a new kind of place, one outside the old English class system—somewhere modern and new, where the old ways of keeping people 'in their place' held no writ. It was progress made concrete (literally). Bannister, the tool designer from Glasgow, recalled being looked down upon by people in the old town when he first came to Stevenage, but he spoke as though such petty snobbery were a peculiar throwback to an older way of living rather than something that impinged directly on his own well-being. He was adamant that class was just a question of money, and he wanted more of that: 'money decides what you are. I won't change myself but the money will make a difference.'[35] Others just felt that class didn't have much meaning in the context of new-town living. Bob Stewart, a toolroom superintendent who had moved out from Harrow, said: 'I come from a working-class family, but in the maze of class at Stevenage you don't know where you are: I'm in a kind of unclassed position.'[36]

But by the late 1950s some people were already beginning to have doubts about Britain's long-term future. The humiliating withdrawal from Suez shook their confidence in Britain as a world power, but it was only among disgruntled,

[31] Ruskin Papers, RS1/303, Interview 8, p. 1.
[32] Ruskin Papers, RS1/302 [no number], 15 November 1959, Q. 7, p. 1.
[33] Ruskin Papers, RS/303, Interview 35, p. 1.
[34] Ruskin Papers, RS1/305 [no number or date], p. 1.
[35] Ruskin Papers, RS1/303, Interview 8, p. 3.
[36] Ruskin Papers, RS1/305 [no number or date], p. 2.

imperialistic Conservatives that these doubts were felt strongly enough to register in the social science field notes of the late 1950s and early 1960s. For this group, 'decline' was already more tangible than 'progress' and, as Bill Schwarz has suggested, racial fears often went hand in hand with regret about the loss of empire.[37] A machine operator from rural Kent spoke angrily of Britain being 'trodden on' by 'little dictators like Nasser' before declaring: 'The Conservatives would look after the Empire more than what Labour would.... There's so many foreigners in this country aren't there?... They cause a lot of trouble here. I've nothing against the coloured people coming but I think they ought to stop in their own country.'[38] There is no suggestion that these comments were rooted in direct personal experience; immigrants were attacked as symbols of national decline: 'if we were still governing India they wouldn't be in such state that they would need to come over here'.[39]

But only a few Conservatives appear to have been sufficiently invested in the hierarchies of empire to question the dominant narrative of postwar progress. The party itself remained strongly committed to the idea of technocratic progress in the 1950s. In 1955 it published an election leaflet called 'The Future Is Being Decided *Now*', which trumpeted the virtues of atomic power and diesel locomotives, concluding with the slogan 'keep *PROGRESS* going... BY VOTING *CONSERVATIVE*'.[40] And at the 1959 election its leaflet 'Building for the FUTURE' began with a quotation from Iain McLeod: 'Leave the Socialists to their bickerings and their old-fashioned theories. They are as out-of-date as bows and arrows are. Let them stay in the past where they belong. WE turn to the future... tomorrow is ours.'[41] Many party supporters echoed this confident progressivism. At Stevenage, an electronics engineer spoke lyrically about a decade of Conservative rule: 'There's been a nice red glow, a beautiful sunset from the Tories. [The] standard of living has gone up. Freedom from controls and so on. Money is freer, production has improved and the quality of goods is higher.' He also took an optimistic view of broader social change, declaring: 'Public life has changed—we're getting more truthful; manners are better'; and he felt that immigration 'should carry on as it is now. We're going out to their countries after all.'[42] In 1959 we also find workers directly quoting Conservative election propaganda when they explain their decision to vote Conservative. Eric Forrest, a young plastics technician, directly echoed advertisers Colman, Prentis, and Varley's slogan 'Life's better under the Conservatives—Don't let

---

[37] Bill Schwarz, *The White Man's World: Memories of Empire*, vol. 1 (Oxford, 2011), 9–52.

[38] Ruskin Papers, RS1/303 [no number], 14 Nov. 1959, p. 6; paraphrased in Samuel's notes on 'The Conservatives as Elite', RS1/301. Samuel drew on this research for Raphael Samuel, 'The Deference Voter', *New Left Review* 1.1 (1960), 9–13.

[39] Ruskin Papers, RS1/303 [no number], 14 November 1959, p. 6.

[40] Labour History Archive, Manchester, uncatalogued box 'General Election 1955, Conservative and Liberal Manifestoes', Conservative Party, 'The Future is Being Decided NOW', election leaflet, 1955 (GE 10).

[41] Labour History Archive, Manchester, uncatalogued box 'General Election 1959, Election addresses, Conservative Leaflets and Guides', Conservative Party, 'Building for the FUTURE', election leaflet, 1959 (EL 20).

[42] Ruskin Papers, RS1/302, Interview 47, 1–2.

Labour ruin it', which had been plastered over thousands of billboards in the run-up to the recent general election.[43] Forrest explained: 'we've done very well under the Conservative government, and people don't want to take a chance of Labour ruining it. The Labour Party could probably do as well or better but people aren't prepared to take the chance.'[44] Labour still sought to mobilize memories of mass unemployment, but new narratives about the causes of postwar 'affluence' carried more weight with many.[45] As an instrument maker and stalwart Labour voter from Kentish Town put it, 'Young people who've never voted before haven't seen what happened before the war.'[46]

INTO THE 1960s

Even in the 1960s, when the winding up of empire was in full swing and the credibility of the country's old patrician elite in free fall thanks to public scandals such as Profumo, a powerful belief in the inevitability of shared progress continued to run through mainstream popular discourse.[47] In their famous study of affluent workers in the southern English boom town of Luton, John Goldthorpe and David Lockwood interviewed workers who were convinced that their rulers were corrupt and decadent, or that the country was heading for ruin if calls to 'modernize' went unheeded; but they found few who doubted that they and their loved ones would continue on a steady course to greater levels of prosperity and material comfort.[48] Indeed they found at least one man continuing to spout the Tory election slogans of 1959. Asked to explain his voting intentions, 'Mr Prosperity voter', as they dubbed him, declared boldly: 'I'm doing all right with the Tories, I've never had it so good.'[49]

The Luton workers were specifically instructed to look ten years ahead and asked: 'What improvement in your way of life would you most hope for?' Most wanted to own a car or a house; or, if they already had these things, they hoped for a better car and a more desirable house. Many just said that they hoped for more money, shorter hours, and longer holidays, reinforcing Goldthorpe and Lockwood's argument about the 'instrumentalism' of British industrial workers (although it is

[43] Jon Lawrence, *Electing Our Masters: The Hustings in British Politics from Hogarth to Blair* (Oxford, 2009), 164; Richard Rose, *Influencing Voters: A Study of Campaign Rationality* (London, 1967), 38–44.
[44] Ruskin Papers, RS1/302, 'Forrest' interview [no date or number], p. 2 (Q22).
[45] David Butler and Richard Rose, *The British General Election of 1959* (London, 1960); Stuart Middleton, '"Affluence" and the Left in Britain, c.1958–1974', *English Historical Review* 129.536 (2014), 107–38.
[46] Ruskin Papers, RS1/303, Interview 35, p. 1.
[47] Jon Lawrence, 'Paternalism, Class and the British Path to Modernity', in Simon Gunn and James Vernon, eds, *The Peculiarities of Liberal Modernity in Imperial Britain* (Berkeley, CA, 2011), 163–80; Frank Mort, *Capital Affairs: London and the Making of the Permissive Society* (New Haven, CT, and London, 2010), esp. ch. 7.
[48] John Goldthorpe and David Lockwood, *Affluent Worker in the Class Structure, 1961–1962* [data collection]. UK Data Service, 2010. SN 6512, doi: 10.5255/UKDA-SN-6512-1 (hereafter Affluent Worker), Luton Home Interviews (hereafter LHI), Case 82, Q64; also LHI, Case 121, p. 32.
[49] Affluent Worker, LHI, Case 177, p. 45.

striking that they put as much emphasis on quality of life as on money).[50] Hardly anyone raised doubts about the likelihood of 'improvement', although respondents turned out to be quite happy to challenge the premise of other questions.[51] A factory worker who had moved out from London said that his main hope was to '[b]e a grandfather. That'll be an important...be a grandfather twice, put that down.' Then, turning to material things, he commented: 'Can't see as we could improve all that much, apart from a new TV, new 3 piece suite [etc.], but they're the things that come along normally in life.'[52] For him at least, material progress was now 'normal'. But, again, a few people sounded notes of doubt: elite debates about 'decline' did not go wholly unregistered.[53] A middle-aged factory worker from Luton said: 'The only thing I hope to have is a caravan or bungalow near the coast—get away occasionally for a holiday, providing we keep prospering in this country.'[54] An Irishman who had moved to Luton in the early 1950s took the bleakest view, declaring: '[there's] not much the ordinary W[orking] C[lass] man can hope for. Health and happiness. I'm quite satisfied to earn my living "by the sweat of my brow".'[55] He, at least, had not internalized the postwar master narrative of progress in either its social democratic or its Tory register.

But, if most workers in 1960s Britain did expect improvements, we nonetheless find some interesting parallels with pre-Second World War attitudes. Perhaps most striking is the number of workers who suggested that 'security' was the key to a happy future. Less had changed than we might imagine since Mass Observation had investigated the meaning of 'happiness' in late 1930s Bolton.[56] As one man put it: 'Security in my job. That brings everything else.'[57] Or, as another put it: 'Security is the highest thing.'[58] But by no means did everyone *feel* secure, despite the booming conditions of the local economy and the high employment levels in the town.[59] A man who called for '[m]ore security at work' complained that 'It's a crying shame that a firm can make you redundant at 50.'[60] Crucially, many made it clear that they saw owning a house as a means to achieve security and independence, and looked forward to the freedom they would feel once they had paid off their mortgage.[61]

---

[50] John H. Goldthorpe, David Lockwood, Frank Bechhofer, and Jennifer Platt, *The Affluent Worker in the Class Structure* (Cambridge, 1969). For a post-materialist analysis of car workers' mentalities, see Jack Saunders, 'The British Motor Industry, 1945–77: How Workplace Cultures Shaped Labour Militancy', unpublished PhD thesis, University College London, 2015.

[51] Jon Lawrence, 'Social-Science Encounters and the Negotiation of Difference in Early 1960s England', *History Workshop Journal* 77 (2014), 215–39.

[52] Affluent Worker, LHI, Case 102, p. 44.

[53] Jim Tomlinson, *The Politics of Decline: Understanding Post-War Britain* (Harlow, 2001); David Edgerton, *Warfare State: Britain 1920–1970* (Cambridge, 2005).

[54] Affluent Worker, LHI, Case 121, p. 44.   [55] Affluent Worker, LHI, Case 49, p. 44.

[56] Ian Gazeley and Claire Langhamer, 'The Meanings of Happiness in Mass Observation's Bolton', *History Workshop Journal* 75 (2013), 159–89.   [57] Affluent Worker, LHI, Case 11, p. 44.

[58] Affluent Worker, LHI, Case 140, p. 44.

[59] Jack Saunders, 'The Untraditional Worker: Class Re-Formation in Britain, 1945–65', *Twentieth-Century British History* 26.2 (2015), 225–48 stresses the persistence of insecurity in 'affluent' Britain.

[60] Affluent Worker, LHI, Case 128, p. 44.

[61] Affluent Worker, LHI, Cases 42, 73, and 78, p. 44.

It was probably the broadly positive view of future progress that explains why almost three-quarters of Luton's shop-floor workers said they would like to run a business, and more than a third claimed to have already done something to make it happen.[62] Men talked about going self-employed as central heating contractors or car mechanics, or else retiring early to run a pub, guest house, or village shop with their wives.[63] As with owning their own homes, they stressed the attraction of feeling 'independent' or, more prosaically, of being their 'own governor'.[64] One declared that he wanted to 'engage in some business where I wouldn't be limited'; another just wanted to say goodbye to six o'clock shifts.[65] Significantly, no one said that he or she wanted to be rich. Their dreams were about escaping the indignities of the Fordist production line.[66] Although they were strongly future-oriented, this was less about 'getting on' than about 'getting off'.

The impressive ethnographic work conducted as part of Richard Brown's study of the Swan Hunter shipyard at Wallsend in the late 1960s also threw up strong examples of the deep popular roots of historicist thinking. Time and again, the shipbuilders spoke about the past as a way of signalling present-day progress. There was little sign here of the nostalgic sensibility often said to dominate working-class memory from the 1960s onwards.[67] Here at least, stories about the bad old days in the 1930s were still being mobilized to underscore the extent of postwar gains. John Wilkie, a foreman joiner, recalled that between the wars work had been so scarce that '[foremen] got packets of cigarettes with ten bob inside. One used to live next door and vegetables were left on his doorstep.'[68] Another joiner recalled that in the past 'It was common for women to have black eyes every week,' and he signalled his disapproval by explaining that 'much of this behaviour, and the drinking that went with it, was indulged in so as not to look soft in front of mates'.[69] But historical framing was also a technique that could allow people to register social change without passing judgement, as when Wilkie recalled that people 'used to disapprove of women who worked... when I was young the girls at the Ropery... were known as Haggy's Angels. I wouldn't go out with one of them, my mother would have had a fit.'[70]

Popular belief in social progress underpinned one of the more important changes in twentieth-century British working-class culture: the growing belief that one's

---

[62] John H. Goldthorpe, David Lockwood, Frank Bechhofer, and Jennifer Platt, *The Affluent Worker: Industrial Attitudes and Behaviour* (Cambridge, 1968), 132.

[63] Good examples include Affluent Worker, LHI, Cases 127, 136, 137, 165, 184, and 218.

[64] Affluent Worker, LHI, Cases 130, 150, 165, 191.

[65] Affluent Worker, LHI, Cases 123, 130, 137; Affluent Worker, Luton Work Interview, Case 67.

[66] See the discussion in Selina Todd, *The People: The Rise and Fall of the British Working Class, 1910–2010* (London, 2014), 258–61.

[67] Carolyn Steedman, 'State-Sponsored Autobiography', in Becky Conekin, Frank Mort, and Chris Waters, eds, *Moments of Modernity: Reconstructing Britain 1945–1964* (London, 1999), 41–54; Chris Waters, 'Autobiography, Nostalgia, and the Changing Practices of Working-Class Selfhood', in George K. Behlmer and Fred Leventhal, eds, *Singular Continuities* (Stanford, CA, 2000), 178–95.

[68] Modern Records Centre, University of Warwick, Qualidata: Shipbuilding Workers (MSS.371), Boxes 1 to 15 (hereafter Shipbuilding Workers), Box 4, File FM08.

[69] Shipbuilding Workers, Box 1, File 8, p. 50.　　[70] Shipbuilding Workers, Box 4, File FM08.

children should enjoy a better and, just as crucially, a *different* life from the one you had known. In *Family and Kinship*, Michael Young records a woman telling him: 'You always want to give your children better than what you had. People are more educated today; they know they can have better if they want to.'[71] In her work on young women's lives between the wars, Selina Todd has suggested that this was one of the key drivers of social change in mid-century Britain.[72] Significantly, less than a third of the shipbuilding workers claimed that they would advise a school-leaver to come into their industry.[73] They explained this largely in terms of structural shifts that had opened up new opportunities unavailable in their youth; but rising expectations were also part of the story. An old welder spoke proudly of a son who had received twelve job offers before he had finished sixth form and was now a computer expert for a major UK bank. The man stressed that he had never wanted his son to follow him into the shipyard, but he also insisted that '50 years ago there was no choice... there were only two jobs to be had in Wallsend "the pit or Swan Hunters shipyard".'[74]

Given that the British shipbuilding industry was in long-term decline (and in fact stood on the brink of decimation at the time when Brown's research was conducted), it is striking how few men at Swan Hunters read the state of the nation off from the state of their own industry. Men were full of stories of high wages to be earned elsewhere in England or Germany, and this knowledge may have helped to preserve a broadly progressivist outlook. But there were signs of growing disillusionment, and it is striking that these, too, could be framed historically. For instance, after watching a programme about slum housing in London, John Robinson, a ship's joiner, denounced the pernicious influence of Freemasons, feudal landlords, and capitalists, before declaring: 'After all this time the working man still doesn't have a decent home to live in.... It's the second time that we have been going to build a nation fit for heroes to live in, and it's taking a bloody long time as far as I can see.'[75] Like many of his workmates, Robinson was bitter that Wilson's Labour government had not done more to help working people and angry that it now proposed to legislate to reduce trade union powers. Again, Robinson turned to history to underscore his point: 'I can remember Barbara Castle saying "Never mind the bread, what about a bit of jam?", but that was before she was in power, now we're back to bread with no jam again. That lot, they're fifth columnists they are. They're out to make sure there will never be another Labour government.'[76] Others railed against the idea of a Labour government planning 'to start sending the bailiffs after an honest man who withdraws his labour. I ask you.'[77] The disconnection between everyday politics and party politics could hardly have been sharper.

[71] Young and Willmott, *Family and Kinship*, 7.
[72] Selina Todd, *Young Women, Work and Family in England, 1918–1950* (Oxford, 2005).
[73] Selina Todd and Hilary Young, *Digitisation of R. Brown Orientation to Work and Industrial Behaviour of Shipbuilding Workers 1968–1969: Manual Workers' Questionnaires* [data collection]. UK Data Service, 2007. SN 6586, UKDA, Essex, doi: 10.5255/UKDA-SN-6586-1, questions 109 and 111.
[74] Shipbuilding Workers, Box 1, File 18 [welder interview], p. 3.
[75] Shipbuilding Workers, Box 1, File 8, p. 40.   [76] Ibid.
[77] Shipbuilding workers, Box 1, File 8, p. 43 (17 April 1969).

FRACTURED STORIES

In short, the mobilizing myths of postwar social democracy were starting to fray even before the economic dislocations of the 1970s and 1980s tested them to destruction. Among the younger generation, workers were beginning to tire, as one Tyneside shipbuilding worker put it, of hearing stories 'about the old days on the dole and the soup kitchens'.[78] But it was during the 1970s that popular belief in the inevitability of progress began to break down. As the long postwar boom came to an end, amid rising unemployment, rampant inflation, and falling living standards, the certainty that people were embarked on a shared journey towards prosperity began to evaporate. It was in 1978 that Eric Hobsbawm famously asked whether 'the forward march of labour' had been halted—but arguably what sealed the fate of postwar social democracy was the more fundamental collapse of popular belief in 'the *people's* forward march'.[79] What we might call vernacular social democracy broke down as people struggled to make sense of experiences that could not easily be reconciled with the broad-brush, optimistic view of change that had taken hold after the war. Everyday speech still resounded with stories about a journey away from the indignities of poverty and domestic service, but these stories ceased to assume a shared, progressive future. Instead they became a staple of the burgeoning heritage industry, shaping the representation of the past not just in stately homes and industrial museums across the country but also in mainstream popular culture. *Downton Abbey's* anachronistic portrayal of domestic service as a historically doomed aberration is just the latest example. If 'the People' could still be imagined as a collectivity with a common identity and purpose, this was now anchored firmly in the past.[80]

Understanding how this happened and why more narrowly individualist conceptions of advancement and 'progress' came to predominate in English popular culture poses considerable historical challenges. One problem is that the English community study went out of fashion in the 1970s.[81] The only major study from this period that has left extensive field notes is Ray Pahl's pioneering mixed-methods project on the Isle of Sheppey, off the north Kent coast, undertaken between 1978 and 1988. Pahl wanted to understand how people from a range of backgrounds were coping with the challenges of a faltering economy and high inflation. The bulk of his interviews were conducted after the severe recession of 1980–1. Unemployment on the island was over 20 per cent, and even among those in work there were many who had faced redundancy or the threat of redundancy in the recent past.

---

[78] Shipbuilding Workers, Box 1, File 6, p. 21.

[79] Eric Hobsbawm, 'The Forward March of Labour Halted?' *Marxism Today*, September 1978, 279–86; Martin Jacques and Francis Mulhern, eds, *The Forward March of Labour Halted?* (London, 1981).

[80] Robinson, '"Different and Better Times"?'.

[81] Margaret Stacey, 'The Myth of Community Studies', *British Journal of Sociology* 20.2 (1969), 134–47; Colin Bell and Howard Newby, eds, *Community Studies: An Introduction to the Sociology of the Local Community* (London, 1971).

Perhaps unsurprisingly, acute economic insecurity had implications for how people conceptualized the future. People began to question whether their children's lives would really be better than their own. Mrs Alsop, the wife of a self-employed heating contractor, is a good example. The family had known considerable prosperity in the 1970s, but a collapse in work during the recession had forced them to turn to social security. By 1982 Mr Alsop was earning good money again, though only by working long hours away from home, and the memory of economic hardship remained strong. Mrs Alsop talked about how she felt 'lowered and degraded' having to go to the social security office, and feared that her children faced an equally grim future: 'When I think of my kids having to grow up like this, I feel sorry for them. The jobs are just getting less and less aren't they?'[82]

One of the more remarkable features of the Sheppey project is the series of long, informal interviews Pahl conducted with the couple he called Linda and Jim.[83] Jim lost his job as a ship's lighterman in the recession of 1980 and survived on benefits and casual employment throughout the next three years. It is striking how this experience changed Linda's orientation towards the future between the first interview in 1978 and those conducted in the 1980s. Kim, the couple's eldest child, had been just about to leave school in 1978, and Linda was still optimistic about her future:

> my sisters' girls are all in the factory, but I don't want to see mine end up in the factory. It's good money, it's better pay than any other job but I think it's boring to sit and sew...I'd like mine to have jobs where they can either go and meet different people and see different places and [do] something a bit interesting.... we was always conditioned into doing domestic, like cleaning or washing up and working in cafes and things like that, you know, I don't want that, you know, I'd like them to do something a lot more interesting.[84]

Speaking five years later, when both Kim and her husband had been unemployed for three years, Linda was much less sanguine about the future. She still wanted her children to enjoy a better life than she had known, but this now simply meant hiding the privations of unemployment from the younger children as much as possible; it did not mean imagining a better future. Recounting how her brother 'went up the wall at me' for buying the youngest child a bike for Christmas, she explained: 'You try and make it better for them because no doubt they're going to have it hard enough when they get older.'[85] The expectation of intergenerational progress had been broken.

---

[82] Ray E. Pahl, *Changing Sociological Construct of the Family, 1930–1986* [data collection]. UK Data Service, 2004. SN 4872, doi: 10.5255/UKDA-SN-4872-1, Box 10, Household Work Strategies Study (hereafter Sheppey Study), HWS1.1982, pp. 7 and 10.

[83] Ray Pahl, *Divisions of Labour* (Oxford, 1984), ch. 11, 'Polarization of Workers' Lives: Jim and Linda; Beryl and George'; Jane Elliott and Jon Lawrence, 'Linda and Jim Revisited: Narrative, Time and Intimacy in Social Research', in Graham Crow and Jaimie Ellis, eds, *Revisiting* Divisions of Labour*: The Impacts and Legacies of a Modern Sociological Classic* (Manchester, 2017), 189–204.

[84] Sheppey Study, Box 5, Linda and Jim interview 1, May 1978, p. 12 (ellipsis in the original transcription).

[85] Sheppey Study, Box 5, Linda and Jim interview 6, February 1983, p. 6.

Clearly Linda was at the sharp end of the economic dislocations of the early 1980s, and their impact on her ability to imagine a benign, progressive future was particularly profound (though it has many echoes across Pahl's study, such as from the boilermaker who commented: 'Yes, skilled worker until you are unemployed, then you are nothing—just a figure').[86] But my argument is not that faith in the future generally collapsed, and not even that from the 1980s only narrowly individualist conceptions of the future held sway. Rather, I am arguing that conceptions of a *shared* future collapsed in this period. What we are really dealing with here is the breakdown of the social democratic concept of 'the People', which had been forged in the populist patriotic rhetoric of the Second World War and underwritten by the postwar settlement.

Economic dislocation played its part in this story, but just as important was the breakdown of the socially conservative, conformist social system that made it possible to imagine 'the People' as a coherent abstraction at all. Immigration helped to unsettle simplistic models of 'the People', but we should not exaggerate its importance.[87] More significant was the growing reluctance to accept socially policed norms about personal lifestyle. A young nurse from a Midlands mining community told Pahl that she welcomed the freedom to live as she chose in Sheppey (what she chose was a life of sex equality in which she and her husband shared the domestic responsibilities). She rejoiced at having escaped the 'conformist lifestyle' of her home town.[88] For her, progress took place on an intimate rather than a societal scale. A middle-aged couple who also insisted that they had always shared domestic tasks explicitly measured progress by the criterion of their neighbours' having finally come to terms with their right to live as they chose: 'People used to think it was odd then [when their children were young] ... but they don't so much any more.'[89]

Another of Pahl's Sheppey cases nicely captures the radical new social forces that undermined dominant postwar conceptions of 'the People'. Debbie was a 32-year-old mother of two, twice divorced, whom the interviewer described as a 'working-class women's libber'. She rejected marriage and housework and proclaimed that she would never be dependent on a man again. Determined to 'better herself' through study and travel, she was clearly strongly oriented towards the future. She wanted success and personal fulfilment, and she was confident that hard work would bring both. But her conception of the future was not purely individualist. She also had what we might call a vernacular feminist vision of the future, in which 'the next generation of girls,' including her own daughter, would not be as 'disillusioned' and put upon as her own had been. For her at least, past, present, and future were still connected, but her master narrative was now about women's liberation from 'male oppressors' rather than about 'the People's' liberation from past injustice.[90] A remarkable story simply as an example of how second-wave

---

[86] Sheppey Study, Box 10, HWS4.331, 1982, p. 6.
[87] Jon Lawrence, 'Why the Working Class Was Never "White"', *New Left Project*, 26 December 2014.
[88] Sheppey Study, Box 10, HWS26.084, pp. 2–3.
[89] Sheppey Study, Box 10, HWS28.039, p. 3.
[90] Sheppey Study, Box 10, HWS24.391, 'Mrs X'.

288 *Jon Lawrence*

feminism could touch ordinary women's lives, it is no less potent as an illustration of how new social movements destabilized postwar social democratic conceptions of historical change.

For the most part we do not find party propaganda reproduced in the testimony from Sheppey; not even the powerful 'common-sense' phrases honed by Saatchi and Saatchi in the late 1970s and 1980s. By 1983 Conservative propaganda was confidently proclaiming that, thanks to Thatcher's leadership, Britain now had 'a very great future as well as a great past'.[91] But it was the snatches of vox pop commentary in other parties' broadcasts that came closest to echoing the way Sheppey people spoke about the future in interviews with Pahl. Perhaps appropriately in a constituency where the newly created Social Democratic Party easily pushed Labour into third place in 1983, its broadcasts came closest to capturing local attitudes. In one, a student complains that Mrs Thatcher 'doesn't hold out much hope for young people', and then a housewife called Alaine Hopkins struggles to voice her fears about her children's future:

> it's the insecurity to the future, um, with our children. I just don't know how they're going to live. That's what I live with is the fear to when they're older and [how] they're going to live—lead their own lives, what future they've got. There's just no future at the moment. Something's got to be done.[92]

But there is no suggestion here that politics was shaping the language of everyday life—on the contrary, this was a new party turning to the everyday to make its appeal appear more grounded and authentic.

In the 1980s British social science had yet to take what might be called its narrative turn. Investigators like Pahl could be attentive to respondents' upbringing and general backstory, but they rarely showed any sustained interest in the ways in which people constructed their life stories.[93] In 1982 Pahl was clearly surprised to encounter a couple who were determined to tell 'their life story at great length', noting that 'they insist that I have to understand their backgrounds in order to understand why they are like they are'.[94] But from the 1990s onwards, with the dissemination of new ideas about narrative identity, it became common to frame the entire social science encounter as a life story.[95] This new emphasis on narrativity imposed an explicitly historical framing on people's testimony. Just like working-class autobiographies written under the influence of history from below in the 1970s and 1980s, such life-course interviews could take a strongly nostalgic form. As Ben Jones has observed, sometimes a nostalgic framing could be mobilized to

91 Labour Party Archive, Manchester, uncatalogued Box, 'General Election 1983', Conservative Party Election Broadcast, 26 May 1983, p. 3 (BBC transcription).
92 Labour Party Archive, Manchester, uncatalogued Box, 'General Election 1983', SDP/Liberal Alliance Election Broadcast, 31 May 1983, pp. 1–2 (BBC transcription).
93 Jane Elliott and Jon Lawrence, 'The Emotional Economy of Unemployment: A Re-Analysis of Testimony from a Sheppey Family, 1978–1983', *Sage Open* 6.4 (2016), 1–11, doi: 10.1177/2158244016669517.
94 Sheppey Study, Box 10, HWS28.039, p. 1.
95 Jane Elliott, *Using Narrative in Social Research: Qualitative and Quantitative Approaches* (London, 2005).

give rhetorical weight to present discontents.[96] Arguably, this was what older residents had been doing in postwar Bermondsey and Bethnal Green. But nostalgia can also serve to underscore the perceived *discontinuities* of recent history. In such accounts the past appears as a 'golden age' now irretrievably lost. Yvette Taylor's study of Tyneside women's lives conducted in 2007–8 offers some striking examples in this genre, for instance the receptionist Mrs Thomas, who commented:

> the community I grew up with. That isn't there anymore. That's where you left your back door open and your granny fetched you up, that doesn't happen. Not in my experience. In all of my married life, that hasn't happened but it did in my youth. I think people live behind...I can honestly say I don't know the names of anyone in our street except the next-door neighbours. After twelve years; that's sad![97]

In fact Mrs Thomas was so close to one of her next-door neighbours that the two of them organized an informal job share with a local firm, adjusting their working hours to suit themselves. However, this lived community barely registered in her testimony. It was from memories of childhood that Mrs Thomas felt able to weave a stable sense not just of self-identity, but of *belonging*, something she clearly found lacking in her present life. But her nostalgic framing accentuated the 'pastness' of the past. Mrs Thomas could mobilize memories of an earlier 'shared journey' to critique the present order, but her discontinuous sense of history necessarily carried few, if any, implications for the future. By no means did all Taylor's respondents share this orientation to the past, but it is, nonetheless, a striking example of the ways in which postmodern sensibilities about time and the self could be found as part of everyday 'common sense' by the early twenty-first century.[98]

CONCLUSIONS

We need to be wary about constructing an overly simple story about the changing 'voice of the people', but it is nonetheless possible to draw some broad conclusions about how people have woven their everyday experiences into broader narratives about societal as well as personal change. During the long postwar boom the dominant popular narrative of change appears to have been broadly social democratic; not only did people internalize the modernists' faith in the inevitability of social progress but, crucially, they saw progress as a shared entitlement. Progress was to be the people's reward for the sacrifices (and, let us not forget, the victories) of two world wars.

[96] Jones, 'Uses of Nostalgia'.
[97] Y. Taylor, *From the Coalface to the Car Park? The Intersection of Class and Gender in Women's Lives in the North East, 2007–2009* [computer file]. Colchester, Essex: UK Data Service, SN: 7053, Interview 19.
[98] On postmodern perceptions of 'history', see Peter Mandler, *History and National Life* (London, 2002); Martin L. Davies, *Historics: Why History Dominates Contemporary Society* (Abingdon, 2006); Emily Robinson, *History, Heritage and Tradition in Contemporary British Politics: Past Politics and Present Histories* (Manchester, 2012). For discussion from the different angle of the political problems this throws up for the left, see Geoff Eley's chapter in this volume.

By the 1960s there already were signs that the purchase of this narrative was loosening. The so-called rediscovery of poverty fuelled complaints that postwar promises to 'the People' had not been honoured. But belief in the possibility of shared progress remained strong—this was still an argument *within* social democracy. However, the concept of 'the People' was already beginning to lose the power to capture the popular imagination when the economic difficulties of the 1970s and the polarizing policies of the 1980s finally undermined the coherence of the postwar social democratic narrative.

But this was not primarily the result of political discourse recasting popular attitudes. Thatcher did not need to win a great discursive or ideological battle; she could rely on the social and economic dislocations of the 1970s and 1980s, coupled with her opponents' misjudgements, to do her work for her. It is doubtful whether popular values changed fundamentally in the 1980s, but popular understandings of history, and hence of imaginable futures, changed dramatically.[99] Crucially, the British people no longer saw themselves on a common journey towards a 'progressive' future. One major reason was that, across large swathes of society as much as in elite discourse, history had become just a story about the past rather than a key to imagining alternative futures. This was a change rooted not in shifts in party political discourses, which were largely playing catch-up by the 1980s, but rather in what we might call vernacular politics—in the stories people told themselves to make sense of their rapidly changing lives. Reanalysing the field notes of major social science projects suggests that, even before the rise of the Internet and social media, there were signs of a sundering of the connection between past, present, and future in popular culture. The social theorist Manuel Castells has described this phenomenon as late modernity's characteristic sense of 'timeless time'.[100] Its implications for politics are profound and sharply underscore the limits of the 'autonomy of the political'. But progressives need not despair. If popular conceptions of time and politics represent vernacular attempts to make sense of experience rather than simply pale reflections of dominant public discourse, it follows that fundamentally resetting the terms of economic life and public policy will re-establish conditions in which more solidaristic and communal conceptions of 'progress' can flourish.

ACKNOWLEDGEMENTS

I wish to thank staff at the Churchill Archive Centre, the London School of Economics Library, the Modern Records Centre (Warwick), the Bishopsgate Institute, the UK Data Service, and the Alfred Sloman Library, Essex for allowing me access to the social survey

---

[99] Ivor Crewe, 'Has the Electorate Become Thatcherite?', in Robert Skidelsky, ed., *Thatcherism* (London, 1988), 25–49.

[100] Manuel Castells, *The Information Age: Economy, Society and Culture*, vol. 1: *The Rise of the Network Society* (Oxford, 1996); Rosa, *Social Acceleration*.

transcripts used in this paper, Mr Toby Young for permission to quote from the Michael Young Papers, and participants at the 'History after Hobsbawm' conference and at seminars in Canberra and Sydney, and David Cowan for helpful comments on earlier versions of this paper. This research was made possible by the generous support of a Leverhulme Trust Major Research Fellowship (MRF-2012-048).

16

A Visit to the Dead
Genealogy and the Historian

Alison Light

Family history is everywhere in Britain, on television shows—like the BBC's extremely popular *Who Do You Think You Are?*—in the newspapers, which frequently carry family stories and old photographs, and above all in the form of software, maps, books, magazines, and huge events such as family history fairs, where gatherings of thousands of people share knowledge and buy things. It is a booming business across Europe, North America, and Australia in particular and has had a huge impact on information science and on the practices of archivists and researchers. Local record offices in Britain, once dusty, daunting, and silent, have been transformed; they are now frequently hubs of manic activity where researchers who ask to see a map of village boundaries, say, from the sixteenth century or the records for the enclosures of fields in the late eighteenth are as likely to be tracking their ancestors as to be writing a doctoral thesis. Family history is, in the simplest terms, public history: everyone can do it. It is one of those activities where people try to find meaning in doing historical work, in looking at documents from the past and interpreting them. And it takes place largely outside universities or colleges. Academic history, even popular academic history of the kind Eric Hobsbawm practised, has usually had little time for family history; nonetheless, as in the case of 'history from below' or 'people's history', which began in Britain in the adult education movement, family historians bring their own experiences and memories to their researches. They usually create extensive personal archives of documents as they collate marriage, birth, and death certificates and download material from the ever-proliferating digital sources—court and trial records, local militia lists, commercial and telephone directories, the roll call for the battle of Waterloo, wills, employment records for the railways and the postal service—to name but a few. In turn, family histories may be deposited in record offices and become a further resource for others. Family historians make a multitude of contacts through the numerous genealogy websites; theirs is usually collaborative work, meant to be shared.

For many people, however, 'doing' family history is a private consumer experience. It is a way of time-travelling safely from the armchair, as you hug a laptop, without leaving your home. Since the 1990s family history has become one of the fastest growing activities in the United Kingdom, a child of the new digital technology and of the World Wide Web. It has been estimated that ten years ago only 13 per cent of Britons had looked into their family history; this figure has since increased to around 40 per cent of the population, and tracing family history is the third most popular activity on the Web after shopping and pornography (and equally addictive, apparently).[1] Professional historians have usually been scathing or dismissive about it, criticizing its packaging of history, its relentless siphoning of the past back to the individual searcher in the form of lists of surnames and trees: 'find.*my*.past', as one of the current websites styles itself (my italics). Myopic and solipsistic, family history is deemed history 'lite' or 'comfort-zone history'—terms that often conceal a lofty masculine dismissal of a feminized activity, seen as sentimental or unobjective. Tristram Hunt, for instance, a historian who has served as shadow secretary of state for education, dismissed genealogy programmes on television as 'an indulgent search for identity and understanding', preferring a more bracing approach: 'television history, done well, should be more of an ice-bath than a comforting warm soak'.[2] There are other issues. Family history has flourished in postindustrial Britain at a time when family members are far-flung and fewer of us actually live in families. Discovering long-lost ancestors online may create links between the living, but this virtual family is a social network without the pain and responsibility of the family we grew up with. Indeed, our virtual family may be infinitely preferable to the families in which we live; grander perhaps, or more victimized, apparently more interesting, more appealing. 'We all have half a dozen possible ancestries to choose from, and fantasy and projection can furnish us with a dozen more,' writes Raphael Samuel, wondering whether people turn to 'make-believe identities in the past'[3] because they can no longer find a home for their ideal selves in the future. Is family history a sign of the morbidity of our culture, as Jacques Derrida and others have argued? Is the frantic search for origins a measure of the deathliness of a museum culture? Or is it rather the reverse, a sign of the vitality of the historical imagination?

Until thirty-odd years ago in British society, genealogy was the home of anti-quarians, cranks, and snobs. A family tree used to belong only to the wealthy. It testified to a continuous history that was based on their claim to land and property and on the assertion that thereby, in effect, they owned the past; often displayed in churches as memorials, family trees were also essential to the avowal of a right to arms. But, with the coming of the Internet, family history has been democratized and need not involve spending money. Some websites are free in record offices and allow people to find their forbears at least as far back as 1841, the first useable census of the nation. Given that in 1900 over 75 per cent of the population might be classified as working-class, chances are that most family historians will find that their British ancestors were not lords but labourers, not duchesses but domestic servants, what used to be called 'the common people'. If nothing else, therefore,

---

[1] 'Great-Auntie Ruth's Family Secrets', *Guardian*, 27 December 2008, where Dr Nick Barratt, historian and chief genealogist for the BBC, reports that websites such as ancestry.co.uk have seen a 500 per cent increase in business since 2005.

[2] 'The Time Bandits', *Guardian*, 10 September 2007.

[3] Raphael Samuel, *Island Stories: Unravelling Britain* (London, 1998), 272, 221.

family history changes the clientele of history; it peoples the past with those 'unknowns' who are usually absent, given little agency, or treated en masse.

But family history is not social history, though the two share much common ground. Nor is its primary concern 'the history of the family', its changing constitution or definition over time, though it overlaps with and can learn much from demographic or population studies. For most people, family history begins in the archives of our lives, with the stories, photographs, or objects that have been passed on through the generations or that survive as evidence of a life. Recalling memories—their own and those of their relatives—is often a prompt for family historians, who soon realize how unreliable their sources can be; and, if family history is a species of life-writing, it is usually unable—unlike conventional biography—to find much detail about an individual life. It proceeds in stops and starts and is obviously patchy. Family history means showing one's hand: the historian is implicated and cannot hide behind the fiction of impersonality.[4]

Family history is one arena where academic historians could find ways to share work and to engage with the wider public, with archivists, with museum workers, with those in the media, and with local and community historians. But what—if anything—can university-based historians learn from family history and its practitioners? Family historians play fast and loose with periodization; they make their own emotional connections and personal links across time; they individualize homogenizing categories of class, disaggregating group identities, and they cheerfully cross disciplinary boundaries, asking moral and metaphysical as well as historical questions about the place of the dead in our memories and our cultures. As someone who has gone in pursuit of her own ancestors, I found that family history could revitalize the histories that we have of people's lives, especially those of the poorer sort. It can also make us think about the limits, forms, and purposes of writing history.

* * *

Several years ago I began my own family history.[5] My motives were mixed. My father was dying of cancer and I imagined it, in part, as an act of restitution or reparation, since he knew little about his ancestry, or even about his closest relations. We had almost no information about our forbears; no names beyond those of my grandparents', a tiny handful of letters and photographs, no diaries; no family graves, no heirlooms, no 'ancestral place' or village. Whoever they were, these ancestors had come through history travelling light. I wanted to know what this lack of belongings meant. How were 'belongings'—possessions—and 'belonging' related? I knew, or thought I did, that they had been poor, but who were 'the poor'? And why had they been poor? I hoped that a family history would provide some continuity, if not stability, and a thread back into the labyrinth of the past.

---

[4] For a larger discussion, see Hilda Kean, *London Stories: Personal Lives, Public Histories* (London, 2004). She begins her own family history with a discussion of such ephemera in working-class lives.
[5] Alison Light, *Common People: The History of an English Family* (London, 2014).

What I found was a history of migrations. The nineteenth century in Britain, as Eric Hobsbawm argued in his essays on *Labouring Men*, was a century of movement.[6] Indeed, as my own researches, working back from my grandparents, confirmed, the poorest sort were on the move long before 'industrialization'. Among my forbears were four main groups: artisans in the building trade, especially masons and bricklayers, men who looked for work in the places that were emerging or expanding (pubs called The Bricklayers' Arms or The Carpenters' Arms were to serve as informal labour exchanges); boatmen, watermen, and sailors (including those who maintained the ship's fabric, like carpenters, or who looked after the crew as cooks or sickbay attendants); all manner of labourers, forest workers, carters, and dockside workers; and, finally, servants, mostly women, who frequently changed situations. Family history particularized the scale and meaning of the comings and goings of individuals and their families. Their crossing of county boundaries also meant that I had to migrate from my armchair and my computer, mimicking their journeys by travelling to the local archive centres that held the older records of their lives, in particular the baptism, marriage, and burial registers, first kept by the parish priest at the prompting of Thomas Cromwell, vicar general to Henry VIII in 1538 (though not all parishes immediately complied). Bafflingly, I found that one of my mother's paternal ancestors, Maria Hosier, had been born in the 1780s in Newfoundland, while her family was from Dorset on the south coast of England. In Dorchester, at the Dorset Record Office, a wall of books on Newfoundland explained the mystery: the Hosiers moved in the early eighteenth century from nearby Corfe, building up a brewing business, and then turned to the sea because of the cod fishing that made Poole a major entrepôt for much of the late eighteenth and early nineteenth century. Maria's father was one of many merchant mariners from Poole, who did well out of the 'cod rush'—a citizen of the North Atlantic who made continual journeys from Poole to Newfoundland and married in the new settlement of St John's; his brother, Giles, did likewise, building a grand house in Bonavista. In 1782, when the American colonists gained independence from the mother country, the British kept Newfoundland and granted New England fishing rights on the Grand Banks; after the defeat of Napoleon, unbridled American competition halved the price of cod and the Newfoundland trade began to founder. The Hosiers lost their fortune and Captain John Hosier returned to England, where Maria sought her fortune in the fashion trades, in the new Regency spa town of Cheltenham. Once the fad for spas went to the continent, Maria found herself finishing off boots in the poorest part of town. The family hit rock bottom when her daughter, Mary, a servant, gave birth in a workhouse, dying shortly after. Mary's child, Sarah, also became a domestic servant; she crossed over 200 miles from Wales to England before she was married in Surrey in the 1880s.

[6] Eric Hobsbawm, *Labouring Men: Studies in the History of Labour* (London, 1968). His essay 'The Tramping Artisan' begins by reminding us that 'the story of nineteenth-century labour is one of movement and migration' (34). As the title of his book suggests, women were yet to enter the picture; considering the roving life of the bricklayer, Hobsbawm assumed that it eventually ceased once he was 'saddled with wife and family' (47).

The Hosiers' story reminds us that the sea and seafaring—and the huge communities they involved—are a central part of 'our island story', yet to be fully integrated with other accounts of people's lives in the British past.[7] It casts a different light on the relation to the village or on the centrality of the parish—its administrative unit run by the church and by local officers—which British historians have often emphasized as the source of the strongest feelings of belonging among the 'labouring poor'.[8] My lot were always leaving. Settlement laws under the parish administration of the Poor Law ought to have tied them to the parish. It operated as a kind of 'border control', preventing migrants who fell on hard times in new places from claiming relief, and frequently taking them back to where they came from if they became a 'burden' on the rates. A sailor town like Portsmouth, however, Britain's premier naval base during the French wars, was made by incomers from the villages and beyond. Most of my mother's maternal ancestors were Irish, arriving there in the 1800s, renting rooms or even beds in the town, before and after setting sail. The men moved between ship and shore, disappearing from view for long stretches, often travelling the globe. The women remained in a nest of streets around the docks; or they, too, followed their men to other port districts, such as Hull and Birkenhead. Such peregrinations were part of life. My mother's mother, an orphan who had never known what became of her father, was the child of one such far-flung family. I discovered that he had died 350 miles away from Portsmouth, on the Tyne near Newcastle, a ship's porter who had fallen down the quay steps at North Shields and had been buried locally in a pauper's grave.

Also unattached to their parish were those dissenters deliberately at odds with the Church of England and whose non-conformity was the cornerstone of their identity. The bricklayer Lights formed a staunch Baptist community in the tiny Wiltshire village of Shrewton in the late eighteenth century—a community in opposition to 'the State church'. In the 1820s and 1830s, Charles Light, a bricklayer, was one of those 'mechanic preachers' who set themselves to teach the village children. Charles ran a Sunday school with a roll of about 200 pupils. In Shrewton, his obituarist noted, 'many owed all the education they possessed to these schools'.[9] Yet the school does not appear in the only official record of the village, the *Victoria County History*. Family history will surely discover other such enterprises, enlarging our knowledge of literacy and the labouring classes. Charles's brother, Henry, my direct ancestor, was an itinerant preacher. When the Lights also migrated to the boom town of Portsmouth, they immediately joined other local Baptists—a shared faith counted for more than village ties. Taking the long

---

[7] Until recently naval historians have largely concentrated on ships and warfare, national policy, or the administration and growth of 'the senior service', their accounts leaning heavily towards the glory days of Nelson and Collingwood; less has been written about the later navy or about sailor towns in general, though this is beginning to change: see Isaac Land, *War, Nationalism and the British Sailor, 1750–1850* (Basingstoke, 2009), which, as part of a new wave of 'coastal history', suggests other approaches. Family historians can help to make many of the links, peopling communities on ship and shore.

[8] See, for example, Keith D. M. Snell, *Parish and Belonging: Community, Identity and Welfare in England and Wales, 1700–1950* (Cambridge, 2006).

[9] Obituary of Charles Light, *Baptist Union Handbook* (1889–90), 149.

view, family history can follow their different paths across the nineteenth century and into the twentieth. One branch of the family established and built churches; its members made religion their route into business, becoming landlords, builders, and contractors of substance; they entered into local politics and eventually became Poor Law Guardians, local councillors, and justices. As the non-conformity of this older generation of migrants became more comfortable and less confrontational, their descendants sought a reinvigorated faith: in the 1880s my great-grandfather joined the Salvation Army, one of the many fruits of revivalism. He never achieved the prosperity of his kin and remained a master bricklayer. Meanwhile those who—like his son, my father's father—eschewed religion altogether remained jobbing bricklayers without the safety net of the wider family or church.

Most of my ancestors were in temporary or seasonal work or took on many jobs within a year (the same would be true of my father, also in the building trade). Family history made me think about the illusion and the ideological force of the census categories, which attempt to fix place, and also 'occupation', in a version of the nation and who counted. Looking more closely at a life or a family over time can help us to distinguish the fine discriminations between destitution and relative respectability rather than resort to an effacing and generalizing description of 'the poor'; it can identify groups, give them names and connections, and flesh out their life stories, if only a little, in all walks of life. The 'vagabond' or tramp was somebody's son or brother; his life has a context, a past and a future. Another group among my forbears consisted of squatters on the edge of a forest in the early nineteenth century; they built conical mud huts on the scrubland that bordered the trees. The Bennetts lived on Shirrell Heath, close by Waltham Chase in the Meon Valley, near Droxford in Hampshire, part of the old hunting ground of the bishops of Waltham. In the 1830s their address was simply given as 'the forest'.[10] They lived doing forest work, but were often underemployed or unemployed for large parts of the year. Part of the 'penumbral' or 'unsettled poor',[11] their lives as makeshift as their homes, they relied on the forest resources in order to survive, collecting firewood to sell for a few pence and making 'tea' from leaves. On the fringe of communities or in extraparochial districts, such migrant workers were often disliked and attacked for their 'encroachments' by the more legitimate 'commoners'—as well as by the powers-that-be, which were in the throes of an agricultural push to 'improve' the commons and so-called wastes. Waltham Chase had long been a resort for the desperately poor; their numbers swelled after Waterloo, when servicemen with no pay or jobs were discharged in Portsmouth (the Meon valley is on the other side of Portsdown Hill, which flanks the port). As the Hampshire labourers grew increasingly impoverished, the area became a hotspot for unrest, especially during the rick-burnings and machine breaking of the Swing Riots in November 1830. As late as 1846 1,000 labourers and their

---

[10] In Waltham Chase, the nearest parish church was four miles away, at Droxford; a chapel of ease was built in the forest in 1828, where the Bennetts baptized their children. Many forests were extraparochial and the lack of close regulation made squatting more possible.

[11] See Steve Hindle, *On the Parish? The Micro-Politics of Poor Relief in Rural England, c.1550–1750* (Oxford, 2004) for further discussion of making shift in a forest economy.

wives assembled, on Shirrell Heath, literally on the Bennetts' doorstep, to protest against the Corn Laws. The vicinity, described by one contemporary, was still a 'wild heath, with here and there a few wretched mud huts'.[12]

Charlotte Bennett, one of my father's great-grandmothers, was among those in the last generation to grow up in the forest; she married Robert Brown, a timber feller and forest labourer. When they, too, travelled to the naval base of Portsmouth to find work, they joined Robert's older sister, Caroline, who had left earlier. Family history so often reveals this pattern, then as now, of new migrants finding kin. It serves as a salutary reminder to historians that those backstreets and slums that were such alarming terra incognita to social investigators were a face-to-face community for those who dwelt there, criss-crossed with family networks. Robert became a dockyard labourer, and eventually a foreman; Charlotte took in washing. She had been gone twelve years when her father, John Bennett, now officially designated 'farm and wood labourer', died in 1858. Another dozen years and Waltham Chase was enclosed; within a decade or two all the timber was cut down.[13] Two new villages with brick houses and smallholdings—Shedfield and Shirrell Heath—spread over area. Those of Charlotte's relatives who remained became market gardeners, carting their produce overnight to Portsmouth, their strawberries to the local station for the London train. In bad years they ploughed runner beans back into the ground.[14] The history of the forest and its ecology; the theft of firewood and the growth of a new, modernizing capitalist economy; the history of protest; the life of the slums and its links to rural migration—all can be brought to life through the fortunes of one family: the world in a grain of sand.

Once the branches proliferate, families become neighbourhoods and groups, and groups take shape around the work they do and the places where they find themselves doing it. Without local history to anchor it, family history is adrift in time, but the local is always connected to a wider world; the apparently parochial to the national; the national to the international. Without these connections and inflections, the moves that people make are often meaningless, and a family history that is more than merely a list of names and dates needs to come up for air. I could follow the precariousness of a family's existence over time through the boom and bust of industries, or see how national policy played out at the human level. Take Mary Edwards, for example, one of my great great-grandmothers. She was a lace-maker from Northamptonshire, an area renowned for its lace made by women who sat in their doorways, crouched over their pillows and bobbins from daybreak to dusk. Mary left the county in the 1830s, at the time when hand lacemaking was in decline; changes in fashion, the decision to allow French lace back into the country after the Napoleonic Wars, together with the new machines, all put paid

[12] Grace Emery, *Some of the History of Shedfield Parish* (Southampton, 1991), 26. Waltham Chase had a long history of protest and unrest: E. P. Thompson, *Whigs and Hunters* (London, 1975).
[13] Waltham Chase was finally enclosed in 1870. Alun Howkins reminds us how long enclosures continued and how little their effects have been studied by comparison with those of earlier periods: Alun Howkins, 'Uses and Abuses of the English Commons, 1845–1914', *History Workshop Journal* 78.1 (2014), 107–32.
[14] Emery, *Some of the History of Shedfield Parish*, 51.

to the old lacemaking and threw thousands of women on the poor rates. After she married Richard Whitlock, a farm labourer from another of the lacemaking villages, they moved across counties, to Herefordshire, where he became a gamekeeper. In another move to Worcestershire, Mary's son, William Whitlock, joined the railway police—another occupation that demanded mobility. He married Louisa Dowdeswell, born in the mid-nineteenth century, the daughter of a needle maker. 'Dowdeswells' was well known in the town of Alcester, Warwickshire, the home of needle making in the Midlands. Developing from a cottage industry, these factories were not enormous operations, like the textile mills or factories in the north of England, but small-scale enterprises where every family member mucked in, working in temporary lean-tos or huts out of the back of their homes. The needle makers' sheds and the family-run factories that fuelled Britain's turbo-capitalism invite parallels with the rural manufacturing of twenty-first-century India and China, where peasants and newly landless labourers are undergoing their own version of an 'industrial revolution'. The local looks different in the light of the global.

Family historians work differently from other historians and this can be usefully unsettling. Most historians begin from a point in the past, advancing gradually forward, covering a few decades, perhaps half a century at most, slowly accumulating a chronology like moss. Family historians, by contrast, are history's speed freaks. They accelerate wildly across the generations, cutting a swathe through time, like the Grim Reaper himself. In the course of an hour's research, surfing the Web at home or scanning the records in a local Family History Centre, they watch individuals die, marry, and be born in hectic series; a dizzying sequence of families fall away and rise up, eras go and come, wars fizzle out and flare, cities turn back to fields. Places—however static they may appear, especially on maps, which have their own reasons for that fixity—become a kind of *flow*. Communities, the village as well as the town or the city, no longer feature as tight containers but are staging posts through which individuals and families move at variable speeds.[15] 'Periodization', too, starts to wear thin. In families time is generational, repetitive, and cyclical. Families are differently affected by war and peace; events in women's lives differ from events in those of men. Family history is a sort of long form that sees a generation emerging, individual life stories and overlapping narratives tracked at an uneven pace. Researchers need a split screen in the mind that refuses compartmentalization and allows them to look at a community horizontally, as it were, at the variety of ways people were living in a culture at any one time. Such synchronicity cuts across the easy divisions and oppositions we use to write with: the city and country, pre-industrial and modern, the male and the female worlds of work and home—the family historian will find it hard to ignore the women in the family and their fortunes. Tracing the lives of siblings and cousins, history is played out at home as a generation emerges with its hopes and disappointments, its

[15] David Rollison makes some of these points, arguing against the view of communities as settlements in a relatively unchanging landscape; see David Rollison, 'Exploding England: The Dialectics of Mobility and Settlement in Early Modern England', *Social History* 24.1 (1999), 1–16. For the idea of communities as 'staging posts', see Charles Phythian-Adams, *Re-Thinking English Local History*, (Leicester, 1987).

random tragedies, its enormous efforts to make a living within the bounds of what is possible.

The family, in other words, is a bridge. What looks like different social groups becomes connected. In 1824 there was not a single railwayman in Britain; but by 1847 there was a permanent staff of around 47,000, and by the 1870s one of around 275,000.[16] My paternal ancestors, the Whitlocks, were Worcestershire farm labourers. In early photographs of their deeply rural world, the smock-wearing men with broken teeth and old clay pipes seem quite a different breed from the smart new Victorian railwaymen in uniform, peaked caps, and shining boots. But, as the railways were cut into the countryside, plenty of men 'went over the fence' from the neighbouring farms. The Whitlock farmhands had brothers and sons who joined the ranks as railwaymen or went into uniform as postmen or police constables (the police force, we tend to forget, was originally made up of country boys, rural migrants who might wind up on the beat in Whitechapel or in the Birmingham slums as easily as they might remain anywhere local). In 1900 my father's mother, Evelyn Whitlock, had brothers and sisters in the metalwork factories and mills on the edge of Birmingham; cousins at a village saddlery; family that worked in the heat and din of the small local needleworks; others working as carters with horses on a farm. Her father, William, began life as a farm labourer and became by turns village policeman, railway policeman, and then metalworker in a factory. Evelyn's two grandmothers were still alive when she was growing up, but they lived very different lives: one, Prudence Dowdeswell, formerly a needle maker, ran a pub in Alcester; the other, Jane Whitlock, was a live-in caretaker for a baronet in a country house close to London. Jane had travelled a 150 miles from the farm in Worcestershire, where she had lived and worked for forty years (she was probably evicted from their tied cottage after her husband died). Her daughter had married a coachman and moved to London, to serve the Dashwood family, which found Jane work: one old lady alone with the gardener, keeping an eye on the shrouded furniture and on the family silver while the family was at its townhouse in Regent's Park—even the barest facts of a family history are suggestive. Seen across some sixty or seventy years of census information, a life holds many surprises: people make choices, though not always in circumstances of their own choosing.

Britain was the first industrialized nation to create populations of migrant workers who serviced capitalist investment. Their stories now resonate with those of thousands of 'economic migrants' across the globe. At the other end of the scale, family history is one way into the specificity of local community history, often overturning our assumptions by revealing how provisional or fluid that community has been; how swiftly traditions could be invented or rejuvenated. In 1900, at the turn of the century, my grandmother, Evelyn Whitlock, William and Louisa's daughter, grew up in Frances Road, in an area called Cotteridge, which later became part of Birmingham, Britain's second largest city. To the untutored eye, her

---

[16] Frank McKenna, 'Victorian Railway Workers', *History Workshop Journal* 1 (1976), 26–73, here 26.

street looks indistinguishable from all those rows across Britain of terraced houses without front gardens, huddled together, close to the railway and the canal, reliant on the local pub and on the corner shop. Yet one glance at the census for 1901 shows Frances Road to be brand new, peopled by workers from all over the country: from Devon and Cornwall in the far west, from Newcastle upon Tyne 400 miles to the north. People like Fred and Eliza Fairhead were born in the same village in the heart of rural Norfolk in the east. Fred drove his 'dray', collecting goods to and from rail stations. They had their children en route: a son from their Sheffield days and a daughter born in York. The horse and cart of their neighbour, Bill Smith, has taken him and his family hundreds of miles from his tiny woodland village of Little Dewchurch in Herefordshire to the seaside resort of St Leonards in Sussex on the south coast, where he and Fanny had their son Thomas, then back to Llanwarne, in his home country on the Welsh borders, where little Beatrice was born seven years before; then they moved on. This is what the Industrial Revolution has meant: thousands of people on the road. Within a generation, though, 'the Cotteridge', as the district was affectionately known, saw itself as 'traditional' working class.

Genealogy, as I have suggested, has never been neutral. Those who claimed a stake in the past, who saw themselves as 'old families' that 'went back a long way', usually ratified this claim through land and property. The history of the working poor, which I found in my own family's past, was, by contrast, one of landlessness and temporary tenancies. Such experiences of discontinuity may go some way towards explaining the insularity of many communities with an often fierce and even violent attachment to streets and neighbourhoods and the displacement of feelings of fury and envy onto other excluded groups, of different race or ethnicity. Family history may help us to historicize the many 'makings' of the English working classes, including its diasporas, and can also challenge the nostalgia about place that animates so much of British culture as a whole—and, in particular, certain notions of English national identity. My family history has turned out to be a history of migrants, who were uprooted and displaced by economic forces or left their villages and towns in the hope of betterment. They might become patriots in times of war (though vast numbers were, of course, dragooned or press-ganged into fighting for England), but their Englishness could also rapidly be sacrificed when starvation threatened or emigration offered a new life. Some of my ancestors left the rural poverty of the Dorset village for Canada. Others, inevitably, were among those shipped to the colonies against their will (Maria Hosier's son, Richard, was transported to Van Diemen's Land for stealing a bag of bread and beef in 1842).[17] These migrations are central to the history of the largely southern working classes, as played out across at least two centuries. They need to be woven into the story of industrial capitalism, with its many shifts of populations that connected regions of the country to a far wider economy. Family history is one way into this

[17] He left the hulks at Sheerness to board the *Asiatic* in May 1843, arriving in Van Diemen's Land four months later: see Tasmania State Library Archives, CON33/1/42; CON14/1/24.

traffic of people and of goods, emphasizing as it does the human beings who made the wealth of the country, even if they did not partake equally in its dividends.

* * *

Writing family history can provide a way into the excitement of original documents and into all the pleasures and pitfalls of empirical research; its inconclusiveness can reveal the legerdemain with which historians produce a generally seamless, apparently artless narrative—how they choose arbitrary beginnings, how often death becomes a destination. Once it is more than a mere list of names and places, it makes direct and intimate links between the local history of places and national, even global, narratives. Writing one's own family history, paradoxically, estranges one from one's ancestors; it can show that their concerns were different from ours and offers an opportunity to move beyond identifications with the people in the past, to questioning and unravelling who we are and where we came from. But, while family history adds much to our knowledge, rendering interesting information on, say, the movement of people or illegitimacy rates, this is not, for the majority of researchers, what drives them on. Although family history can be used by others as a species of collective biography,[18] it is generally as a personal project that family historians begin their work, drawing on family stories and memories, looking for missing people, or asking awkward questions about their family's past. The stories of poorer people and migrants are especially likely to unravel, or be full of, loose ends—disappearing husbands and wives, children left behind or brought up by relatives, relationships that were never officially registered, trails that go cold. But every family has its myths and its skeletons in the closet: the lost fortune or the ancestral home; the children born on the wrong side of the blanket; the fortune swindled, the prison sentence hidden. Family myths, the secrets and lies, suppressions and absences, are a different kind of inheritance.

Romances about the past, often fantasies of self-aggrandisement, these 'myths we live by', as oral historians have suggested, contain emotional truths every bit as historical as the documentary evidence.[19] My mother's father told his children that he came from a wealthy family in Surrey but that he had been cut off and disinherited; he had got the family servant pregnant, had married her, and then had run away to sea. I found out that his father was a farm carter and his mother was Sarah Hill, the granddaughter of Maria Hosier, whose family was one of North Atlantic citizens. Sarah died in a mental hospital of 'mania' when he was sixteen. He was a milk boy at the time and all his cousins and uncles were either labourers on farms or people on the roads. Around 1900 the mental hospital was called the pauper asylum, and the pauper lunatic was even more of a non-person that the workhouse orphan, a kind of social death. Sarah was never mentioned and none of his five daughters took her name, or even knew it. My grandfather's romance about his past hid, I think, his shame and fear but also allowed him to reinvent himself. Such stories, 'make-believe identities', tap into the reservoir of feelings of inferiority,

---

[18] Melanie Nolan, *Kin: A Collective Biography of a New Zealand Working-Class Family* (Christchurch, 2005), looks not at her own family but at that of the McCulloghs, trade unionists and socialists.

[19] Raphael Samuel and Paul Thompson, eds, *The Myths We Live By* (London, 1990).

resentment, belligerence. They give us glimpses into the psychological and emotional legacies of being poor, of the inequalities and injustices that are part of what we call class feeling. They bespeak the astonishingly fertile and vigorous ways people have of resisting official versions of their lives. Family history, like oral history, ought not to debunk or dismiss but needs to respect the tall stories people tell to make themselves look big in a national history that so often diminishes them and their lives. It can also suggest ways in which those emotional legacies shaped later generations.

Family historians may discover material that is disturbing, even offensive, to other family members. The family is far from being a sanctum; it is a place of power relations. Yet there can also be much rejoicing when one finds a black sheep or a forbear notorious enough to have left a record, singled out from the rest (provided that his or her notoriety is not based on too heinous a crime). Writing about the poorest sort brings its own problems, however. Nearly all my forbears were among the poorest workers in Britain, in seasonal or temporary jobs or in multi-occupations. They were often subjected to the Poor Laws and were spending time—months, even years—in the workhouses and the mental asylums set up for the newly designated paupers in the second part of the nineteenth century. Their stories—like that of Sarah Hill, born in a workhouse and dying in a madhouse— come to us filtered through the lens of the nineteenth-century stage and novel. The slums, too, have their own glamour, their ready-made cast of victims and villains ('Dickensian' is a word often used to convey a generic, literary sense of period as an image: think of *Oliver Twist* or *Hard Times*). Like cliché, genre reassures us at the cost of reflection and makes the past predictable. Poverty is easily turned into period drama, where an emotional response to the wretchedness of lives in the past is paramount, or into a version of 'poverty pornography' akin to that of current television shows which cater to the emotional satisfactions of gawping at our fellow citizens who live on state benefits or apply for social housing.[20] Historians can widen the optic, provide the political context for the creation of the workhouse system or the asylums; but they can also counter with particularisms and local detail, making ordinary and unexceptional what first appears melodramatic and heightened; they can argue against the more conservative view that sees individuals in isolation, blaming chance or moral character alone, or fate.

Family historians have their own mythologies, not least about the family itself. As any longitudinal study will show, 'family' is a chameleon: it changes shape and colour to adapt to time and place. It waxes and wanes with the age of the inhabitants: prosperous newly weds grow into a house full of children and servants, only to shrink again over time; the less comfortable take in lodgers or apprentices, or are themselves lodgers; the elderly in turn join their children, board with other families, or have to make shift for themselves, working into their eighties. Neighbourhood and workmates may be every bit as intimate and important as family members; other attachments, like those between people of the same sex, have to be read between the lines. Yet it is hard to look coolly at the fantasy of the

---

[20] An example would be *Benefits Street*, first aired on television on Channel Four in January 2014, featuring the residents of James Turner Street, Birmingham.

family as sufficient unto itself, as if the family were somehow outside history, made of victims and heroes, forged through strong will, and wrecked only by dire accident. No family was more extended, it turned out, than my mother's: the Irish seafaring Murphys, who lived in the same few streets around the harbour and docks in Portsmouth for most of the nineteenth century and well into the twentieth. The web of kin and connections was not enough to keep them all afloat, however, no matter how hard they worked and how many different jobs they juggled; my grandmother landed in the workhouse as a little girl. In my family there was a constant traffic between what felt like respectability and what was endured as poverty; the same people could find themselves moving between different states within a short time in their working lives. Family history can challenge the view that hardworking families on low pay coping with high rents can succeed whatever the state or government does; or that social mobility is a matter of individual willpower and self-help; or that only the lazy and feckless fall into poverty; or that 'the poor' existed in separate classes. But, of course, it need not.

Family history, in other words, offers many versions of what Benedict Anderson called, in a now justly well-worn phrase, 'imagined communities'. Telling a story about one's self or about one's ancestors is always a way of having a place in historical narrative, of counting; but it need not have radical potential. I would query any assumption that family history is necessarily a tool that leads historians to a more open-minded view of the past or to a less 'top-down' version of it. Its political valency, like that of all history, depends on the historian, the uses to which it is put, and the audience being addressed.[21] Genealogy has long been central to the political projects of the right and has often nurtured fantasies about blood and belonging, being profoundly conservative in its view of the family and of the nation, looking to restore lost origins, and dreaming of a once whole society, or imagining bloodlines from roots, specious lineages with their own systematic and sometimes murderous exclusions.

More commonly and less drastically, family historians may give their own Whiggish accounts of history, emphasizing those who were the successes of industrialization, promoting the virtues of the work ethic or of their *embourgeoisement*. Memoir writing can be 'restorative' too, as it looks back to the vanished world of childhood in particular and wants to preserve it as a lost Eden rather than reflect on the nature of memory or deliberately probe the feelings of loss and estrangement.[22]

Family history is a trespasser and is at its most productive, perhaps, when it refuses to be put off by the hedges that academic historians put around their 'fields'. As I wrote my family history, the book often grew in my mind not with an argument but with a vision: I saw two brothers on the road, leaving their village to

---

[21] Tanya Evans discusses this question in relation to changing versions of Australian national history: Tanya Evans, 'Secrets and Lies: The Radical Potential of Family History', *History Workshop Journal* 71 (2011), 49–73. See also Tanya Evans, *Fractured Families: Life on the Margins in Colonial New South Wales* (Sydney, 2015).

[22] I have borrowed this distinction between a 'restorative' and a 'reflective' nostalgia from Svetlana Boym, *The Future of Nostalgia* (New York, 2001).

migrate to the town. I tried to conjure other visions and images, so as to break up the relentless narrative of social history and the forward march of chronology, creating some breathing space in which the present, as it was lived, was full of roads not taken; to allow the rhythms of poetry, or to explore some of the sensual and subjective elements that fiction can give us: the feeling of being there, say, as a girl in a port town in the mid-nineteenth century, or of crossing the Atlantic to Newfoundland. If at times I felt as if every person I encountered was a potential novel, I was nonetheless frequently brought up short. Each 'character' was someone's grandmother, great-grandfather, or brother, and there were limits to the liberties I could take. The historian's job has a moral and ethical basis, but family history more than any other history writing, perhaps, is a visit to the dead, a paying of our respects to the past.

Ancestor worship is as old as the hills, and family history may be a modern-day secular way of appealing to our ancestors as mediators between past and present, as those ghosts and invisible presences who still speak to us and may need to be exorcised, appeased, forgiven. Family histories, shot through with loss and longing, piling up the detail about missing generations, may offer a form of mourning and a way of anticipating or acknowledging our own passing into history. During my work I often returned to what the poet Joseph Brodsky wrote in one of his lyrics, 'what's the point of forgetting if it ends in dying?',[23] with its surprising reversal of our expectations. What's the point of remembering, we might more usually ask, if we are all going to die anyway? The historian's task is always Sisyphean, shoring up fragments against the ruins of time. Family history's own efforts at the reclamation of the past remind us of the human burden and privilege of remembering *because* 'it ends in dying'. Underpinning the search for ancestors is perhaps an existential, philosophical inquiry, which writing history cannot ultimately answer—the meaning of an individual life in the great flow of time.

---

[23] Joseph Brodsky, 'Song', in idem, *So Forth* (London, 1996), 5–6.

CONCLUSION

17

A 'Slight Angle to the Universe'

Eric Hobsbawm, Politics, and History

Geoff Eley

An undergraduate in Cambridge in the early 1930s, Margot Heinemann (1913–92) received 'the most brilliant English First of her year—perhaps of the 1930s'.[1] After watching the hunger marchers pass through Cambridge, she became a lifelong communist, staying with the party, like Eric Hobsbawm, until the very end. From 1936 until 1953 she was working politically for the Communist Party of Great Britain (CPGB) more or less full time, mainly at the Labour Research Department (LRD), delivering research for the trade unions, especially the coal miners. Like Hobsbawm's, hers was a life made and lived inside the party, though to a degree different from his. John Cornford, the legendary communist poet killed in Spain at the age of 21, wrote her, just before his death, a love poem that began 'Heart of the heartless world'. Later, from 1949 on, she began a long-term relationship with Hobsbawm's Birkbeck colleague, the eminent communist crystallographer J. D. Bernal (1901–71). Having shared the dissidents' critique during the party crisis in 1956–7, she, like Hobsbawm, decided against leaving the party, though she remained outside its leading committees until the late 1970s—by then a very different epoch. In 1959 she published *The Adventurers*, a well-received novel that encapsulated the communist predicament of the time.[2] She was by then developing a new career as a lecturer in English at Goldsmith's, having made her way through school teaching in 1959–65; eventually she moved in 1976 to a fellowship in Cambridge at New Hall, which is where I knew her. After the nuts and bolts of the industry, trade, and wages analyses of the 1940s and 1950s at the LRD, she now turned to seventeenth-century literature and drama, producing an equally impressive body of scholarship in that area while she wrote historically about

---

[1] Eric Hobsbawm, 'Address at the Funeral of Margot Heinemann, 19 June 1992', in David Margolies and Maroula Joannou, eds, *Heart of the Heartless World: Essays in Cultural Resistance in Memory of Margot Heinemann* (London, 1995), 216–19, here 217. Subsequent details are taken from David Margolies and Maroula Joannou, 'A Chronology of Margot Claire Heinemann', ix–xiii in the same volume.

[2] See Andy Croft, 'The End of Socialist Realism: Margot Heinemann's *The Adventurers*', in Margolies and Joannou, eds, *Heart of the Heartless World*, 195–215; also Alan Sinfield, *Literature, Politics and Culture in Postwar Britain* (Berkeley, CA, 1989), 258: 'This is the most positive and astute representation of working people that I have seen in the period; it is rarely discussed.'

communism earlier in the century and kept up with her politics. She died in 1992, a year after the CPGB dissolved.

There are several reasons for beginning this essay with Margot Heinemann. The first is that, by Hobsbawm's own account, she enacted a notable commitment to holding together those parts of life—the personal, the intellectual, the political—that are often kept distinct. This was an ideal Hobsbawm himself wanted to follow. 'Margot', he wrote in *Interesting Times*, was 'one of the most remarkable people I have ever known...Through a lifetime of comradeship, example and advice, she probably had more influence on me than any other person.'[3] Or, in his Funeral Address: 'My personal debt to her is that she, more than any other single individual I can think of, taught me, by her example, what being a communist meant, or should mean, especially for intellectuals.'[4] These statements act as a pendant to Chapter 9 of Hobsbawm's autobiography, 'Being Communist', a brilliantly distilled treatment of its subject.[5]

Second, Heinemann's life reminds us that history can be made away from the obvious thoroughfares. Those who make history in meaningful ways only selectively appear in the books. They remain, as the famous title put it, 'hidden from history'.[6] 'If you look at the leading book on Cambridge between the wars,' Hobsbawm said, 'she is not in it. John Cornford and Bernal are, Klugman and Kiernan are, and so are Kettle and myself, but not Margot Heinemann...If she is in any of the histories of the CP, I've missed her.'[7] Since 1992, thanks to Kevin Morgan, Nina Fishman, John Callaghan, Geoff Andrews, and more, things are much improved.[8] Yet it is still common enough to find women, however brilliant, missing from the pertinent accounts.[9] Even *Interesting Times*, after so striking a tribute, reports nothing about what Heinemann actually did. For a life lived so consistently and productively in ways not without importance for the writing of a range of twentieth-century histories, whether in relation to Eric Hobsbawm, to British communism, to the broader history of the left, or to the complicated place of women in the shaping of a certain progressive–modernist intelligentsia, this invisibility is an interesting problem. There is thus a question to be explored here

---

[3] Eric Hobsbawm, *Interesting Times: A Twentieth-Century Life* (New York, 2002), 122.

[4] Hobsbawm, 'Address', 216.   [5] Hobsbawm, *Interesting Times*, 127–51.

[6] Sheila Rowbotham, *Hidden fom History: 300 Years of Women's Oppression and the Fight against It* (London, 1973).

[7] Hobsbawm, 'Address', 218.

[8] e.g. Geoff Andrews, Nina Fishman, and Kevin Morgan, eds, *Opening the Books: Essays on the Social and Cultural History of the British Communist Party* (London, 1995); Kevin Morgan, Gidon Cohen, and Andrew Flinn, *Communists and British Society, 1920–1991* (London, 2007); John Callaghan, *Cold War, Crisis and Conflict: The CPGB, 1951–1968* (London, 2003); Geoff Andrews, *End Games and New Times: The Final Years of British Communism 1964–1991* (London, 2004); Nina Fishman, *The British Communist Party and the Trade Unions 1933–1945* (Aldershot, 1995).

[9] We might call this the Rosalind Franklin effect. Franklin (1920–58), a British biophysicist and X-ray crystallographer, made crucial contributions to the discovery of the DNA double helix but was subsequently written out of the account. Effectively marginalized by Francis Crick, James Watson, and Maurice Wilkins, who shared the Nobel Prize in 1962, she was later restored to the narrative. See Brenda Maddox, *Rosalind Franklin: The Dark Lady of DNA* (New York, 2002); and the more polemical Anne Sayre, *Rosalind Franklin and DNA* (Minneapolis, MN, 1975). On leaving King's College, as it happens, Franklin was recruited to Birkbeck by J. D. Bernal.

about the mechanisms of generational transmission, about how the political goods of one time are passed down to another or not. Given the iconoclasm and general turbulence of the period, an old communist of Heinemann's vintage might easily have been perceived by the 1970s as a predictable and superseded political voice, for example. The continuing influence of an internationally prominent public intellectual like Hobsbawm may be grasped more readily than the resonance of those whose lives were more locally and institutionally bounded. Yet, notably in those more modest settings, the effects of cross-generational conversations should never be underestimated. Among the sixteen contributors to Margot Heinemann's memorial volume, strikingly few came from her own generation—just two, Victor Kiernan and Christopher Hill—while most of the rest were younger scholars who came to maturity in the 1980s. To take another illustration, Tilda Swinton, while an undergraduate at New Hall in the early 1980s, was inspired by Heinemann to join the Communist Party.[10]

Third, Heinemann and Hobsbawm belonged to that cluster of generations for which the Second World War became the defining life experience. Here, of course, the war means not just the European conflict of 1939–45, but the far wider, globally unfolding international disorder that began in 1931; and not only the international military defeat of fascism, but also the visions of domestic societal change that were always the indispensable antifascist correlate. In this particular imaginary, in other words, 'the war' or '1945' meant programmes of social reconstruction conceived in response to the world capitalist crisis and to the social misery of the Depression. Under the circumstances of the time, the rhetorics of antifascism (the anti-Hitler coalition, the good war, the antinomies of 'barbarism and civilization'), for all their elisions and simplifications, captured a space of collective agency that proved perhaps uniquely resonant and long-lasting in the broadest of popular–democratic terms. People born in 1917 emerged from the war still in their twenties, formed in the immediacy of hardships and dangers, thankful for survival, and looking to a future of citizenship and security. That future was to be assembled via social planning and the welfare state. Reconstruction would honour the role of ordinary people in the nation's survival, not just rhetorically but through a new ethics of the public good. For the first time across Europe, moreover, democracy would become universal, not just because interwar dictatorships and authoritarianism became dismantled and defeated, but because women finally received citizenship in the vote.[11]

Despite all later disappointments, this embedding of democracy was a lasting gain. Hobsbawm returned repeatedly to the plenitude of the moment, with its

---

[10] 'I tell you exactly what turned me into a commie: the great Margot Heinemann and her like when I was at Cambridge. I had the great, great fortune of being taught by her and Raymond Williams and that generation of leftwing intellectuals'. Simon Hattenstone, 'Tilda Swinton: Winner Takes All', *Guardian*, 22 November 2008 (at http://www.theguardian.com/film/2008/nov/22/tilda-swinton-interview, accessed 17 October 2015).

[11] For an elaboration, see Geoff Eley, *Forging Democracy: The History of the Left in Europe, 1850–2000* (New York, 2002), 278–328; Geoff Eley, 'Finding the People's War: Film, British Collective Memory, and World War II', *American Historical Review* 106.3 (2001), 818–38.

sense of tangible responsibility for the future, linked as it was to the unfolding of a great and unifying cause, in a time when everything meshed together. It was from this ground that he explained his decision to remain a communist. As he said at Heinemann's funeral:

> we did not waste our lives, even though many of us lost their hopes. In the first place we, the communists and what was at the time the only communist state in the world, the USSR, won the most important negative victory of this century. We defeated fascism, which would have won the Second World War but for the USSR and the great national anti-fascist mobilizations of which we were the champions and the pioneers. This was the great achievement of Margot's generation.

He then said more, invoking the essential domestic accompaniment: 'we were concerned with the world revolution and the Soviet Union only indirectly. Directly we were concerned with our own front in the battle, which was here.' He continued:

> Well, the future of the industrial workers in an age of deindustrialization is problematic, and so, in an era of transnational capitalism, is the future of the unions. But it is as true now as it ever was that a country without unions is a country of social injustice. Margot worked for the unions, and especially the miners, and she has a right to ask that her life be judged by that and what she did for British workers and not by what Stalin did in Russia. And what she did as a British communist was good.[12]

This was something far more than dogged and determined loyalty to a cause, although, as Roy Foster pointed out in his fine obituary essay, Hobsbawm did place the highest value on the sustaining of loyalties—to friendship, to collegiality, to *Past & Present*, to Birkbeck, to a certain idea of Cambridge even. 'His adherence to the Party', Foster wrote,

> was a commitment to a comradeship which had played a vital part in the identity and life of someone who had lost both parents by the age of fourteen, and then moved to a new country... the fidelity to joint endeavour, and to the friends of his youth, had been acquired during the displacements and engagements of his early life, and he never lost it.[13]

This was loyalty, above all, to the energies and purpose of a very particular time. Partly that really meant 1917 and its utopian charge, 'the dream of the October Revolution'. But it had as much to do with the endangerment of the early and later 1930s, the sense that history was at an exceptionally fateful pass. Christopher Hill, another close comrade of Heinemann's and Hobsbawm's, described his own earliest foray into the English Revolution in 1940 as having been written out of great urgency, 'very fast and in a good deal of anger', under circumstances of extreme national danger, where it amounted to 'my last will and testament'.[14] Such times inscribe themselves indelibly into the script of a life, however unpredictably its

---

[12] Hobsbawm, 'Address', 217–18.
[13] Roy Foster, 'Eric Hobsbawm', *Past & Present*, 218 (2013), 3–15, here 14.
[14] Tim Harris and Christopher Husbands, 'Talking with Christopher Hill: Part I', in Geoff Eley and William Hunt, eds, *Reviving the English Revolution: Reflections and Elaborations on the Work of*

future trajectory may yet be composed. Around 1970, I remember asking Martin Kettle, definitely a party insider but already at that time something of an errant child, why, given Hobsbawm's published criticisms of Stalinism, he hadn't just left; and Martin answered, well he's more important to them than they are to him.[15] That may well have been true. Yet Hobsbawm's own considered reflections bespeak an emotional cathexis—not just to the community of commitment in its psychic dimensions, but as the continuing recognition of an existential locatedness inside a powerful life experience shaped around a compellingly told collective story.[16]

Fourth, I want to flag this question of cathexis, of continuing investment in a cause, per se. That is, what are the stakes of political commitment for a long haul of that kind? Why does it matter that we are willing to take one kind of visible stand or another? What *difference* does it make? During the first two decades of the Cold War, these questions translated into very sharply drawn fields of confrontation and engagement—academically, within institutions and across particular disciplines; historiographically, field by field and controversy by controversy; and, intellectually, across wider territories of the public culture. During the later 1960s and the 1970s, with the expansion of higher education, a certain liberalizing of the overall climate, and a definite strengthening of the intellectual left, these terms of engagement became less cramped and more hospitable for a wider diversity of intellectual work attached to a left-wing politics of knowledge. But then, by the turn of the 1980s, an unexpectedly virulent right-wing counterattack was also already well under way, so that very quickly a very different and less favorable 'battle of ideas' was joined.[17] So how are the commitments and exigencies of starkly differing conjunctures to be connected together? What were the terms of equivalence and possible reciprocity between the political languages of the

---

Christopher Hill (London, 1988), 99–103, here 99; Geoff Eley, 'John Edward Christopher Hill (1912–2003)', *History Workshop Journal* 56 (2003), 287–94.

[15] See here Martin Kettle, 'How Did My Communist Family Get It So Wrong? Because Politics Was Their Religion', *Guardian*, 22 January 2016, reacting to the publication of David Aaronovitch, *Party Animals: My Family and Other Communists* (London, 2016). The views expressed in Kettle, as generally in the adulatory reviews of Aaronovitch's book, differ from my own. For more measured reflections and analysis, see Morgan, Cohen, and Flinn, *Communists and British Society*, and John McIlroy, Kevin Morgan, and Alan Campbell, eds, *Party People, Communist Lives: Explorations in Biography* (London, 2001).

[16] Eric Hobsbawm, 'The Present as History', in *On History* (New York, 1997), 228–40, here 229, 230: 'Every historian has his or her own lifetime, a private perch from which to survey the world. ... My own perch is constructed, among other materials, of a childhood in the Vienna of the 1920s, the years of Hitler's rise in Berlin, which determined my politics and my interest in history, and the England, and especially the Cambridge, of the 1930s, which confirmed both.' And then: 'for me, 30 January 1933 is a part of the past which is still part of my present. The schoolboy who walked home with his sister that day and saw the headline is still in me somewhere. I can still see the scene, as in a dream.' Or, answering the question of why he became a communist: 'I mean from the start it was obviously an emotional and profoundly felt conviction. You felt that the world was going to hell and you felt that world revolution would be the only way of saving it. And you may understand that if you were a teenager in Berlin during the rise of Hitler.' See also Christian Tyler, 'Post-Mortem on a Bloody Century', *Financial Times*, 8–9 October 1994.

[17] Stuart Hall, 'The Battle of Socialist Ideas in the 1980s', in idem, *The Hard Road to Renewal: Thatcherism and the Crisis of the Left* (London, 1988), 177–95 (originally published in Ralph Miliband and John Saville, eds, *The Socialist Register 1982*, London, 1982, 1–19).

popular–democratic postwar, as I described them a little earlier above, and those new ones coalescing during the 1970s and 1980s inside the 'post-1968'? How should we think about the *bridging* of generations in that sense? Where was the coherence of a new political formation that combined them both likely to be found?

So far in this essay I have been considering some political dimensions of Hobsbawm's lifetime as a historian—Hobsbawm's own politics and some ways of understanding them. I have been pointing to certain continuities across a very particular twentieth-century life, a life emblematic, too, of larger political formations, whose main features were complicated and variable, but with meanings nonetheless portable across wide parts of society. I have centred those thoughts around the century's long mid-point in the Second World War; on the languages linked to the urgencies of antifascism; on the kinds of mobilization and coalitioning associated with the Popular Front, which Hobsbawm himself returned to again and again, not just as a very specific formation of the 1930s and 1940s but as a paradigmatic bundle of strategic precepts and protocols that were good for all time.[18] Then, more abstractly, I have reflected a little on the meanings of keeping loyalty to a cause over the longer term, on the importance of seeking to understand the mechanisms of generational transmission, and on the disjunctions and dissonances that can occur when times change, as they inevitably do.

But 'Hobsbawm and politics' calls us to a second set of questions, to do with the particular treatments of politics in his works; and this is what I will turn to now. What can his writings tell us about the nature of politics and about how politics takes place? In the space available I will focus on the writings of the 1960s and 1970s, which to my mind contain the most interesting extended reflections, forming the best place to begin.

What we find in these writings is an extremely classical conception of the axiomatic indebtedness of politics to what Marxists of the earliest generations called the role of the 'economic factor' in history. Part of this conception was the grand progressivist schema of the advance of human society from lower to higher stages of development, realizing ever-growing complexity in the structuring of economic life and enabling the eventual replacement of scarcity with abundance. The primary warrant for this thinking was the urban–industrial transformation of European society, directly observed by Marx and Engels and conceptualized as the transition from feudalism to capitalism, which Hobsbawm took explicitly as the ground for writing on the nineteenth century. On that ground, he reserved a kind of first-order priority—ontologically, epistemologically, analytically—to the underlying importance of the economic structure in conditioning everything else, including the possible forms of politics and law, institutional development, and social consciousness and belief. The common expression for that determining relationship had been, of course, the architectural language of 'base and superstructure',

---

[18] See especially Eric Hobsbawm, 'Fifty Years of People's Fronts' [1985], in idem, *Politics for a Rational Left: Political Writing 1977–1988* (London, 1989), 103–17, along with 'Labour's Lost Millions' [1983], 'Labour: Rump or Rebirth?' [1984], and 'The Retreat into Extremism' [1985], respectively 63–76, 77–86, and 87–99 in the same volume.

in which the spatial metaphor of ascending and sequential levels also implied the end point in a logical chain of reasoning.[19] But, if that can be abstracted from Hobsbawm's writings of the 1960s through to the 1970s, it then gets gradually harder to pin him down, so that by the 1990s a more eclectic and elusive relationship to those standpoints is left.[20] His understanding of *determination* always allowed a great deal of space to unevenness and complexity, including to what used to be called the 'autonomization of the superstructure' (*Verselbständigung des Überbaus*); and in any of the particular works (e.g. throughout the *Age* volumes, or in the writings on nationalism) there was enormous subtlety in the practice of any detailed political, ideological, or aesthetic treatment. But now, reading his last thoughts—beginning perhaps with the *Past & Present* 50th anniversary lecture, which sketched out the framing for his autobiography, along with *Interesting Times* itself, each published in 2002—it becomes unclear how confidently he retained the stronger conviction in the directionality of history that ran through most of the earlier writings.

This is the first of the places where Hobsbawm's history seems vulnerable—in his approach to general questions of social determination, that is. Several others may be mentioned briefly, each going back to classical materialism. One is a fairly unbudging *Eurocentricity*. It seems odd to be writing this about someone who was so impressively internationalist, who knew so much about other parts of the world, especially Latin America, and whose *Age* tetralogy was distributed so impressively across its global settings, all of which made him a 'world' or 'international historian *avant la lettre*'.[21] But he did say this:

> *Everything* that distinguishes the world of today from the world of the Ming or Mughal emperors and the Mamelukes originated in Europe—whether in science and technology, in the economy, in ideology and politics, or in the institutions and practices of public and private life. Even the concept of the 'world' as a system of human communication embracing the entire globe could not exist before the European conquest of the western hemisphere and the emergence of a capitalist economy. This is what fixes the situation of Europe in world history, what defines the problems of European history, and indeed what makes a specific history of Europe necessary.[22]

---

[19] See Eric Hobsbawm, 'Marx on Pre-Capitalist Formations', in idem, *How to Change the World: Reflections on Marx and Marxism* (New Haven, CT, 2011), 127–75. Originally written as the introduction to *Pre-Capitalist Economic Formations* (London, 1964), the earliest English translation of sections from Karl Marx's *Grundrisse der Kritik der politischen Ökonomie* (Moscow, 1939–41; Berlin, 1953), this was also Hobsbawm's most significant contribution to Marxian scholarship. For a sovereign summary, appositely written in 1968, at the apex of Hobsbawm's classical Marxist period, see Eric Hobsbawm, 'What Do Historians Owe to Karl Marx?', in idem, *On History* (New York, 1997), 141–56.

[20] See the 1983 lecture 'Marx and History', in Eric Hobsbawm, *On History* (New York, 1997), 157–70. Responding in 1994 to the question of 'what it meant to be a "Marxist historian"', Hobsbawm answered: 'the best way to tackle history was still to study the way human beings collectively earn their living, to understand the social structures and institutions they develop' (quoted in Tyler, 'Post-Mortem on a Bloody Century').

[21] Jan Rüger, 'Britain, Empire, Europe: Re-Reading Eric Hobsbawm', and Natasha Wheatley, 'The Compass of International History: Eric Hobsbawm and After', *Journal of Modern European History*, 12.1 (2014), respectively 417–23 and 424–32, here 419 and 424: each uses a version of this phrase.

[22] Eric Hobsbawm, 'The Curious History of Europe', in idem, *On History* (New York, 1997), 224.

Another attenuation concerns *gender*. Hobsbawm was too good a historian, too capacious a thinker not to have seen the importance of women's emancipation and women's rights either to the project of the left, to the reach of democracy, or to the histories of social transformation he wanted to write. The chapters dealing with women in *Age of Extremes* and its predecessor are good examples, though the same could not be said of the two earlier volumes—an absence that eloquently marks the distance travelled in the historical profession, as in the thinking of the left, between 1975 and 1987. In one final conversation, Roy Foster reports him as choosing '[t]he women's revolution' as 'the most influential revolution in his lifetime'.[23] Yet to say that Hobsbawm recognized the importance of gender as 'a useful category of analysis' would certainly be a stretch.[24]

Next, there was an *underlying developmentalism* in Hobsbawm's work that was extremely problematic, most evidently in two of the works that were most inspiring in their time: *Primitive Rebels* (1959) and *Bandits* (1969).[25] To read these books again, still more to teach from them, as I did recently under the aegis of the University of Michigan's Anthropology–History Joint PhD Program, is to be struck by the road travelled since the late 1970s not just anthropologically, but also historiographically, in terms of microhistory and *Alltagsgeschichte* and many other genres of intervening work and thought, but most especially beneath the impact of postcolonial studies and more particular schools like subaltern studies. As Natasha Wheatley says in a brilliant commentary, the subalternists 'were thinking from within the same Marxist tradition as Hobsbawm, and trying to wrestle with those categories and that compass from their perspective in South Asia'. She then cites Ranajit Guha, who shared both Hobsbawm's Marxism and his interest in peasant rebels (including a comparably precocious knowledge of Gramsci):

> In his luminous work, *Elementary Aspects of Peasant Insurgency*, Guha took issue with Hobsbawm's conception of the pre-political peasant, and the normative development sequence implied in that category, in which European notions of secularization and modernization were necessary prerequisites for true political consciousness.[26]

---

[23] Foster, 'Eric Hobsbawm', 12.

[24] The reference is to Joan W. Scott's foundational essay 'Gender: A Useful Category of Historical Analysis', in eadem, *Gender and the Politics of History* (New York, 1988), 28–50. The essay was first published in 1986, the year before Hobsbawm's *Age of Empire* appeared. See also the impassioned response of three feminist historians to Eric Hobsbawm, 'Man and Woman in Socialist Iconography', *History Workshop Journal* 6 (1978), 121–38—all three in subsequent issues of the same journal: Sally Alexander, Anna Davin, and Eve Hostettler, 'Labouring Women: A Reply to Eric Hobsbawm', *History Workshop Journal* 8 (1979), 174–82; Tim Mason, 'The Domestication of Female Socialist Icons: A Note in Reply to Eric Hobsbawm', *History Workshop Journal* 7 (1979), 170–5; and Maurice Agulhon, 'On Political Allegory: A Reply to Eric Hobsbawm', *History Workshop Journal* 8 (1979), 167–73. Hobsbawm's original essay was republished as 'Man and Woman: Images on the Left', in idem, *Uncommon People: Resistance, Rebellion, Jazz* (New York, 1998), 94–112.

[25] Eric Hobsbawm, *Primitive Rebels: Studies in Archaic Forms of Social Movement in the Nineteenth and Twentieth Centuries* (Manchester, 1959); Eric Hobsbawm, *Bandits* (London, 1969).

[26] Wheatley, 'The Compass of International History', 431. For my own discussion, see Geoff Eley, *A Crooked Line: From Cultural History to the History of Society* (Ann Arbor, MI, 2005), 137–48. See also Ranajit Guha, *Elementary Aspects of Peasant Insurgency in Colonial India* (Delhi, 1983); and Ranajit Guha, 'The Prose of Counter-Insurgency', in idem, ed., *Subaltern Studies II* (Delhi, 1983),

The language of *Primitive Rebels*—primitive, archaic, premodern, pre-political—grates almost audibly on contemporary sensibilities. Hobsbawm's grasp of heterogeneous temporalities and his imaginative empathy for the movements concerned were revelatory for those who read this pioneering book at the time. Yet his appraisal of the rebellions of Andalusian and Sicilian peasants is still, in the end, organized by a directional and progressivist conception of a political efficacy based on a developmentalist schema of necessary stages (backward to advanced), one that centres around a particular understanding of how modern politics has to be conducted.[27] What the Andalusian peasants *really* needed, in other words (as he always argued in relation to the Spanish Civil War) was a *communist party* (or 'the necessity of organization').[28] Something of this standpoint remained, perhaps, in what Wheatley calls 'the paradigmatic methodological metaphor' of the 'bird's eye view' in *Age of Extremes*—the 'zoom-out effect' and the 'distant gaze', with its imputations of mastery and command. Wheatley continues, citing Dipesh Chakrabarty: 'Appealing to the bird's eye view does not release us from the problems of place; universalisms, too, are situated knowledges.'[29] Seeing this does *not* require withdrawing into 'localism' or any parochial resistance to generalizing and theory. What we now call the cultural turn has enabled understandings to which Hobsbawm stayed brusquely immune—about subject positionality; about the locatedness of identity; about the lived particularities of place, region, and body; about the inevitable in-betweenness of any actually existing community; and, indeed, about the complex interrelations of all those things to the more universal formations of class, gender, nation, globe, and 'the West'. This brings us to the ambivalences between, say, an avowed internationalism or the cosmopolitanism of an adopted standpoint on the one hand and, on the other, the affective realm of historically formed cultural ties, so essential to 'history and politics' in Hobsbawm's case—that is, Vienna, Berlin, central Europe, Jewishness, Cambridge, communism.

Finally, among Hobsbawm's attenuations, there was the bluntness of some of his thinking about aesthetics, culture, and the arts. His breadth and acuteness of knowledge were remarkable; his chapters on the arts in the *Age* books are fabulous; his indebtedness to British social anthropology enabled the originality of his readings of the formation of working-class culture, of nationalism, and of 'the invention of tradition', which Roy Foster claims rightly as pioneering a version of cultural history; he was the author of *The Jazz Scene*. Yet he could voice all the mid-century communist's scorn for commercially produced mass culture: rock was 'an art of amateurs and the musically or even the alphabetically illiterate'; 'in twenty years time', he wrote in the *New Statesman* in 1963, 'nothing of [the Beatles] will

1–42 (reprinted in Nicholas B. Dirks, Geoff Eley, and Sherry B. Ortner, eds, *Culture/Power/History: A Reader in Contemporary Social Theory*, Princeton, NJ, 1996, 336–71).

[27] Hobsbawm, *Primitive Rebels*, 2.

[28] Eric Hobsbawm, '1956' (interview with Gareth Stedman Jones), *Marxism Today*, November 1986, 229–31, here 230.

[29] Wheatley, 'The Compass of International History', 432. See Dipesh Chakrabarty, 'Preface to the New Edition', in idem, *Provincializing Europe: Postcolonial Thought and Historical Difference* (Princeton, NJ, 2007), ix–xx.

survive'.[30] On a different ground, at the high cultural end of the spectrum, his
ill-considered 1999 polemic against twentieth-century high modernism, reprinted
unrepentantly as 'The Avant-Garde Fails' in *Fractured Times*, drew an exasperated
and wholly justified riposte from Martin Jay in *Artforum*.[31] There is much to be
said, clearly, about the relationship of politics to culture here.

Each of these comments is meant to mark out some of the ground where
Hobsbawm's understanding of politics—the approach to politics we can find in his
works—will need to be assessed.[32] In the remainder of this essay I return to the
issue broached earlier, namely: What is the relationship between the 'postwar' and
the 'post-1968'?

As a voice in politics, aside from his unrepentant communism, it was for his
arguments about the Labour Party in *The Forward March of Labour Halted?* that
Hobsbawm ultimately became best known.[33] With this intervention, I would
argue, he was drawing a line under his earlier attachment to an avowedly *revolutionary* tradition, in this case 'the spirit of October'. The bookends of that process
were *The Forward March* in 1978 and *Revolutionaries* in 1973, which gathered his
political commentaries of the 1960s.[34] In the space separating these two texts, he
crystallized the defence of the antifascist heritage, where my discussion in this essay
began. It was then that he formalized his belief in the strategic permanence of the
Popular Front idea, thereby distancing the direct-action, insurrectionary version of
revolutionary politics that derived from 1917. We can see this being worked out in
a variety of ways. The writings on Gramsci date from these years; likewise those on
the Popular Front and antifascism per se. It was then that he began identifying
more strongly or openly with the heritage and vision of Palmiro Togliatti, with the
'Italian road to socialism', and with the Eurocommunism of the Historic
Compromise.[35] This was also the force of his contrast between the German (KPD)
and the French (PCF) Communist Parties: if the one stayed beholden to an
intransigently class-political militancy and sectarian isolation, the other could
draw on the wider resources of the French republican tradition and build the
broader coalition that became the Popular Front. Even so, in Hobsbawm's view,

[30] Gregory Elliott, *Hobsbawm: History and Politics* (London, 2010), 44, 45.

[31] Martin Jay, 'Eric J. Hobsbawm, 1917–2012', *Artforum*, February 2013; Eric Hobsbawm, *Behind
the Times: The Decline and Fall of the Twentieth-Century Avant-Gardes* (London, 1998); Eric
Hobsbawm, *Fractured Times: Culture and Society in the Twentieth Century* (London, 2013), 241–57.

[32] For general assessments, see especially Perry Anderson, 'The Vanquished Left: Eric Hobsbawm',
in idem, *Spectrum: From Right to Left in the World of Ideas* (London, 2005), 277–320; Elliott,
Hobsbawm; Wheatley, 'The Compass of International History'.

[33] See Eric Hobsbawm, Martin Jacques, and Francis Mulhern, eds, *The Forward March of Labour
Halted?* (London, 1981)—an anthology of a debate carried out in *Marxism Today* and *New Left Review*
in response to Hobsbawm's 'The British Working Class One Hundred Years after Marx', delivered as
the Marx Memorial Lecture in 1978. Subsequent thinking may be tracked in Eric Hobsbawm, *Politics
for a Rational Left: Political Writing 1977–1988* (London, 1989).

[34] Eric Hobsbawm, *Revolutionaries: Contemporary Essays* (New York, 1973).

[35] See especially Eric Hobsbawm, 'The Dark Years of Italian Communism', in idem, *Revolutionaries*,
31–42; Eric Hobsbawm, 'In the Era of Anti-Fascism 1929–45', 'Gramsci', and 'The Reception of
Gramsci', in idem, *How to Change the World: Reflections on Marx and Marxism* (New Haven, CT,
2011), respectively 261–313, 314–33, and 334–43; and Eric Hobsbawm and Giorgio Napolitano,
The Italian Road to Socialism (London, 1977).

the PCF's particular Stalinism still impeded its ability to follow through on that chosen path—it could never consistently shed the proletarian reflexes acquired in the 1920s in order to find the political creativity that he thought the Italian Communist Party (PCI) came to display so well.[36] His essays on guerilla war and Latin American peasant movements tend in a similar direction, bridging from *Primitive Rebels* to a less developmentalist take on such popular agitations. His commentaries on the Chilean Popular Unity are key in this regard. All in all, these writings brought him to the place where *The Forward March* marked out his sense of the possible.[37]

There was another side to this. *Revolutionaries* concludes with two essays on 1968, which dismissed not just the possible effectiveness of the student movements but also their *seriousness*, and still more their lack of concretely realizable programmes.[38] Hobsbawm returned to 1968 on its tenth anniversary for a brilliant conspectus of that year as a whole.[39] But otherwise he had rather little to say about how the political meanings of 1968 might be processed—about how such far-reaching political upheavals might have redrawn the agenda, not least (as he argued in 1978) because they extended precisely across all three of the great divisions of the globe, the industrialized capitalist countries, the socialist countries, and the underdeveloped countries of the Third World.[40] *Interesting Times* contains a snippet of barely four pages, notable for its grumpy declaration of generational incomprehension and for the decision never ever to wear blue jeans. 'And where did it all lead?' he asked rhetorically, and answered: 'In politics, nowhere much.'[41] Later he paused occasionally to direct a few barbs at 'identity politics', which he took to be 1968's main legacy. He never modified the verdict that he delivered in the early 1970s: neither single-issue mobilizing (like 'consumer agitations and environmental campaigns'), nor countercultural lifestyle radicalism, nor 'frenzied ultra-left gestures' could ever remotely come close to the leadership once provided by parties (and communist ones in particular).[42]

This has to count as his biggest failure. For, however one judges 'the broad democratic alliance' (his redeployed version of the Popular Front) as a response to the straitened circumstances analysed in *The Forward March* under the shadow of Margaret Thatcher, this strategy still needed to be carefully spelled out, with

[36] See Eric Hobsbawm, 'French Communism' and 'Confronting Defeat: The German Communist Party', in idem, *Revolutionaries*, respectively 16–24 and 43–54.

[37] See Eric Hobsbawm, 'Peasants and Politics' [1973] and 'Peasant Land Occupations' [1974], in idem, *Uncommon People: Resistance, Rebellion, Jazz* (New York, 1998), respectively 146–65 and 166–90; Eric Hobsbawm, 'Guerillas in Latin America', in Ralph Miliband and John Saville, eds, *The Socialist Register 1970* (London, 1970), 51–61; Eric Hobsbawm, 'Chile: Year One', *New York Review of Books*, 23 September 1971; Eric Hobsbawm, 'The Murder of Chile', *New Society*, 20 September 1973 (with subsequent correspondence on 27 September 1973).

[38] Eric Hobsbawm, 'May 1968' and 'Intellectuals and the Class Struggle', in idem, *Revolutionaries*, respectively 234–44, and 245–66.

[39] Eric Hobsbawm, '1968: A Retrospect', *Marxism Today* 22.5 (1978), 130–6.

[40] Ibid., 130.   [41] Hobsbawm, *Interesting Times*, 258–62, quotations at 261.

[42] Hobsbawm, 'Intellectuals and the Class Struggle', 265. See also Eric Hobsbawm, 'Identity Politics and the Left', *New Left Review* 217 (1996), 38–47, and Eric Hobsbawm, 'Identity History Is Not Enough', in idem, *On History* (New York, 1997), 266–77.

sympathetic attentiveness in particular to the new cultural politics that materialized from the preceding decade. Yet, while patiently making his case in the essays, short articles, and interviews of the 1980s, Hobsbawm never pressed beyond certain registers of generality, where discussion of Labour Party programmes, policies, and values was measured against the emerging patterns of working-class life and the detailed findings of electoral sociology. With his unrivalled command of the larger picture, grounded as always in comparative distinctions and an understanding of national, regional, and local particulars, such commentaries were never short of insights and illumination. But he thought only very schematically about how the necessary breadth of democratic politics might be gained. The new forms of political practice, the new sources of political meaning, and the new horizons of political aspiration—everything separating the New Left from the old, whether in the shifting terms of political intervention (the personal is political) or in the complicated dynamics that brought national politics into the intimate and ordinary locations of everyday life—had little imprint on his thinking. For that to occur, precisely the meanings of 1968 had to be faced. The nettle of *identity* had to be grasped—not in the fragmentary, solipsistic, and disaggregating manner he scorned, but as the basis for the broadest possible unity of 'the whole people', in exactly the Gramscian terms he wished to embrace. In pitting 'identity politics' *against* the antifascist success story of old, Hobsbawm badly reduced how questions of political subjectivity might be approached. Let me explain briefly what I mean.

Concurrently with Hobsbawm's *Forward March*, the pertinence of class to politics was passing more generally—and very radically—into question. By the 1990s, the working class of history was coming to be seen less as a collective actor in the manner of earlier traditions of labour history, whether Marxist or not, than as a particular kind of story told about the past.[43] Especially compelling in its time, such critiques claimed, the 'rise of the working class' had worked remarkably well as an inspiring but fictive projection, the narrative ordering of past time for the purpose of fashioning and securing a particular collective identity, one that was capable of rallying masses of people politically for a cause. But now, in the late twentieth century, after deindustrialization and capitalist restructuring had worked their changes, class had to be seen as only one possible affiliation out of many. Class supplies only one nexus of key relations, practices, and meanings among a more dispersed array of sites and connections that place an individual in the world. Earlier materialist accounts, in this view, missed the fragmented and particularized

---

[43] Huge literatures are involved here. Hobsbawm's *Forward March* was followed in France by Alain Touraine, *L'après socialisme* (Paris, 1983) and by André Gorz, *Farewell to the Working Class* (London, 1982); in West Germany by Rolf Ebbighausen and Friedrich Tiemann, eds, *Das Ende der Arbeiterbewegung in Deutschland? Ein Diskussionsband zum sechzigsten Geburtstag von Theo Pirker* (Opladen, 1984). Debates were summarized by Michael Schneider, 'In Search of a "New" Historical Subject: The End of Working-Class Culture, the Labor Movement and the Proletariat', *International Labor and Working-Class History* 32 (1987), 46–58. For the new approach, see Patrick Joyce, *Visions of the People: Industrial England and the Question of Class, 1840–1914* (Cambridge, 1991); Patrick Joyce, *Democratic Subjects: The Self and the Social in Nineteenth-Century England* (Cambridge, 1994); and Patrick Joyce, ed., *Class* (Oxford, 1995).

bases from which people actually negotiate some workable coherence for their social and cultural lives. Class now appears as just one term among others in the mobile and contingent play of political appeals and affiliations. It ceases to form the social historian's main ground, from which all other questions have to be viewed.[44]

That leads us instead to the many different forces acting on and through the lives of ordinary people, through which they may be able to recognize themselves. How we see ourselves as a basis for action, how we become addressed as particular kinds of publics, is not fixed. We recognize ourselves variously—as citizens, as workers, as consumers, as parents, as lovers and sexual beings, as enthusiasts of sports and hobbies, as audiences for music and film, as believers in religious and other creeds, as generations, as objects of policy and surveillance, as subjects of race and nation, and so forth. Such recognitions are structured by power relations of various sorts. They are gendered by assumptions that place us as women, men, or something in between.

This fragmentary, complex, non-fixed quality of selfhood has become a commonplace of present-day identity talk. But politics is usually conducted *as if* identities were stable and fixed. The operative question then becomes this: How does identity settle and congeal; how is it worked upon; how does it acquire continuity over time; how is it fashioned into concentrated, resolute, or reliable shapes? How do some forms of identity begin to coalesce into more generalized forms of collective self-recognition, while others remain inchoate or unassimilable? That is, how is *agency* produced? Under what circumstances, in particular places and times, can people begin thinking of themselves as a particular *kind* of collective agency, political or otherwise? If people occupy such widely different social positions, then how do they find themselves shaped into acting subjects, understanding themselves in justified or possible ways?[45] How, between the 1940s and 1960s, did such a wide predominance of the British people come to recognize themselves in the meanings of 1945, and how, during the 1970s and 1980s, was that common understanding so effectively dismantled and replaced with something else, indeed so successfully that it became harder and harder (as Stuart Hall said in 1987) for anyone *not* to think of themselves as 'just a tiny bit of a Thatcherite subject'?[46]

Politics here is about *domesticating the infinitude of identity*.[47] It is the effort at stabilizing identity, 'ordering' it into a strong, programmatic direction. If we are to

[44] For a full elaboration of this context of argument, see Geoff Eley and Keith Nield, *The Future of Class in History: What's Left of the Social?* (Ann Arbor, MI, 2007); also Geoff Eley and Keith Nield, 'Farewell to the Working Class?' *International Labor and Working Class History* 57 (2000), 1–30, with comments by Don Kalb, Judith Stein, Stephen Kotkin, Barbara Weinstein, Frederick Cooper, and Joan W. Scott (31–75) and our own attendant reply (76–87).

[45] For one guide through the pitfalls of theorizing identity, see the now classic article by Linda Alcoff, 'Cultural Feminism versus Post-Structuralism: The Identity Crisis in Feminist Theory', in Nicholas B. Dirks, Geoff Eley, and Sherry B. Ortner, eds, *Culture/Power/History: A Reader in Contemporary Social Theory* (Princeton, NJ, 1993), 96–122.

[46] Stuart Hall, 'Gramsci and Us', in idem, *The Hard Road to Renewal: Thatcherism and the Crisis of the Left* (London, 1988), 165.

[47] This formulation is indebted to Ernesto Laclau, 'The Impossibility of Society', in idem, *New Reflections of the Revolution of Our Time* (London, 1990), 89–92, and to the wider body of his writings; see especially Ernesto Laclau, *On Populist Reason* (London, 2005); Ernesto Laclau, 'Why Do Empty Signifiers Matter to Politics?', in Jeffrey Weeks, ed., *The Lesser Evil and the Greater Good: The Theory*

think of identity as being decentred, then politics becomes precisely the process of trying to *create a centre*. As a drive for coherence, to produce various forms of consistency and completeness, politics requires working on identity's many complicated referents, especially those that are social. It requires focusing on the systems of meanings and representation by which people organize their relations with the material world, through which they manage their relationship with the social and historical circumstances of their lives. Politics works on this imaginary field by seeking to make stable and unitary sense of the fragmentary, divided, and antagonistic aggregations of social relations and social spaces we call 'society', 'the nation', or the 'people.' Again: this is what has to happen to individuals and groups before their multiple and complex relations to the world can be organized into a political identity sufficiently centred to be capable of motivating action.

It was unclear why Hobsbawm needed to disparage the challenge of these questions. A version of the process just described—that is, arriving at a common language of politics with enough binding coherence to hold a movement together over time—had been key to the breadth and resilience of the antifascist outlook of the 1930s and 1940s as Hobsbawm had wanted to understand it, after all. Yet he seemed impeded from building such a language again by drawing on the political goods of the 1960s and 1970s in a manner resonant with the New Times movement.[48] This was a failure of what earlier I called generational transmission. Hobsbawm was surprisingly inattentive to the ways in which oppositional ideas, the access to a critical intelligence, or just a dissentient sensibility could be kept alive across changing times; how commitments might be preserved in the face of unexpected transformations and a generally bad conjuncture; how well-tried ideas and practices might be redeployed for the new exigencies that catch us by surprise. He tended to see the grassroots militancies of 1968 and its aftermath ('identity politics') as distractions from what he saw as the real stuff of politics—'just incoherent fragments that do not add up to a winning coalition', in the words of a fellow sceptic who scornfully dismissed 'these revolutionaries organizing from below, these civic committees, these street activists, these incorrigible utopians'.[49] We know that in a crisis, when people take to the streets, images circulate, language is used, actions coalesce that draw on existing reservoirs of knowledge. But how is such memory assembled? How is the continuity produced, especially when the bearers are tiny dissenting networks whose influence now suddenly blossoms? How are traditions reproduced, *not* in some unchanged and seamless form, but as incitements and unconsciously reworked purposes, redeployed in a different time and in a different setting?

---

and the Politics of Social Diversity (London, 1994), 167–78; and Ernesto Laclau, 'Populism: What's in a Name?', in Francisco Panizza, ed., *Populism and the Mirror of Democracy* (London, 2005), 32–49.

[48] Here my reference is to the motivating commitments of the grouping associated with *Marxism Today* and the Eurocommunist tendency of the Communist Party of Great Britain in the 1980s, to which Hobsbawm likewise subscribed, albeit in one of its less radical versions. See Stuart Hall and Martin Jacques, eds, *New Times: The Changing Face of Politics in the 1990s* (London, 1991).

[49] Donald Sassoon, 'All Shout Together', *Times Literary Supplement*, 6 December 2002, 6.

How do we make connections between needs and desires as they circulate through the micropolitics of the local and the everyday, in workplaces, neighbourhoods, schools, offices, hospitals, dance halls, cinemas, sports arenas, and streets, and thence to the national public sphere and polity, where any lasting efficacy has to occur? If the *local* and the *practical* can become *national* in that sense, particularly in the midst of spectacular, unanticipated events like 1968, then the ideas in question—that is, the usable political knowledge, the understandings of how political actions get mounted, the perceptions of the possible, the necessary resources of hope—will come from widely differing times.[50] Some will be familiar and well tried, enacting the value of the already given, their appeal and prestige deriving from the successes of an earlier period. Others are seemingly fresh, bursting suddenly into voice. Moreover, the ideas arrive not only tidily arranged, as motions to be voted by committees, but also in a turbulent mess, as unexpected and discomforting intrusions, as demands and expressions not easily welcomed into the fold. The normative practitioners seldom adjust easily. Here is Sheri Berman, a leftish political scientist, on the unimportance of the legacies of 1968 for 'the left and democracy'. Local activisms, extra-parliamentary social movements, and spontaneous direct action, she argues, produce no coherence but only 'an amorphous longing for change'. Thus to misrecognize their 'anarchic radical spirit' as the basis for any kind of effective left politics 'seems romantic at best'.[51] Here is the echo of Hobsbawm's dismissal of 1968, his 'nowhere much'.

But this profoundly misses the point. Participatory activism, however 'unrealistic' its own political desire, has always been essential to whatever 'staying power' a national movement comes to possess. Without those local cultures of aspiration, their utopian impulse, the successes of any reforming parliamentarianism are inconceivable, as the slightest acquaintance with the history of twentieth-century left movements quickly confirms. However we judge the hard-nosed pragmatism of leaderships, locally based activism was vital to everything that helped to make people into socialists or communists—to centre their political selves—so that movements could build their support into a lasting and solidly grounded continuity over time. In that sense, there are always tensions and gaps between what the supporters want and what the leaders think they can get. Yet writing the history of one to the exclusion of the history of the other is the sound of just one hand clapping. It is staggeringly naïve. Popular democratic movements have always been most effective when *both* are moving in the same time—when the 'committee room' and the 'streets' can be moved into acting together. For contemporary social democrats like Berman, *realistic* political action is confined only to the highly circumscribed spheres of social administration, parliamentary proceduralism, and the rule of law. Expecting anything more, they warn, exceeds what the political can bear. But the politics of democratic breadth Hobsbawm wanted to see accomplished

---

[50] I build here from arguments in Raymond Williams, *Resources of Hope: Culture, Democracy, Socialism* (London, 1989).

[51] Sheri Berman, 'The Left and Democracy: The Triumph of Realo-Politik', *Dissent* 50.1 (2003), 99–102, here 100, 101.

in the 1980s required looking precisely *beyond* those normative limits. It meant regrounding the Popular Front in *precisely* those new collective activisms of the 'post-1968'—peace movements, ecology, women's liberation and new feminisms, gay and lesbian activism, antiracism and multiculturalism, solidarity with immigrants and refugees, squatting, rave cultures and alternative scenes, anti-inequality and anti-corruption campaigns, anti-roads protests, DIY politics, and so forth. This is what I mean by the challenge of generational transmission.

It is *here* that 1956 and Hobsbawm's decision to stay with the party acquire their meaning. His early and continuing political formation discouraged an engagement with some key challenges arising from the contemporary capitalist transformations, authorizing selective perceptions of what to take seriously or not. How this worked was complicated. The New Times project of the 1980s materialized from inside the Communist Party and not just among the younger post-1968 recruits, for example. The appeal of Eurocommunism cut across generations rather than between them. If during the late sixties and seventies intellectual and political tensions were apparent, then the presence of that older Marxist generation—Hobsbawm and the rest of the former Communist Party Historians' Group and their equivalents across the academic disciplines—proved invaluable for the freshly radicalized student cohorts. While Trotskyists and other sectarians among the latter drew harder and faster lines, certain spaces remained open—History Workshop, for example, or *New Left Review*, where Hobsbawm and other old communists continued contributing across many decades. In this very broad sense, the goods of the past were surely being transmitted. But, as Hobsbawm's aversions suggest—his dismissal of everything that 1968 commonly connotes—there were limits. Nor, conversely, was breaking with the party any guarantee of openness and sympathy in that regard, as John Saville and Edward Thompson, two of the key dissidents from the mid-1950s, were each to make plain.[52] But another key voice of 1956—not a member of the party, significantly, but certainly an architect of New Times—did show what working through the legacies of 1968 might mean.

More than anyone, Stuart Hall bridged between those two eventful markers of the long postwar, namely 1956 and 1968.[53] In contrast with the dissident

---

[52] There is no space here to outline the difficulties of the 'old' New Left (the dissident communists of 1956–7) with the new radicalisms crystallizing from 1968, including notably the feminisms. They were aggressively on display in a plenary of the Thirteenth History Workshop at Ruskin College, Oxford on 1 December 1979, when Thompson (as one of the main speakers) and Saville (in the discussion) each upheld the superior virtues of an older mode of political debate (i.e. 'hard and firm polemic' as against 'charitable and generous and sisterly and brotherly' discussion). See Dennis Dworkin, *Cultural Marxism in Postwar Britain: History, the New Left, and the Origins of Cultural Studies* (Durham, 1997), 239–40, quoting Saville. Thompson shocked even his intellectual allies with the angry theatrics of his assault on the two other speakers, Stuart Hall and Richard Johnson. Published versions of the three papers appeared in Raphael Samuel, ed., *People's History and Socialist Theory* (London, 1981), 376–408. See also Martin Kettle, 'The Experience of History', *New Society*, 6 December 1979, reprinted in Raphael Samuel, ed., *History Workshop: A Collectanea, 1967–1991: Documents, Memoirs, Critique, and Cumulative Index to 'History Workshop Journal'* (Oxford, 1991), 107. The fullest account of the occasion and its meanings can be found in Dworkin, *Cultural Marxism*, 232–45.

[53] For a fuller development of this argument, see Geoff Eley, 'Stuart Hall, 1932–2014', *History Workshop Journal* 79 (2015), 303–20.

communists around *The Reasoner/New Reasoner* and despite any other convergence, Hall and his collaborators around *Universities and Left Review* (*ULR*) saw 1956 far more clearly as an opening towards a new cultural politics, to a space of action and thought beyond any existing ground of either classical Marxist or older Anglo-British socialist and popular radical traditions—in other words, beyond the ground where Hobsbawm, too, was crafting his social histories of the time.[54] With its new corporate organization, fresh dynamics of accumulation, and rampant consumerism, postwar capitalism was in the process of transforming contemporary Britain—social structure, labour markets, residential patterns, spending habits, educational chances, forms of mass leisure and entertainment, in short, the entire given terms of class belonging and their meanings for politics. As Hall put this later, reflecting on 1968:

> We raised issues of personal life, the way people live, culture, which weren't considered the topics of politics on the left. We wanted to talk about the contradictions of this new type of capitalist society in which people didn't have a language to express their private troubles, didn't realize that these troubles reflected political and social questions which could be generalized.[55]

These recognitions broke the given boundaries of politics apart, making culture into a decisive site, 'not a secondary, but a constitutive dimension of society'. It was through cultural analysis that the most effective critique of the new capitalism would have to be mounted—by tracking 'the impact of "commodification" in areas of life far removed from the immediate sites of wage-labour exploitation'. And to track it would change the stakes for politics. If 'the discourse of culture' was becoming 'fundamentally necessary to any language in which socialism could be redescribed', then the left would have to think differently from before.[56] From his particular communist perch, Hobsbawm was not able to see these connections, whether in the 1980s, in 1968, or in 1956, however capaciously his new version of the Popular Front was to be cast. There is an irony here, because knowing how to bridge between ordinary desires and large-scale events had always been essential to the history Hobsbawm wanted to write, from *Primitive Rebels* and *Labouring Men* through *Workers* to *Uncommon People*. But this was as vital for the 'post-1968' as it had been for the 'post-1945'.

---

[54] See Eric Hobsbawm, *Labouring Men: Studies in the History of Labour* (London, 1964), especially 'Labour Traditions', 371–85. For the contrast between the dissident communists and the *ULR*, see Raymond Williams, *Politics and Letters: Interviews with* New Left Review (London, 1979), 362: 'The *ULR* people ... were more oriented to what was happening now in the rapidly changing society of contemporary Britain—while the people coming from *The New Reasoner* were more aware of the whole international Marxist tradition, but with a sense of being less close to some of the extraordinary transformations of scene in England. This was the period of the emergence of the dominant cultural styles appropriate to consumer capitalism, with qualitatively new kinds of magazines, advertisements, television programmes, political campaigning. The 'New Left' cultural intervention, incomplete as it then was, outlined a necessary new kind of analysis of a new phase of capitalism.'

[55] Stuart Hall, as quoted in Ronald Fraser, ed., *1968: A Student Generation in Revolt* (New York, 1988), 30.

[56] Stuart Hall, 'The "First" New Left: Life and Times', in Oxford University Socialist Discussion Group, ed., *Out of Apathy: Voices of the New Left 30 Years On* (London, 1989), 11–38, here 25, 27.

At one level, Hobsbawm knew this. Could the Portuguese communists have imagined holding together when their party was outlawed in 1926, he asked, if they had known they were going underground for almost half a century? No one has written more brilliantly about the relationship between locally textured political identities and loyalty to a cause on the one hand, and the appeal of nationally organized movements and programmes on the other hand. All of his work moved with compelling acuity between carefully measured generalization and the telling instance, with details culled from an astonishingly wide array of often recondite sources, so that the ability of some particular movement to keep the emotional commitment of its supporters came vividly alive. Two of the best examples are the essays on 'Religion and the Rise of Socialism' and 'What Is the Workers' Country?', from 1978 and 1982 respectively.[57] These are virtuoso performances of learning, insight, political wisdom, imaginative sympathy, and largeness of vision. But why did this have to stop with 1968? To cite some examples from my own *Forging Democracy*, why should people like Mary Kay Mullan in contemporary Derry, or the Exodus Collective in Dagenham, or any other bearers of the new politics in the 1980s not deserve the same devotion of imaginative and sympathetic understanding?[58]

I want to close with a kind of counterexhibit. In *Revolutionaries* there is an essay that sits oddly with the rest of the *oeuvre*, namely a 1961 review of Ernst Bloch's two-volume and 1,657-page treatise *The Principle of Hope*—a work written in 1938–47 during Bloch's US exile, published in Germany in 1959, and eventually translated into English in 1986. In 1961 Hobsbawm greeted Bloch's utopianism as a powerful resource against the 'end of ideology' theorists of the 1950s. He found Bloch's thought beautifully in tune with the new spirit of the times, what he called 'the passionate, turbulent, confused but hopeful atmosphere of that international phenomenon, the intellectual "new left"'. By the close of Bloch's 'superb work', he said at the end of his review, 'Blake fuses with Marx, and alienation ends in man's discovery of his true situation. For it is not every day that we are reminded... that hope and the building of the earthly paradise are man's fate.'[59] How does this fit with the later disdain for 1968? It returns us, I think, to that matter of cathexis. 'Without the political project to which [I] committed [my]self as a schoolboy, even though that project has demonstrably failed, and as I now know, was bound to fail,' he wrote early in *Interesting Times*, '[my] life would lose its nature and its significance.' Then comes this: 'The dream of the October Revolution is still there somewhere inside me, as deleted texts are still waiting to be recovered by experts, somewhere on the hard disks of computers.'[60]

So, if in one dimension Hobsbawm wanted to brush history with the grain, in another he always 'stood at a slight angle to the universe'.[61] It was never just his remarkable qualities as a historian that made him so inspiring as a model, but the

[57] See Eric Hobsbawm, *Workers: Worlds of Labor* (New York, 1984), 33–48 and 49–65.
[58] See Geoff Eley, *Forging Democracy: The History of the Left in Europe, 1850–2000* (New York, 2002), 381–83, 479–81.
[59] Eric Hobsbawm, 'The Principle of Hope', in idem, *Revolutionaries*, 136–41, here 136, 141.
[60] Hobsbawm, *Interesting Times*, 55–6.   [61] Ibid., 416.

consistency of his stance as a politically engaged intellectual. One might agree or disagree with various parts of his persona in that regard, but over a long lifetime he continued to live obstinately inside an ethics of commitment that seems worth aspiring to emulate. While *Interesting Times* closed on a sombre note, his final sentences were admirably direct: 'Still, let us not disarm, even in unsatisfactory times. Social injustice still needs to be denounced and fought. The world will not get better on its own.'[62]

---

[62] Ibid., 418.

Index

Index